Software Development on the SAP HANA Platform

Unlock the true potential of the SAP HANA platform

Mark Walker

[PACKT] enterprise
PUBLISHING
professional expertise distilled

BIRMINGHAM - MUMBAI

Software Development on the SAP HANA Platform

First published: July 2013

Production Reference: 1040713

Published by Packt Publishing Ltd.
Livery Place
35 Livery Street
Birmingham B3 2PB, UK.

ISBN 978-1-84968-940-3

www.packtpub.com

Cover Image by Sujay Gawand (sujaygawand@gmail.com)

Credits

Author
Mark Walker

Reviewers
Sridhar Sunkaraneni
Joselyn Quintero Veliz

Acquisition Editor
Edward Gordon

Lead Technical Editor
Madhuja Chaudhari

Technical Editors
Jalasha D'costa
Arvind Koul
Vaibhav Pawar

Project Coordinators
Abhishek Kori
Wendell Palmer

Proofreader
Mario Cecere

Indexer
Tejal Soni

Graphics
Valentina Dsilva

Production Coordinator
Manu Joseph

Cover Work
Manu Joseph

About the Author

Mark Walker has been working with computers since a very early age, starting out with programming the Sinclair ZX Spectrum. After graduating from Cardiff University, he moved to France, starting a 17-year (so far) career in SAP development, first on the SAP ERP, then moving to SAP BW in 2004. He specializes in process optimization, especially in the SAP BPS and BI-IP modules. He's been following SAP HANA since its release in 2011, and is a certified HANA Application Associate since early 2012.

Mark has been working for the last six years for Censio, a consultancy in Paris, France, which has expertise in SAP, Microstrategy, Business Objects, and Microsoft BI technologies. During that time he's worked on several end-to-end projects for some prestigious clients, and done some missions in SAP's name.

In November 2012, he published *SAP HANA Starter, Packt Publishing*, a small book about getting a foothold in the SAP HANA world.

I would like to thank all those people who have helped me throughout my career, and especially my wife, who puts up with the many hundreds of hours I spend in front of a keyboard, tinkering.

About the Reviewers

Sridhar Sunkaraneni is a senior business intelligence / SAP business planning and consolidation consultant. He holds a master's degree in Computer Science from University systems of Maryland, USA.

Sridhar has more than eight years of experience in Information Technology and has been working with SAP products since 2005. He is certified by SAP AG for the SAP BusinessObjects Business Intelligence and SAP Business Objects Data Integrator, SAP HANA products. Sridhar has expertise providing solutions in the areas of SAP NetWeaver Business Warehouse (BW), SAP SAP BI, SAP HANA, and SAP BPC.

I want to thank the entire team of Packt Publishing who coordinated the process of publishing this book.

Joselyn Quintero Veliz is a Venezuelan Financial Expert and SAP Financials Senior Consultant, with professional experience in technology, oil, construction, manufacturing, and banking industries. Managing both business and technology environments, she is able to transform financial requirements into successful IT solutions. She possesses a certification of In-Memory Technology Databases for SAP HANA, issued by the Hasso Plattner Institute in Postdam, Germany.

At this moment, Joselyn works as SAP Process Excellence Senior Consultant in Deloitte, helping companies to take advantage of the latest SAP technologies to reach ambitious business goals.

In her free time, Joselyn spreads her personal financial knowledge in Latin America, through her website `www.joselynquintero.com`. Joselyn also works in philanthropic initiatives as Spanish translator in Animal Foundation Platform, promoting the ethical treatment and reducing violence against stray animals.

I want to first thank the author of the book for sharing valuable knowledge in these pages, providing useful information for people around the world. Secondly, thanks to Packt Publishing for promoting high-level knowledge, and for inviting me to be part of this project. Last, but not least, I appreciate my family and friends for the support and the patience, and for not being around for the hours this book required my focus. We worked as a team, and we made it!

www.PacktPub.com

Support files, eBooks, discount offers and more

You might want to visit www.PacktPub.com for support files and downloads related to your book.

Did you know that Packt offers eBook versions of every book published, with PDF and ePub files available? You can upgrade to the eBook version at www.PacktPub.com and as a print book customer, you are entitled to a discount on the eBook copy. Get in touch with us at service@packtpub.com for more details.

At www.PacktPub.com, you can also read a collection of free technical articles, sign up for a range of free newsletters and receive exclusive discounts and offers on Packt books and eBooks.

PACKTLIB

http://PacktLib.PacktPub.com

Do you need instant solutions to your IT questions? PacktLib is Packt's online digital book library. Here, you can access, read and search across Packt's entire library of books.

Why Subscribe?

- Fully searchable across every book published by Packt
- Copy and paste, print and bookmark content
- On demand and accessible via web browser

Free Access for Packt account holders

If you have an account with Packt at www.PacktPub.com, you can use this to access PacktLib today and view nine entirely free books. Simply use your login credentials for immediate access.

Instant Updates on New Packt Books

Get notified! Find out when new books are published by following @PacktEnterprise on Twitter, or the *Packt Enterprise* Facebook page.

Table of Contents

Preface

Welcome to the world of development with SAP HANA. More than just the latest technological buzzword, even more than the result of SAP's marketing effort, SAP HANA is a complete development system, including a database system, complete development environment, and application server.

While SAP HANA is often considered as an extension of SAP's BW data warehouse, and more recently of their ERP system, in this book we will see that it can be used for pure development purposes, and indeed, provides tools ideally suited to this use case.

From loading data to modeling it into reusable objects through authorizations, creating reporting applications, and developing a website with the system, the journey we will be taking together will allow us to explore the multifaceted system that is SAP HANA.

What this book covers

Chapter 1, So, What Is This SAP HANA Thing Anyways?, introduces SAP HANA and examines the characteristics that make it special.

Chapter 2, SAP HANA Studio – Installation and First Look, describes the SAP HANA Studio—the software you will use throughout the book, and every day you work with SAP HANA—to do database modeling and development work. You will also discover three different ways of getting access to a SAP HANA server.

Chapter 3, Your First SAP HANA Development – An Attribute View, starts your development journey with SAP HANA, building an attribute view, the first building block of database development with the system. Your attribute view will use data extracted from several tables, joined together to provide description for a customer in the system, in a coherent way.

Chapter 4, Painting with Numbers - An Analytic View, will create the next step of SAP HANA database development—an analytic view, showing how this object can use and present numeric information, combined with the description of this information provided by an attribute view.

Chapter 5, Let's Get Graphical - Graphical Calculation Views, continues our database development work, introducing the notion of graphical calculation view, which is an object providing aggregation and combination functionality. This object can use data from one or more analytic views to present it to your users for consumption.

Chapter 6, You Talking to Me? - Scripted Calculation Views, is where you will learn that in SAP HANA, for each function you can perform using the graphical designers provided by Studio, there is a way of doing the same job by writing code. In this chapter, you will create a calculation view using SQL Script, the SAP HANA SQL scripting language. This calculation view will fulfill the same function as the one you created in *Chapter 5, Let's Get Graphical - Graphical Calculation Views*.

Chapter 7, Hey! That's My Data! - Authorizations in SAP HANA, introduces the notion of authorizations in the SAP HANA system, allowing you, as a developer, to dictate who can access which object in the database, and even which values (that you have created in the different modeling views) can be seen by which of your users. You will learn that user groups can be created by developing authorization roles; you will create a database user to be able to test the authorizations you create.

Chapter 8, On Another Level - Hierarchies in SAP HANA, examines the notion of hierarchies as they apply to data visualization, showing the different hierarchy types you can create with SAP HANA. You will learn how a hierarchy can affect the data your users can see, providing automatic subtotals and aggregation.

Chapter 9, Deploying your Reporting Application to Reporting Software, will show how you can deploy the SAP HANA data models that you will create in three different tools: SAP's Lumira, Tableau, and Microsoft Excel so that your users can analyze their data. You will see the differences between the three tools, both in their approach, their capabilities, and their requirements.

Chapter 10, Data Provisioning Using Data Services, explains how you can use another of SAP's tools, Business Objects Data Services, to import data into your SAP HANA instance in an easy way.

Chapter 11, Application Development Using the XS Engine, is where you will learn how you can create web applications using SAP HANA's inbuilt application server, the XS Engine. From a simple "Hello, World" application to database access with your web-based application, to user interface development with SAP's SAPUI5 HTML-based framework, you will learn all the techniques needed to develop Internet or intranet applications on the SAP HANA system. You will also learn about accessing the data in the SAP HANA database from your XS Engine applications.

Appendix, So Long and Thanks – Where to go from here, gives an overview of all that you will have learned throughout the book, and gives some tips and pointers on your possible next steps in the SAP HANA development world.

What you need for this book

This book is designed to be self-contained, and by the time you reach the end, you will be provided with all the information you need to procure the software discussed, from the SAP HANA server to the client software, Studio, right through to the reporting software discussed in *Chapter 9, Deploying your Reporting Application to Reporting Software*. The only thing you will need is a PC, with Windows and Java installed.

Who this book is for

This book is aimed at anyone who wants to start working with SAP HANA to create reporting software or intranet and Internet applications:

- SAP HANA consultants, project managers, and end-user clients wanting to know how they can get the most out their SAP HANA system
- Database developers on another database system looking to switch over to this revolutionary technology
- SAP BW and SAP ERP consultants trying to understand what this new database will change for them in their everyday lives

Conventions

In this book, you will find a number of styles of text that distinguish between different kinds of information. Here are some examples of these styles, and an explanation of their meaning.

Code words in text are shown as follows: "We have in the `ORIGIN` and `DESTINATION` columns, seven values and they're all the same."

A block of code is set as follows:

```
$.response.contentType = "text/html";
var conn = $.db.getConnection();
var pstmt = conn.prepareStatement( "select * from \"_SYS_BIC\".\"book/
CUST_ATTR\"" );
var rs = pstmt.executeQuery();
var body;
```

New terms and **important words** are shown in bold. Words that you see on the screen, in menus or dialog boxes for example, appear in the text like this: "Click on the **SAP HANA available hardware configurations** link."

[Warnings or important notes appear in a box like this.]

[Tips and tricks appear like this.]

Reader feedback

Feedback from our readers is always welcome. Let us know what you think about this book—what you liked or may have disliked. Reader feedback is important for us to develop titles that you really get the most out of.

To send us general feedback, simply send an e-mail to `feedback@packtpub.com`, and mention the book title via the subject of your message.

If there is a topic that you have expertise in and you are interested in either writing or contributing to a book, see our author guide on `www.packtpub.com/authors`.

Customer support

Now that you are the proud owner of a Packt book, we have a number of things to help you to get the most from your purchase.

Downloading the example code

You can download the example code files for all Packt books you have purchased from your account at `http://www.packtpub.com`. If you purchased this book elsewhere, you can visit `http://www.packtpub.com/support` and register to have the files e-mailed directly to you.

Errata

Although we have taken every care to ensure the accuracy of our content, mistakes do happen. If you find a mistake in one of our books—maybe a mistake in the text or the code—we would be grateful if you would report this to us. By doing so, you can save other readers from frustration and help us improve subsequent versions of this book. If you find any errata, please report them by visiting `http://www.packtpub.com/submit-errata`, selecting your book, clicking on the **errata submission form** link, and entering the details of your errata. Once your errata are verified, your submission will be accepted and the errata will be uploaded on our website, or added to any list of existing errata, under the Errata section of that title. Any existing errata can be viewed by selecting your title from `http://www.packtpub.com/support`.

Piracy

Piracy of copyright material on the Internet is an ongoing problem across all media. At Packt, we take the protection of our copyright and licenses very seriously. If you come across any illegal copies of our works, in any form, on the Internet, please provide us with the location address or website name immediately so that we can pursue a remedy.

Please contact us at `copyright@packtpub.com` with a link to the suspected pirated material.

We appreciate your help in protecting our authors, and our ability to bring you valuable content.

Questions

You can contact us at `questions@packtpub.com` if you are having a problem with any aspect of the book, and we will do our best to address it.

1

So, What Is This SAP HANA Thing Anyways?

If you have an interest in the computing field of databases, business intelligence, or in-memory technology, you'll have most probably come across the term **SAP HANA** several times over the last couple of years. Over the course of the next 300 pages or so, we'll be taking a journey together through the SAP HANA development landscape, looking at most of the functions that SAP HANA provides us developers, in order to provide our users with a new outlook on their data and their daily workload.

The book is split into four main sections:

- Chapters 1 and 2: Introduction and installation
- Chapters 3, 4, 5, and 6: Database development in SAP HANA
- Chapters 7, 8, 9, and 10: Ancillary functions useful to most developments
- Chapter 11: The XS Engine for website development

In this chapter we'll take a fairly high-level look at SAP HANA and the technology that underlies the system. We'll start with a couple of comparisons to more traditional database systems, and then examine each of the advances in technology that have made SAP HANA's performance possible.

But what really is SAP HANA? The simplest answer to this question is that SAP HANA is a relational database system, just like Oracle or SQL Server, or MySQL. That's it, really? Not very exciting, when you think about it.

Of course, if that was the whole answer, then this book would be very short, so what else is there to tell?

Let's start with a very simple example of what SAP HANA can do for its users.

Time for action – statistics about internal commercial flights in the USA from 1998 to 2011

SAP markets their HANA database as being really, really fast. But how fast is it really, when there is a large amount of data in the system? The author decided to do a couple of tests to find out. Rather than creating some "fake" data, it was decided that using publicly available information would be better. This means that anyone else wanting to do some performance tests can repeat the experiment.

The US government, as a part of their "open" data initiative of making data available for analysis, released all the data concerning commercial flights inside the USA, starting in 1998 and going right through to the present day. You can find this at `http://www.transtats.bts.gov/DL_SelectFields.asp?Table_ID=236&DB_Short_Name=On-Time`.

After a couple of days of downloading the data (49 GB of CSV files), tidying it up a bit, and then loading it into SAP HANA and MySQL, it was possible to do a handful of comparisons on the two different database systems. To be fair, it has to be said that the MySQL machine has only 8 GB of memory, but it has an SSD, while the SAP HANA machine has 128 GB, but "real" disks.

As an indication of SAP HANA's data loading performance, each data file of around 1.5 GB and around five million lines, loaded using SAP HANA's native IMPORT FROM CSV FILE instruction, took approximately 45 seconds (on an average). That means around 100000 lines are loaded every second.

The first thing to note is the sheer data volume—we're talking about over 140 million lines of data, which is a reasonable dataset size. Many companies have this much data in their `orders` or `stock movement` tables, so doing a couple of stress tests on this dataset allows extrapolation on the performance which we can expect when we use SAP HANA for large applications.

Without explaining all the data fields available, we have some interesting information, such as the origin and destination airports, as well as the flight delay at departure and on arrival. With these fields, we can perform some interesting queries.

We'll start by taking a look at something relatively simple: count the number of flights leaving Los Angeles airport, per year. The SQL statement to achieve this is as follows; the syntax is same in any relational database. Don't worry, we won't be spending 300 pages writing SQL code.

```
SELECT YEAR, COUNT(*) FROM FLIGHT.ONTIME WHERE ORIGIN = 'LAX' GROUP
BY YEAR
```

First up, let's see how MySQL fares with this query (age before beauty, as they say):

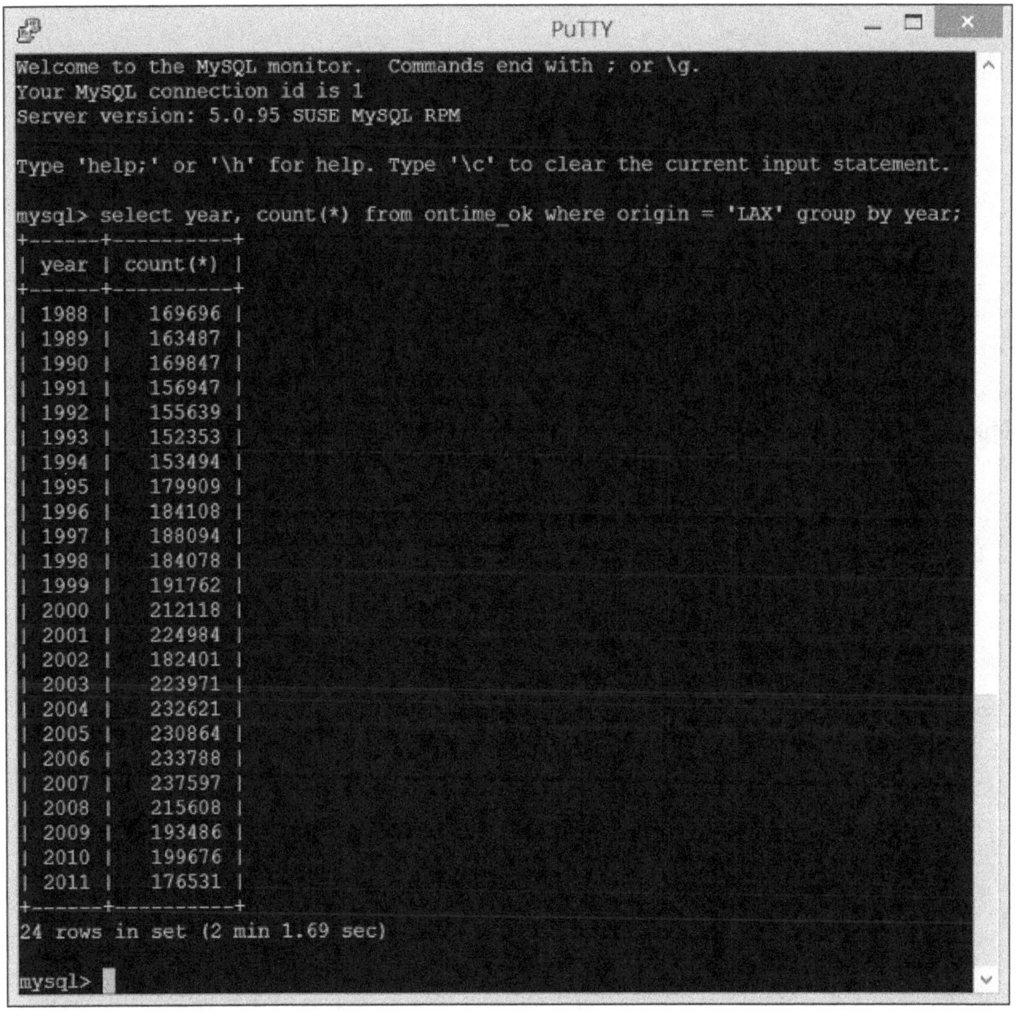

Two minutes for MySQL. Not bad at all. We could probably optimize this, at least a little, by creating an index on the `ORIGIN` and `YEAR` columns though.

Now how does SAP HANA do on the same query and same dataset:

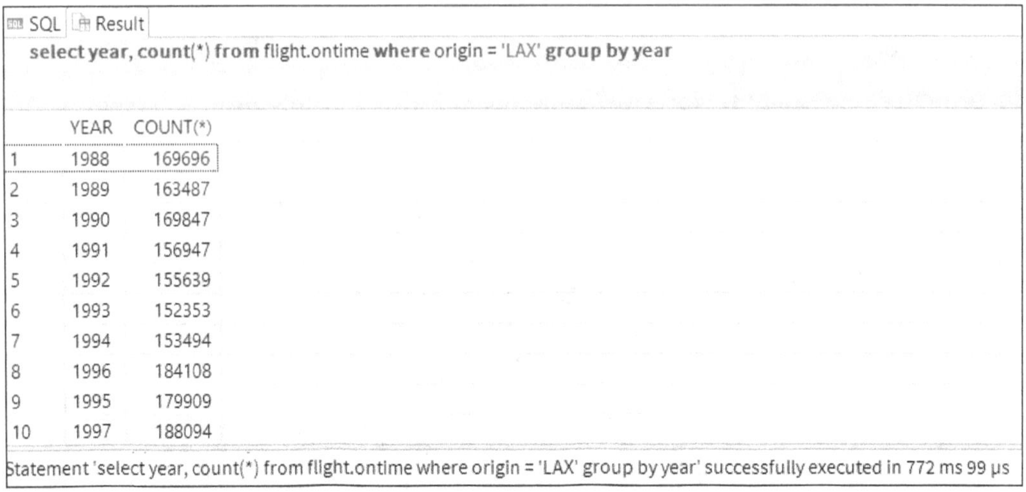
SQL Result

select year, count(*) from flight.ontime where origin = 'LAX' group by year

	YEAR	COUNT(*)
1	1988	169696
2	1989	163487
3	1990	169847
4	1991	156947
5	1992	155639
6	1993	152353
7	1994	153494
8	1996	184108
9	1995	179909
10	1997	188094

Statement 'select year, count(*) from flight.ontime where origin = 'LAX' group by year' successfully executed in 772 ms 99 µs

Well the results of the SQL are the same—which proves no cheating is going on. The time taken to resolve a query on SAP HANA is slightly under 800 milliseconds and around 160 times faster than MySQL. Impressive stuff.

How about something a little more taxing? Let's count the number of flights per day of the week, and then sort them by the number of results.

To see how MySQL fares with this query, check the following screenshot:

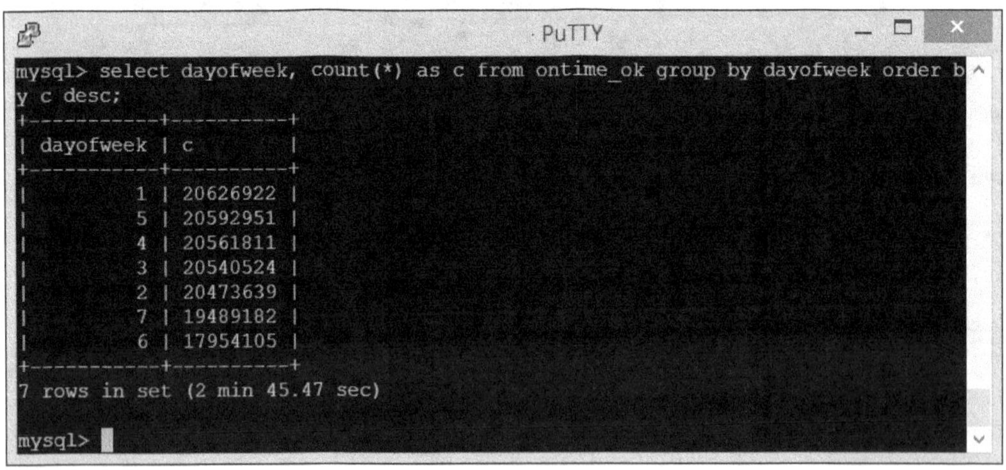
PuTTY

```
mysql> select dayofweek, count(*) as c from ontime_ok group by dayofweek order b
y c desc;
+-----------+----------+
| dayofweek | c        |
+-----------+----------+
|         1 | 20626922 |
|         5 | 20592951 |
|         4 | 20561811 |
|         3 | 20540524 |
|         2 | 20473639 |
|         7 | 19489182 |
|         6 | 17954105 |
+-----------+----------+
7 rows in set (2 min 45.47 sec)

mysql>
```

Not too shabby I suppose. MySQL looks at the full 140 million-line dataset in less than three minutes. How much time does SAP HANA take for the same query?

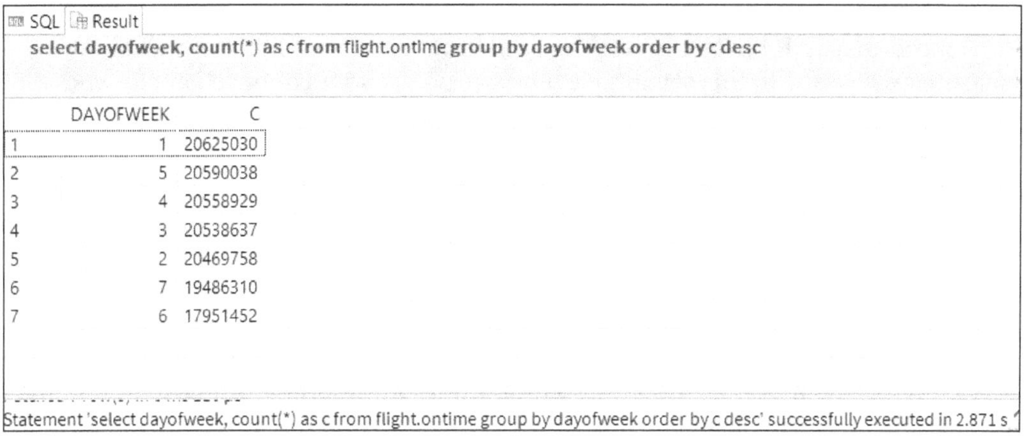

Once again, we can see that SAP HANA returns the result in a couple of seconds, where MySQL needs nearly three minutes to do the same.

If we were to summarize these results, we could say that with SAP HANA:

- The machine, working more efficiently, is less busy for less time, and can therefore do more work

With a more efficient database such as SAP HANA, your servers will be able to do even more work, getting necessary information into your users' hands faster, enabling them to spend more time analyzing data, rather than waiting for it.

What just happened?

We've just glanced through the simplest usage of SAP HANA: a "standard" (if rather fast) database. SAP HANA can be used to replace legacy databases in more or less any situation: the system provides connectors for several standard database-access protocols (ODBC and JDBC, notably), so just by unplugging your MySQL, PostgreSQL, or SQL server database, and replacing it with SAP HANA, you'll be getting immediate speedups.

Understanding the performance of SAP HANA

We noticed that SAP HANA is very fast, but how exactly are these performance measures achieved? In this section we'll take a look at some of the characteristics that make up a SAP HANA server and just how the performance that we have just seen is achieved.

Massively parallel execution

The first thing that SAP HANA does to speed up SQL queries is to break them down into manageable chunks. For the dataset we used in the previous examples, there were 140 million lines. The server that the `SAP HANA` database was running on in the previous example had 12 processors, so to speed up the queries, SAP HANA split the data into 12 chunks (of just under 12 million lines each) and ran the 12 queries all at the same time. Once the results from each subquery came in, SAP HANA then combined the results to provide the overall result.

The advantages of working in this way are immediate: today's computers, especially servers, have several CPUs, each of which has many CPU cores. By putting as many cores to work as possible, SAP HANA maximizes the power which the server can provide to every incoming query.

Most traditional databases claim to work in a similar manner—they run a handful of processes, and so are able to serve several queries at the same time. But there's a critical difference to this: nobody gets the full power of the server. In our example, the only time the server would be fully used is when 12 queries arrive all at the same time (and when a query only takes 800 milliseconds to serve in HANA, this would be relatively rare).

If we imagine a server as an image, it might look like the following image for a query on a legacy database:

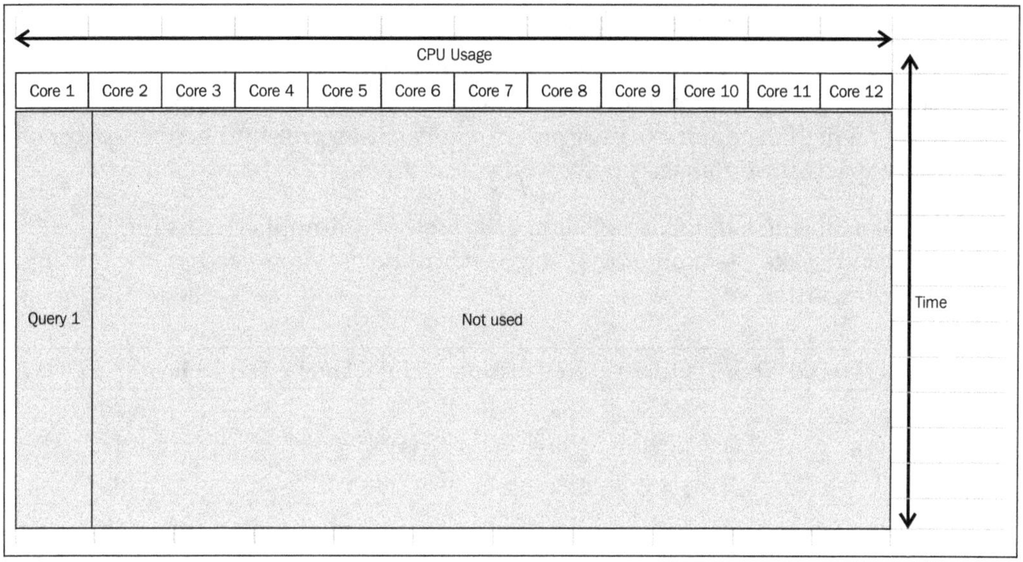

We can see that the server runs the query on one of the CPU cores, and the other 11 sit idle waiting for work.

The same query running on SAP HANA might be shown something like this:

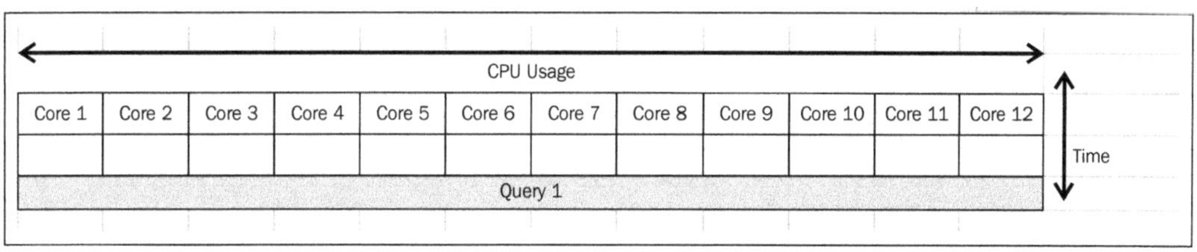

The query is running on all 12 CPU cores, making the most possible use of the server's power—and returning results around 12 times faster.

If the only innovation were parallel execution of queries, then on our example server shown here, SAP HANA would be faster 11 times out of every 12 queries received if all queries were received at exactly the same time. In all other scenarios, SAP HANA would systematically return query results faster than the legacy database.

Of course, parallel execution isn't the only trick up SAP HANA's sleeve, there's also....

Column-oriented table storage

In any given database, no matter how sophisticated, simple, fast, or slow it is, when it is boiled down, you end up with files of information on the computer's hard disk. The speed at which the database program can get at, interpret, and generally unravel these files impacts the database's perceived speed directly.

Let's picture a table in a database system. This table is a simplified (just for comprehension's sake) version of the table used in the previous section, concerning the US flight records.

Date	DayOfWeek	Origin	Destination	FlightTime	DepDelay	ArrDelay
19880101	5	LAX	JFK	305	10	15
19880102	6	LAX	JFK	301	3	4
19880103	7	LAX	JFK	311	-4	7
19880104	1	LAX	JFK	282	37	15
19880105	2	LAX	JFK	300	0	0
19880106	3	LAX	JFK	294	4	-2
19880107	4	LAX	JFK	284	16	0

In just about every database system used today (with some exceptions, mostly research projects at universities and a couple of relatively small open-source projects), data is stored in the files basically as you would expect, and might look something like this on disk:

```
198801015LAXJFK3051015198801026LAXJFK30134198801037LAXJFK311-
47198801041LAXJFK2823715198801052LAXJFK30000198801063LAXJFK2944-
2198801074LAXJFK284160
```

The fields have been laid out in the file as they appear in the table, starting with the first row, first field, then second field, and so on to the end of the first row. The operation is then repeated for the other rows in the table. While this is fairly unreadable to us, to a computer program, interpreting this file structure is no trouble at all.

Storing data in this way has one huge advantage for a database server: when you need to add a new line to a table, you just open the file, skip to the end, and write out your data. Adding data to the file is extremely fast.

Inversely, however, reading data can be relatively slow. If we ask the database for the time of the flight from LAX to JFK on the 6th of January 1988 (294 minutes), it has to read the data from the file, parse it until it gets to the `Date` field which contains 19880106, then skip to the next `Origin` field, check it contains LAX, then the `Destination`, checking it contains JFK, then to the `FlightTime` field to return the result.

Imagine the work necessary when there are millions of lines in the table.

Databases use indexes to speed up these searches. We might create an index on the `FlightDate` field, which would contain the address of the first character of the data for a given flight date. In the first line of the table, the `FlightDate` field starts at position 1 in the file. For the second line, it is position 23, and for the third line, position 43. Our index file might therefore look like this: 19880101-1, 19980102-23, 19930103-43, and so on.

This will speed up our data reads, especially if we create an index for FlightDate, Origin, and Destination in the case of the example query we've been looking at. The database system will open the index file (which is a lot simpler than the real data file), find the starting character of the needed data, then open the real data file, skip right to the correct place in the file, and read the data.

Of course, this increase in speed when reading data has one large drawback, we now have two files to maintain when we insert data. The data file must be updated and then any index files need to be updated, too. The more indexes we create to improve reading performance, the more we degrade the writing performance of our database. This, traditionally, has been a big problem in databases used both for transaction creation (so called OLTP, or online transaction processing) and reporting (OLAP, or online analytic processing). To put things simply, writing data and reading data are just not easily optimized at the same time on the same server.

If a query comes in for which there is no index, then the whole data file has to be read anyway, leading to the database administrator's worst nightmare: a "full table scan". This does just what its name suggests, it reads the whole data file (since no index exists there might be another line for 19980106 right at the end of the file, but we won't know that until we've read the whole file).

As you've probably figured out by now, this storage system is not usually how SAP HANA does things. As well as being able to use row-based tables, SAP HANA usually stores data in a column-oriented manner.

Consider a data table such as the following one existing in the database:

Row1-Field1	Row1-Field2	Row1-Field3
Row2-Field1	Row2-Field2	Row2-Field3
Row3-Field1	Row3-Field2	Row3-Field3

Rather than storing the data as:

Row1-Field1, Row1-Field2, Row1-Field3, Row2-Field1, Row2-Field2, and so on.

A column-oriented database stores data as:

Row1-Field1, Row2-Field1, Row3-Field1, Row1-Field2, Row1-Field2, and so on.

If we take another look at the example table we saw earlier in this chapter, that would give us a storage file something like this:

> This layout is shown for example purposes, this layout type is true for some column-oriented databases, but SAP HANA does not store the data files exactly like the following storage file, it takes the storage to another level that will be explained in a moment.

```
1988010119880102198801031988010419880105198801061988010756712 34LA
XLAXLAXLAXLAXLAXLAXJFKJFKJFKJFKJFKJFKJFK30530131128230029428 4103-
43704161547150-20
```

What difference does this way of storing data make? When you read the table to do reporting, for example, all the values of a column are stored together, so if we need to find "all the rows for January 6th, 1988" then we don't need to look at the whole file, just the first part, which contains the first column. There's no need to read, skip forward, check, read, skip forward, and so on.

SAP HANA takes this one step further, storing each column in a separate file:

Col1:19880101198801021988010319880104198801051988010619880107
Col2:5671234
Col3:LAXLAXLAXLAXLAXLAXLAX
Col4:JFKJFKJFKJFKJFKJFKJFK
Col5:3053013112823002942844
Col6:103-4370416
Col7:1547150-20

If SAP HANA needs to answer the query we saw earlier (the time of the flight from LAX to JFK on the 6th of January 1988), then the server can again cut the query into several components:

FlightDate = 19880106
Origin = LAX
Destination = JFK
Information to return = FLIGHTDATE

These components can be run in parallel, one CPU handling each of the tests, finding the row numbers which match:

FlightDate = 19880106 - Matching row(s) = 6
Origin = LAX - Matching row(s) = 1,2,3,4,5,6,7
Destination = JFK - Matching Row(s) = 1,2,3,4,5,6,7

Finally all that needs to be done is to find the union of each sub-result set (row 6), and return the final result (which is 294 minutes).

Of course, if reading is optimized then we can wonder whether writing to the database is much slower. As it happens, by storing each column in a separate file, SAP HANA can provide the optimum speed we saw originally in the row-based database system. When a new database row needs to be added to the table, SAP HANA just has to open each individual file, add the appropriate column-value to the end of the file, and then close the file. This can even be done to the columns in parallel.

As we can see, storing data in columns can greatly speed up queries on the database, but column storage allows SAP HANA one more trick which would be difficult with a row-storage database and that is...

Data compression

If we take another look at our example table (admittedly, the example is rather extreme), we have in the `ORIGIN` and `DESTINATION` columns, seven values and they're all the same. It's rather a shame to store all seven values; it would be much more space-friendly to store each unique value, and a list of the rows it was present in, something like this:

```
Col1:19880101198801021988010319880104198801051988010619880107
Col2:5671234
Col3:LAX(7)
Col4:JFK(7)
Col5:305301311282300294284
Col6:103-4370416
Col7:1547150-20
```

The database could see that in column 3, there are seven occurrences of the value LAX. The space used by this column has just been divided by seven. Imagine the space savings on a database table of 200 million sales order lines, all of which are in USD. The savings in disk space, and therefore in the time it takes for the disk to find data are potentially huge.

It has to be noted that compression has an impact on performance, especially when data is added to the database. Column files need to be uncompressed, new data added, and then recompressed to maintain both compression quality and optimum read speed. In order not to penalize users when data is written to the database, SAP HANA keeps two separate versions of a column file. The main storage contains the compressed table contents, and the delta storage contains data freshly added to the database and which hasn't been compressed yet. When the system is idle, or when the delta storage represents a certain percentage of the main storage, the table is recompressed in the background.

Of course, we could ask why data compression is such a big deal when disks are so cheap nowadays, and that's where SAP HANA's (probably) best playing card can be brought out.

In-memory technology

SAP HANA tries as much as possible to not serve data from hard disks. They're just too slow. Whenever a table is requested in a query, SAP HANA loads the whole table into memory, and from then on, serves the query results directly from memory. Reading from memory has been, for many years, a few orders of magnitude faster than reading data from hard disks (SSDs have clawed back some of the hard disk losses, but they're still much, much slower than main memory).

Keeping all the data in memory means that accessing it is at least 150 times faster.

Of course, this means that SAP HANA can't really be run on "just any old server". How many machines have you seen with, say 128 GB of RAM? 256 GB? 1 Tera? Not many, and that's why SAP HANA isn't sold as a piece of software you can "just install".

SAP HANA as an appliance

SAP only sells HANA as an appliance. You cannot purchase SAP HANA as a DVD set from SAP. You have to purchase an appliance which is a certified server configuration from one of the SAP's hardware partners such as Dell, Cisco, or IBM. The hardware partner builds the machine to SAP's specifications, has it certified by SAP as conforming to the requirements of the SAP HANA database, and then installs SAP HANA on it. You can purchase the SAP HANA license from SAP, but the software and the hardware are actually sold together as a bundle: an appliance.

This method allows SAP much greater control over the SAP HANA ecosphere, guaranteeing a certain level of performance from the database, and keeping support calls to a reasonable level.

Since the servers are all configured to a certain level, SAP can more easily tell customers what performance they are likely to achieve from their SAP HANA installation.

Full information about SAP partners' available configurations for SAP HANA appliances are available from the `sap.com` website at `http://www.sap.com/solutions/technology/in-memory-computing-platform/hana/partners/index.epx` and click on the **SAP HANA available hardware configurations** link.

This document requires a **SAP Service Marketplace** login for downloading, but here is a sample screenshot:

SAP HANA PAM: Supported Hardware Platforms for SAP HANA Single Node 2/7

HW Vendor	Server System	CPU	Log volume (1*Memory)	Data volume (4*Memory)	Memory	File System	Operating Systems
Cisco	UCS C260 M2	2*Westmere EX Intel E7-2870 (2,4 GHz)	6* 100 GB SSD, configured as RAID 10	8* disks 600GB 10k rpm , configured as RAID 0+1	128 GB RAM	ext3	SLES 11 SP1, SP2 or SLES for SAP 11 SP2
Cisco	UCS C260 M2	2*Westmere EX Intel E7-2870 (2,4 GHz)	6* 100 GB SSD, configured as RAID 10	8* disks 600GB 10k rpm , configured as RAID 0+1	256 GB RAM	ext3	SLES 11 SP1, SP2 SLES for SAP 11 SP2
Cisco	UCS C460 M2	4*Westmere EX	2* Fusion-io ioDrive 320 GB, or	10* disks 300GB 10k rpm,	512 GB RAM	ext3, xfs	SLES 11 SP1, SP2

Summary

You now have a general idea of what makes SAP HANA different from traditional database systems. SAP HANA is a complete system: a massively-parallel, column-oriented, in-memory database appliance, offering several technological differences to other database systems in order to give superior performance over a number of use cases.

There are several other functions offered by SAP HANA, such as complex data models handled natively, an integrated development environment, and other features. These make the system a complete, integrated option allowing businesses to rethink their database management, and allowing users faster access to their data, and ultimately allowing them to spend their time analyzing the data, not waiting for it.

In the next chapter, we'll be taking a closer look at the SAP HANA development environment, the SAP HANA Studio. This is an Eclipse-based tool giving access to all aspects of the SAP HANA appliance.

2

SAP HANA Studio – Installation and First Look

In the previous chapter we took a quick look at what SAP HANA is under the hood. In this chapter we'll be getting a little more personal with SAP HANA itself. We will be looking at several aspects of the system, including:

- The different ways of acquiring access to a SAP HANA server
- Downloading and installing the SAP HANA Studio
- An overview of the functions provided by the SAP HANA Studio
- Importing some data into the SAP HANA server

> The examples in this book were all made and tested with SAP HANA release SP5, made available in November 2012. The Studio version used was release 45. If you use an earlier version of either the server or the Studio, some features will not be available (the whole of *Chapter 11, Application Development Using the XS Engine*, notably). Additionally, some of the screenshots reproduced in this book will not look exactly the same. The features, however, all work with at least release SP4 of the SAP HANA server, and release 38 of the Studio.
>
> If you use a Studio and/or server release after release 45/SP5, there is a fair chance that the screenshots won't look the same either. The features and concepts should all work just fine however, though you might need to click on a different button or menu entry.

Getting access to SAP HANA

If you want to do any development work on SAP HANA, the first thing you need is access to a server.

There are currently three ways to access a SAP HANA machine. They have been listed in decreasing order of price:

- Purchase a SAP HANA license from SAP, and then a SAP HANA appliance from a hardware partner
- Sign up for the SAP HANA One license on a cloud-based service
- Ask SAP nicely for a free 30-day trial of SAP HANA on CloudShare

Each of these options will give you access to SAP HANA, in slightly different ways.

Purchasing a SAP HANA license and appliance

This is obviously the most expensive option, and only really feasible if you are an end user client of SAP who wishes to use SAP HANA as the database for enterprise applications.

The purchase of a SAP HANA license gives access to the SAP In-Memory download section on the **SAP Software Download Center** (**SWDC**) website, as shown in the following screenshot:

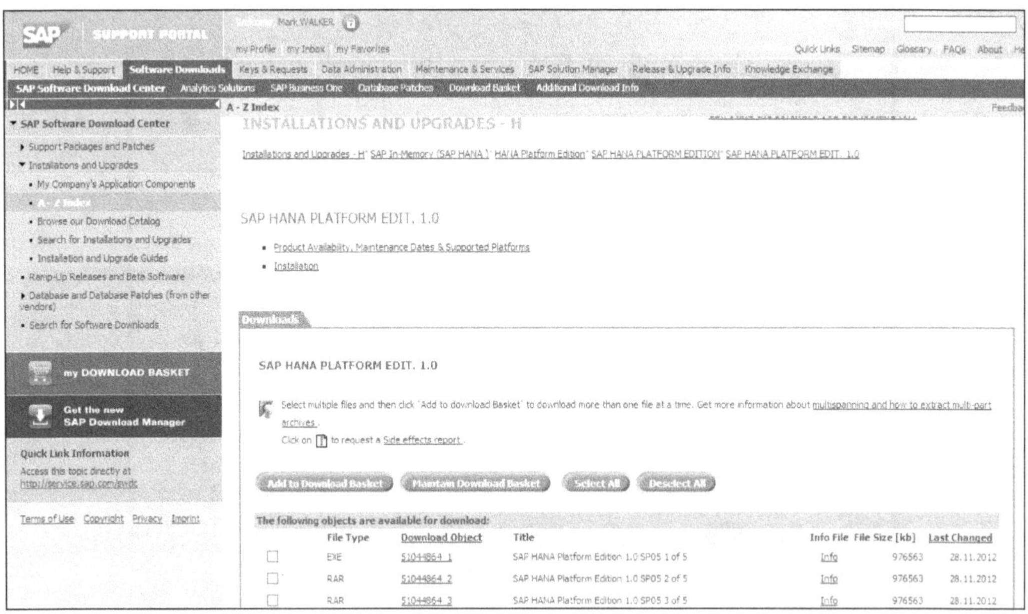

In order to access the SWDC website, you'll need a SAP Service **Marketplace** login and password (also known as an **S-User**, or **OSS username**).

You can access the SWDC at `https://service.sap.com/swdc`.

The SAP HANA section can be found by following the path **Software Downloads | Installations and Upgrades | A-Z Index | H | SAP In-Memory (SAP HANA)**.

If your Marketplace username is not authorized to access the SAP HANA downloads, you will see a **Not available content** error. If this is the case, you might like to look at the second option for SAP HANA access, via a cloud-based service.

The downloads available include upgrades to the SAP HANA server, as well as downloads for the client software, the SAP HANA Studio. Unfortunately, the Studio cannot be downloaded on its own—the whole SAP HANA bundle needs to be downloaded. The bundle contains updates to the server software as well as the Studio (for Windows and Linux) and driver components for all supported architectures. This represents nearly 5 GB of data, and might take a little while, depending on your network connection. Once the download has finished, decompress the archive—it's a Windows self-extracting archive. The following screenshot shows the subfolders created after extraction, containing the software for different uses and different machines:

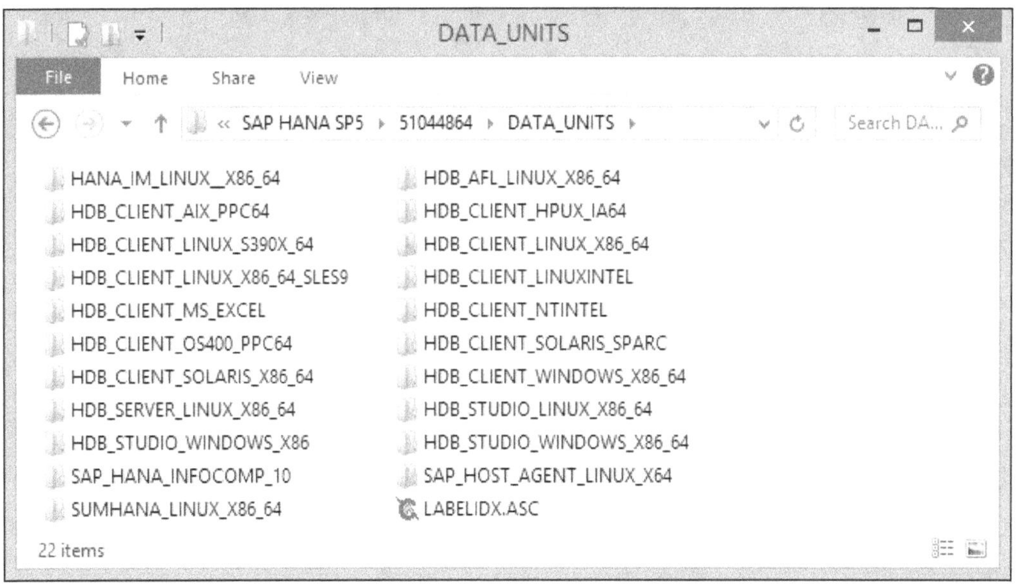

The SAP HANA Studio installations can be found in the following folders:

- `HDB_STUDIO_WINDOWS_X86` and
- `HDB_STUDIO_WINDOWS_X86_64`

Once you have located these folders, you can skip to the *Running the installation* section.

Accessing SAP HANA in the cloud

If you don't have access to a real SAP HANA appliance on-site, you can purchase access to SAP HANA via a cloud-based service. In this way you don't have any up-front payment to make, and you pay for SAP HANA only when you use it. This might be a viable solution for testing, validation, or infrequently-used servers.

On the **SAP Community Network** (**SCN**) website, you can see the list of supported cloud services, as well as the prices for each, and the technical specifications of their virtual machines. The web address for this information is `http://scn.sap.com/docs/DOC-31722`.

At the time of writing, the website looked like this:

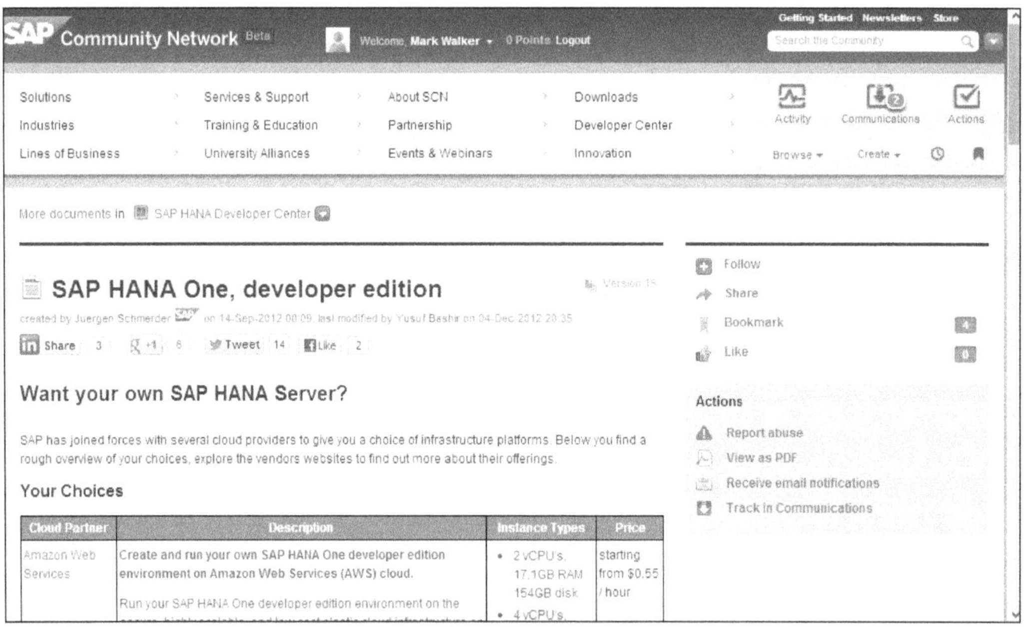

The setup documentation is very complete, and provides a step-by-step procedure for creating your account with your chosen service provider, and then setting up your HANA instance on their systems.

Just follow the instructions to get set up.

Once you have access to SAP HANA in the cloud, you can download the Studio software. The download link is at the bottom of the same page. Alternatively, a direct link to the Developer edition of the Studio software is `http://www.sdn.sap.com/irj/scn/go/portal/prtroot/docs/webcontent/uuid/10e6e3ff-6081-2f10-e690-829e62f29a26`.

Once you've access to your SAP HANA instance and downloaded the software, you can skip to the *Running the installation* section.

Getting a free 30-day trial of a SAP HANA instance from SAP

If you are just starting out with SAP HANA, and don't necessarily want to spend money on testing the system, you can ask SAP for a free 30-day trial of the system. This will give you 120 hours of server time (five calendar days), which you have to use within a 30-day period. The server can be accessed in the cloud, following the instructions you will receive in the invitation e-mail from SAP.

To request access, just go to `http://scn.sap.com/docs/DOC-28191` for full information. The form you will need to fill in is at `http://www.sdn.sap.com/irj/sdn/index?rid=/webcontent/uuid/a01f2bae-82d8-2e10-f3ac-b33d4c919918`.

The form will ask you to enter an access code. If you don't have one, just leave the form blank. The access code is only needed if you received an e-mail from SAP asking you to test SAP HANA, not the other way round!

If you access SAP HANA from the free trial, you don't need to download the Studio, as SAP preinstalls it on your virtual machine. You can therefore skip the following *Running the installation* section, and go straight to the *Welcome to the SAP HANA Studio* section.

Running the installation

Now that you have the SAP HANA Studio software downloaded, you can install it on your PC. The installation itself is very simple, but there are a couple of prerequisites:

- If you are installing on Linux, there is only a 64-bit version of the software available. You must be running a 64-bit version of Linux.
- If you are installing on Windows, you have the choice of either 32-bit or 64-bit. Choose the same version of the Studio as your version of Windows. If you don't know which version of Windows you are running, you can open the **Control Panel** and select **System** (this works with versions of Windows from Windows XP right up to Windows 8). The Windows version is listed under **System type**, as we can see here in the following screenshot:

- You must have Java installed on your machine. Recent versions of Windows do not have Java preinstalled, so you'll need to download it yourself from `http://www.java.com`.

Once you have satisfied the prerequisites, you can run the installer. Just run the `hdbsetup` program in the installation folder. The only information you'll need to provide is the destination folder, and you can usually leave this as-is:

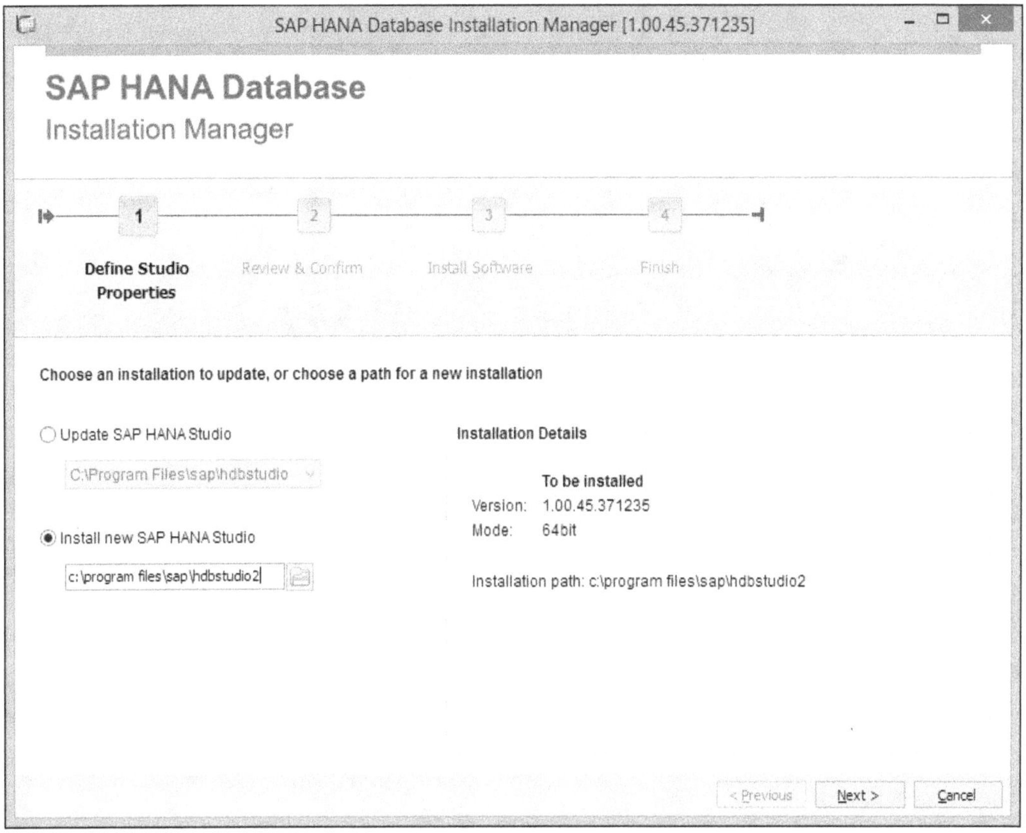

The installation will only take a couple of minutes, and you will be left with a Start menu folder called `SAP HANA` containing one entry, that of `SAP HANA Studio`.

If you run this entry now, we can get familiar with the Studio software.

Welcome to the SAP HANA Studio

When you run the Studio for the first time, you are presented with a welcome screen presenting the main functions of the program, as shown here:

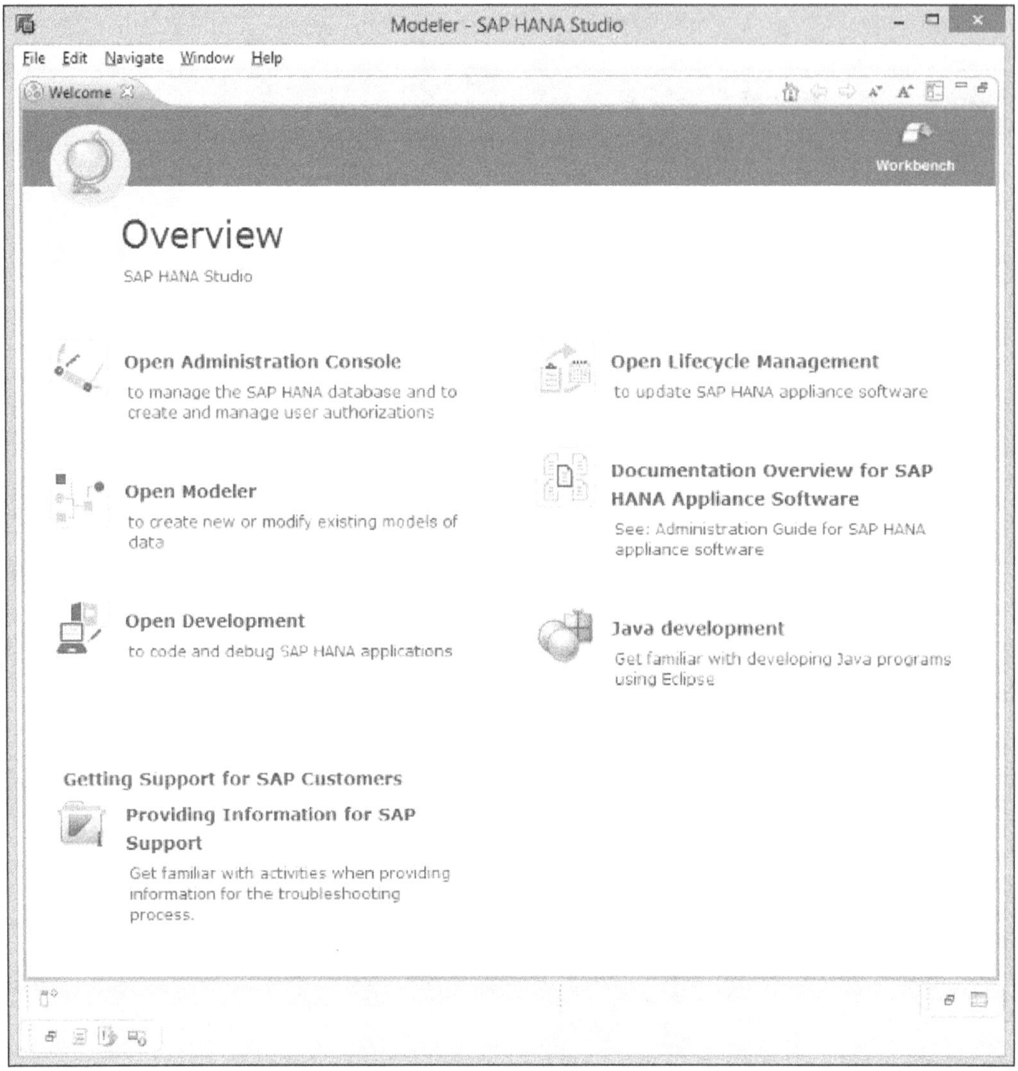

There are seven options on this screen (until release 38 of the Studio, only the first four were present):

- **Open Administration Console**: This will open a **perspective** (layout) allowing administration of the server, from User creation, to Authorization handling. No development of objects can be done in this view.
- **Open Lifecycle Management**: This perspective gives you access to functions for updating the server software. When a new version of SAP HANA is released, you can use this function to apply patches to your existing installation to bring it to the new version. Once more, no development can be done in this view, nor can any administration task be carried out, except updating the server.
- **Open Modeler**: Undoubtedly, the view where you will spend most of your time, this is where the SAP HANA information models are created. We will be looking in detail at the different types of information models later in this book, as well as how they all link together to form applications. The **Modeler** is probably the most important part of the SAP HANA Studio, and it's this view that contains the most functions and options.
- **Documentation Overview for SAP HANA Appliance Software**: The SAP HANA Studio doesn't come with any inbuilt documentation or help system, so this option opens an internal web browser to the `sap.com` website, on the SAP HANA **Help** page. All functions of the Studio, the SAP HANA system as well as the SQL syntax used by SAP HANA are described fully on this webpage. The advantage to this system is that **Help** is always up-to-date. The downside is that you must be connected to the Internet in order to see **Help**.

> If your network blocks access to specific websites, you'll need to ask your administrator for access to the following websites in order to be sure to see information from SAP about HANA (including the **Help**): `*.sap.com`.

- **Open Development**: Starting with SAP HANA SP5, web development is possible directly on the HANA appliance. This means that the whole application can be run directly on top of the SAP HANA box, and you don't need to use any external languages or tools to do so. This option opens up the SAP HANA development perspective, for Web application development. Functions available in this perspective will be discussed at length in *Chapter 11, Application Development Using the XS Engine*. If you have a SAP HANA version earlier than SP5, this functionality is not available.

- **Java Development**: The SAP HANA Studio is built upon Eclipse, the open source Java development environment (which is why Java is a prerequisite for installation). Using this perspective, you can do Java development inside the SAP HANA Studio, and since the installation includes JDBC drivers, you can connect directly to the HANA server from your Java applications.
- **Providing Information for SAP Support**: This option opens a pop up window explaining the best way to explain any problems you might have, with the Studio or with HANA itself. SAP receives thousands of support enquiries per year, and most of them need several round trips to and from the client and SAP before the problem is understood by the technician sufficiently well to be able to provide support. By following the instructions in this guide when you need to ask for help from SAP, you are improving your chances of getting the right answer to your question, faster.

Since the functions available in the **Administration Console** are available also in the **Modeler** perspective, we won't be looking in any detail at the **Administration Console**. Open up the **Modeler** perspective now and we'll take a detailed look at the different panels that are available, and what they do.

The Modeler perspective

Here is the **Modeler**, as it will appear the first time you run it:

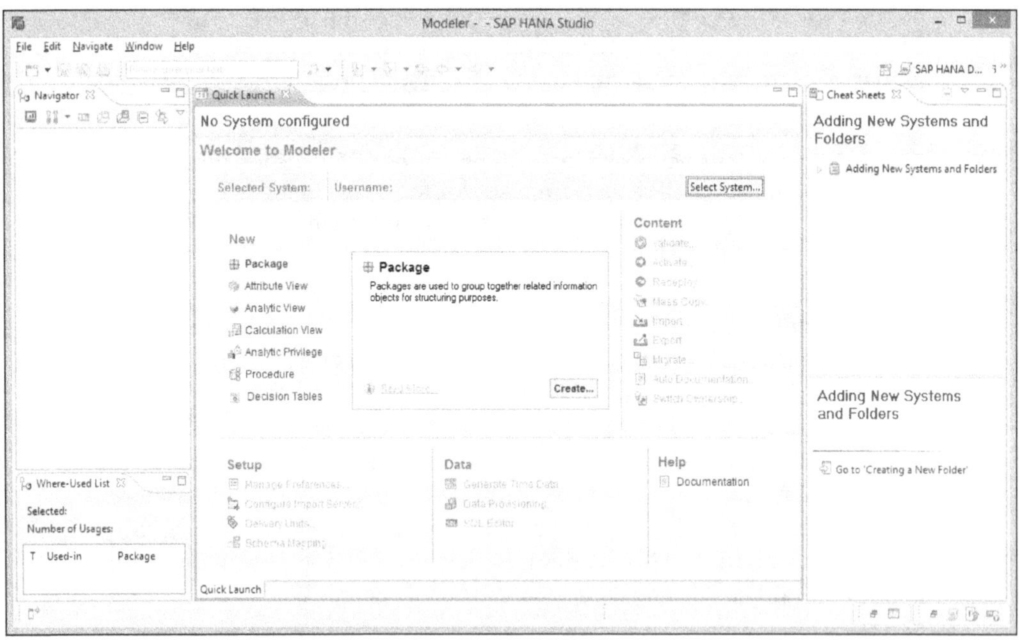

The **Modeler** perspective is split into several panels:

- **Menus**: As with most software these days, menus are used to hold the different options available to you. The different options will be explained throughout the book as we come across, or need them. When a given option is not appropriate, it is disabled. If you take a look at the menus now, you will see that nearly all the options are disabled.
- **The button bar**: Like the menus, the button bar provides rapid access to different options appropriate to the development being done. Again, right now they are nearly all disabled, except the very first one **New**, which allows you to create a new project.
- **The Navigator panel**: The **Navigator** panel, when filled-in, will contain the list of SAP HANA servers configured on your machine. This panel provides a tree-like structure, inside which you will see the different types of objects available for the SAP HANA servers you configure. For example, you will see the different tables you create in the database, as well as the HANA modeling views. At the top of the **Navigator** panel, there is a row of buttons that provide quick access to the different functions this panel provides.
- **Where-Used List**: If you are familiar with SAP ERP or SAP BW development, you will have come across the notion of where-used list before. This function shows you where the object currently selected in the **Navigator** panel is used. For example, if you have an **attribute view**, and you use it in an **analytic view**, selecting the attribute view in the **Navigator** panel will list the analytic view in **Where-Used List**.

> The notions of the attribute view and the analytic view will be discussed in detail in *Chapter 3, Your First SAP HANA Development - An Attribute View*) and *Chapter 4, Painting with Numbers - An Analytic View.*

- **Quick Launch**: Occupying the largest part of the screen is the **Quick Launch** panel. This panel provides, as its name suggests, a quick way to run most of the development tasks available in the Studio. As we can see in the previous screenshot, it allows you to create new objects and perform actions on existing objects (such as validating they are correct, or importing and exporting them). You can also configure your Studio software and perform other administration tasks, such as generating calendar data. By default, SAP HANA knows nothing about the calendar, such as which week is in which month, and which month is in which year; this data has to be created before you can do calculations on date and time information.

- **Cheat Sheets**: Depending on the action you are currently performing, the **Cheat Sheets** panel will provide helpful ways to perform the most common tasks you might need to do. Here, for example, we've just installed the Studio and it knows that we won't be able to do any useful work until we connect it to a SAP HANA server. Therefore, the **Cheat Sheet** panel is offering to help us add a new server to the **Navigation** panel.

Connecting to the SAP HANA server

Now that we've taken a look at the different panels available in the Studio, we can connect to our SAP HANA server.

> You'll need the connection information for your server at this point. This includes:
>
> - The address of the server
> - The SAP HANA instance number
> - Whether you connect using a username and password, or using **Single sign-on** (**SSO**) and the SSO method if appropriate
>
> If you don't know this information, ask your system administrator.
>
> Additionally, for the examples in the book to work correctly, you will need the authorization to create schemas and tables, as well as modeling objects. When your system administrator asks the authorizations you need, you can say that they are:
>
> - PUBLIC
> - CONTENT_ADMIN
> - MODELING
>
> Authorizations will be covered fully in *Chapter 7, Hey! That's My Data! – Authorizations in SAP HANA*.

In order to create a connection to your SAP HANA server, you can proceed in one of the following two ways:

- Follow the **Cheat Sheet** panel's **Adding a New Systems and Folders** wizard. This will take you step by step through the creation of a new connection in the Studio.
- Right-click in the **Navigator** panel, and select **Add System** from the menu.

Both methods will lead you to the same **System** dialog, as shown in the following screenshot:

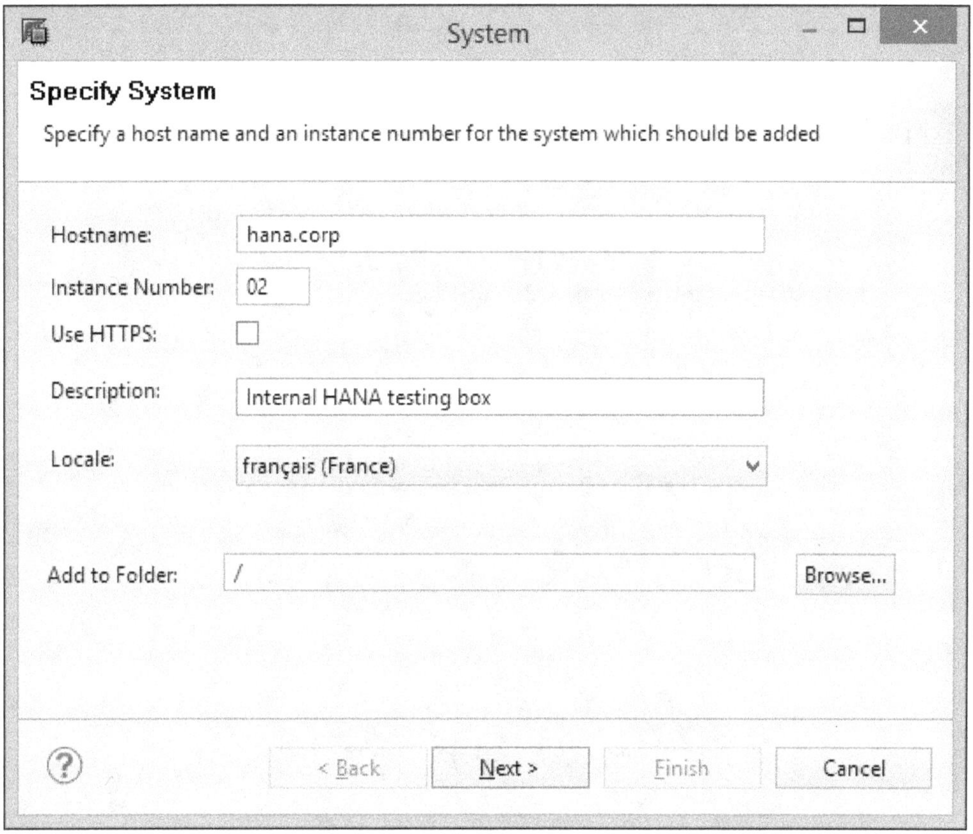

We can see in the screenshot that we are adding a server on the machine at the address **hana.corp**, with an instance number of **02**.

The instance number allows for several copies of the SAP HANA database to run on the same machine at the same time. You might, for example, have one copy of the database running for development tasks, and another copy for validation that the developments are correct. In this way you have one instance where the state of development might be relatively unstable because developers are continually making changes to the information models, and a second instance where only developments that are considered complete are present, and which is therefore more stable.

Clicking on **Next** will make the Studio validate that it can connect to the server whose address you specify, and will prompt you for your connection information:

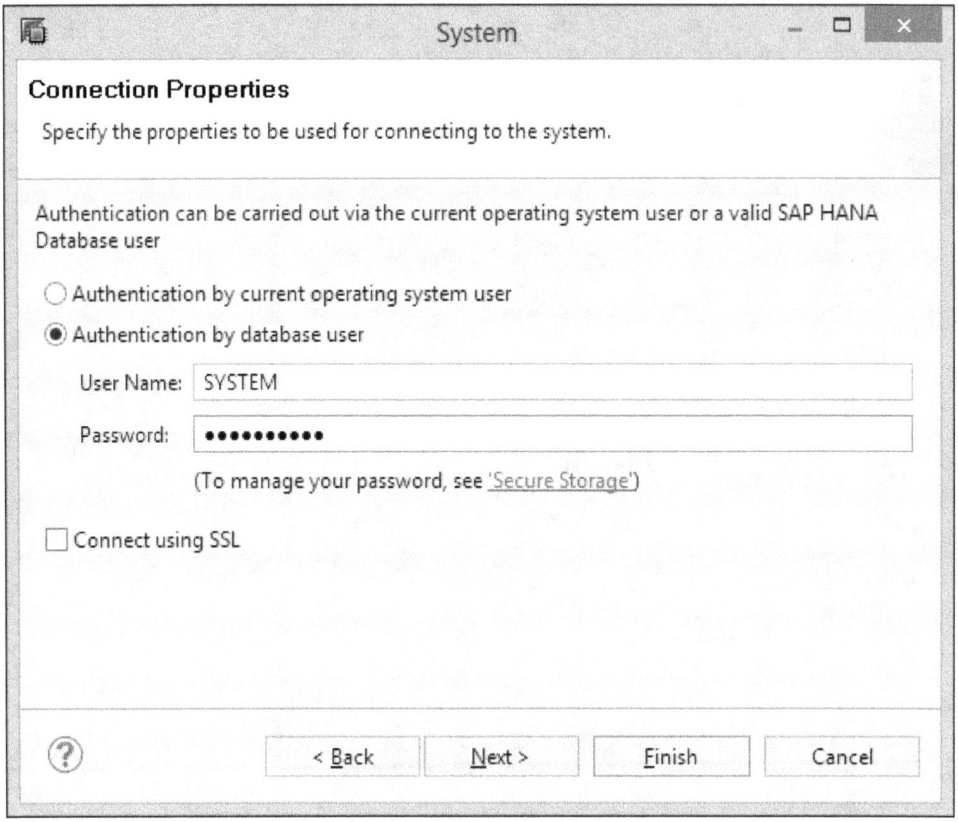

In this example, we're connecting to the server using a provided username and password. We also have the possibility of connecting using our Windows login credentials, if the system administrator has configured the server to allow this.

Clicking on **Finish** will add the connection information to the Studio, so that from now on we won't have to enter the information any more. The SAP HANA server will be added to the **Navigator** panel, and we'll see the different types of object stored in the database, as shown in the following screenshot:

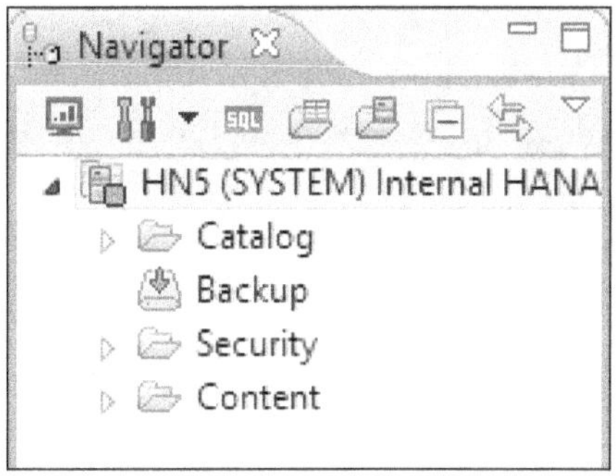

Our server (**HN5**), to which we connect using the **SYSTEM** user, has been added to our Studio. On this server, there are three families of objects (`Catalog`, `Security`, and `Content`), as well as an option to examine the backup status of the server (`Backup`).

The `Catalog` folder contains pure SQL objects such as schemas, tables, database views, and so on. These are the same types of objects you would find in any given database; they are not specific to SAP HANA.

The `Security` folder contains the information related to the security and authorizations in the SAP HANA server. For example, it contains the list of authorization roles and users, and allows manipulation of these objects. We'll be looking in detail at the authorization concept in SAP HANA in *Chapter 7, Hey! That's My Data! - Authorizations in SAP HANA*.

Finally, the `Content` folder will contain the SAP HANA information models we create. These objects are specific to SAP HANA, and represent our developments on the server. Creation of these objects will be covered in detail in *Chapter 3, Your First SAP HANA Development - An Attribute View* to *Chapter 6, You Talking to Me? - Scripted Calculation Views*.

Importing sample data

The first thing we need to do in order to begin developing data models in SAP HANA is to import some sample tables and data. Some data has been prepared for this book, which will enable us to use all the features of the SAP HANA Studio and develop a reporting application. You don't have to use the sample data if you don't want to; you can follow the examples in the book using your own data if you prefer. However, if you use the data that's been prepared, you'll be able to see the example application unfold, using the different functionalities that SAP HANA provides.

> **Downloading the example code**
>
> You can download the example code files for all Packt books you have purchased from your account at `http://www.packtpub.com`. If you purchased this book elsewhere, you can visit `http://www.packtpub.com/support` and register to have the files e-mailed directly to you.

This sample data will allow us to build a large range of data models, and will show the different features available in SAP HANA and SAP HANA Studio. The notion of speed of execution will not be covered; if we wanted to stress-test the database, we'd need millions of lines in tens of tables, which would not be feasible from a development perspective. If you need to test the performance of SAP HANA, please feel free to do so on a large dataset you prepare with your own data, or data you acquire freely from the Internet.

> The data used in *Chapter 1, So, What Is This SAP HANA Thing Anyways?*, to show SAP HANA's performance (information on commercial flights in the USA) can be acquired by download, contact the author directly by e-mail for the download link. Please bear in mind that the download size is over 5 GB, and represents nearly 50 GB of files on the disk, not counting the size taken by the data once loaded into SAP HANA.

The data prepared for this book represents the **Revenue** by **Customer** over three **Years**. Each customer is assigned to a **Sector** (large, small, or tiny customers), and a **Country**. Countries have been organized into **Regions** (the UK is in Europe, for example). The textual representations of the different objects are available in the data in different languages (English and French) represented by the `Lang` field. Additionally, each table has a field called `MANDT`. This field will be familiar to SAP ERP developers, as it represents the notion of **session client** or **instance**, where one given SAP ERP machine can have multiple instances of the software running at once, on the same database. The `MANDT` field allows for data from different instances to be kept separate.

Once the archive has been uncompressed, you will be provided with a folder structure containing the tables, their data, and the information SAP HANA needs to correctly recreate the information, as shown in the following screenshot:

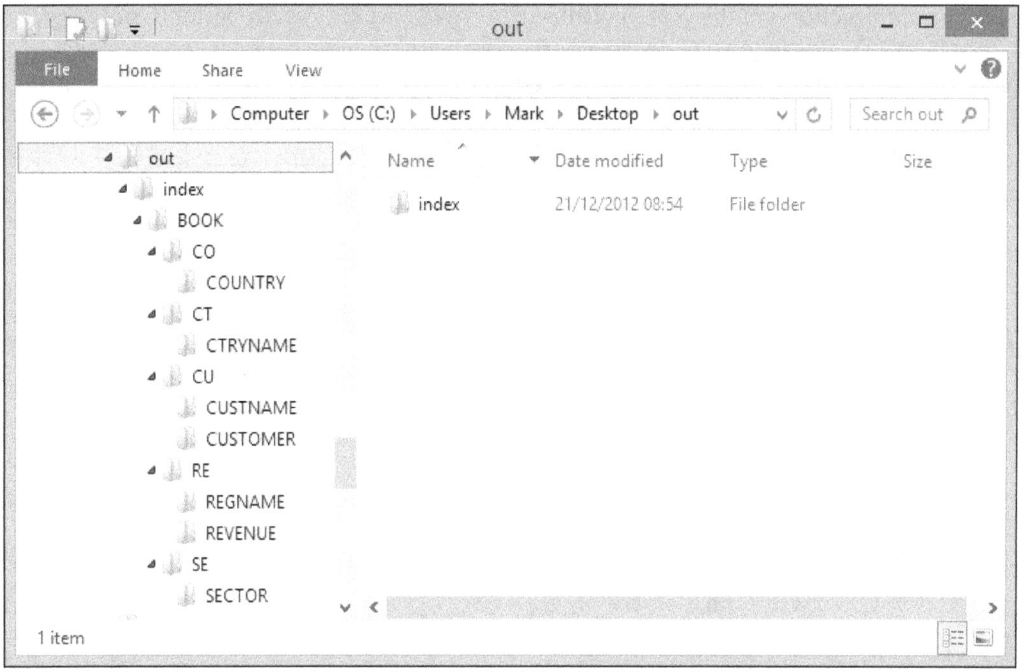

Inside the `index` folder is a folder called `BOOK`, which is the name of the database schema. Inside this folder are the seven tables; each table is represented by a folder, inside of which are several files describing the design of the table, its contents, and other metadata used by SAP HANA. We'll be importing this information into our SAP HANA server in a moment, but let's first take a look at how these data files were created.

SAP HANA object export

> This section deals with exporting data from SAP HANA. You don't need to do any of the actions in this section, they are just listed for reference, in case you need to use the export function later in your own developments.

This directory structure was created automatically by the SAP HANA Studio's **Export** functionality. This function allows the creation—either on the HANA server or on the local PC—of files representing the contents of the SAP HANA system.

The Export function can be called either from the **Quick Launch** panel (**Content** | **Export**), or from the menu (**File** | **Export**). The first thing to select is the type of object to be exported from the large selection of object types provided by the Studio, as shown in the screenshot:

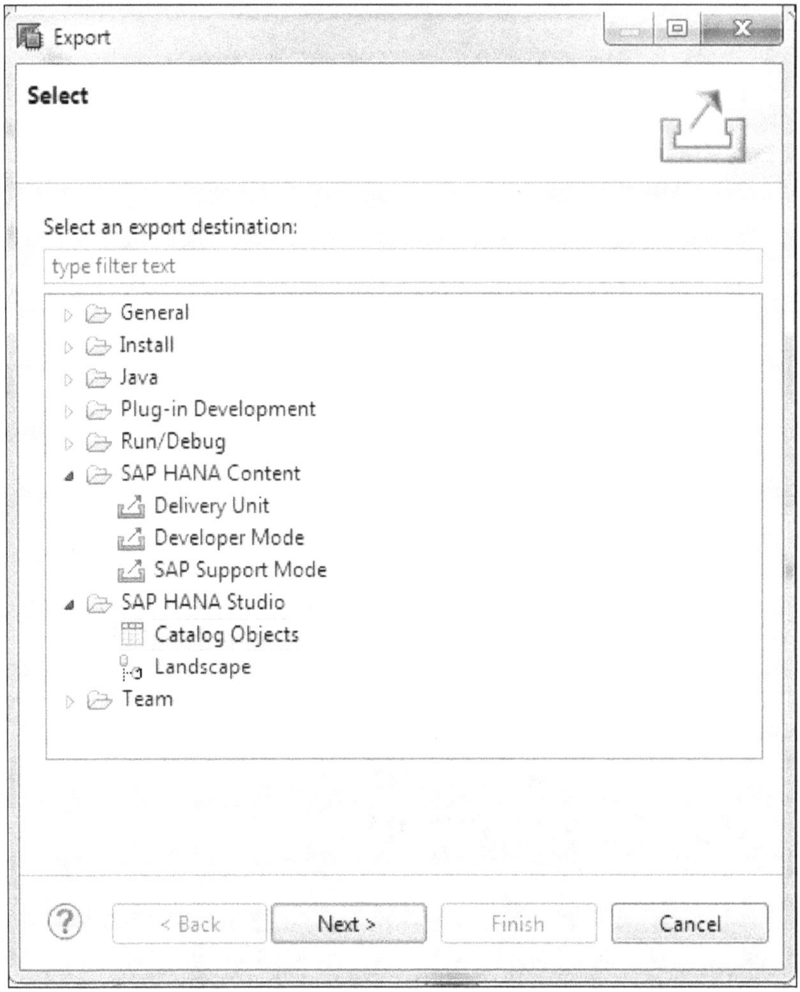

Several of the export options shown in the screenshot are provided by the Eclipse tool, while others (the `SAP HANA Content` and `SAP HANA Studio` folders) are specific to SAP HANA. In order to export tables and their data the option used was **Catalog Objects**. This option allows export of tables, schemas, and database views (but not SAP HANA modeling objects).

The names of the objects to be exported need to be selected next. These have to be selected by name using the text field at the top of the following dialog box:

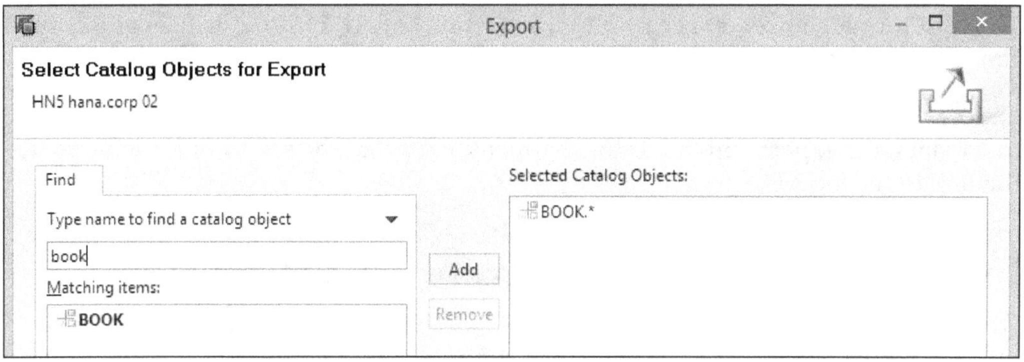

We can see in the screenshot that a search was done for all objects containing the word "book". The only matching object was the **BOOK** schema, and once it was added to the **Selected Objects** list, the Studio proposed to export the schema and all of its subobjects (this can be seen by the asterisk).

The final stage in the export process is the destination selection:

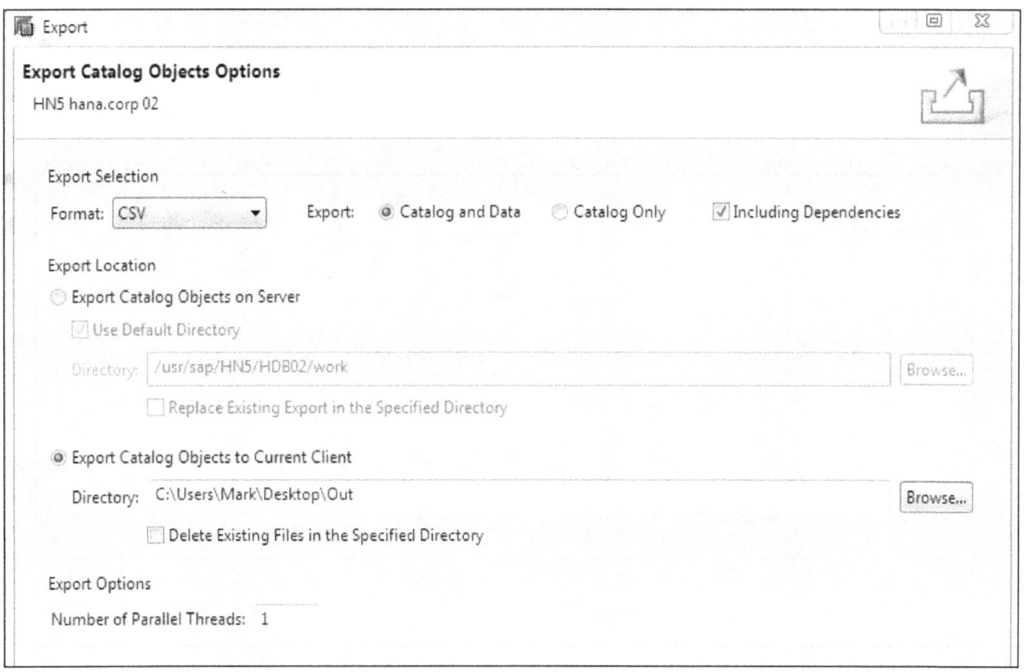

As we can see in the screenshot, export can be done either to the SAP HANA server or to the local PC, in either the **CSV** or **BINARY** format. The BINARY export is easier for SAP HANA to re-use on import, and takes up slightly less space in the data files. The CSV format, however, is easier to use outside of SAP HANA, as files of this type can be opened in many different tools, such as Microsoft Excel.

Export to the local PC can only be done on limited quantities of data. If there is too much data, the export will fail. If this happens, export to the server and then transfer the files to the local PC.

Importing exported data into SAP HANA

Once data has been exported from one SAP HANA instance, it can easily be imported into another. We'll be using this function here to import the sample data we downloaded earlier.

The **Import** function can be launched, just like the Export function, either from the **Quick Launch** panel or from the menu (**Content** | **Import** or **File** | **Import**, as appropriate).

The first screen of the **Import** dialog is identical to the first screen of the **Export** dialog we saw earlier. This screen allows us to select the type of data we are importing. As in the previous section, we are importing **Catalog Objects**.

On the second screen of the dialog, we choose the location containing the data to be imported, as we can see here:

The folder to select is the one that contains the `index` subfolder. By selecting this level, the Studio will be able to detect the schema name and the table names. Once we click on **Next**, the Studio will present us with a list of importable objects in the selected folder, and we can choose those we wish to import:

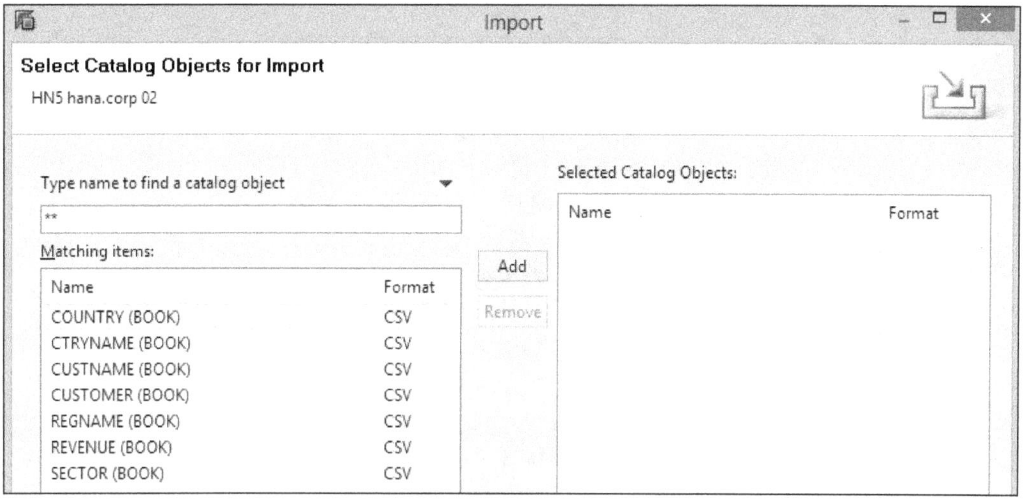

In order to use the sample data for the examples in this book, select all the tables in the **Matching items** list, and click on **Add** to add them to the **Selected Catalog Objects** list. Click on **Next** to go to the following screen, where we can choose whether to import just the description of the tables (**Catalog Only**) or the table contents as well (**Catalog and data** – this is the option we need). Click on **Finish** to run the import.

The import itself will only take a couple of seconds, and once it's done, just refresh the **Navigator** panel (by clicking on the server name and then pressing the *F5* key) to see the new **BOOK** schema under the **Catalog** node, and then the tables we just imported listed under the **Tables** node. The result should look similar to this screenshot:

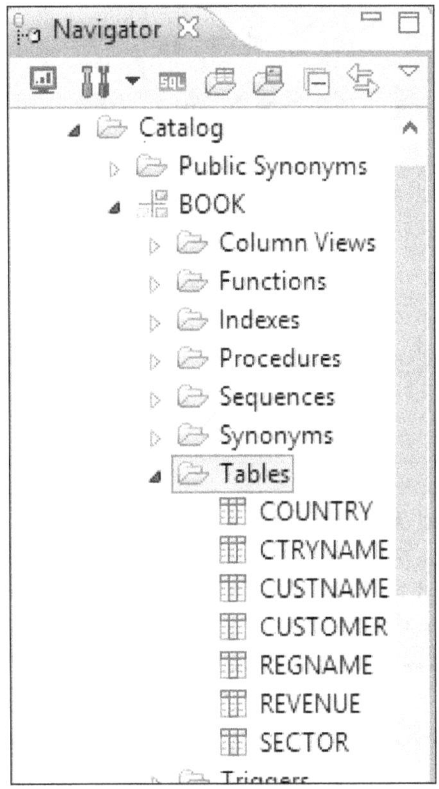

Previewing the sample data

Now that the data for the examples in the book is in our SAP HANA system, we can take a few minutes to examine it and get familiar with it.

Here is a visual representation of the sample data:

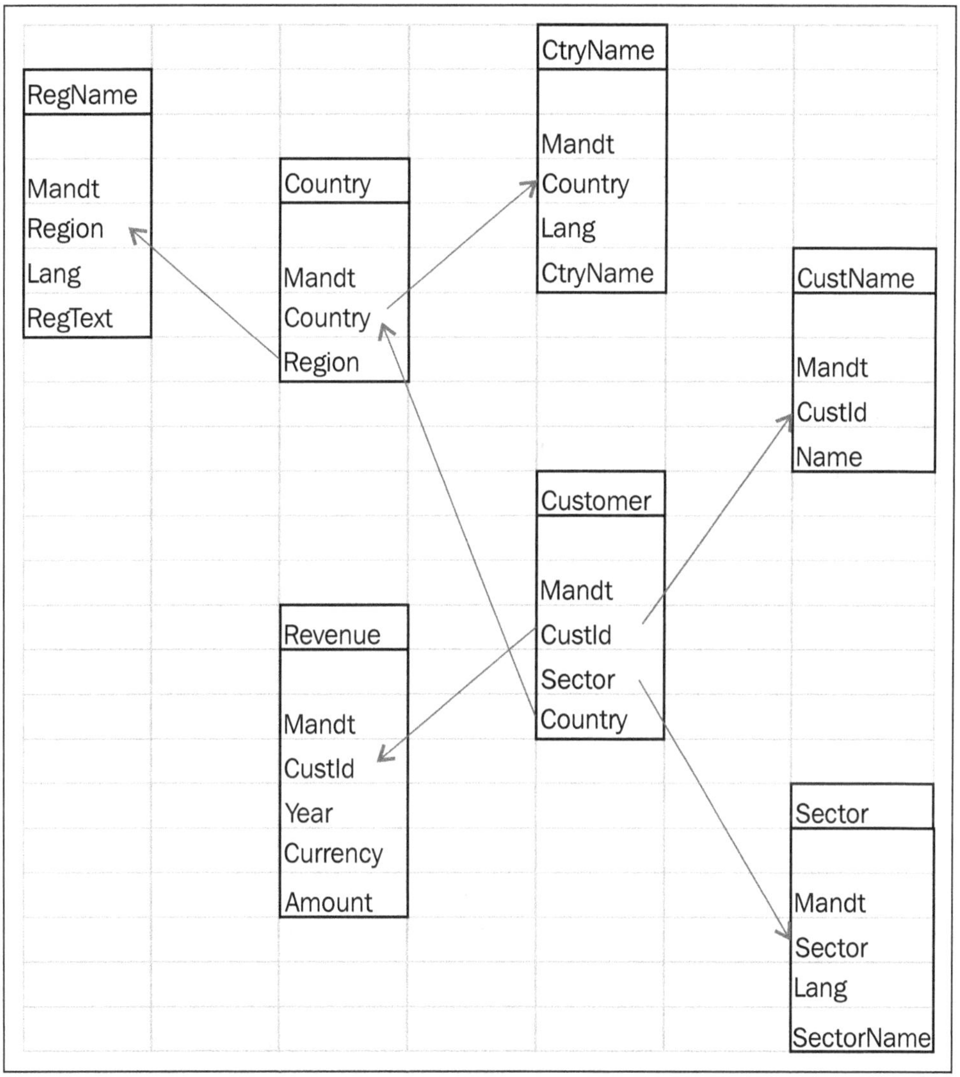

The Studio offers a very useful **Data Preview** tool, which can be used to see the contents of tables (and indeed any modeling view we create later). To access this function, just right-click on the table (or view) name, and select **Data Preview**. The following is a screenshot showing the contents of the `CUSTOMER` table we just imported, so that you can compare it with the data in your SAP HANA system:

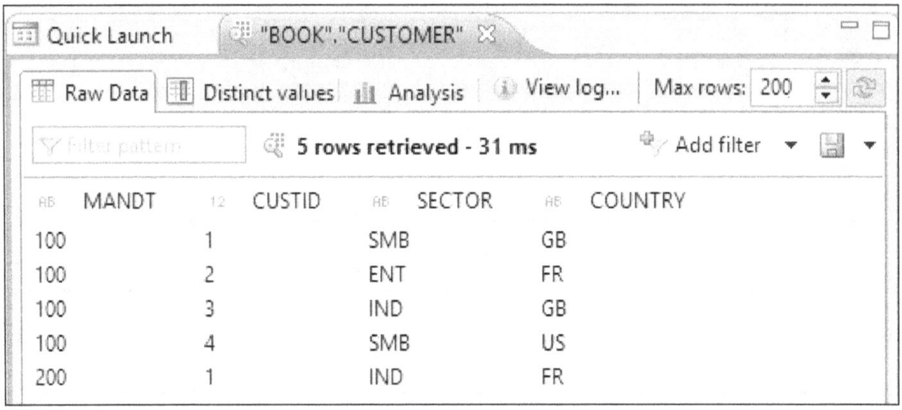

The Data Preview function does what its name suggests, it shows you the raw data in the underlying table. There are other possibilities offered by this tool, which we will see in detail later.

You might like to take a few minutes to have a look at the data in each of the tables we imported, and compare what you see to the schema of the links between the tables on the previous page. When you are happy that you understand the data, and the joins between the tables, we can move on to the next step, which is the creation of an attribute view. This will be examined in detail in the next chapter.

Summary

In this chapter, we have taken a look at the different options available to access a SAP HANA instance, from purchasing a license and a machine (very expensive) and accessing an instance on the cloud (relatively expensive), to a trial account offered by SAP (free).

Next, we installed the SAP HANA Studio, the administration and modeling tool used to interact with the SAP HANA server. We looked at the different functions offered by the software, and the parts of the user interface.

Finally, we imported some sample data into our SAP HANA instance. This data will be used throughout the book as a reference for the models we create, and using the Data Preview function in the Studio, we took a first look at the data itself.

In the next chapter, we'll be building our first data model in SAP HANA, an attribute view. This will allow us to gather data from several tables together in one place, creating one virtual table we can then re-use in other developments.

3

Your First SAP HANA Development – An Attribute View

Over the past few pages, we've taken a look at the SAP HANA Studio, imported some data and taken a look at it. We are now in a position to do some SAP HANA development work. After some initial housekeeping to prepare the Studio for our developments, we'll be taking a closer look at our tables and data, the links that exist between them, and how SAP HANA can gather the data into one place for intelligent use later.

Creating a delivery unit

Before we can create any of our developments per se, we have to do a little housekeeping. The very first thing to create is called a delivery unit. This object is basically a container, and is used to transport your developments from the development machine, through to quality and in to production without making any changes (and hence possibly avoiding unnecessary errors) in any machine other than development. It is the basic box used to transport objects together. For readers familiar with development in the SAP **Enterprise Resource Planning** (**ERP**) or SAP **Business Warehouse** (**BW**) environments, it is the equivalent to the notion of transport order.

> This first step is not strictly obligatory; however, it is something you will need to do for nearly every development. It is part of the SAP HANA best practices for development.

From the **Quick Launch** panel, under **Setup** at the bottom, select **Delivery Units**, as you can see in the following screenshot:

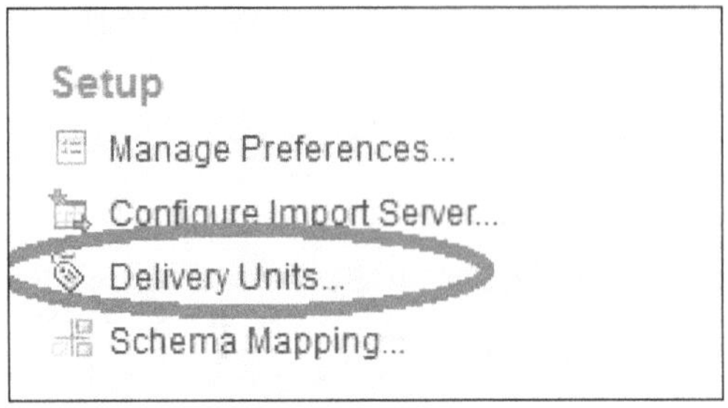

The **Delivery Units** dialog will open. There might be some delivery units already present in the list—we'll create a new one for our development.

Just click on **Create** now to see the **New Delivery Unit** dialog.

> At this point you might receive an error stating that you cannot create a delivery unit because the content vendor is not defined for your SAP HANA system. If this is the case, close the two dialog boxes that are open and we'll define the content vendor.
>
> In the **Navigator** panel, double-click on the system name to see the administration tab which will be placed alongside the **Quick Launch** panel. Select the **Configuration** tab. You will be presented with a list of configuration options. In the filter box, type `vendor`, to restrict the selection:

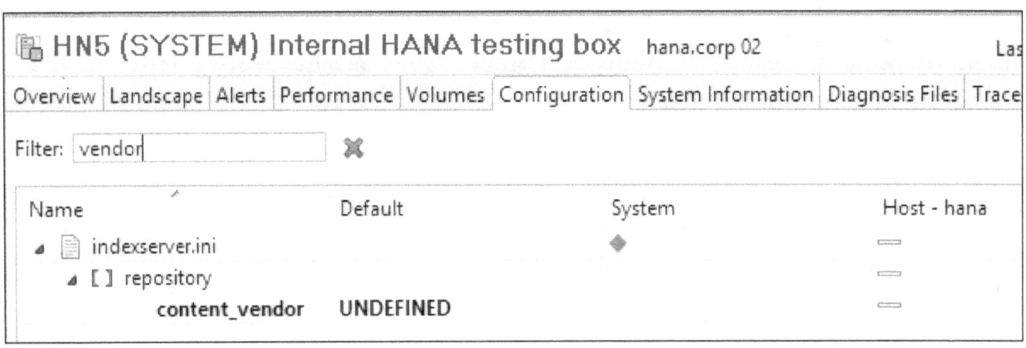

> Double-click on the `System` column, next to the word **UNDEFINED**, then type in some representative string to be the content vendor. The value does not actually have any meaning for SAP HANA, it just identifies, for a given delivery unit, who created it. Once you have entered a value, click on **Save** to see the results, which should look something like the following:

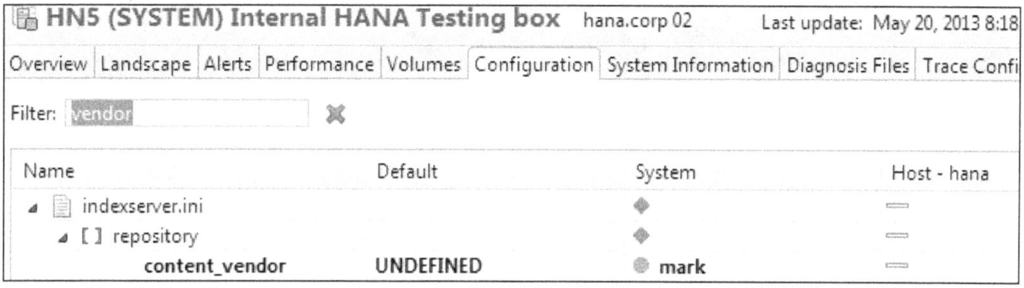

> Your value will now be present in the `System` column. You can at this point close the **Administration** tab. Now reopen the **Delivery Units** dialog, and click on **Create** once more to create our delivery unit.

The **New Delivery Unit** dialog asks for several pieces of information, as we can see in the following screenshot:

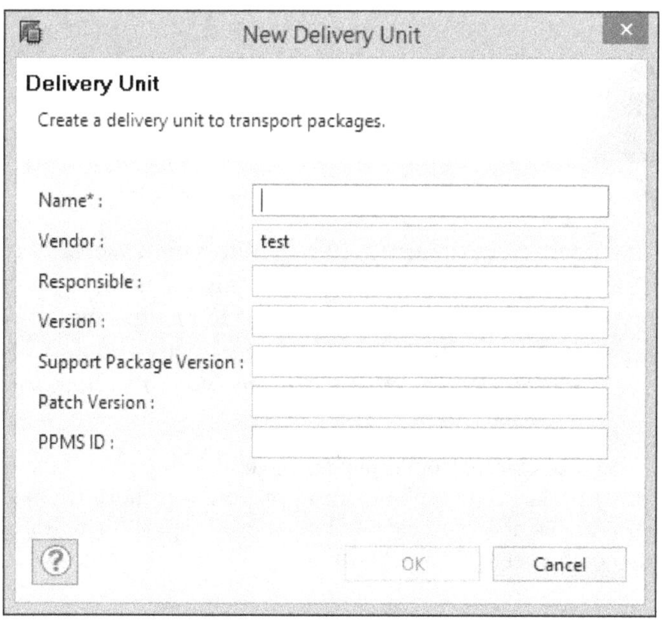

The only mandatory field is **Name**, and you can enter any meaningful (for you) value here. Something like `BOOK` might be appropriate. Delivery unit names can only contain capital letters (A-Z), numbers (0-9), and the underscore (_) character. If you attempt to type any other character, the system will warn you that your entry is invalid, and will deactivate the **OK** button.

The **Vendor** field is filled automatically from the `content_vendor` system configuration value. The other fields can be filled or not as you prefer; they are all optional. If you are building an application which you will ship to customers then the **Version**, **Support Package Version**, and **Patch Version** field will be useful to be able to detect which version your customers have installed when they call you for support.

Once you are done, click on **OK** to see your delivery unit listed alongside the others delivered by SAP, as we can see in the following screenshot:

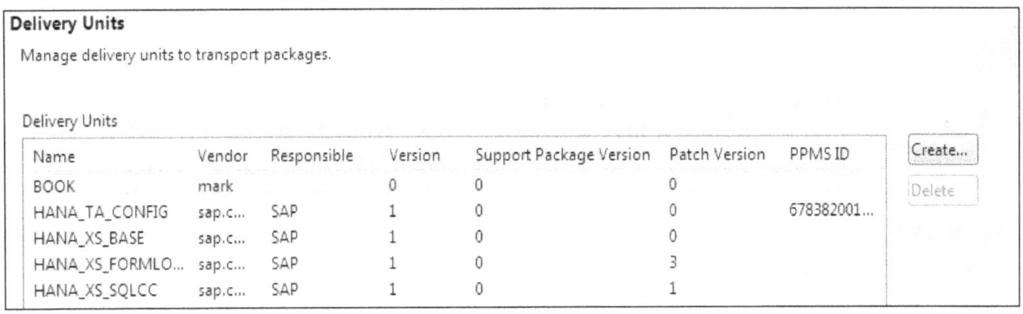

Name	Vendor	Responsible	Version	Support Package Version	Patch Version	PPMS ID
BOOK	mark		0	0	0	
HANA_TA_CONFIG	sap.c...	SAP	1	0	0	678382001...
HANA_XS_BASE	sap.c...	SAP	1	0	0	
HANA_XS_FORMLO...	sap.c...	SAP	1	0	3	
HANA_XS_SQLCC	sap.c...	SAP	1	0	1	

You can now click on the **Close** button at the bottom of the **Delivery Units** dialog. Your delivery unit has been created.

Creating a package

We are still not in a position to do any actual development work. In order to do so, we need to create a package. This object is once again a container, only it is not used for transportation purposes. A package serves just to group objects. For example, you might create one package for your sales reporting objects, and another one for your HR reporting developments. Packages are more for your use than for SAP HANA's.

> You can use objects from one package in developments belonging to another package (if you have the appropriate authorizations). Be careful if you do this however, as you'll need to transport (using the delivery units) both packages together in order for everything to work correctly.

From the **Quick Launch** panel of the **Modeler** perspective, select **Package**, then click on **Create** to see the **New Package** dialog:

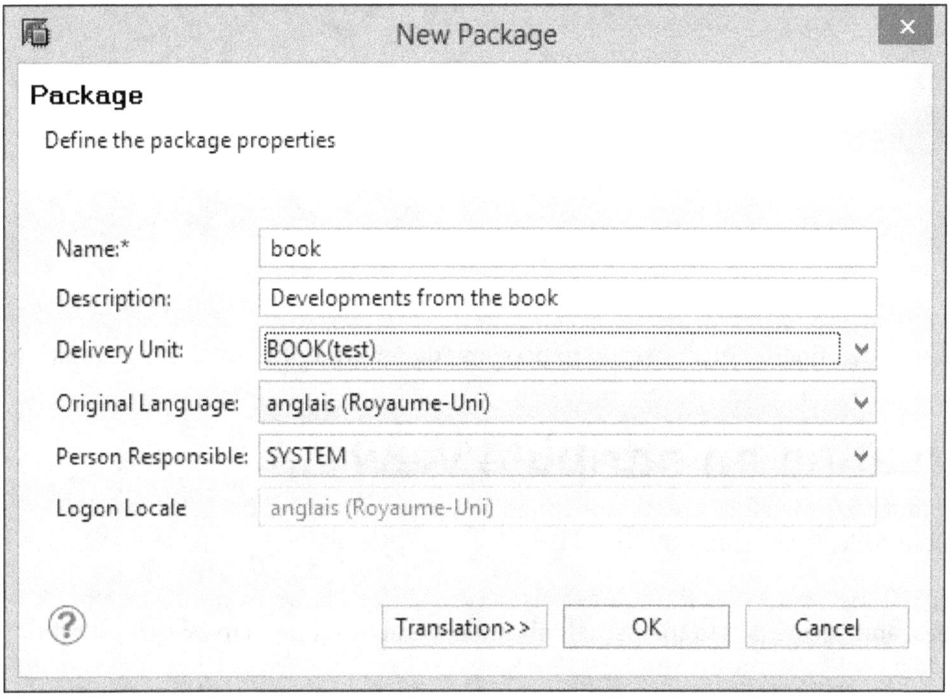

Once again, the only information you need to provide is a **Name**. This must be in lowercase letters. The **Description** field will be filled automatically for you (by copying the **Name** you enter)—but you can change it if you like, as has been done in this case.

The **Delivery Unit** field can be filled or not as per your preference. If you are doing test developments, it might be unnecessary for you. In the screenshot we've just seen, the **Delivery Unit** named **Book** created in the previous section has been selected.

The other fields present are used for multi-language developments—where you create the objects in English, say, and need them to be correctly translated into French.

The **Person Responsible** field, which will be prefilled with your username, serves to know who is in charge of the objects in the package.

Just click on **OK** to create the package.

If you now expand the **Content** node in the **Navigator** panel from the **Modeler** perspective for your SAP HANA system, you will see the package listed as follows:

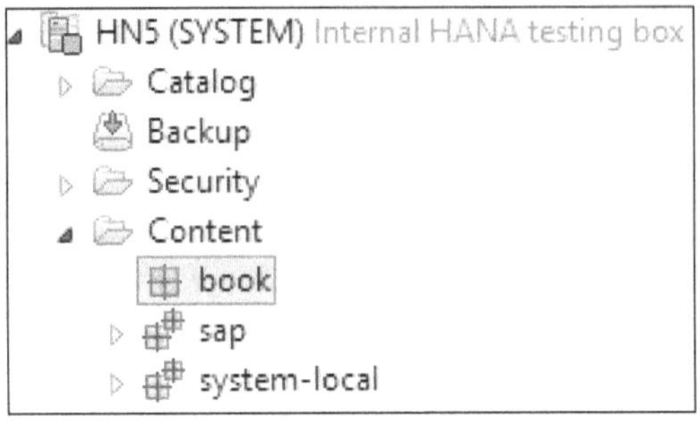

We are now, finally, in a position to do some development work. Let's get started!

Creating an attribute view

The first object we'll be creating is called an attribute view. This is the basic building-block for nearly all SAP HANA developments.

An attribute view takes the characteristic (text) information from one or more tables, and presents it to the user. It allows several operations to be carried out on data such as the following:

- Information can be filtered on specific values
- Tables can be joined together
- Certain fields can be hidden from the user if they are not appropriate to the current development

> Attribute views have one major restriction: they cannot work with numeric information. You cannot, for example, use a `SALARY` or `REVENUE` field in an attribute view. To work with numeric information, we'll use an analytic view, which we'll be looking at in *Chapter 4, Painting with Numbers – An Analytic View*.

In our attribute view, we'll be using the data from our `CUSTOMER` table. This table has four fields: `MANDT`, `CUSTID`, `SECTOR`, and `COUNTRY`. We'll only be using three of these fields in our development, so our attribute view will serve to hide the field we don't need—`MANDT`.

From the **Quick Launch** panel, select **Attribute View**, then **Create**, to view the **Attribute view creation** dialog:

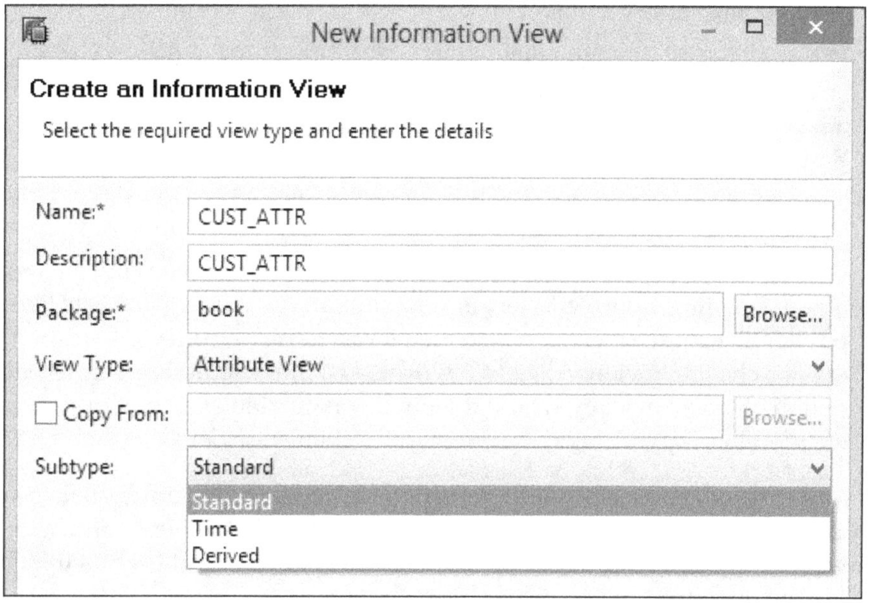

We need to give our view a **Name** (only uppercase letters, numbers and the underscore character are allowed) and a **Description** (which automatically takes the value of the **Name** field). Additionally, we need to specify in which **Package** this object is to be created. In the preceding screenshot we can see that the **Package** we created in the previous section was selected.

The **View Type** field allows for creation of attribute or analytic views. We'll be looking at analytic views in the next chapter, so leave **Attribute View** selected for now.

To save time in creating several similar views, or views on the same base table, we can create our views by copying an existing view. To do this, just check the **Copy From** checkbox, then select the source view using the **Browse** button. This is a function we'll be using in a later development.

Finally, we need to choose the type of attribute view we are creating:

- **Standard**: The basic attribute view, exposing different fields of one or more base tables.
- **Time**: A specific attribute view used to hold time information, including the link between a specific date and a month, for example. By default, SAP HANA has no notion of time, so it does not know that the date 30 November 2012 is in the eleventh month, or even that it is in 2012. An attribute view of time information is used to provide this basic information to your developments, by running a program which creates the calendar information and stores it.
- **Derived**: As we saw, we can create an attribute view by copying an existing object. Creating a derived view is very similar. A derived view acts like a pointer to a source view; if we create view B derived from view A, then if we make a change to view A, view B will also be impacted. This is different to the notion of create by copy where if view B was created as a copy of view A, and we modified view A later, nothing would change in view B.

The view we are creating here is a **Standard** view, so leave this option selected. The dialog allows selection of tables to add to the view via the **Next** button, but we'll create our view first, and add the base tables later as this allows us to take our time to examine the view.

Click on **Finish** when you are ready.

At this point we are presented with the attribute view creation screen:

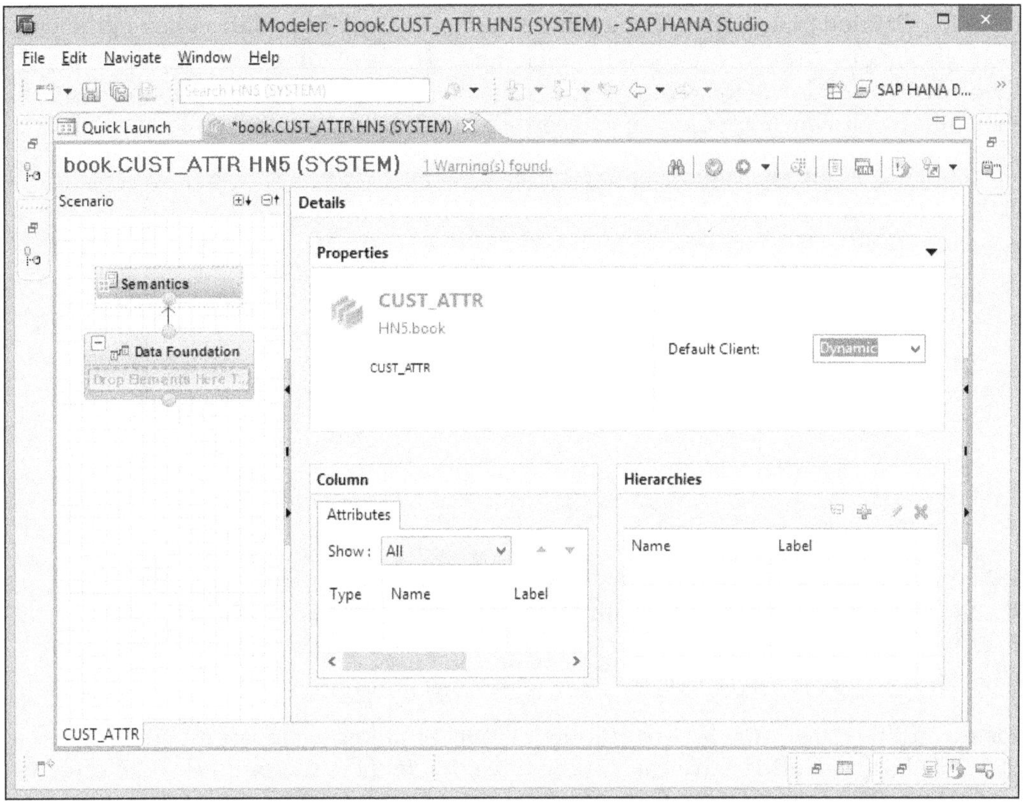

The preceding screenshot shows the different aspects of the attribute view. On the left-hand side of the screen is the **Scenario**. If we follow the diagram from bottom to top (in the direction of the arrow), data will flow from the base tables (in the **Data Foundation**) into the view, represented by the **Semantics** block. The **Semantics** block represents the visible part, the result of the view.

The right-hand side of the screen is split into three panels. At the top, we have some basic **Properties** of the view. At the bottom, there is a panel called **Column**, which will contain the different columns of the view once we have created some, and on the right-hand side, a panel containing any **Hierarchies** used in the view. We'll be looking at hierarchies in detail in *Chapter 8, On Another Level – Hierarchies in SAP HANA*.

As you can see in the screenshot, the view right now contains no data at all, since no tables have as yet been selected. Adding a table to the view is done by drag-and-drop, from the **Catalog** node in the **Navigator** panel, to the **Data Foundation** box in the view, or by clicking on the green plus sign which appears when you hover the mouse over the **Data Foundation** box, and then typing the name of the table to add in the filter of the **Find** dialog which appears, as you can see in the following screenshot:

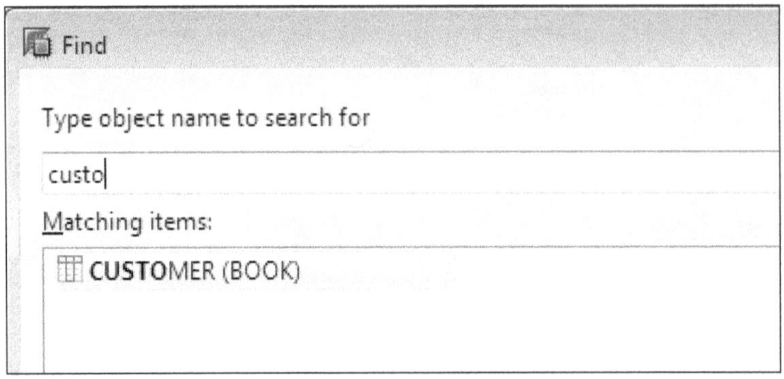

When you start typing the name of a table in the filter box at the top of the dialog, the Studio will search for and list all tables whose names match what you type, making finding tables much easier. Just click on a table name to select it, and then click on **OK** to add it to the view.

Please add the `CUSTOMER` table from the `BOOK` schema to the view now. As soon as the table has been added, we can see the list of its fields in the middle of the screen in the **Details** panel.

At this point we just add to the view the fields needed from the table, by right-clicking on each one, and selecting **Add to Output** from the menu. We only need to add the `CUSTID`, `SECTOR`, and `COUNTRY` fields to our view. Once this is done, your view should look just like the following screenshot:

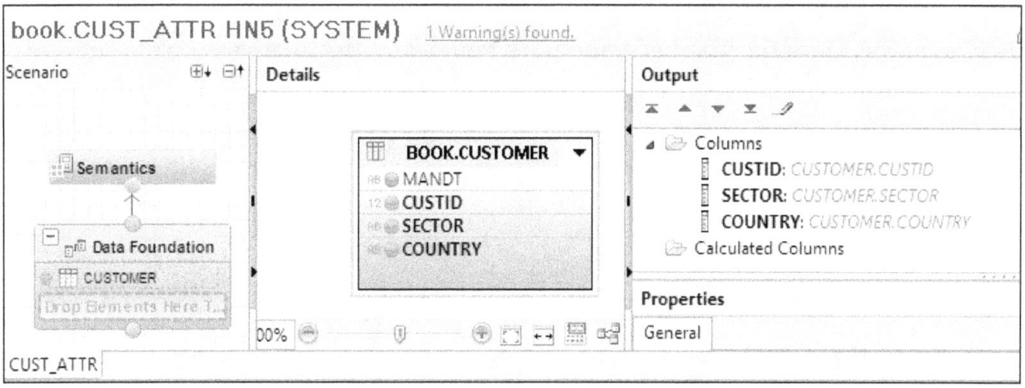

Before we can use our view, we need to define which field or fields will be the key fields. This is exactly the same principle as for a database table; a view needs to have at least one key field, or else you won't be able to use it.

Marking a field as a key field is simple; in the view definition window, click on the **Semantics** block. You will be presented with the grid of fields in the view. In this grid, the first column is `Type`. At the moment, all the fields in the view have a blue icon in the `Type` column, indicating that they are regular fields, as we can see in the following screenshot:

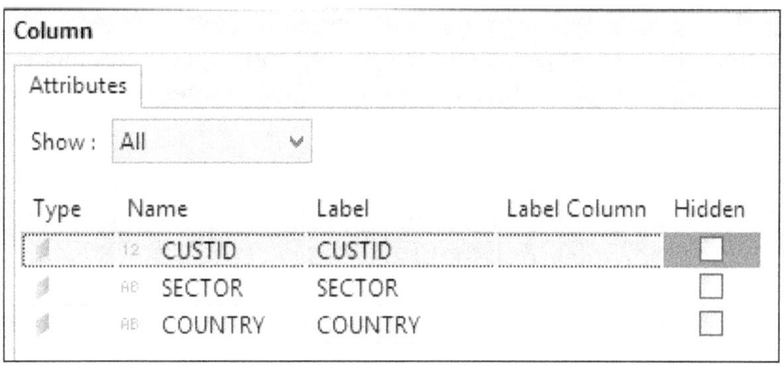

To define a field as a key field, double-click on the blue icon next to the field, and select **Key Attribute** from the menu which appears. This will change the icon, showing (with a little imagination) a key and a green star.

In our view, the key field is the `CUSTID`, so please change this attribute to a key attribute now. Once this has been done, we will obtain the final version of our view, which should look like the following screenshot:

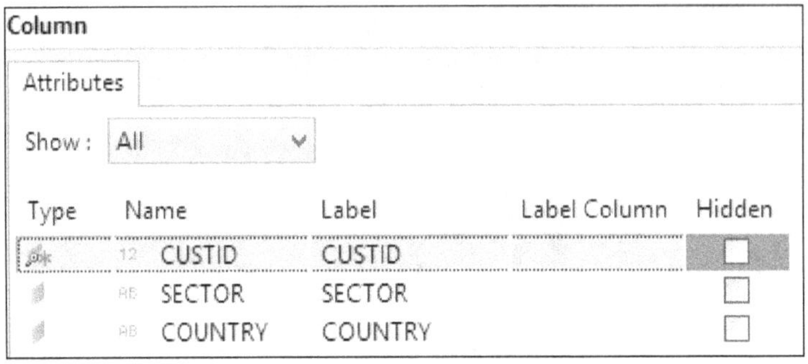

The definition of our first attribute view is finished. Yay! Let's take a look at the contents of the view now. A view is basically like a table; you can take a look at its contents just like you would for a table, using the data preview function we saw in the previous chapter. Before we can do this however, we need to activate the view.

Activation is a concept readers familiar with SAP's ERP or BW software will have come across often. It basically means compilation of the object we have just created visually, turning it into the underlying SQL statements. Activation allows the SAP HANA system to be sure that each object is coherent when the user asks for an object's contents. When an object is created in the Studio (like the view we have just built), only its definition is stored in the database. It does not actually exist as a usable object until it has been activated.

To activate our view, simply click on the round, green, button with the right-facing arrow at the top-right of the view definition panel. The appropriate button is highlighted in the following screenshot:

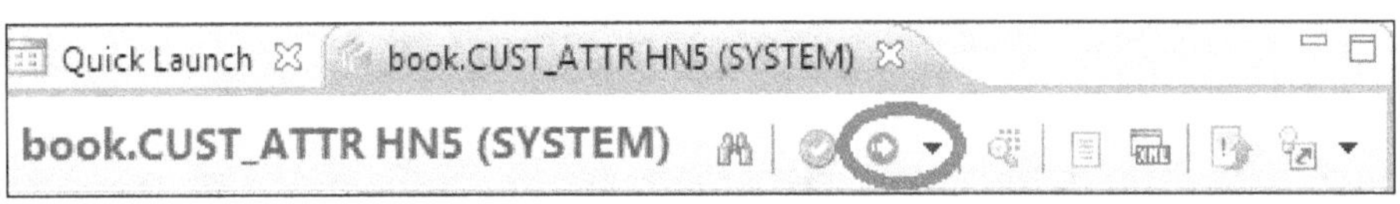

SAP HANA will check that your view is coherent, and then create the runtime version. This system has another advantage—once an object's runtime version exists, none of the changes we make to the object will be visible until that object is activated once more. There can be two versions of an object in the system at the same time, one active and one inactive.

Activation will take a couple of seconds, and you will see in the **Job Log** panel the results of the activation, as we can see in the following screenshot:

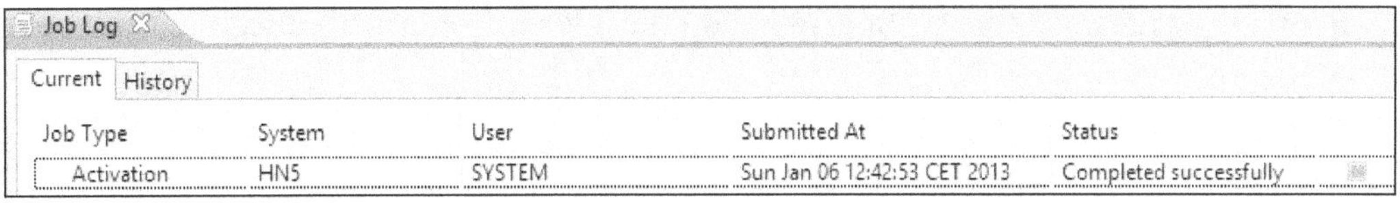

Once your view has been activated, it is ready for use. You will see it listed in the **Content** node of the **Navigator** panel, as you can see in the following screenshot:

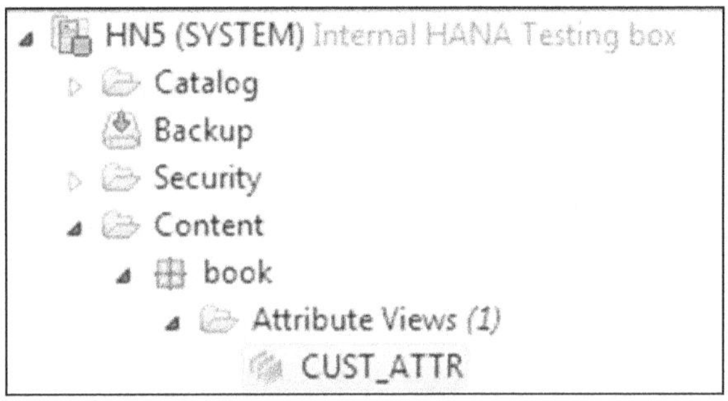

You can now request a **Data Preview** of the view, in the same way we looked at the contents of the tables earlier. The data in the view should look like this (depending on the order you choose the output fields, the columns in the grid might be arranged differently).

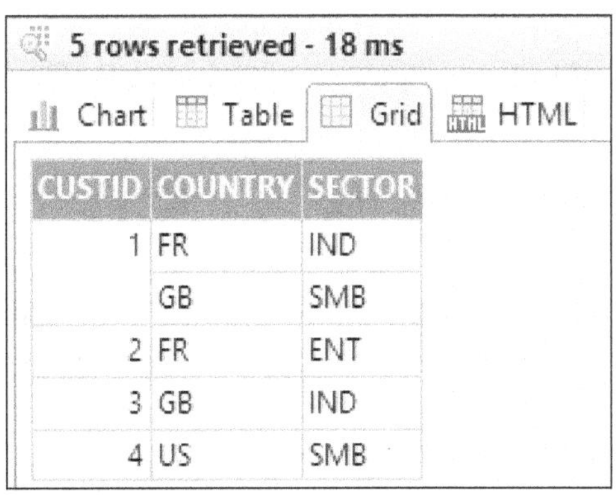

CUSTID	COUNTRY	SECTOR
1	FR	IND
	GB	SMB
2	FR	ENT
3	GB	IND
4	US	SMB

Advanced features of attribute views

In the previous section we created a simple attribute view, using only certain fields from one base table. In this section we will take a look at more advanced features of attribute views.

The client field

If you can still see the data preview screen of the attribute view, and you switch to the **Grid** tab of this panel, you will see that the `CUSTID` number `1` is present twice. This is a problem, especially since this customer is apparently from both the UK and France.

If you recall when we described the data in the previous chapter, we saw the notion of `client` and the fact that there could be two instances of SAP's ERP software running on the same database at the same time, using two different Client IDs. In our example tables, there is data from both the client 100 and the client 200, and this is why the `CUSTID` appears twice.

> It is very important here to note that even though the `CUSTID` is the same, the customer `1` from client `100` is not the same customer as number `1` from client `200`.

Now, we can see the tight coupling that exists between SAP HANA and the SAP ERP software—in the Studio we can indicate to HANA with which client we want to work. For example, we might have a SAP ERP user Tom who works in client 100, and the ERP user Sue might work exclusively in client 200. We can specify in HANA that Tom's user has a default client of 100 and Sue's, 200. We'll see how to create these default values later, in the chapter concerning authorizations.

In the meantime, we can set the default client at the view level. Setting the default client value for a view is simple, just open the view (for example the attribute view we have just created), and click on the **Semantics** block.

As we saw a couple of pages back, the **Semantics** panel has an option called **Default Client**, which by default takes the value **Dynamic**. The different values for the **Default Client** and their meanings are:

- **Dynamic**: Take the default value from the user record, or do no filtering on the client if no value is present.

- **Cross Client**: Do no filtering on the client value—values from all clients will be shown in the view.
- **User-defined**: If you want to force the view to filter on a particular view for the client, you can do this by typing your own value directly into the drop-down list on the **Semantics** screen. In the following screenshot, the view filters directly on the client value of 100:

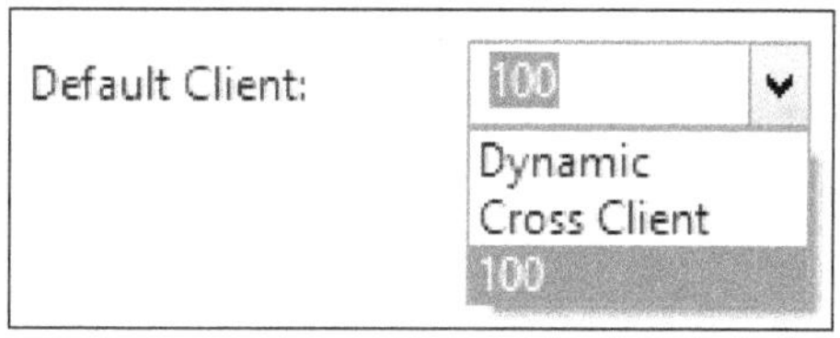

If you filter your attribute view on the **Default Client** of `100` now (and then reactivate!), do a data preview (or refresh the data preview if it is still open), you will see that `CUSTID` number `1` is now present only once in the view.

> If you want to check that the filtering is done correctly, you might like to filter the data on client 200, as a test. In client 100, `CUSTID 1` is from sector `SMB` in Great Britain. In Client 200, however, `CUSTID 1` is in sector `IND` and is from France.
>
> If you do decide to do this test, then please change the view's filter back to 100 at the end, or the following examples won't work correctly!

Joining tables in views

Now that we have an attribute view which extracts the correct data we want from the base table `CUSTOMER`, we can make our view more interesting.

In order to do this, we can take the information from the `CUSTOMER` table, and combine it, or join it, with information from other tables, to provide what is basically a new table, containing information from different sources.

Let's look at the different table joins we can make, and add the different information to our view.

Join types in SAP HANA

Readers familiar with SQL and relational databases in general will already know the points in this section, but we'll just take a couple of minutes to go over the basics.

The examples in this section all refer to joining data between two of our sample tables, CUSTOMER and CUSTNAME, as pictured in the following screenshot:

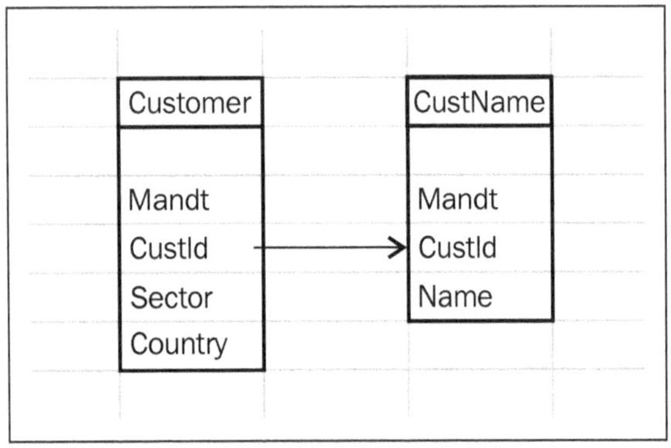

The CUSTOMER table is on the left-hand side, and the CUSTNAME table is on the right-hand side (the placement of the tables is important, as we'll see in a moment).

In order to join data in one database table to data in another database table in SAP HANA, several types of join are possible. They are as follows:

- **Inner Join:** This type of join indicates to SAP HANA that the value in the table on the left-hand side will be in the table on the right-hand side. For example, we can be fairly certain that each CUSTID will have a NAME, so we can do an inner join between the tables CUSTOMER and CUSTNAME. If there is no value in the CUSTNAME table for a value in the CUSTOMER table, and the two tables are joined using an inner join, then no value will be returned—from either of the tables. This can lead to missing data, so be careful when you use an inner join.
- **Referential Join**: This is the same as an inner join, though it assumes that referential integrity is ensured in the database. If values from only the left table are requested, then the system will perform a left outer join (which is fast). If fields from both tables are requested, then the system will perform an inner join.

- **Left Outer Join**: This type of join is used when you are not sure of the existence of values in the right-hand table. In our example, we are certain that in the `CUSTOMER` table we have all the `CUSTID` values. If we are not sure that they all have a `NAME` associated in the `CUSTNAME` table, we can join the two using a left outer join. In this case, we are certain that all the `CUSTID` values would be present when we ask for the contents of our view. If a `CUSTID` does not have an associated `NAME`, then the `NAME` column will be empty for that `CUSTID`.
- **Right Outer Join**: The same as a left outer join, but we are certain that all values from the right-hand table will be present in the view contents, whether or not there is a corresponding value in the left-hand table. In our example, we could be sure to see all `NAME` values from the `CUSTNAME` table, and the corresponding entry in the `CUSTID` column might be empty. This might be useful, for example, if we need a list of customers who don't have a code.
- **Text Join**: A text join is a special join type provided by SAP HANA. It allows a left outer join between a table of master data (our `COUNTRY` table, for example) and a table containing language-dependent texts for that master data (our `CTRYNAME` table). The join is done on one field (`COUNTRY`) and we indicate to SAP HANA which field in the right-hand table contains the language key.

Join cardinality

In addition to the join type between two tables, you will need to indicate the cardinality of the join:

- **1..1**: This indicates that for each entry in the left-hand table, there is one entry in the right-hand table, and vice-versa.
- **1..n**: This option tells SAP HANA that we know that for one entry in the left-hand table, there are 0 or more entries in the right-hand table. For example, if we have a table containing sales orders, and a second table containing sales order lines, then for one entry in the sales order table, there are 0 or more sales order lines
- **n..1**: Basically the same as the 1..n cardinality, but the other way round. We can imagine a `CUSTOMER` table with several `CUSTID` fields, each of which has a `NAME` — if several of our customers are called Smith, we might have only one entry Smith in the `CUSTNAME` table, and several `CUSTID` values pointing to it.

- **n..n**: This cardinality indicates that there are many entries in the left-hand table which link to many entries in the right-hand table. We don't have an example of this join type in our sample data, however we can imagine the join between a `CUSTOMER` and a `PRODUCT` table, where several `CUSTID` values can use a particular `PRODUCTID`, and any given `CUSTID` can use several `PRODUCTID` values.

Completing an attribute view with information from different tables

At the moment, the attribute view will show us the customer ID, the Sector ID and the country code for our customer. In other tables we imported, we have the customer's name, the sector name and the country name.

It would be more useful for our users if, when we ask for the contents of the attribute view, it automatically gets the text values for the different IDs in the base table:

- `CUSTID` links to `CUSTID` in the `CUSTNAME` table, to find the customer's `NAME`.
- `SECTOR` links to `SECTOR` in the `SECTOR` table, to find the `SECTORNAME` - which is language-dependent.
- `REGION` links to `REGION` in the `COUNTRY` table. This allows us to find the Country of the Region. In addition:
    - `REGION` in the `COUNTRY` table links to `REGION` in the `REGNAME` table, to find the `REGTEXT` value, which is language-dependent.
    - `COUNTRY` in the `COUNTRY` table links to `COUNTRY` in the `CTRYNAME` table, to find the `CTRYNAME` value, which is language-dependent.

If our attribute view could undo this spaghetti for us automatically, it would make our developments much easier.

Let's add the first field, the customer name, to the view.

From the **Navigator** panel, find and then open the attribute view we just created if it's not open already. In order to add the customer's name to the view, we first need to add the `CUSTNAME` table, in the same way we added the `CUSTOMER` table, by drag-and-drop.

Once this is done, click on the **Data Foundation** block, and your view will look like the following screenshot:

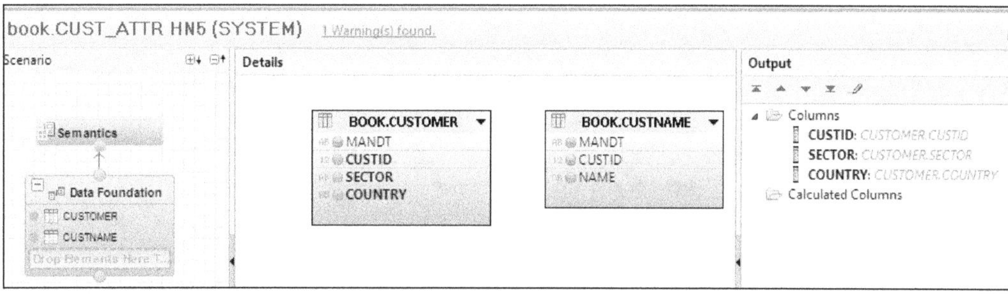

We can now create the join between our two tables. The join is made on the `CUSTID` field, which is in both tables. Make the join by clicking on the `CUSTID` field in the left-hand table (`CUSTOMER`) and dragging the mouse to the `CUSTID` field in the right-hand table (`CUSTNAME`). This will draw an arrow between the two fields.

> There is no need to join the tables on the `MANDT` field. This field represents the default client, and is handled automatically by SAP HANA.

Now that the join has been made, we need to indicate the join type and cardinality.

One `CUSTID` in the `CUSTOMER` table represents one `CUSTID` in the `CUSTNAME` table (because each customer has a name), so the **Join Type** can be **Inner Join** or **Referential**. Also, since a customer has only one name, and one name refers to only one customer, the **Cardinality** is **1..1**. To set these properties, click on the join between the two tables, and select the correct values in the properties panel which appears, as we can see in the following screenshot:

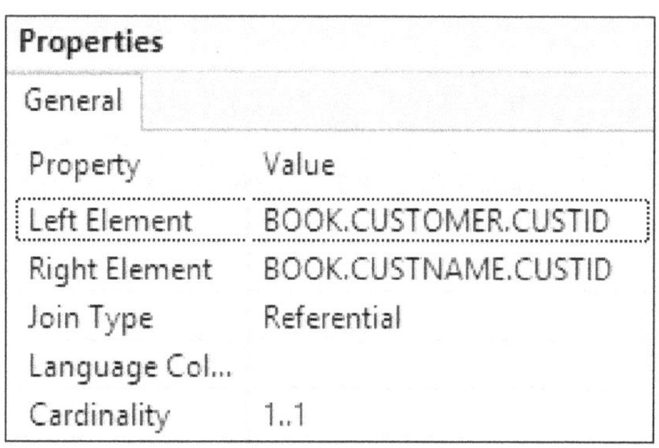

At this point, the view will use both tables, and will calculate the correct join between them, but will not show the customer name, because we haven't added it as an output field yet, so please do that now, by adding the **NAME** field to the view output.

After reactivating the view, and requesting a data preview, we can see that the customer's name is now visible in the output:

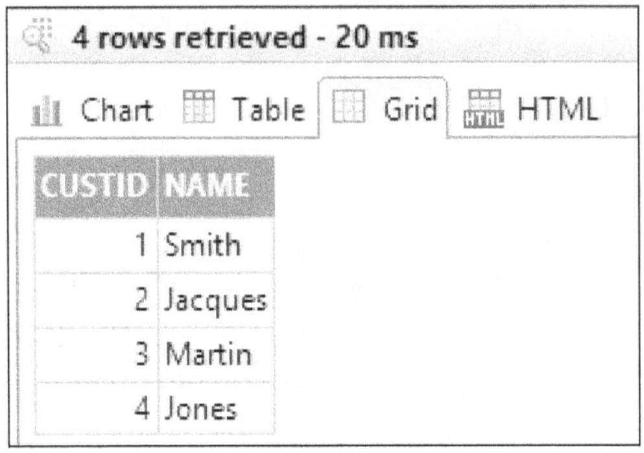

Congratulations! We now have an attribute view based on the `CUSTOMER` table, which will pull information from the `CUSTNAME` table whenever needed. This has greatly improved the usefulness of our view.

We can now add more information to the view, starting with the sector name. Each customer has been assigned to a sector; these represent the rough company size. In the `CUSTOMER` table, we have the `SECTOR` ID field, and the text for the sector is present in the `SECTOR` table.

The `SECTOR` table has a description for each `SECTOR` ID, and these descriptions (the `SECTORNAME` field) have been translated into both English and French. This means that we'll need to create a text join.

Add the `SECTOR` table to the view, and create a join between the `SECTOR` fields in the `CUSTOMER` and `SECTOR` tables now, then change the type of the join to **Text Join**. We now need to indicate which column in the `SECTOR` table contains the language, so that SAP HANA can give us the description in the language we need. The language column is called `LANG`.

> The selection of the correct language is done using the preferences of the connection to SAP HANA. Right now we're using the Studio, so the language that SAP HANA will use is defined by the Studio. In the **Navigator** panel, right-click on the system name, select **Properties**, then in the **Advanced Properties** of the **Database User Logon** section of the dialog that will appear, select the language you wish to use with SAP HANA.
>
> In our example data, only texts for **English** and **French** are available, so according to your preferences, select one of the **English** or **French** variants in the **Locale** list then click **OK** to validate your choice.

If we now add the `SECTORNAME` to the output of the view, reactivate our attribute view, and request a data preview, we can see that alongside the `SECTOR` ID, we have the description for the `SECTOR`, in the language we have selected.

First the current state of our view is as follows:

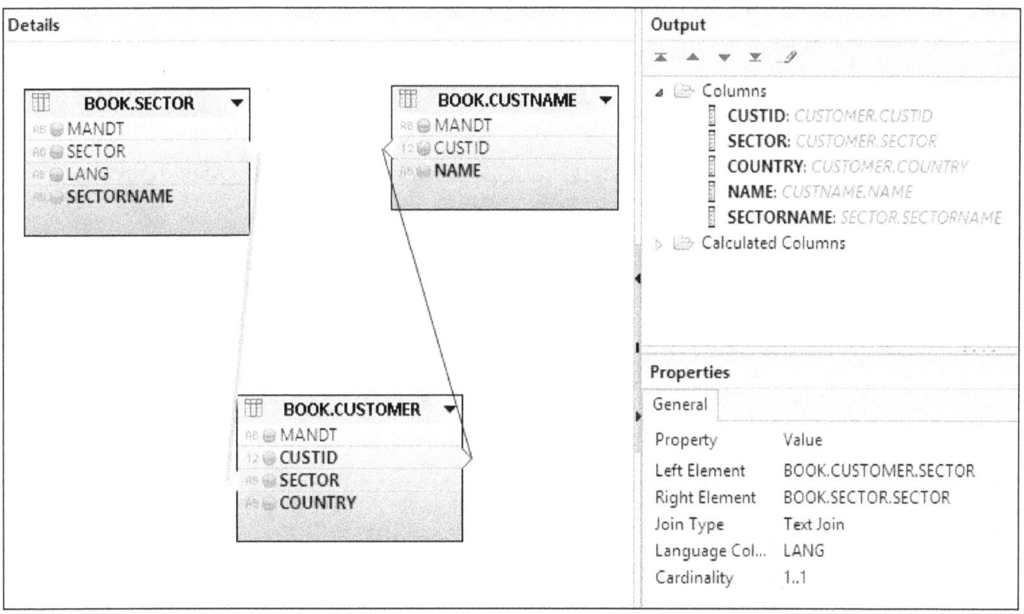

In the previous screenshot, the **Properties** panel refers to the text join between the two `SECTOR` fields (the join on the left hand side of the screen).

Now the result of this view, if our SAP HANA user connects in **English**, then French (to obtain the **Properties** screen, right-click on the system name in the **Navigator** panel, and select **Properties** from the menu. To see the language options, click on **Database User Logon** in the left-hand side panel, then **Additional Properties** on the right-hand side of the screen):

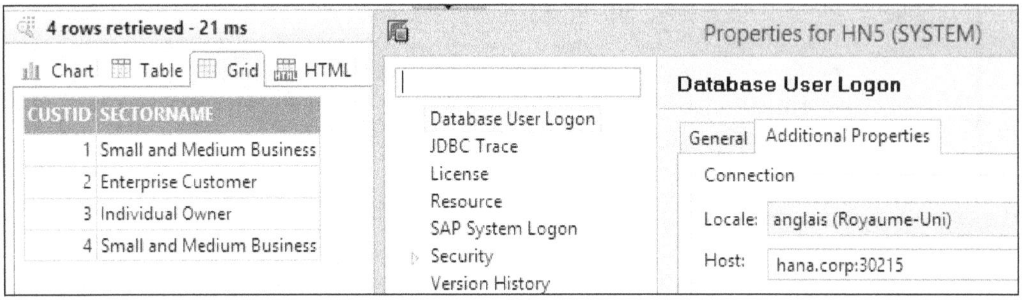

The language selection of the correct text to display was done by SAP HANA automatically at runtime—no changes were made to the view to see the alternative language.

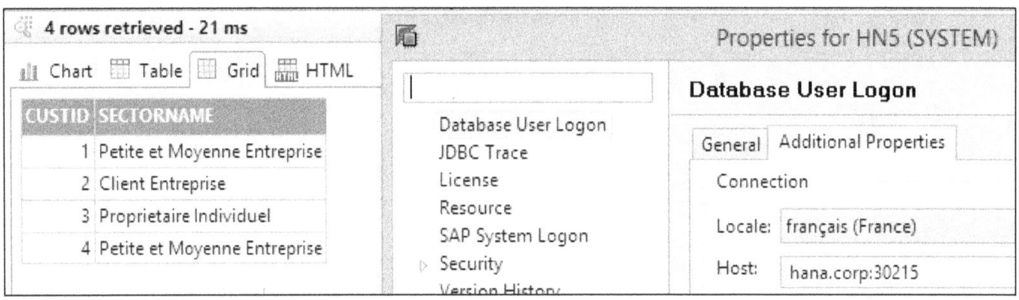

> One point to note is what happens if no description is present in the requested language. Here is the output of the view if we connect to SAP HANA in German:

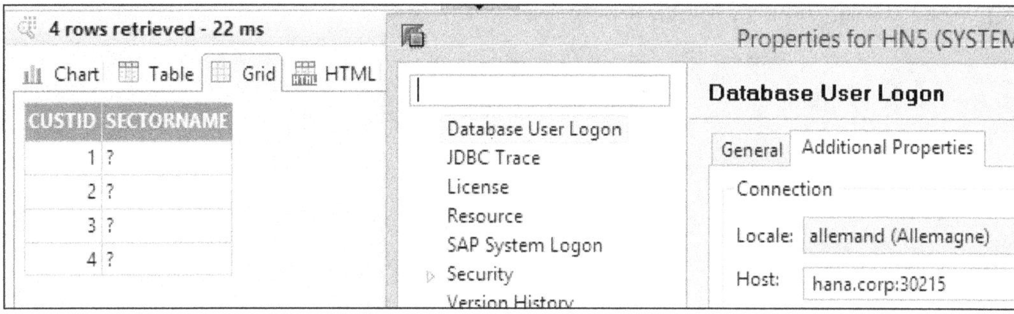

> No description is available in German, so no SECTORNAME can be provided by SAP HANA.
>
> Additionally, the language key must be provided in the base tables as a single letter; in our examples, E for English, F for French, and so on. Longer language specifications (such as EN or FR, or even EN_US, or FR_CA) will not work.

Now that we have looked at simple joins and text joins, we can add the final fields to our view—the country and region descriptions for our customers. We'll need to add the COUNTRY, CTRYNAME, and REGNAME tables to our view.

First we'll create a join between the CUSTOMER and COUNTRY tables on the COUNTRY field. This is an inner join, with a 1..n cardinality.

In order to see the country and region names in our view, we can create text joins between COUNTRY and CTRYNAME (on field COUNTRY), and COUNTRY and REGNAME (on field REGION). Once again, the join types are text join, and the language column is called LANG.

We can now add the following fields to the output of our view:

- REGION from the COUNTRY table
- REGTEXT from the REGNAME table
- CTRYNAME from the CTRYNAME table.

Our view should now look like the following screenshot:

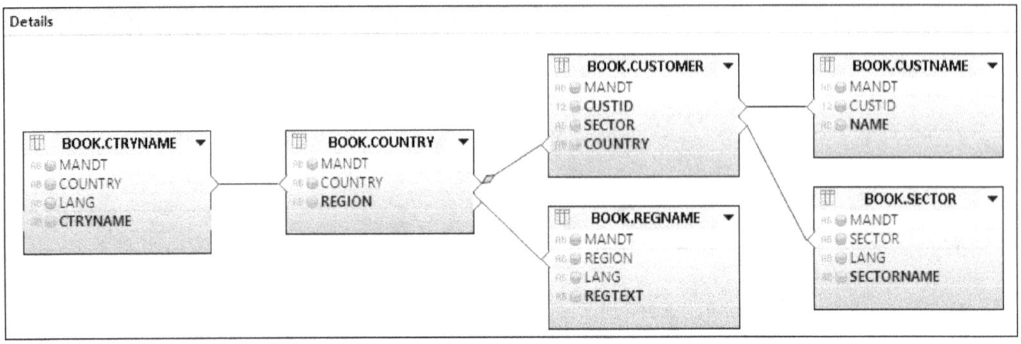

A data preview of the view contents will now give us the information on each customer, as well as the sector name, country name, and region, as we can see in the following screenshot:

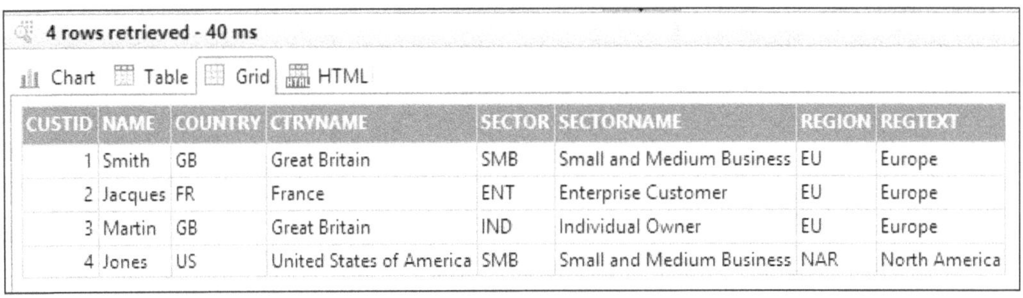

CUSTID	NAME	COUNTRY	CTRYNAME	SECTOR	SECTORNAME	REGION	REGTEXT
1	Smith	GB	Great Britain	SMB	Small and Medium Business	EU	Europe
2	Jacques	FR	France	ENT	Enterprise Customer	EU	Europe
3	Martin	GB	Great Britain	IND	Individual Owner	EU	Europe
4	Jones	US	United States of America	SMB	Small and Medium Business	NAR	North America

At this point, our view is complete. When we ask SAP HANA for information about our customers using this view, the system will pull all related information from the different tables, and present it to us in a coherent and predictable way.

By creating attribute views in this fashion, we are creating reusable building blocks which we can incorporate in further developments. These building blocks allow us to ensure that whenever we use a particular `CUSTID` in a development, all the information we need about this customer is available.

Additionally, if we always use this attribute view instead of adding the base tables, we can ensure that all our developments are coherent.

As an added plus, maintenance is largely reduced—if we make any changes to the base tables, or need additional information about the customer, we need only change our attribute view, and the fields in the view will automatically be available in all further developments which use this view.

Summary

In this chapter, we have taken a look at some of the first building blocks, and the main concepts in SAP HANA development. We started by creating a delivery unit in which to store our developments, then a package to group them together.

We then went on to create a simple attribute view on one table, and saw how SAP HANA manages the notion of client in data, keeping values from one client separate to another.

Next, we built upon our attribute view, using several join types to pull data from other tables and add it to the view. We saw that SAP HANA can automatically handle translations for us, as long as the appropriate text is in one table, depending on the language we choose when we connect to the system.

In the next chapter, we'll be taking a look at a new type of view, the analytic view.

Quick reference

In this section we present a quick reference to the objects covered in this chapter.

Object	Usage	Creation
Delivery unit	Transport developments from one SAP HANA system to another	**Quick Launch** | **Delivery Unit** | **Create** | **Enter Name** | **OK**
Package	Group objects together	**Quick Launch** | **Package** | **Create** | **Enter Name** | **OK**
Attribute view	Pull data from base tables, join tables together, recover descriptions for identifiers	**Quick Launch** | **Attribute View** | **Enter Name** | **Select Package** | **Finish** Add table(s), add field(s) to output, create join(s) between tables, create key field(s), activate.

4
Painting with Numbers – An Analytic View

In the previous chapter, we made our first development in HANA, an attribute view, pulling data from several tables and making sure that wherever we have a code we also have its description. Additionally, when we are looking at a customer ID, associated data (attributes) are also available at the same time.

The main limitation with attribute views is that they cannot work with numeric data, which means that we cannot use a customer's revenue, or the number of orders he has placed, or anything else vaguely numeric in an attribute view and then do calculations on it. To put things simply, an attribute view can't count; it doesn't know that one order in January plus one order in February equals two orders in all.

In order to work with numeric information, we need to use an analytic view. An analytic view allows us to work with numbers, indicate how SAP HANA should aggregate them, and do intermediate calculations on them, directly in the view.

> Readers familiar with the SAP BW system might like to consider an analytic view as the fact table of a BW Cube. An attribute view can be considered a dimension of a cube.

In this chapter we'll be taking a close look at analytic views and the possibilities they offer. We'll build a couple of analytic views, using both simple and more advanced techniques. We'll be building on the attribute view created in the last chapter, using it to provide the textual information to describe the numbers (so-called context).

Creating an analytic view

Let's start by creating a simple analytic view, so we can see how it works. Like an attribute view, we first need to identify the table which contains the information we are to work with. In our example data, we have a `REVENUE` table which contains `CUSTID`, `YEAR`, `CURRENCY`, and `AMOUNT`. As the column names suggest, this data represents the revenue, per customer, per year. Each `AMOUNT` is shown in a given `CURRENCY`, as we can see in the following screenshot:

MANDT	CUSTID	YEAR	CURRENCY	AMOUNT
100	1	2009	GBP	112
100	2	2009	EUR	127
100	3	2009	GBP	120
100	4	2009	USD	158
100	1	2010	GBP	119
100	2	2010	EUR	125
100	3	2010	GBP	121
100	4	2010	USD	163
100	1	2011	GBP	121
100	2	2011	EUR	131
100	3	2011	GBP	137
100	4	2011	USD	171
200	1	2009	EUR	163

Once again, data exists from two clients, **100** and **200**, so we'll need to filter on one of them to get something meaningful.

To create an analytic view, open the **Quick Launch** panel and navigate to **Analytic View | Create**.

> If you can't find the **Quick Launch** panel, then you might not have the Studio's **Modeler** perspective open. If this is the case, navigate to **Window** | **Open Perspective** | **Modeler**, or navigate to **Window** | **Open Perspective** | **Other** | **Modeler**. This will open the panels you last opened when you did modeling tasks (like creating the attribute view from the last chapter).
>
> If at this point you still don't have the **Quick Launch** panel open, then you might have closed it by accident earlier. Since the Studio remembers the panels you were using, if you close one, it will stay closed. To get the panel back, just navigate to **Window** | **Reset Perspective**. This will take the current screen layout (perspective) and reset it to the installation defaults. This can be very useful if you "lose" panels.

You will be presented with the **Create an Information View** dialog, which is identical to the one we saw when we created an attribute view in the previous chapter:

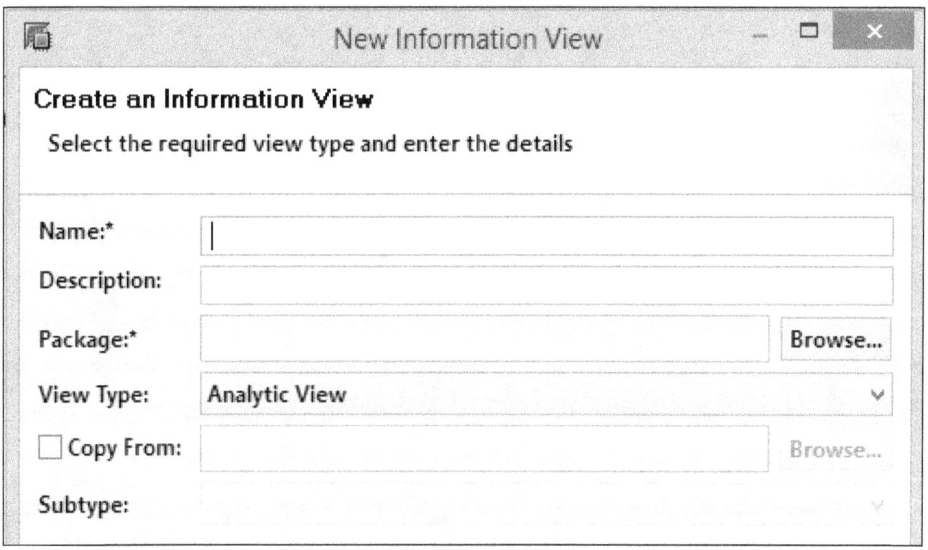

As you can see in the preceding screenshot, an analytic view needs the same information as an attribute view for creation. Just give it a **Name**, an optional **Description**, and select (by clicking on the **Browse** button) the **Package** which will contain the view. The analytic view we are creating will contain customer revenue, so you might like to give it a descriptive name, such as `CUST_REV`. The package for our developments is called **book** (unless you called it something else).

As we can see, the **View Type** field has been prefilled with **Analytic View**, and there is no **Subtype** available. Unlike attribute views, analytic views do not have a **Subtype**.

We can, once more, create a view by copying an existing view if so desired. We don't have any existing views as yet, so we won't be using this option. Click on **Finish** when done.

At this point we are provided with the now-familiar view creation screen:

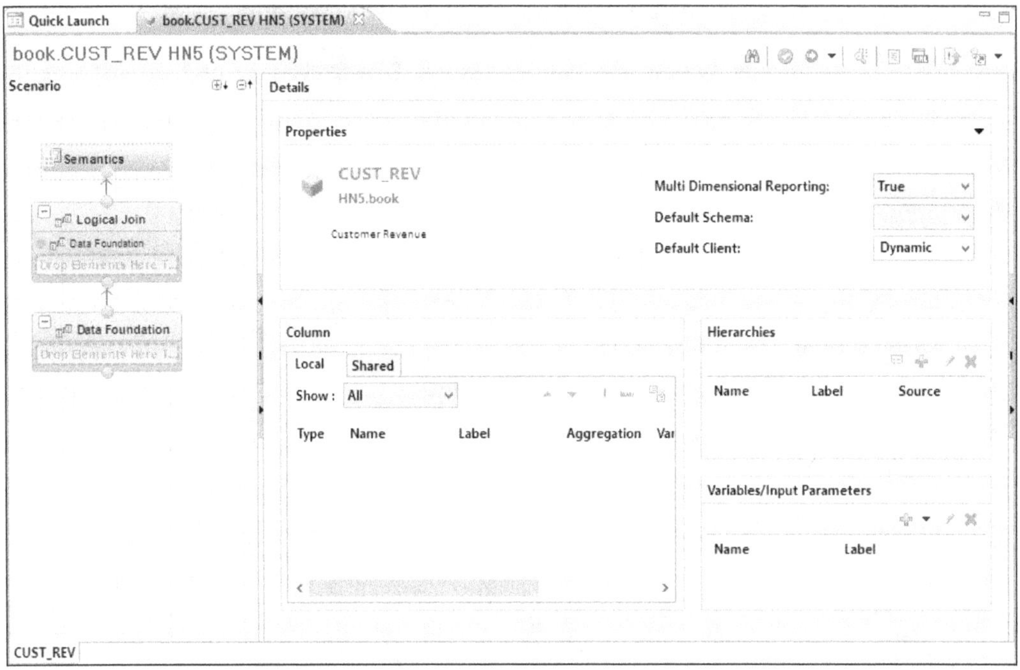

As for our attribute view, we have the data flow diagram to the left-hand side of the screen, with the **Data Foundation** at the bottom. This will contain the base tables with the information we wish to present to our user.

Above this block is the **Logical Join**. This block is where we can create joins between our base tables, in much the same way as we did for our attribute view. In addition, this block allows us to incorporate attribute views in our analytic view. In this way, we have access to all the work we did on our attribute view, and can use all the information describing our customer alongside their revenue information.

> You might like to think of this reuse of blocks as a bit like Lego. You create one small model, and then use it inside another model, and so on. Attribute views can be used inside any number of analytic views, and analytic views, in turn, can be used inside other views. Taking the time to create the basic building blocks for your application will save a lot of time later on, and make your application a great deal easier to understand and maintain.

Finally, the topmost block of an analytic view is the **Semantics** block. This is where we define the output fields of the view, as well as the view's technical information, as we can see in the screenshot.

Adding a Table to an Analytic View

In our example data, the table which contains the data which we will be using is the `REVENUE` table. This table contains, for each `CUSTID`, for the years 2009, 2010, and 2011, the revenue for this customer. Please add the `REVENUE` table to the **Data Foundation** block of the analytic view now, in the same way you added a table to the attribute view we built in the previous chapter; either by drag-and-drop from the **Catalog** node of the **Navigator** panel, or by hovering your mouse over the **Data Foundation** block, clicking on the green plus sign button which appears, and then using the **Find** dialog to select a table.

We can now, in the **Data Foundation** block, add the data fields to the output of the view, once more by right-clicking on each field and selecting **Add to Output** in the menu. We need to add `CUSTID`, `YEAR`, `CURRENCY`, and `AMOUNT` to our view.

If the information needed for analysis is all contained in the base table (if for example, the `REVENUE` table contained the customer name) then no further action is needed. We can just activate the view, and use it as it is.

> In order for an analytic view to activate correctly, it must contain one measure field. We'll examine these in detail in a minute.
> By default all numeric fields you add to an analytic view will be considered measures, so your `AMOUNT` field is one, for example.
> If no measures are found in the analytic view, activation will fail.

In our example, we will be doing some more work with the analytic view, but for now, we'll activate it so that we can take a quick look at some points. You might get tripped-up by them at some point during your development work, so taking a look at them now is appropriate.

Attributes and Measures – what a difference an icon can make!

Activate your analytic view now, and then open a data preview of the view. Have a look at what happens when `CUSTID` is added as a value to the data preview:

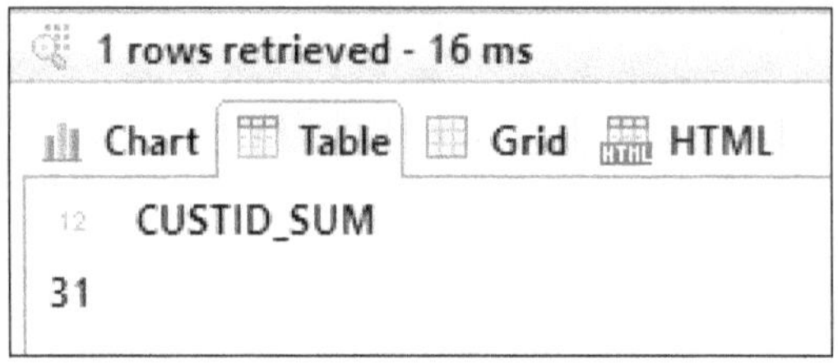

CUSTID_SUM
31

Since `CUSTID` is a numeric field (it is defined as an `INTEGER` in the base `REVENUE` table), SAP HANA quite correctly assumes that as a value you will want to sum the values when you display it.

> This behavior is called the default aggregation for the field. By default all numeric fields have an aggregation of `SUM`, so their values will be summed according to the characteristics used to display them. In our `REVENUE` table, the `CUSTID` field has four values of `1`, and three values of `2`, `3`, and `4`, for a total of `31`, which explains the value of **31** in the screenshot we have just seen. If we add the **YEAR** field to the labels axis, we can see the **CUSTID_SUM** changing, to represent the total seen per year (a total of **11** in **2009**, **10** in **2010**, and **2011**):

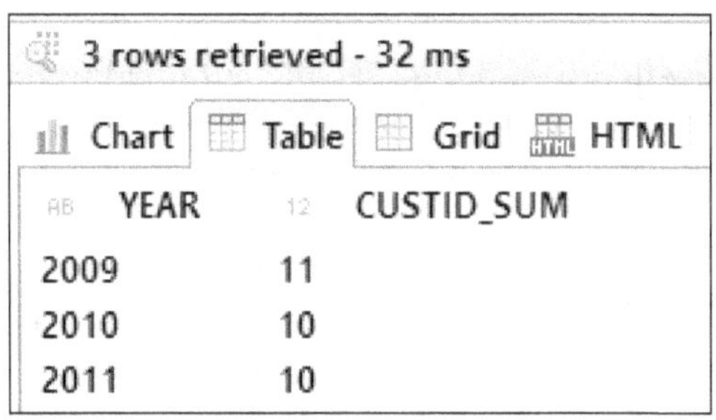

YEAR	CUSTID_SUM
2009	11
2010	10
2011	10

> As we can see, the default aggregation for a numeric field applies to the values seen according to the characteristics used. This is especially important for aggregation values of `MAX` or `MIN`, or when in a report, we ask the system to give us the average.

Of course, `CUSTID` is not a numeric field at all, so we need to indicate this to our analytic view. We would not want our reporting software to decide to sum `CUSTID` values—this makes no sense.

If you now return to the `CUST_REV` definition tab, and click on the **Semantics** block, you will see the four fields we added to our view:

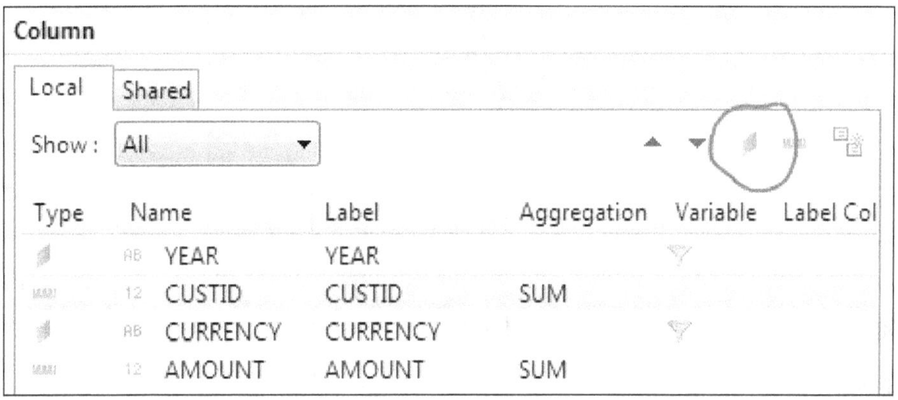

The first column of the table showing the fields is the column type. This can be either Attribute (a blue diamond shape) or Measure (an orange ruler). **CUSTID** was determined by SAP HANA to be a measure, since it is a numeric field. We need to change this to attribute. We can do this in one of two ways:

- Click on the field, and then on the blue diamond button at the top of the panel (highlighted in the screenshot)

- Click on the **Measure** icon on the line itself, and then select **Attribute** from the menu that appears:

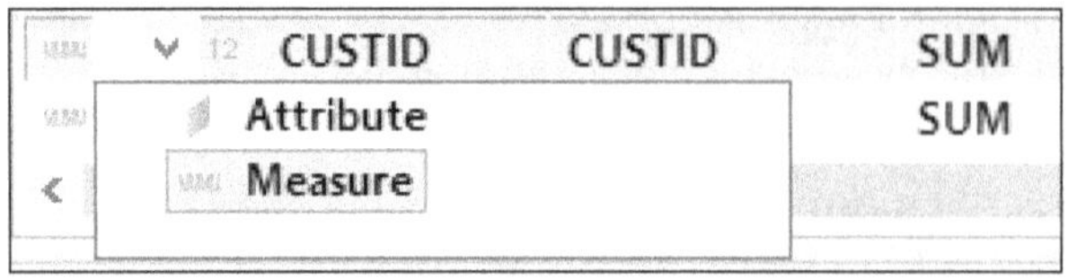

If we reactivate our view, then ask for a data preview once more, we will see that upon adding **CUSTID** to the values pane, SAP HANA will no longer try to sum the values, but will give a count of the individual values instead, which is much more useful:

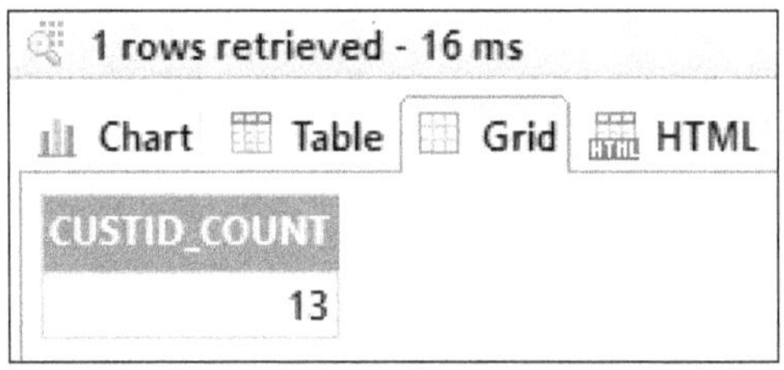

Adding an attribute view to an analytic view

Let's take a closer look at the **CUSTID_COUNT** value. SAP HANA says there are **13** individual values. If we were to add the attribute view we created in the previous chapter, we could have the customer's name (and all the other information we gathered together) alongside their revenue.

Adding an attribute view to an analytic view is basically the same as adding a table.

Our `CUST_REV` analytic view currently looks like the following screenshot:

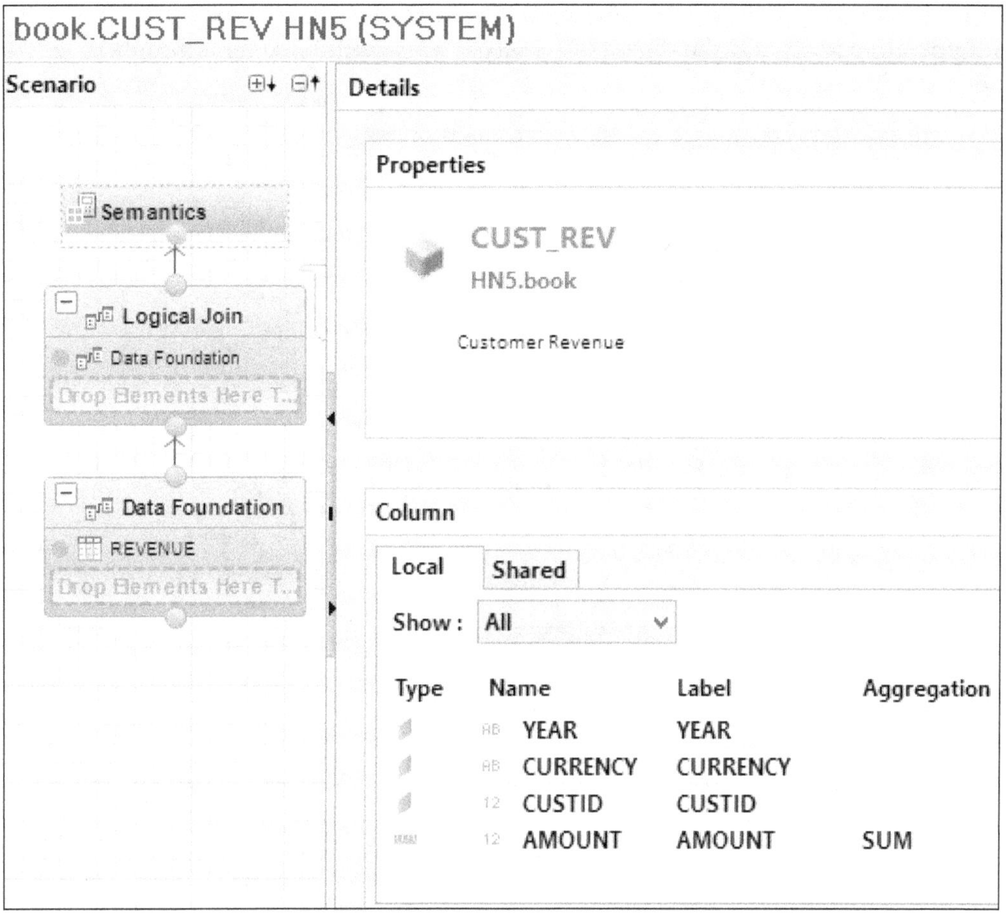

In the **Data Foundation** we have our `REVENUE` table, and we've added the **YEAR**, **CURRENCY**, and **CUSTID** fields as attributes, and the **AMOUNT** field as a measure.

In the screenshot, we can see a **Logical Join** block, and it's here that we can add an attribute view (or several, if we compartmentalize our developments further).

As when we added tables to either our attribute view from *Chapter 3, Your First SAP HANA Development – An Attribute View*, or to our analytic view in this chapter, if you hover your mouse over this block, a popup window with a green plus sign will appear, allowing you to select an attribute view for addition. Alternatively, you can add your attribute view using drag-and-drop, from the **Navigator** panel, in the same way as we added the `REVENUE` table.

Please add the `CUST_ATTR` attribute view we created earlier, to the `CUST_REV` analytic view now, and the `CUST_REV` analytic view will look something like the following screenshot:

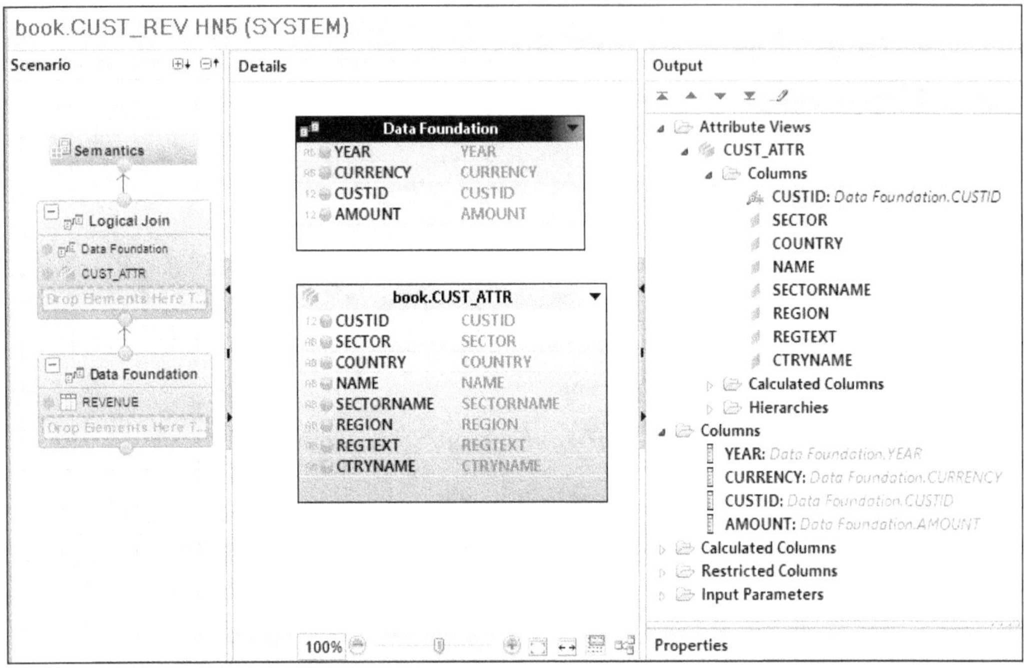

> You can rearrange the blocks in the **Details** view to suit your own preferences, just by clicking on the title of the block (for example **book.CUST_ATTR** in the screenshot) and dragging the block to some appropriate place in the **Details** view. You can also use the auto-arrange button, which is the rightmost button you can see at the bottom of the **Details** view. The Studio will attempt to arrange the layout of the blocks in a useful way.

The only thing we need to do to have access to all the information in our attribute view is to join the view to the `REVENUE` table. This is done in the same way in an analytic view as in an attribute view; just draw a link from the source field in the base table to the corresponding field in the view, and then select the join type. The join type by default will be referential.

You should now have an analytic view which looks like the following screenshot:

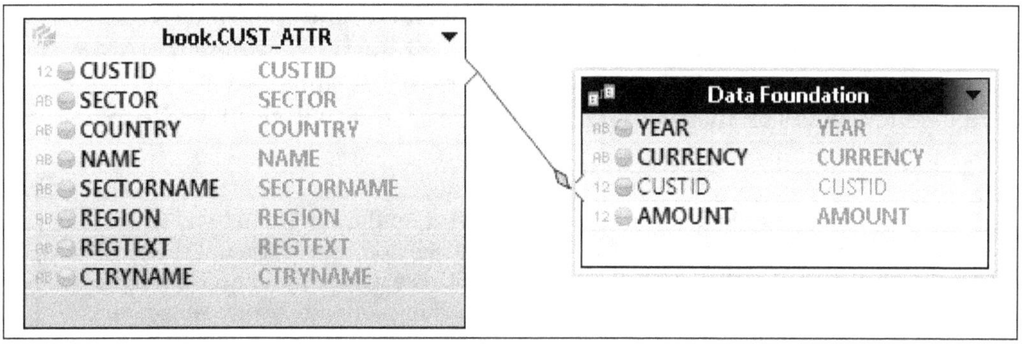

If we activate the view, and ask for a data preview with **CUSTID** as a label and **AMOUNT_SUM** as a value, however, we can see that we have a problem:

CUSTID	AMOUNT_SUM
?	515
2	383
3	378
4	492

SAP HANA is unable to determine the **CUSTID** for some of the values, which means there is a problem with our join. We know that **CUSTID** values **2**, **3** and **4** are all OK, so the problem lies with **CUSTID** number **1**.

As we saw in the previous chapter, problems with join types can lead to missing data, and that is exactly what is happening here. The Referential join assumes that all values in the table on the left-hand side are available in the table on the right-hand side, and that's not the case here. If we change the join type from **Referential** to **Left outer join**, then reactivate and refresh our data preview, we obtain the following result:

CUSTID	NAME	SECTORNAME	AMOUNT_SUM
1	?	Individual Owner	515
		Small and Medium Business	515
2	Jacques	Enterprise Customer	383
3	Martin	Individual Owner	378
4	Jones	Small and Medium Business	492

As we can see, we've regained **CUSTID**, but not **Name**, and there are two different sectors. This tells us that **CUSTID** number **1** has (at least) two different **NAME** values in different **SECTORNAME** fields. The reason is simple—whereas the attribute view filters on the client ID (`MANDT`) of `100`, the analytic view doesn't.

> Even if correcting the join type did not completely solve the problem with our data, it is usually better to set up the join in this way (data table on the left-hand side, attribute view on the right-hand side, conceptually, and a left outer join). This ensures that the **CUSTID** field is filled. Depending on the reporting software used to examine the data, if the database was not able to display the **CUSTID** field, the associated **AMOUNT_SUM** might not show up at all in reporting. It is usually best to ensure that numeric information always appears, even if we don't have the metadata to describe it.

In order to have the analytic view filter automatically on a given client number, we need to proceed in the same way as for the attribute view. In the view definition screen, in the properties for the **Semantics** block, define the appropriate client value. We will see later (in *Chapter 7, Hey! That's My Data! – Authorizations in SAP HANA*) that we can define a default client value for each user in our SAP HANA system, so we don't need to predefine the values in the different views we create.

Right now we need to set the **Default Client** for our analytic view to **100**:

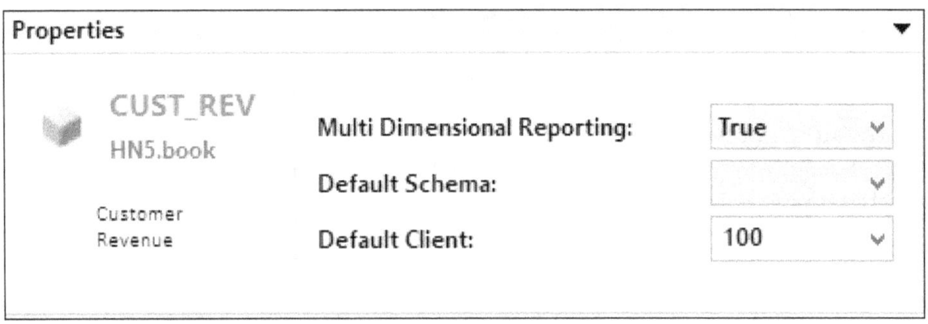

After reactivation, our analytic view will now show the correct data from the `REVENUE` table, and we have access to all the customer information we gathered in our attribute view:

CUSTID	NAME	SECTORNAME	CTRYNAME	REGTEXT	CURRENCY	YEAR	AMOUNT_SUM
1	Smith	Small and Medium Business	Great Britain	Europe	GBP	2009	112
						2010	119
						2011	121
2	Jacques	Enterprise Customer	France	Europe	EUR	2009	127
						2010	125
						2011	131
3	Martin	Individual Owner	Great Britain	Europe	GBP	2009	120
						2010	121
						2011	137
4	Jones	Small and Medium Business	United States of America	North America	USD	2009	158
						2010	163
						2011	171

Advanced features of analytic views

As we have seen so far, an analytic view allows us to use numeric information. We can present salaries, sales amounts, turnover, and all kinds of numbers with an analytic view. We can also join an analytic view to an attribute view, and profit from the metadata they provide, enabling us to describe our numeric information.

Analytic views have a lot more functionality however, making them considerably more powerful. In this section we'll take a look at a few of the functions they provide.

Restricted columns – what they are and how to use them

One feature that an analytic view can provide is a restricted column. This option will create a new column in our view, based upon an existing numeric value, and only populate it for a given line if a specified condition is true.

> For readers familiar with the SAP BW BEx reporting suite, this feature is equivalent to a restricted key figure.

The easiest way to understand the concept is to make a restricted column ourselves, so let's do that now.

In our view, we show `AMOUNT` per `CUSTOMER`. Our users would like to have a new column showing `AMOUNT` per `CUSTOMER`, but only for those `CUSTOMER` values in Europe. For customers outside Europe, our users don't want to have a value in the new column.

We can achieve this with a restricted column.

To create a restricted column, in the view creation screen, click on the **Logical Join** block, and then, in the **Output** panel, right click on **Restricted Columns**, and select **New** from the menu to see the **Restricted Columns** dialog, presented in the following screenshot:

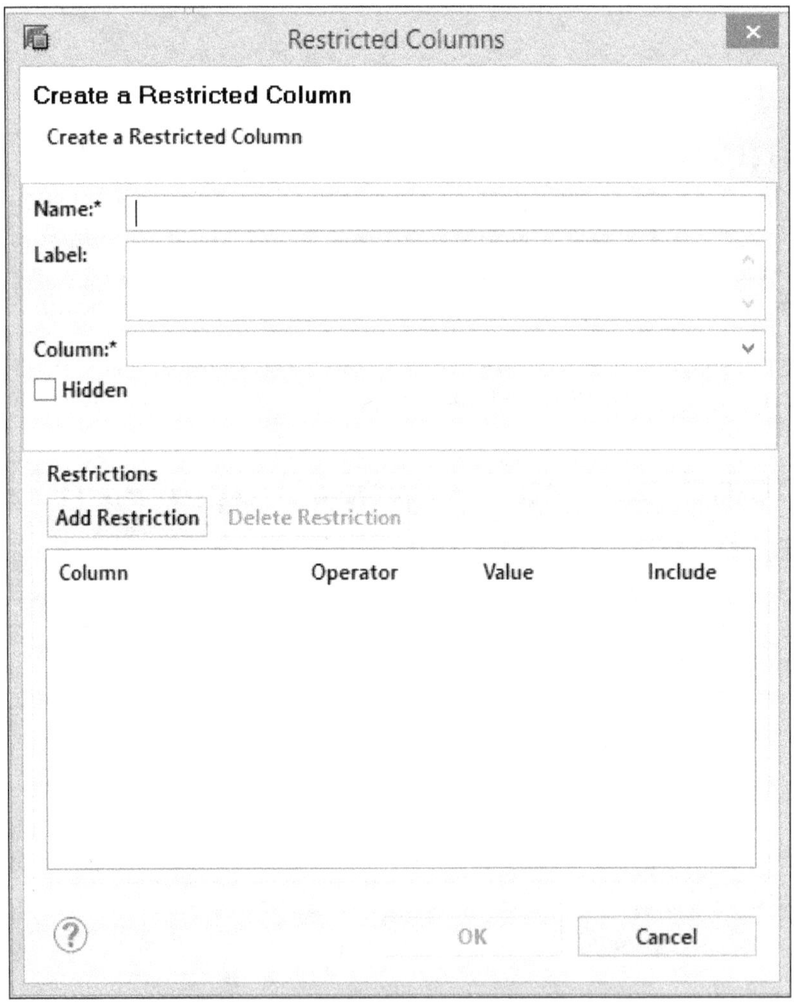

As with most objects in SAP HANA we need to give our restricted column a **Name** and a description (**Label**). The **Name** will become the column name in our view.

Additionally, we need to specify the source **Column** on which the contents of this restricted column will be based. In the drop-down list you will be presented with all the measures configured in the view. In our analytic view, there is only one measure, **AMOUNT**, so select it now.

It is possible, by checking the **Hidden** checkbox, to define a restricted column which is hidden. In this case, your column cannot be used to present information to the user, though you can use it inside other calculations. Think of such a column as a temporary variable you can use in your models. We won't be using this option here.

The last thing we need to define is the restriction on the column. After you click on **Add Restriction**, you can define a source column and a condition on which to test the column contents. In our example, we'll test the contents of the **REGION** column against values which **Equal EU**. The restricted column will copy the contents of the source column (**AMOUNT**) for all lines which match the restriction. All other lines will have no value filled.

You can even, if you require, define several restrictions (all Individual Business Owners (**SECTOR**) in Canada (**COUNTRY**), maybe). The value will only be copied if all restrictions are met at once.

Once your restricted column has been created, save and reactivate the view, then you can request a data preview to see the result, which should look like the following screenshot:

NAME	REGION	AMOUNT	EUROPE_REVENUE
Jacques	EU	125	125
		127	127
		131	131
Jones	NAR	158	?
		163	?
		171	?
Martin	EU	120	120
		121	121
		137	137
Smith	EU	112	112
		119	119
		121	121

As we can see, our **EUROPE_REVENUE** column is filled only for those customers in Europe. Customer **Jones**, from North America, does not contribute to the revenue in Europe.

Calculated Columns

Taking the notion of new columns to the next level, we can create calculated columns. Where a restricted column will only copy a value from an existing source column, a calculated column can create values from scratch, or manipulate existing values.

We'll improve our view by creating two calculated columns:

- The first, a calculated attribute indicating that the data in the view is `REAL` data. This means that what we are showing our users is the data stored in the underlying table.
- The second, `VAT_RATE`, will contain the rate of sales tax (VAT) each customer pays. The value in the column will depend on the country of the customer—19.6 percent for France, 20 percent for Great Britain, and 0 percent for the USA
- The third, `VAT_AMOUNT` will take the `VAT_RATE` we've just calculated, and give us the amount of sales tax paid, assuming that the value in the `AMOUNT` column is inclusive of tax.

To create a calculated column, we just need, as usual, to right click on **Calculated Columns** in the **Output** panel of the **Logical Join** of an analytic view, and select **New** to obtain the **Calculated Column** dialog pictured in the following screenshot:

This is by far the most complex dialog we've seen so far, though it is not actually that difficult to use.

As usual, a **Name** and Description (**Label**) are necessary for our new column. Next we have the **Data Type**. This is the same information necessary when defining a column in a database table—basically is it numeric (and if so, an integer or a decimal number) or text, and then the length and number of decimals if necessary.

The **Column type** box allows you to define your new column as either an attribute or a measure.

> Readers familiar with SAP BW will find this interesting. Unlike SAP BW, SAP HANA can create calculated characteristics (called calculated attributes in SAP HANA), whereas SAP BW can only create calculated Ratios (Measures), at least in the reporting layer.

The bottom half of the dialog window is dedicated to the definition of the column itself. To create a calculated column, you need to write an expression, which is a lot like an Excel formula. SAP HANA allows you, in the **Elements** list, to select existing columns of the view as operands. You can then manipulate these column values with either **Operators** or **Functions**. Once again, if you are at ease writing Excel functions you'll feel right at home here. The function list is somewhat similar, and organized in much the same way as in Excel.

Calculated attribute – DATA_TYPE

Let's create our data type indicator first, as it's the easiest to create.

We will be creating a simple column containing just the word `REAL` on each line. However, we won't be using this information until later in the book.

Our new column will be called `DATA_TYPE`, will be of type `VARCHAR`, length `4` (just enough to hold the word `REAL`).

The expression we need to use to create the column will not be based upon another column, nor will it use any special calculations to generate the value. We'll just put a constant value in the expression. To do so, we need to surround the value with single quotes (if it's text, which is the case here).

Our new column will look like the following screenshot:

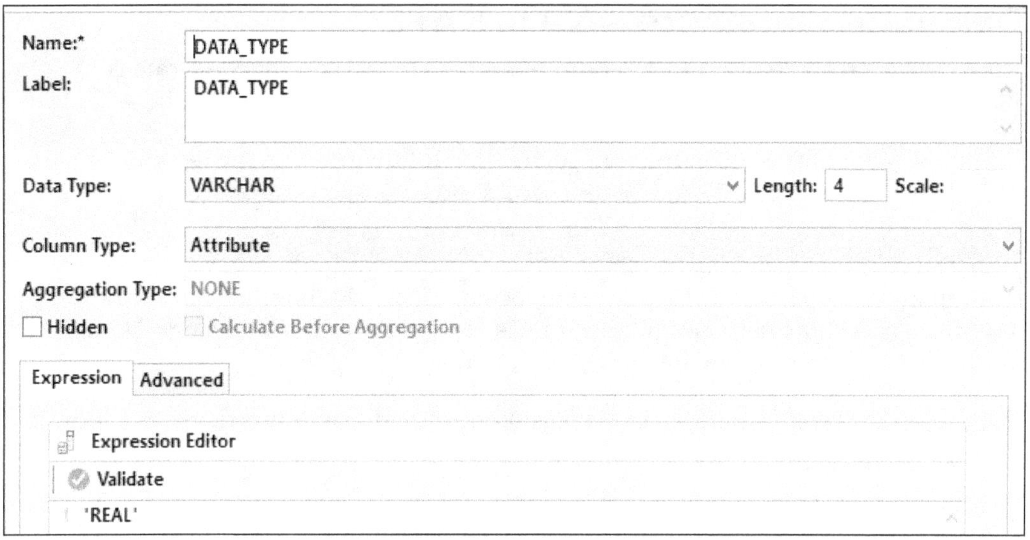

A quick reactivation and data preview shows us that we now have access to the **DATA_TYPE** column in the field list of our view, and as expected it contains the word **REAL** (without the quotes we typed) on every line, as we can see in the following screenshot:

YEAR	AMOUNT	DATA_TYPE
2009	112	REAL
	120	REAL
	127	REAL
	158	REAL
2010	119	REAL
	121	REAL
	125	REAL
	163	REAL
2011	121	REAL
	131	REAL
	137	REAL
	171	REAL

The full usage of this new column will become clear a little later in the book, but in the meantime we can create our two other calculated columns.

Calculated measure – VAT_RATE

Now we can create the `VAT_RATE` column. As we saw earlier, the VAT rate is 19.6 percent in France, 20 percent in Great Britain, and 0 percent in the USA.

We could write this as an expression such as the following in pseudo-code:

```
If country is France, vat is 19.6%, if not, if country is GB, vat rate
is 20%, if not 0%
```

Admittedly, it's not the most legible sentence in the world, but you can see how it works. Full syntax help is available for the expression editor by using the **Help** button at the bottom of the dialog (the question mark).

The correct expression syntax (and this is what you'll have to type in) is as follows:

```
if ("COUNTRY" = 'FR',19.6,if("COUNTRY"='GB',20,0))
```

Note that `COUNTRY` is surrounded by double quotes, indicating to SAP HANA that it is a column name. `FR` and `GB` are surrounded by single quotes, indicating that they are constant values.

Your calculated column **VAT_RATE** should look like the following screenshot:

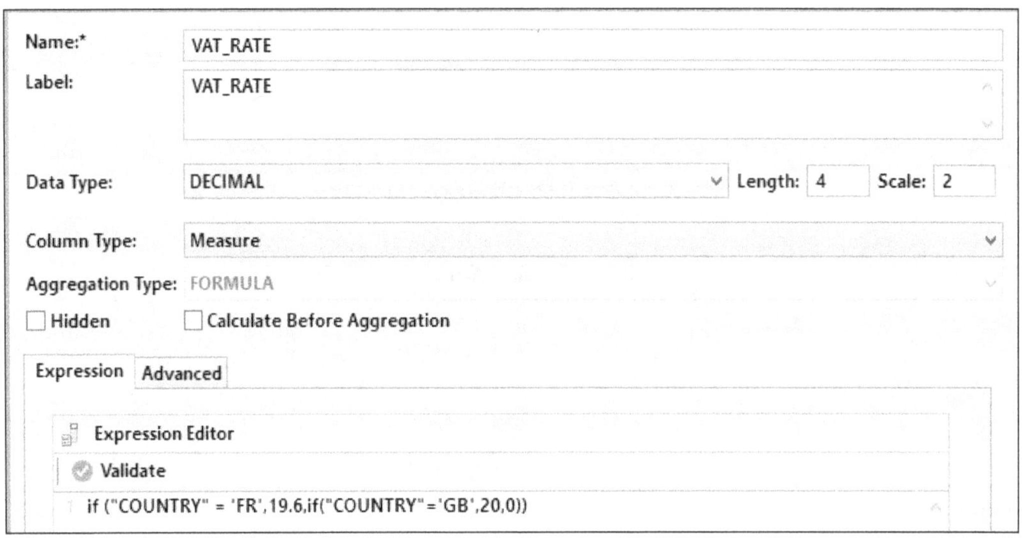

Save the column, reactivate the view and open a data preview to see the results:

COUNTRY	VAT_RATE
FR	19.6
GB	20
US	0

This is exactly what we expected, and exactly what we need for the next step—calculating the VAT amount.

Calculated measure – VAT_AMOUNT

Creating the `VAT_AMOUNT` column is done in exactly the same way as we created `VAT_RATE`. To do this, create another calculated column in the view (called `VAT_AMOUNT`), and enter the following formula:

```
("AMOUNT" * "VAT_RATE")/100
```

As we can see, both `AMOUNT` and `VAT_RATE` are columns—we can use the result of one calculated column in order to calculate another.

> You cannot do cyclic calculations in calculated columns. However, this means that you cannot use the result of column A to calculate column B, to calculate column A.
>
> Additionally, while you can use restricted columns in the expressions of a calculated column, you cannot use calculated columns as the source for a restricted column.

Your second calculated column looks like the following screenshot:

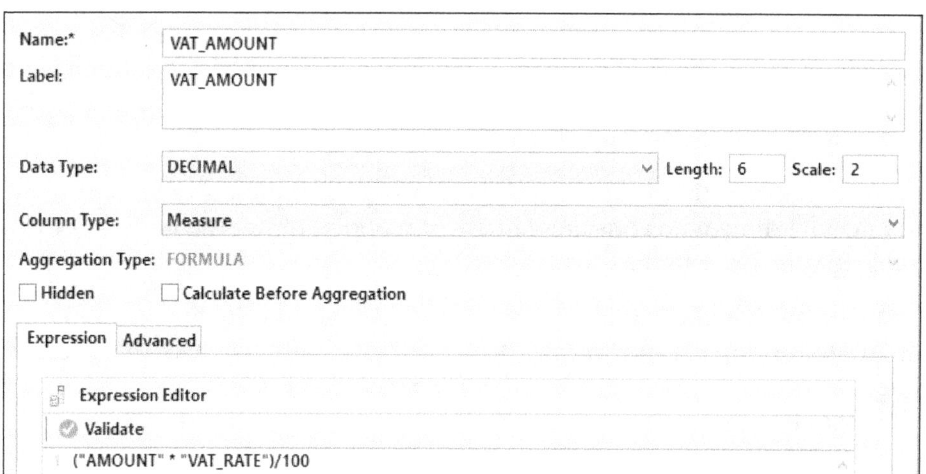

Once again, a reactivation and a data preview will yield the expected results, with another new column giving the amount paid by the customer in sales tax:

NAME	CURRENCY	VAT_RATE	YEAR	AMOUNT_SUM	VAT_AMOUNT_SUM
Jacques	EUR	19.6	2009	127	24.13
			2010	125	23.75
			2011	131	24.89
Jones	USD	0	2009	158	0
			2010	163	0
			2011	171	0
Martin	GBP	20	2009	120	24
			2010	121	24.2
			2011	137	27.4
Smith	GBP	20	2009	112	22.4
			2010	119	23.8
			2011	121	24.2

As expected, our customers in Great Britain paid **20** percent tax, which for customer **Martin** amounted to **24** GBP on an amount of **120** GBP in **2009**. In France the tax rate of **19.6** percent led to **24.89** EUR tax on an amount of **131** EUR for **Jacques** in **2011. Jones** paid no tax at all, since he is living in the USA, his sales tax rate was **0** percent.

Accepting user input

At this point we have an analytic view which pulls data from the underlying table, joins it to an attribute view to recover information about the customer whose revenue we are examining. We have also enhanced this view with a restricted column which is filled only for customers in Europe, and some calculated columns, giving, notably, the amount of sales tax each customer has paid.

One thing to notice is that we have only been able to manipulate data that already exists, or create some with constant values. At no point of time so far has our user been able to contribute to the calculations.

It might happen that at times in reporting, you need your users to enter values. You might for example, leave the `VAT_RATE` for France as a user variable because it changes so often, or you might want your restricted column to filter on a country that the user chooses.

In this section we'll be looking at such a function.

Our existing analytic view shows customer revenue from years `2009` to `2011`, for four customers. We'll take the information from `2011`, ask the user for a percentage by which to increase the amount, and create a new column called `PROJECTED_AMOUNT` for year `2012` using the result.

So as not to complicate our existing analytic view further, we'll start by copying our view, and we'll make all further changes to the copy, not the original view (which we can consider "finished").

Creating a view by copy

The first thing we need to do is create our copy of the analytic view. We'll call it `PROJ_REV`. Since we need a copy of an existing view, we can create the view by copy, it'll save a lot of time. In the **Modeler** perspective, **Quick Launch** panel, select **Analytic View** and then **Create**. Enter the view's **Name**, **Description**, select our **book Package**, and choose to **Copy from** the **CUST_REV** view, as shown in the following screenshot:

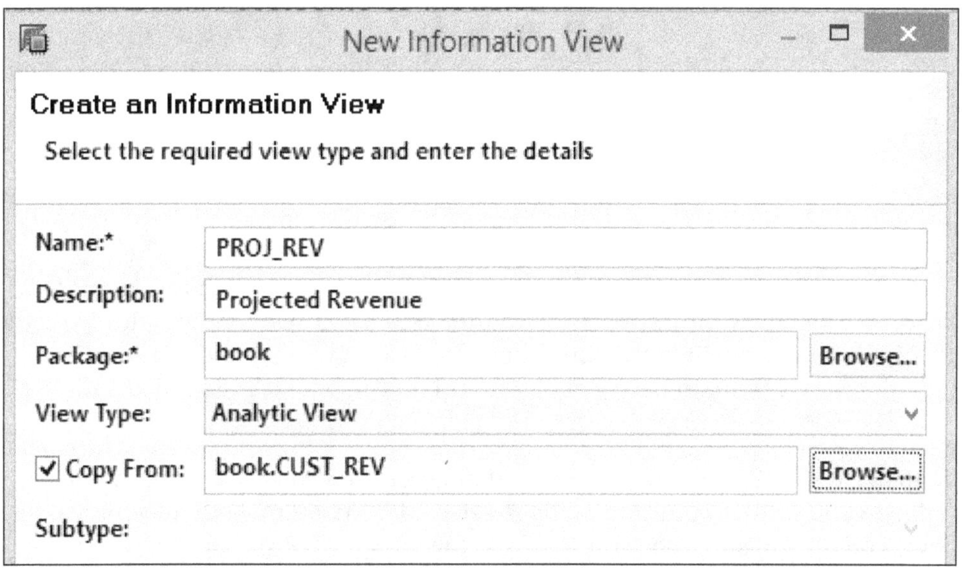

Just click on **Finish** to create the view. There's no need to activate it yet, as we'll be making a few changes.

Filtering view contents

Since in our **PROJ_REV** view we will be calculating 2012's projected revenue, based upon 2011's real revenue, the only data we need to keep from the underlying table is that from 2011. SAP HANA lets us do this by filtering the data.

In the view creation screen, in the **Data Foundation** block, if you right-click on the **YEAR** field, you will see the option **Apply Filter** in the context menu. Select this option now to see the **Apply Filter** dialog, which has been reproduced in the following screenshot:

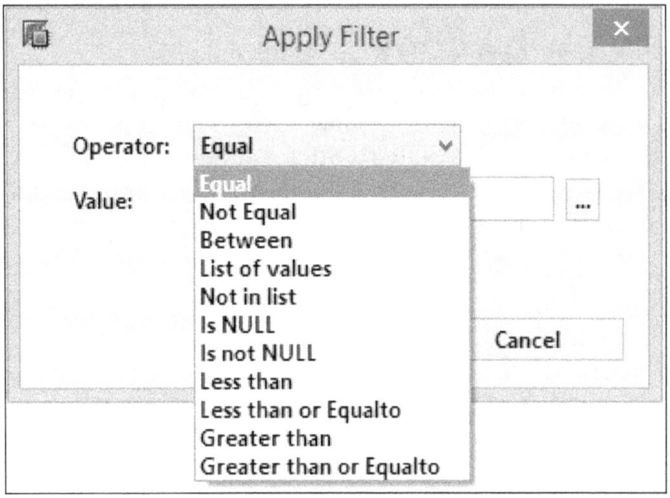

As we can see, the filter option allows us to restrict data according to a condition. We choose a value for the appropriate column and a comparison operator from the list. Only lines which match the condition will be kept in the view. Our condition will be simple; we want to keep only lines with a `YEAR` value `Equal` to `2011`.

Next to the **Value** box is a **Browse** button. This is an intelligent button—if you click on it, then click on **Find** on the resulting dialog, the Studio will show you the list of unique values in the column you have selected. It really makes choosing values easier if you are not sure what is present in the view.

Once you have configured the filter, click on **OK**. You'll see a funnel icon next to the `YEAR` field in the view creation screen in the **Data Foundation** block. If at this point you activate the view and request a data preview, you'll see that as expected, only data from 2011 is present. You don't need to do this yet unless you want to check, as we have a couple more changes to make to the view.

Creating a variable

We have just seen that we can use a hard-coded filter in our view. It might be interesting however to use filters that the user can define at runtime. For example, today you might want to analyze sales data from France, and leave Germany for tomorrow. We could have one analytic view showing the sales data for the whole of Europe, and create a variable allowing us to filter on the requested country at runtime.

Creating a variable is done by clicking on the **Semantics** block, and then in the **Variables/Input parameters** box, click on the green plus sign to create a variable. The **New Variable** dialog will appear, allowing you to define your variable.

An example variable is shown in the following screenshot; this variable requests that the user select a value for the company size at runtime:

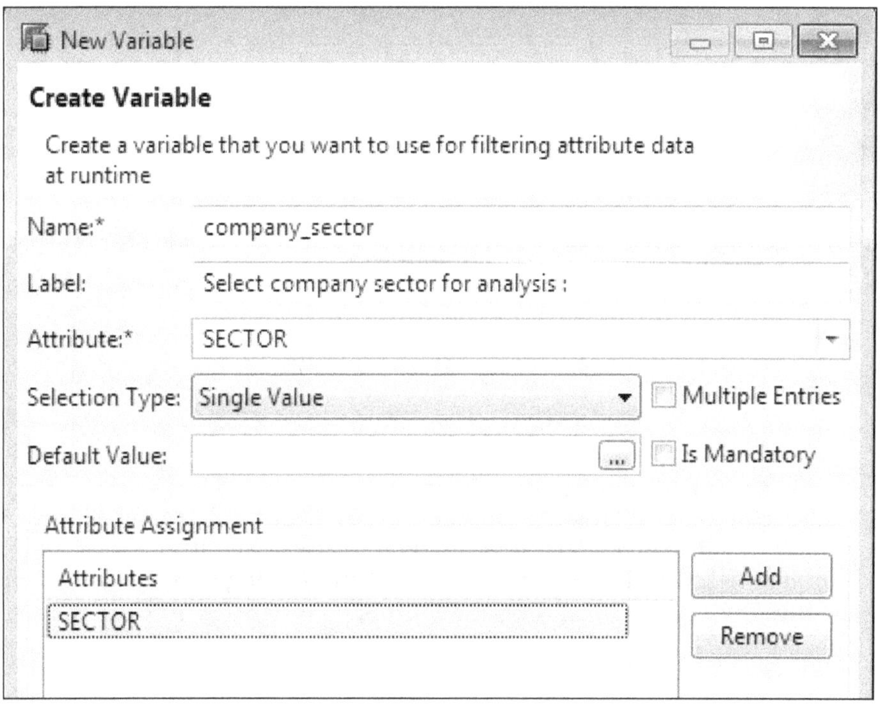

A variable, such as most other objects we create, needs a **Name** and a **Label**. The **Attribute** field defines the type of data on which the variable will filter. In the example, the **SECTOR** field has been selected.

The **Selection Type** option allows us to define whether the user will be able to select either one value (**Single Value**), a **Range**, or **Interval** of values (customer IDs 7 to 13, for example).

We can allow the user to select several values or ranges with the help of the **Multiple Entries** checkbox, can define a default value for the variable with the **Default Value** box, and can require that the user enter a value with the **Is Mandatory** checkbox.

The **Attribute Assignment** list shows which view fields will be filtered using this variable. This will usually be a field of the same type as the **Attribute** field. However if you have an **Attribute** field of type `YEAR`, and you have several `YEAR` fields in your view (`SALES_YEAR`, `FISCAL_YEAR`, maybe), you can choose which field to filter here.

If a variable is defined in your view, and has at least one attribute assigned to it, then you will be prompted to enter or select a value for the filter at runtime. The default variable entry dialog for the variable we've just created is shown as follows:

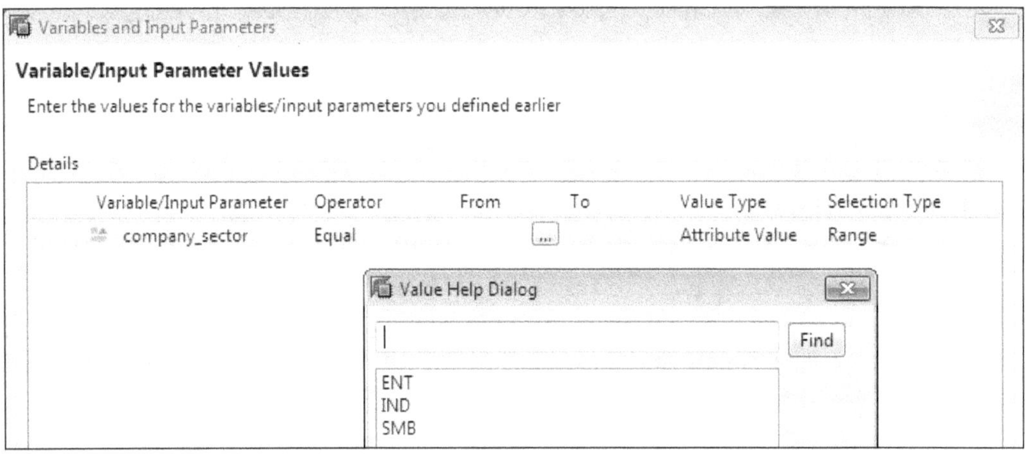

Values for the variable can be entered directly in the **From** column, or the button in the column may be used to obtain the **Value Help Dialog**, which will list all appropriate values when you click on the **Find** button, as we can see in the preceding screenshot.

Creating an input parameter

In our view, we'll be showing projected revenue, calculated according to a percentage increase which we'll ask our user to supply at runtime. This has the advantage of being very flexible—if one user expects us to increase revenue by 10 percent, and another user, a little more pessimistic, expects only a 1 percent increase, we won't need to make any changes to our data models to allow them both to make their simulations. Even better for our users, they won't need us at runtime, the system will handle everything automatically.

In order to allow our users to enter a percentage value, we'll create an input parameter. As usual, a right-click on the appropriate block (**Input Parameters**) in the output panel of our view is enough to bring up the correct dialog:

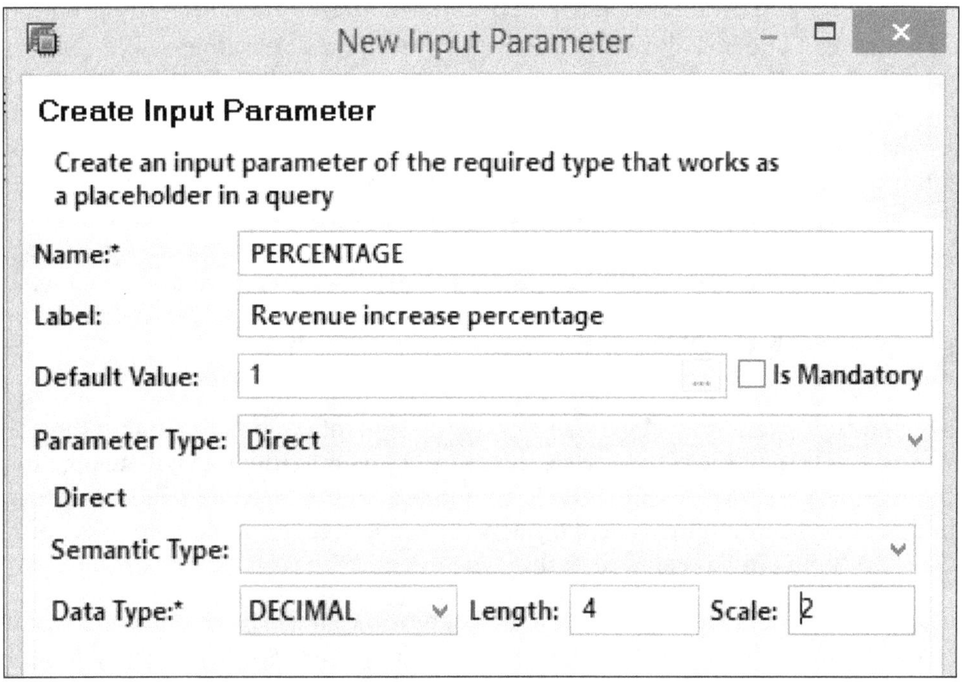

Again as usual, we need to give our object a **Name** and a **Label**. If we wish we can give a **Default Value** for the input parameter. Here, we've entered a **Default Value** of **1**, for a default 1 percent increase.

> Some reporting software does not know how to handle input parameters correctly. Typically, if you query a SAP HANA view from SAP's BusinessObjects software, you will be prompted to enter any input parameters that exist for a view, however if you query the same view from Microsoft Excel, then no prompt will appear. Creating a default value will make sure that at least some value exists, and any calculations you make based upon the input parameter won't break.

We can also decide to make an input parameter mandatory or not by checking on the **Is Mandatory** checkbox. If we absolutely need a value (typically we cannot calculate projected sales without a percentage increase value), then we can decide to make the user entry mandatory, so we can be sure that there's some value at runtime.

The **Parameter Type** box allows us different types of input parameter. We can decide for example to not ask our user to enter a value, but to recover the value from elsewhere. We might, for example, have a configuration table in our system which states that company-wide, the expected revenue increase for 2012 is 2.3 percent. By selecting a **Parameter Type** value of **Derived from Table**, and specifying the table name, field name and the selection conditions, we can recover this configuration value at runtime. This will make our view fairly dynamic, allowing changes to be made in a coherent manner, without needing to modify and reactivate the view.

In our example, the **Parameter Type** is **Direct**, meaning that we want the user to enter a value manually.

The **Semantic Type** box can be either empty (no semantic type), or contain the values **Currency** or **Date**. In these two cases, the prompt given to the user will change to be more appropriate to the data type to be entered. In the case of a `Date` entry for example, the system might present a calendar to the user to enable date selection, rather than typing in the value directly.

Finally, we have the **Data Type** box, which determines the type of data we're asking the user to enter, whether it is numeric or text. We can also specify the field length, and number of decimal places, as appropriate.

In this example, we'll be asking the user to enter a decimal number, with no more than two decimal places, as the percentage increase value.

When you have finished defining the input parameter, just click on **OK** to save it. It'll appear in the **Output** panel of the **Logical Join** box of the view creation screen.

Creating a new calculated column

Now that we have created an input parameter, we can use it to make calculations on the fly in our view.

Create a new calculated column called `PROJECTED_AMOUNT`, type `Decimal`, Length `6` with `2` decimal places, and whose calculation formula is as follows:

```
"AMOUNT" + ( "AMOUNT" * $$PERCENTAGE$$ / 100 )
```

> In the same way column names are surrounded by double quotes and constant values by single quotes, in expressions in SAP HANA, input parameter names are surrounded by double dollar-signs.

A second calculated column we need to create is `PROJ_YEAR`. The data we are calculating is based upon the year 2011. The value in the `PROJECTED_AMOUNT` column is the amount in the `AMOUNT` column, increased by a user-defined percentage. This percentage increase represents the revenue increase year-over-year.

The value in the `PROJECTED_AMOUNT` column, therefore, represents data from 2012.

Please create a new calculated column, called `PROJ_YEAR`, type `VARCHAR`, length `4`, of type `Attribute`, and which has the rather convoluted expression of:

```
string( int( "YEAR" ) + 1 )
```

This expression means:

- Take the value of the `YEAR` column, turn it into a number, add `1` and then turn the result into a `string`.

This is necessary because we need to add `1` to the `YEAR` column, but we cannot do this by default since `YEAR` is not a number. Hence the two typecast functions, `int()` and `string()`.

Your **PROJ_YEAR** column, when activated, will give the following result in a data preview:

YEAR	PROJ_YEAR
2011	2012

Modifying existing calculated columns

As you recall from earlier, we have a calculated column called `DATA_TYPE`, which we have filled with the value `REAL`. While this was true for the `CUST_REV` view, it isn't for this view, which now contains only projected (definitely not real) data.

Please modify the expression for the **DATA_TYPE** column in the `PROJ_REV` view, so that it returns a value of **PROJ**:

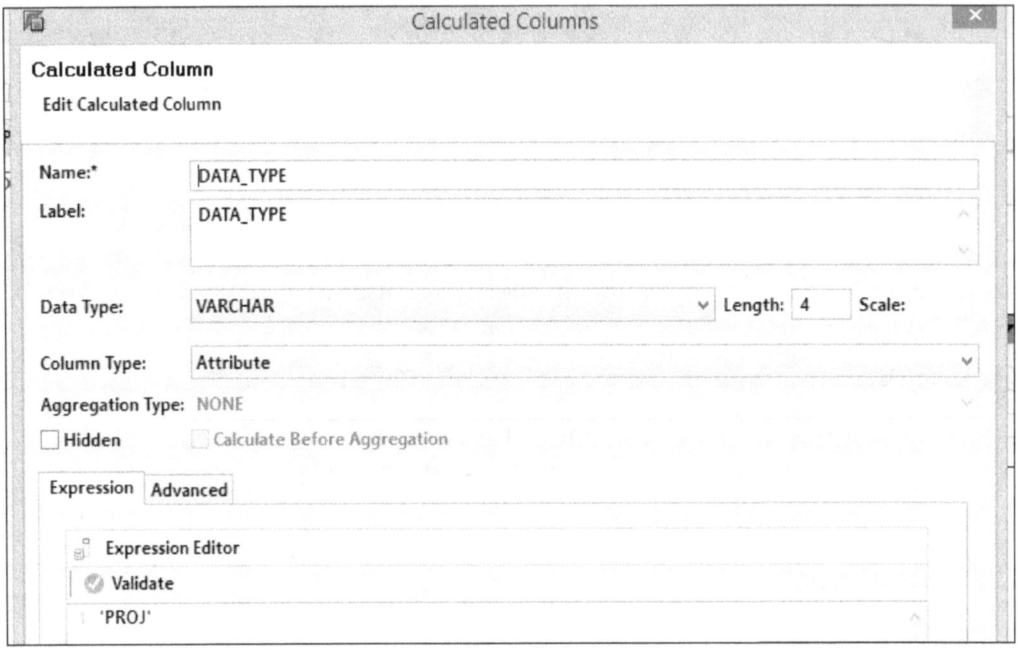

At this point your `PROJ_REV` view should look like the following screenshot:

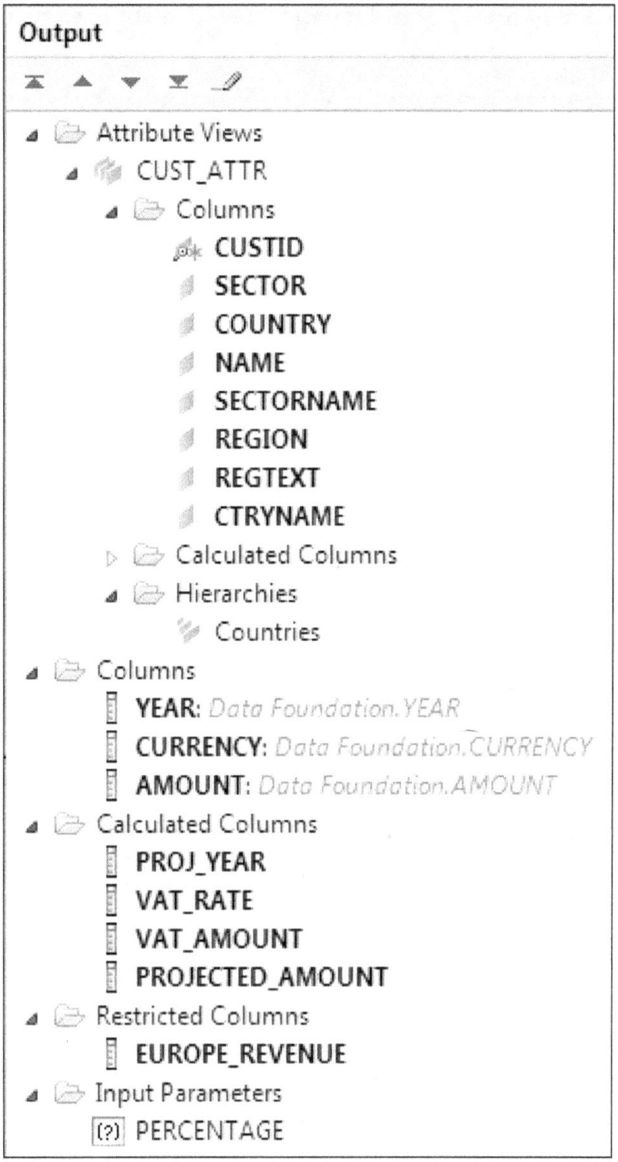

Starting to look fairly full, isn't it?

If we now activate the view and ask for a data preview, everything will come together!

First, we'll be asked to enter a percentage increase (this is the same dialog we saw earlier when we covered variables):

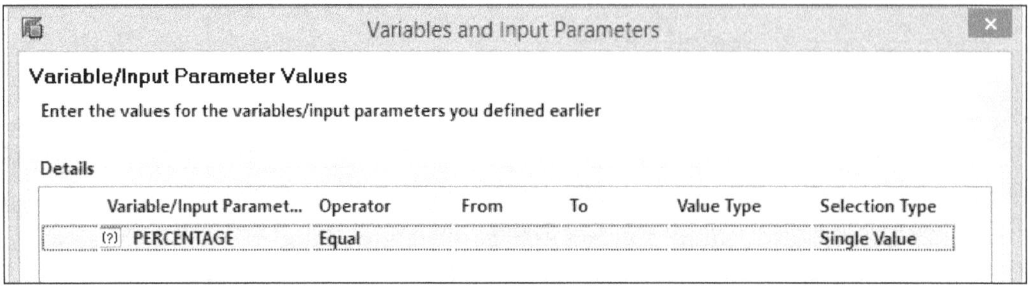

When we enter a value (let's say 5 – there's no need to enter the percent sign, and indeed it would be refused by SAP HANA), and validate, we will be able to see the view's contents:

NAME	YEAR	CURRENCY	AMOUNT	PROJECTED_AMOUNT	VAT_AMOUNT	VAT_RATE
Jacques	2011	EUR	131	137	24.89	19.6
Jones	2011	USD	171	179	0	0
Martin	2011	GBP	137	143	27.4	20
Smith	2011	GBP	121	127	24.2	20

As we can see, the **PROJECTED_AMOUNT** column is equal to the **AMOUNT** column, increased by our user-supplied percentage value.

And our two analytic views are finished!

Summary

In this chapter, we have seen a large number of features of SAP HANA. We started by creating a simple analytic view on a base table, allowing us to access and work with numeric information. We joined the attribute view created in the previous chapter to our analytic view, which brought the customer information, allowing us to describe the numeric information in the view.

We then saw how we could create a column whose value would only be filled if a certain condition was filled (a restricted column). Next we created some calculated columns, whose values ranged from simple fixed values (the `DATA_TYPE`), to a dynamic value depending on the contents of another column (the `VAT_RATE`), to using the results of other calculated columns in calculations (`VAT_AMOUNT`).

Finally, we created a second analytic view by copying the first, and we filtered the data shown (keeping only data from 2011). A variable allowed us to ask the user for an optional `SECTOR` to work on at runtime. After creating a user-supplied input parameter (a revenue increase percentage), we used it to create another calculated column, representing the projected revenue for 2012.

Between the functionalities provided by the attribute view and those we've seen in the analytic view, we can now provide rich reporting functionality to our users, allowing on-the-fly calculations, user intervention, filtering, and different methods of data aggregation.

In the next chapter, we will see the next level of modeling, where the work we've done on our two analytic views will be brought together, providing a coherent reporting object to our user in a graphical calculation view.

Quick reference

The following is a quick overview of the main topics covered in this chapter.

Object	Usage	Creation
Analytic view	Allows representation of numeric data	**Quick Launch** | **Analytic View** | **Create** Add base table with numeric field(s) to work with, join any necessary attribute views, activate.
Restricted column	Copies the value of an existing measure column, only if condition(s) are met	In view creation screen, in the **Logical Join** block, right-click on **Restricted column** and select **New**. Give name, description, select source column, define restriction column and value, save

Object	Usage	Creation
Calculated column	Creates a new column based upon either an existing column, or a hardcoded value	In view creation screen, **Logical Join** block, right-click on **Calculated column** and select **New**. Give name, description, type. Enter expression to define the column (such as an Excel formula)
Filter	Only shows certain rows from the base table	In view creation screen, **Data Foundation** block, right-click on field to filter, select **Add Filter**. Enter filter conditions in box, save.
User parameter	Let's the user participate by entering information which changes the view's behavior at runtime	In view creation screen, **Logical Join** block, right-click on **Input Parameter** and select **New**. Give name, description, type. Give any default value and select mandatory or not, save. Use the parameter in calculated columns, surrounding the parameter name with `$$`.

5

Let's Get Graphical – Graphical Calculation Views

In *Chapter 4, Painting with Numbers – An Analytic View*, we made two analytic views in our SAP HANA system. The first of these pulled the revenue data for our customers from the `REVENUE` table and joined it to our attribute view, giving us information on the customer alongside their revenue. The second analytic view that we created introduced the notion of user input, allowing our users to enter a revenue increase percentage, and then showed the projected revenue for 2012 based upon the real revenue for 2011 in the system.

In this chapter we'll be seeing how we can create a view which joins the information from these two analytic views together, presenting in one place the real revenue from the first view alongside the projected revenue in the second.

What is a graphical calculation view?

A graphical calculation view, as its name suggests, is a graphical editor with building blocks to create a view. We've often seen the concept of building blocks in this book, whereby we create a small initial development which can then be included in a larger one. Graphical calculation views push this concept to its logical conclusion, giving a visual editor to create, organize, and link different blocks together.

This graphical editor is only for our benefit as developers. When we activate our development, it is transformed, as are all objects we create in the SAP HANA Studio, into SQL statements appropriate to SAP HANA. We will see in the next chapter (*Chapter 6, You Talking to Me? – Scripted calculation views*) that we can achieve the same results by writing the SQL ourselves if we need to do more complex calculations in our views.

In the next few sections we'll create a graphical calculation view, seeing the different types of actions we can perform with one.

Creating a graphical calculation view

Like most objects in the SAP HANA Studio, a graphical calculation view is created in the **Quick View** panel of the **Modeler** perspective. If your Studio is closed, please open it now and, switch to the **Modeler** perspective if this is not the default view which opens.

You can get to the **Modeler** perspective by selecting from the Studio menu the option **Window** | **Open Perspective** | **Other** | **Modeler**. There is also a shortcut to opening the modeler, with a button directly on the screen. At the top-right hand corner of the Studio window is a default tab allowing perspective switching. It looks something like the following:

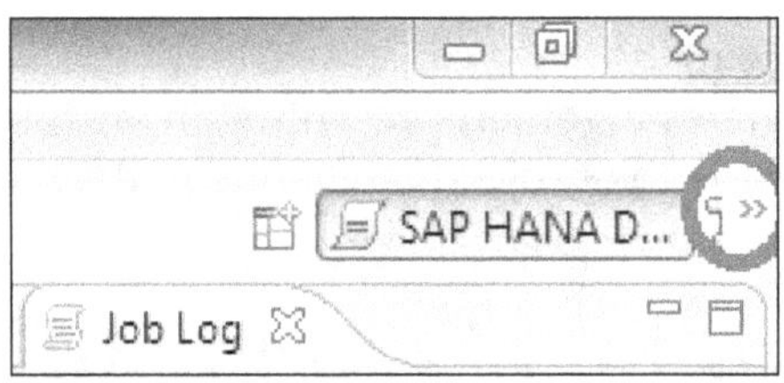

The exact layout of this tab changes depending on user actions, so it might not look exactly as the screenshot represented.

In the screenshot, we can see that the current perspective in use in the Studio is the **SAP HANA Development** perspective, which we will see in great detail in *Chapter 11, Application Development Using the XS Engine*, where we'll do some JavaScript development using the SAP XSEngine.

To open the **Modeler** perspective, click on the right-facing double arrow button (highlighted in the preceding screenshot), then click on the **Modeler** option in the list:

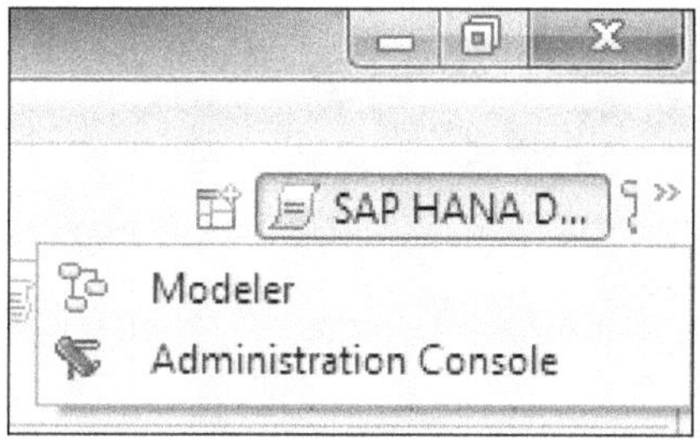

If the **Modeler** perspective is not in the list, you can find it by clicking on the first button we can see in the screenshot, which represents a computer screen with four windows and a plus sign. Click on this button and then select **Other** from the menu to see the full list of perspectives available.

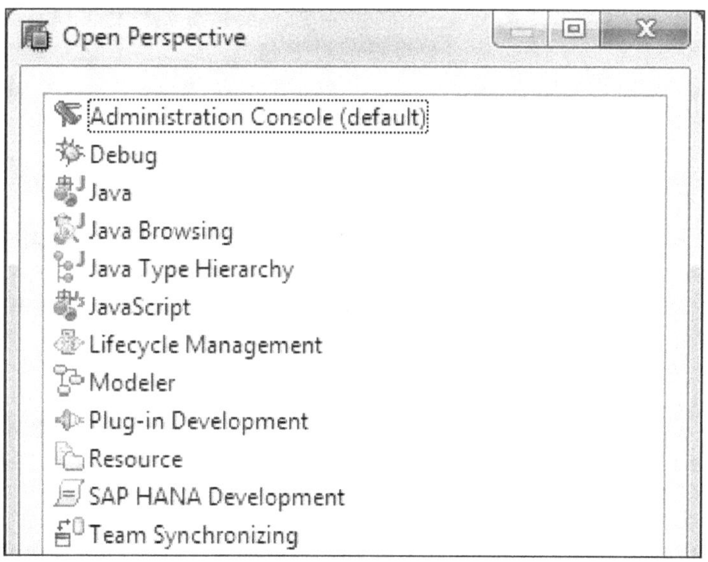

Once you've selected the **Modeler** perspective at least once, it will be present in the quick-switch tab for easy selection later.

Now that the **Modeler** is open, from the **Quick Launch** panel, select **Calculation View**, then select **Create**, to see the **New Calculation View** screen, as we can see in the following screenshot:

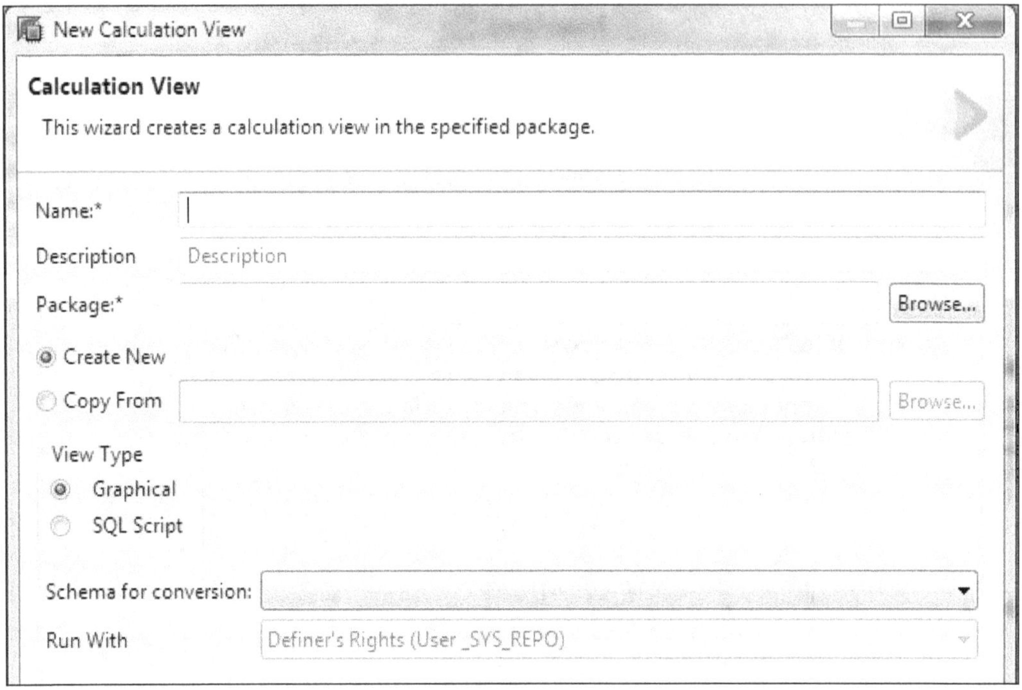

As always, we are asked to give a **Name** and a **Description** for our view, and to select the **Package** in which to store this view. We'll call our view `BOOK_CV_GR` (for Book, Calculation view, Graphic), and put it in the same package as the rest of our developments, the `book` package.

As is often possible in the Studio, we can create our view either from scratch, or by copying an existing view. In this case, we do not currently have any other calculation views to copy, so we'll leave the default option **Create New** selected.

We are asked which type of calculation view we want to create, **Graphical** or **SQL Script**. In this chapter we'll be examining the graphical calculation view, and we'll look at the SQL Script view in the next chapter, so leave the **View Type** at **Graphical**.

The last two options are the **Schema for Conversion**, and **Run With**. The **Schema for conversion** option allows us to select the database schema containing SAP-Standard tables for currency conversion. This option, when active, allows for automatic conversion of amounts from one currency to another.

In order to perform currency conversion in SAP HANA, it is necessary to create the following tables in the database and then populate them with appropriate data:

- `TCURR`
- `TCURC`
- `TCURX`
- `TCURF`
- `TCURT`
- `TCURV`

These tables and their format are identical to the corresponding tables in the SAP ERP, and for readers familiar with currency conversion in SAP systems, the currency conversion functions work in the same way. You are free to create the tables in any way you wish, either manually or using some automated tool. We'll be examining one such tool in *Chapter 10, Data Provisioning Using Data Services.*

The **Run With** option defines with which authorization the calculation view will do its selection on data. The default option, which is the only one available for a graphical view, is to use the system user `_SYS_REPO`.

Click on **Finish** to create your calculation view and see the view creation screen which looks like the following screenshot:

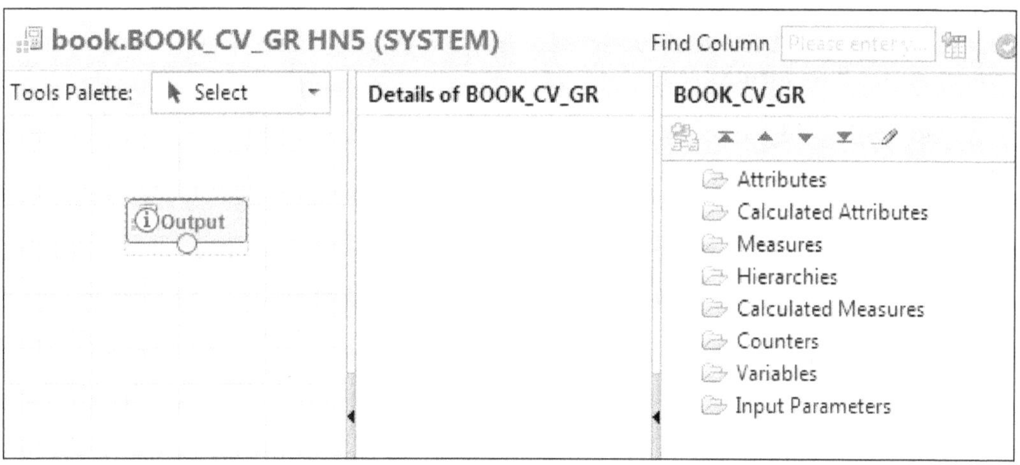

This is the main screen we'll be using for development over the next handful of pages.

On the left-hand side we have the graphical editor, where we'll be adding development blocks. Right now only the **Output** block is available. This block represents the output (the result) of the view. At the bottom of this block we can see a round junction point. This point is where we can attach other blocks in order to define data flows.

> A junction point at the bottom of a block represents the input of a block; one at the top represents data that this block will give to another block. The data flows from the bottom of the diagram to the top.

Let's start building our view now. Development of a calculation view needs the view or table containing the basic data to present to the user to be included, so we'll start there.

Adding analytic views

Our calculation view will be based upon our two analytic views, `CUST_REV` and `PROJ_REV`. In order to add them to the view, we need to have the view definition screen open (this should be the case), and to have the **Navigator** panel open also. By default this panel will be open, docked to the left-hand side of your screen.

If for some reason the **Navigator** panel is not open, you can get it back by choosing **Window | Show View | Navigator**.

Expand the tree in your **Navigator** panel so that you can see the **Content | Book | Analytic Views | CUST_REV** view, and drag it to the calculation view development screen, under the **Output** block.

`CUST_REV` will be added to the calculation view, and will appear as a new block in the window as follows:

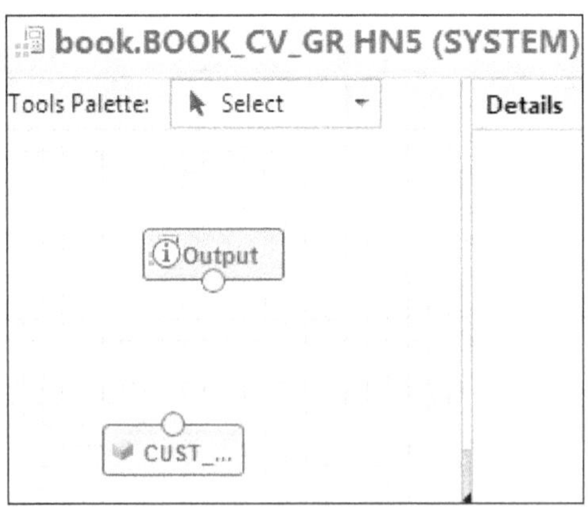

In order to join two blocks together in the view designer, just draw a line from the output node in the source block to the input node in the target block, by drawing a line from the upper junction in the `CUST_REV` block to the lower junction in the **Output** block. Please do this now, and you will obtain the following result:

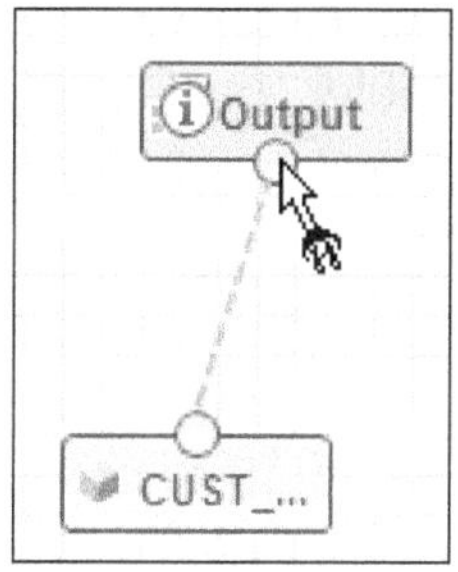

If you need to delete a connection you have made in the designer, just click on it and then press the *Delete* key on your keyboard. We don't actually need the connection we have just made; our calculation view will be considerably richer than this, so please delete the connection now. You will be warned that any calculated columns created in the view will be deleted. We haven't created any yet, so you can safely ignore this warning.

We'll be working with both the real data in the `CUST_REV` view, as well as the projected revenue in the `PROJ_REV` view, so please add the `PROJ_REV` view to our calculation view, alongside the `CUST_REV` view.

The projection block

Since in our view we have both real data and projected data, it would be most useful for our users to know which is which. We will achieve this by using a projection. A projection block allows us to decide with which columns of the analytic view we want to work, and to create additional calculated columns and filters as required.

To add a projection block, just select **Projection** from the **Tools Palette** drop-down box at the top of the view designer window, and a new **Projection** block will be added to the view automatically. You can then drag it to a more appropriate place in the view.

Our first projection will work with the data in the `CUST_REV` view, so we'll create a connection between `CUST_REV` and the new projection block (which should be called `Projection_1`).

Once the connection has been made, if we click on the **Projection** block, we will see in the middle of the screen, in the **Details of Projection_1** panel, the list of fields which have been made available. The list will contain all fields available in the `CUST_REV` view.

Please add all the fields in the list, except the `EUROPE_REVENUE` and `row.count` fields, to the output of the projection before continuing. You can add fields to the output by right-clicking on them and selecting **Add to Output** from the context menu. Your calculation view should at this point resemble the following screenshot:

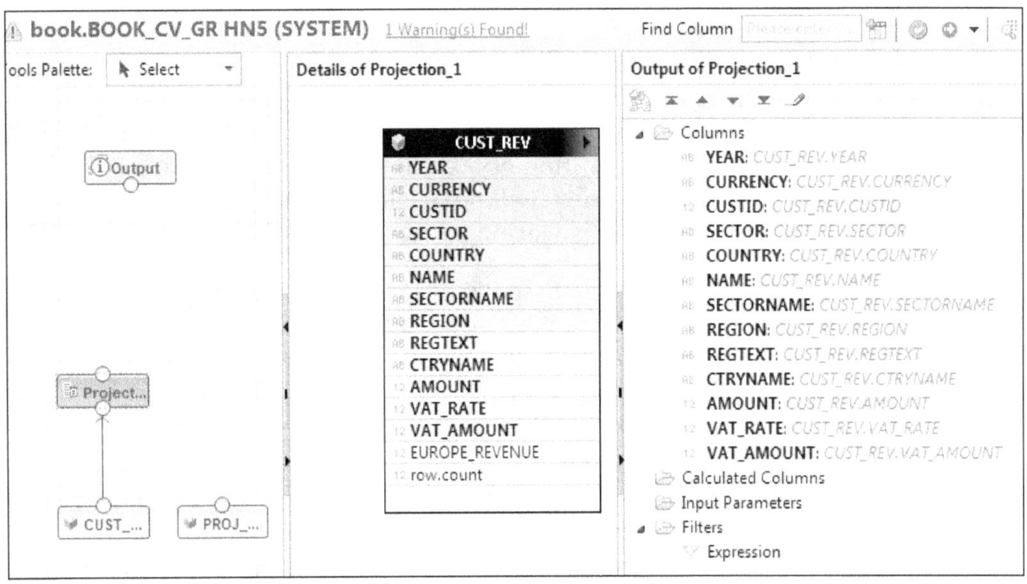

In our projection, we have the possibility not only of deciding not to use certain fields (the `EUROPE_REVENUE` field, for example), but we can, here also, create a calculated column, in much the same way as we created a calculated column in the underlying analytic view.

In this case, we'll create a calculated column to indicate that the data in this projection is real data. This will be useful to our users later, when we display the data from the calculation view, which will contain data from both the `CUST_REV` and the `PROJ_REV` views, and hence will display both real and projected data.

Please create a calculated column, called `DATA_TYPE` which will look like the following screenshot when done:

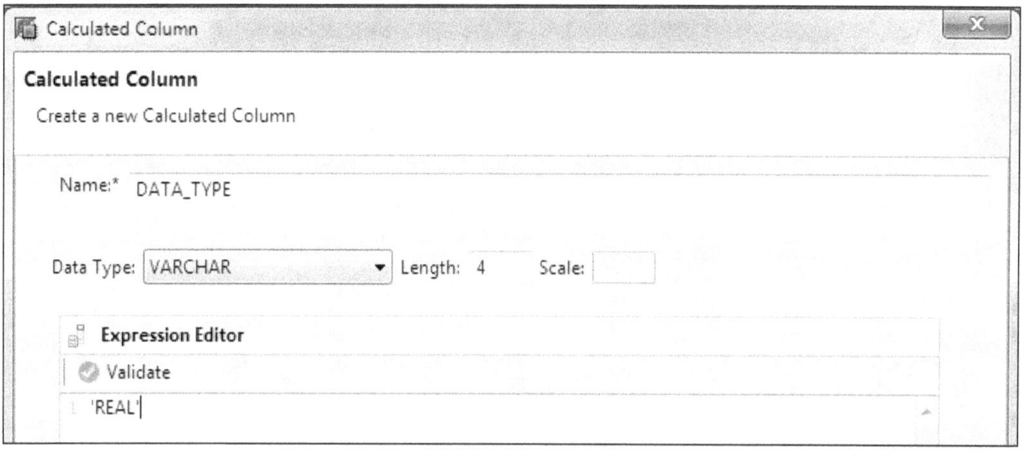

As we can see, the calculated column relies on no underlying data for its contents; it will contain only a constant value, `REAL`.

Once this has been done, we can create a second projection block, this time linked to the `PROJ_REV` view, containing all the columns in the `PROJ_REV` view, except the `EUROPE_REVENUE` and `row.count` fields. Once again we need to create a calculated column in our second projection, called again `DATA_TYPE` but this time containing the value `PROJ`, to indicate that the data in the projection is projected, not real data.

Your calculation view after creation of the second projection block should resemble the following screenshot. The details of the second projection block (`Projection_2`) have been displayed as follows:

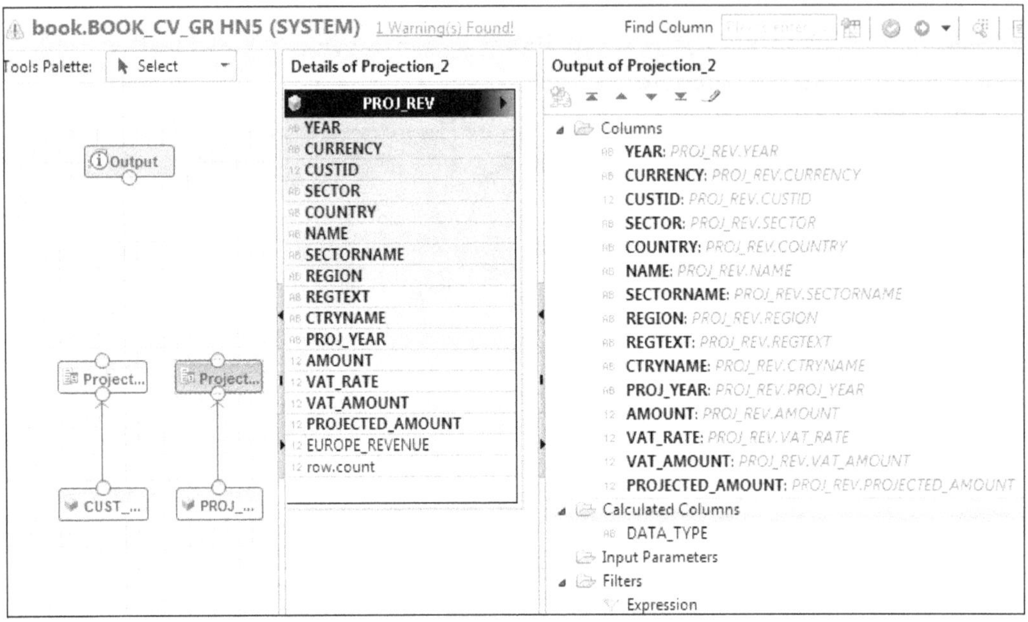

We have just one more action to perform in order to be able to use the data from the `PROJ_REV` view. As you recall from the previous chapter, when we created `PROJ_REV`, we included an input parameter so that the users could select for themselves the expected revenue increase. If we want to be able to use `PROJ_REV` in a calculation view, we have to include this input parameter in the calculation view also.

The Studio is somewhat cryptic about this. You might notice a small warning message at the top of the view definition screen in the previous screenshot. If we click on this message, we will see the following dialog box:

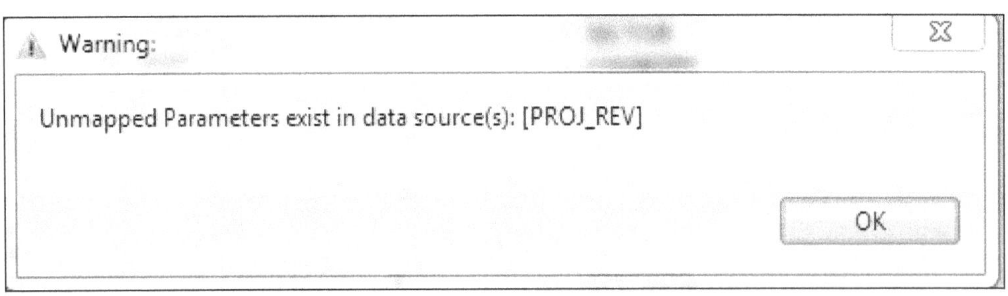

In order to include a user parameter from an analytic view in a calculation view we need to right-click on the **Input Parameters** node in the **Output** panel of the projection for that view (or in the **Output** panel of the **Output** block of the calculation view, both will achieve the same result), and select from the menu the **Manage Mappings** entry. Do not select **New**, as this will create a new input parameter, not reuse the one defined on the underlying view.

The **Map Data Source Parameters** dialog, shown in the following screenshot, will appear:

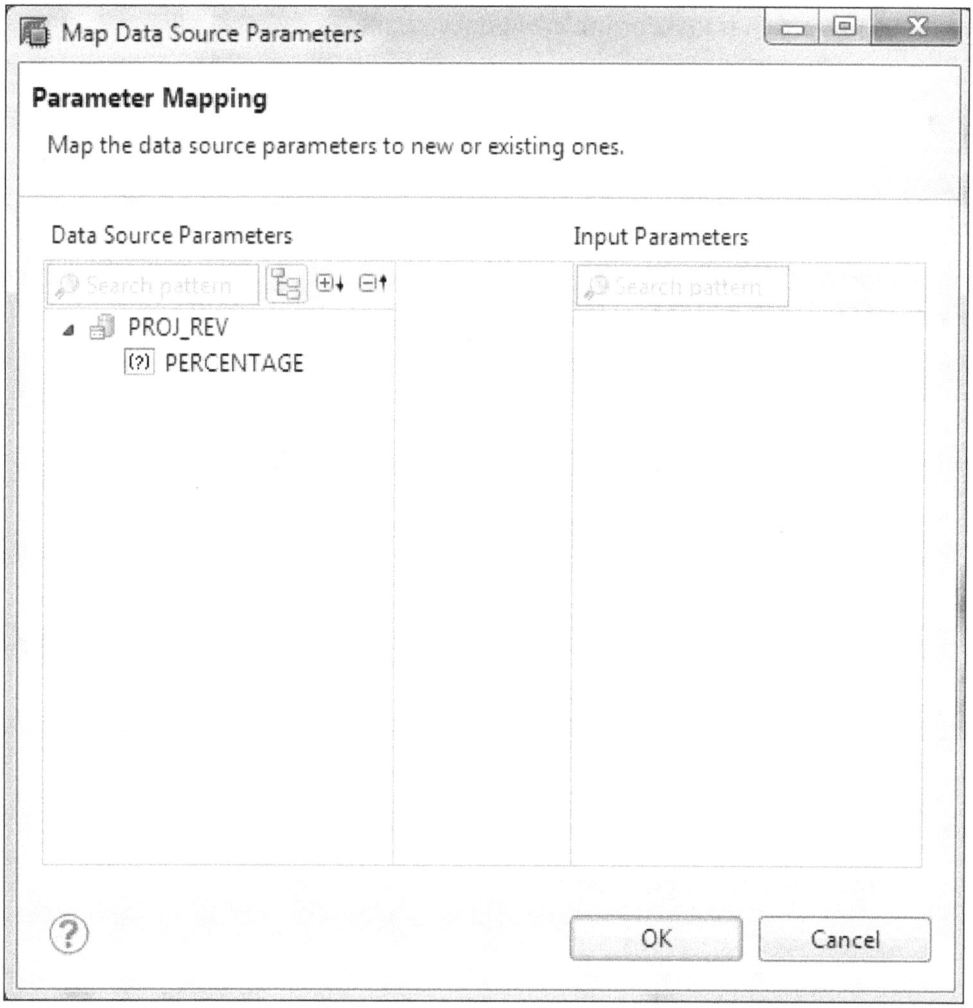

To have access to the **PERCENTAGE** input parameter from `PROJ_REV`, just drag it to the right-hand **Input Parameters** box. A junction line will be drawn between the two, indicating that the input parameter is available for use. You can then close the dialog with the **OK** button.

At this point, we have integrated into our calculation view the data from two underlying analytic views, `CUST_REV` and `PROJ_REV`. We've used two projection blocks in order to select those fields which are useful to us, and exclude those fields from the underlying views which we do not need. We have also created, in each of the projection blocks, a new column called `DATA_TYPE` which indicates whether the data in the projection is `REAL` or projected data.

At this point we can join the data from the two projection blocks together in order to present one unified vision to our users. To do this, we have a choice between creating a join on the data, or a union. We'll look at both of these in the following sections, but first, let's take a look at the aggregation block, which is similar in usage to the projection block.

The aggregation block

An aggregation block performs exactly the same function as a projection block, except that the output of the block is aggregated. Choosing between an aggregation block and a projection block is only necessary when your calculation views contain raw tables (as opposed to the analytic views we have added to ours).

> Output of an analytic view is always aggregated by SAP HANA, whereas output from a raw table isn't, so depending on your needs, a projection block or an aggregation block might be more appropriate.

We won't be using an aggregation block on our development, but let's take a look at how it works.

As we have just seen, a projection block allows us to select only certain columns for output if we so desire.

If we imagine the output of our `REVENUE` table:

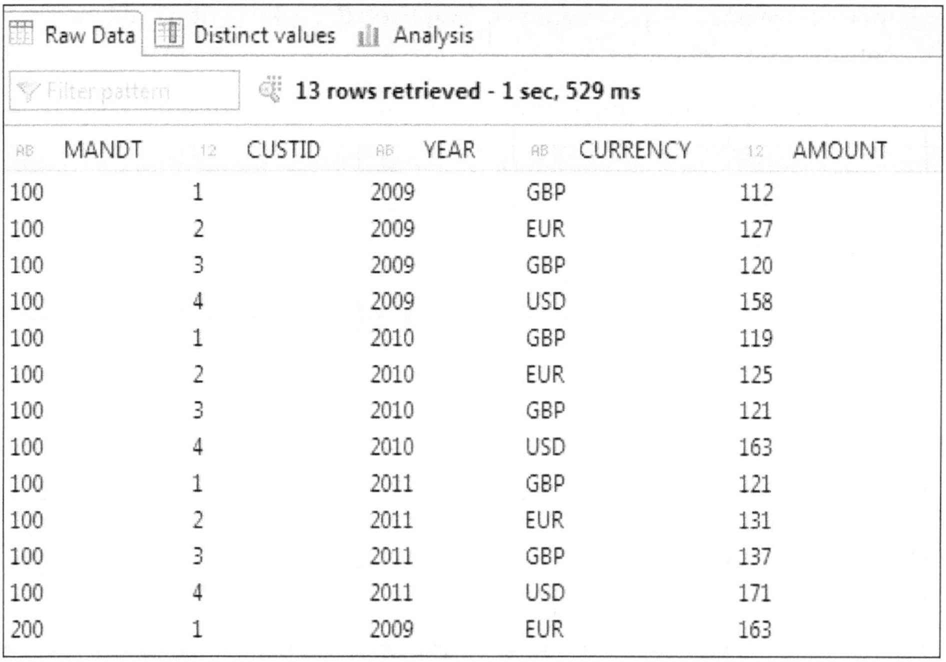

MANDT	CUSTID	YEAR	CURRENCY	AMOUNT
100	1	2009	GBP	112
100	2	2009	EUR	127
100	3	2009	GBP	120
100	4	2009	USD	158
100	1	2010	GBP	119
100	2	2010	EUR	125
100	3	2010	GBP	121
100	4	2010	USD	163
100	1	2011	GBP	121
100	2	2011	EUR	131
100	3	2011	GBP	137
100	4	2011	USD	171
200	1	2009	EUR	163

If we create a projection view in a calculation view, in which we define only the `CUSTID` and the `AMOUNT` fields (omitting the year), we obtain the following result:

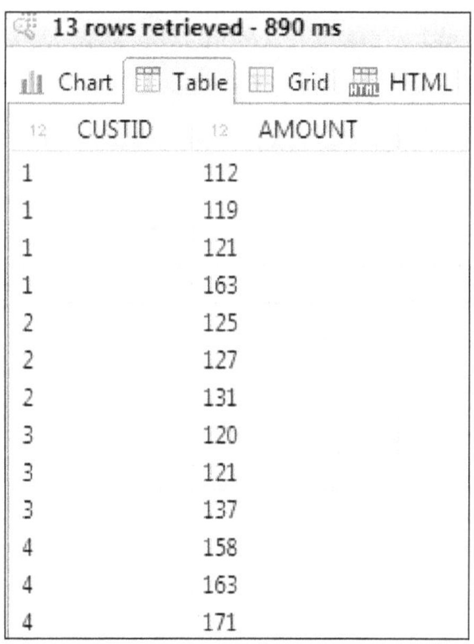

CUSTID	AMOUNT
1	112
1	119
1	121
1	163
2	125
2	127
2	131
3	120
3	121
3	137
4	158
4	163
4	171

Note how we have one line per client per year, even though we don't see the individual values for the years.

If however we were to use an aggregation block instead of a projection block, the result would be slightly different:

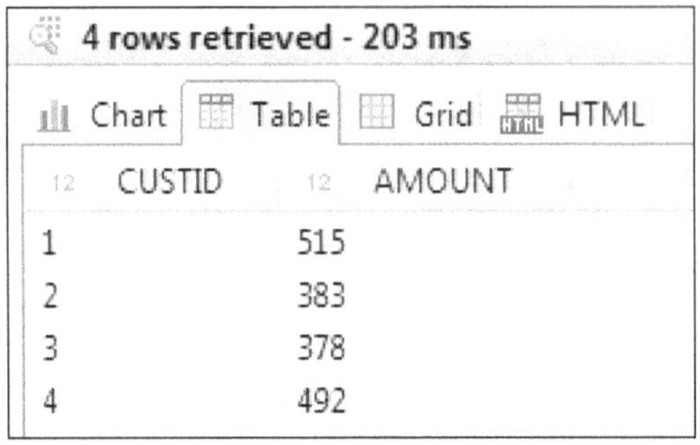

We can see that the aggregation block has aggregated the values, presenting us with the total value, and not the individual lines.

Whether you use a projection or an aggregation block depends on your usage needs:

- If the data is in a table, an aggregation block might be useful
- If the data is in a view, the aggregation block provides exactly the same output as a projection block
- If you have large amounts of data, an aggregation block might improve performance, since it will aggregate results and provide less output lines.

The join block

A join block in a graphical calculation view allows us to gather information from two different sources, which do not necessarily have the same structure or the same fields, and present a unified vision of the data to our user. It works in exactly the same way as a join between two tables.

To create a join block, just select it from the block selection drop down at the top of the view creation screen to add it to the view:

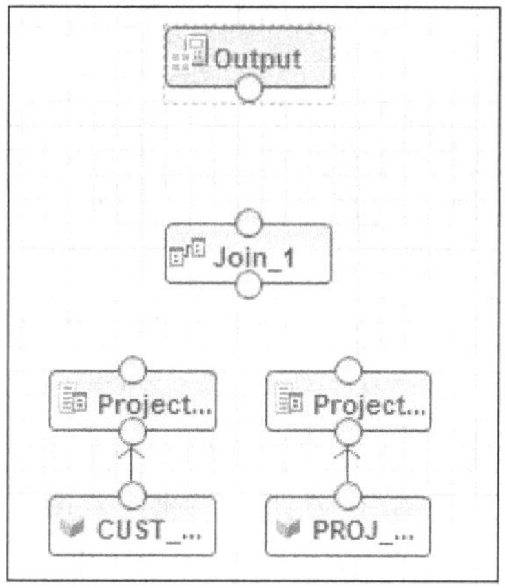

We can then link it to our source blocks (in our case, the source blocks are our two projection blocks) by linking their output node (at the top of the block) to the input node of the join (at the bottom of the block).

If we then click on the join block, we can see the two data sources, and create our join, as usual, by clicking on each field in the list on the left-hand side of the screen, and dragging it to the appropriate field in the list on the right-hand side.

In the following screenshot, we can see that a join block has been added to the view, and the link between the fields in the `CUST_REV` analytic view has been made to the appropriate fields in the `PROJ_REV` view:

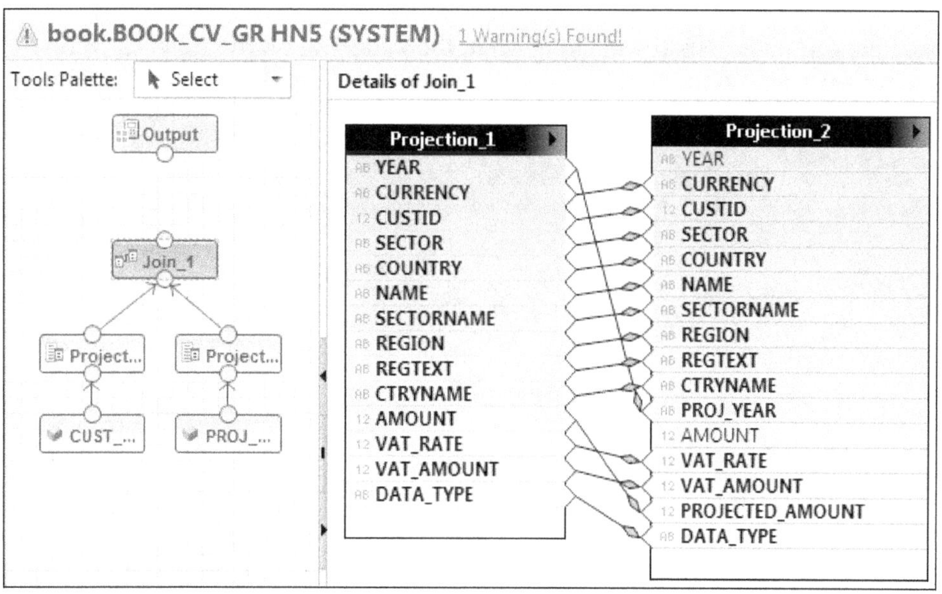

Let's take a moment to examine the screenshot, because it is here that we make the link between real revenue (in the `CUST_REV` view) and projected revenue (in the `PROJ_REV` view). We can see that for information concerning our customer (their `NAME`, `REGION`, and `COUNTRY` for example) we have linked the data in `CUST_REV` to the same data in `PROJ_REV`. This will give us one line of output for our customer, with coherent information.

Note however, that we have linked the `YEAR` field in **Projection_1** (which is `CUST_REV`) to the `PROJ_YEAR` field in **Projection_2** (which is `PROJ_REV`).

In this way when we ask for the contents of the `YEAR` column in our join, it will be filled with either the `YEAR` column of `CUST_REV` or the `PROJ_YEAR` field for `PROJ_REV`. This is how we align the data in our projected revenue view to that in our real revenue view. We have, in effect, renamed our `PROJ_YEAR` column on the fly in the join.

The union block

We can achieve the same results as we have just done with our join block in the view with a union block. This allows the same results, when data from the two sources has the same format.

> It is recommended to use a union block over a Join block when possible, since the union block offers better performance.

Let's delete our join block (by clicking on it, then clicking on the trash can icon which appears next to the block).

Now we can add a union block to the view (by selecting it in the **Tools Palette** dropdown), join it to our two source blocks (again, by drawing a line from their output nodes to the input node of the union block), and define our union:

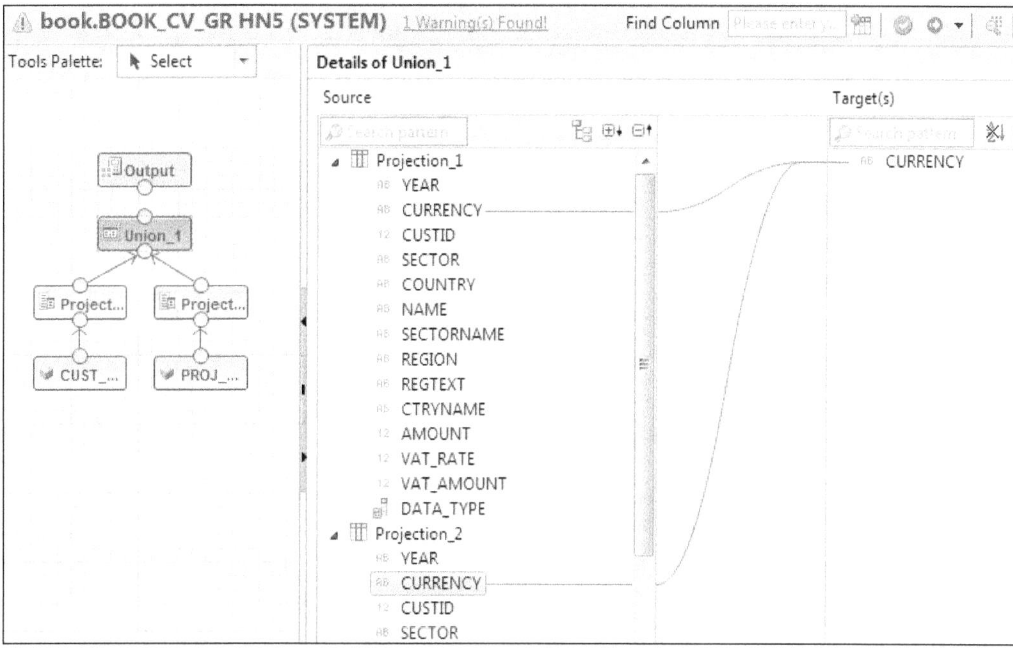

The definition of a union is done in a slightly different way to that of a join. In the union, we add one field from one source (in the preceding screenshot, we added `CURRENCY` from **Projection 1**), by right-clicking on the field and selecting **Add To Target** from the menu.

Then, to indicate to the system that the `CURRENCY` field in **Projection_2** should also link to the same field in the output, we can right-click on it and select **Map To Target** from the menu, to see the **Map To Target** dialog seen in the following screenshot:

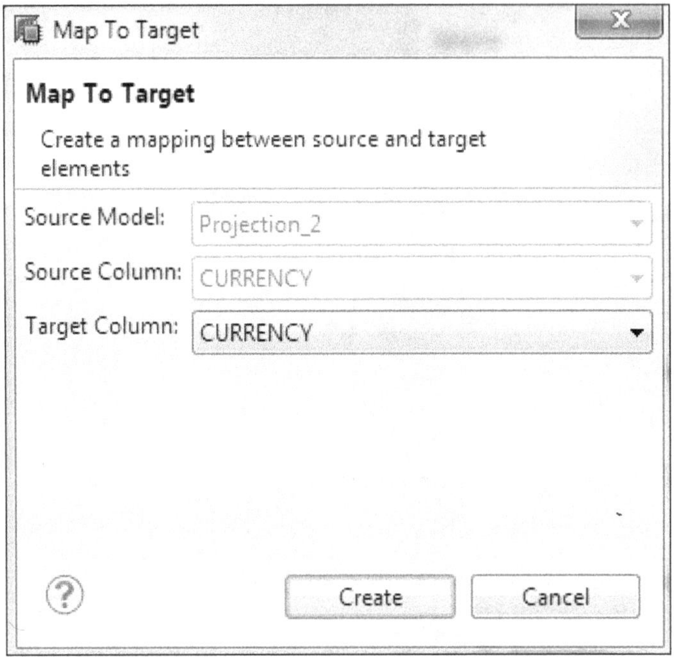

Alternatively, we can drag the field from **Projection_2** and drop it on the field in the output to create a mapping.

If field names in the two source blocks are all the same, or mostly the same, we can ask SAP HANA to do the work for us, and use the **Auto Map By Name** function, which will try to add fields to the output from one source, and either create a mapping if a field with the same name exists in the second source, or create a new output field if not.

This function can be called by clicking on the button with a tree-view representation on it, at the top of the **Source** panel. This button can be seen in the following screenshot:

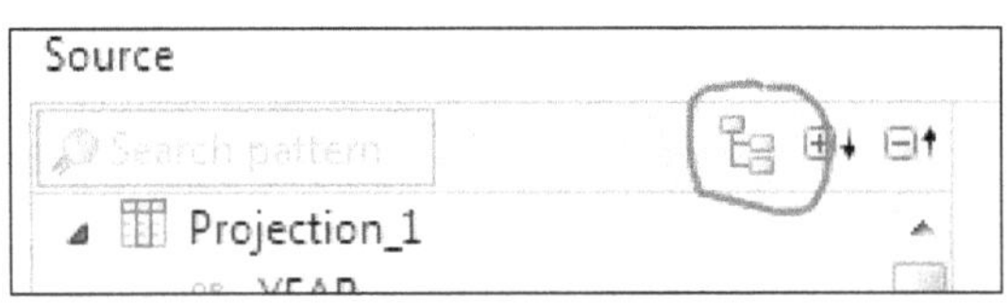

If we use this function on our view, it will do most of the work for us, however we will need to correct the mappings for the `PROJ_YEAR` and `PROJECTED_AMOUNT` fields, since we want to map them to the `YEAR` and `AMOUNT` fields, respectively.

Select the **Auto Map By Name** option now, and your view should look like the following screenshot:

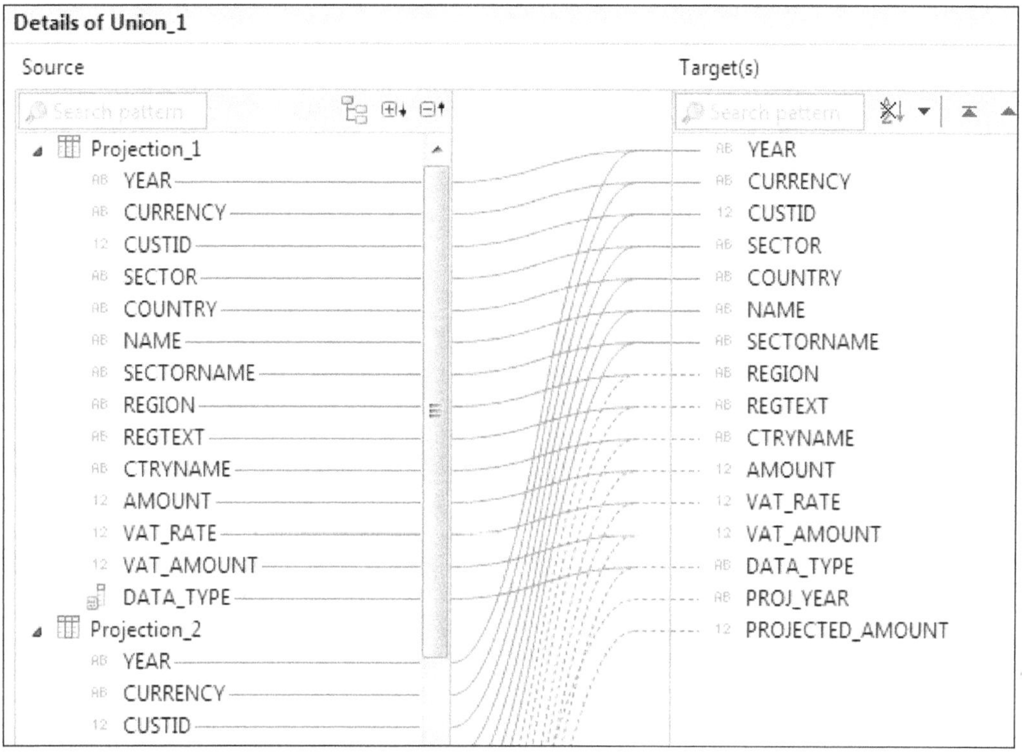

Please remove from the **Target(s)** panel the `PROJECTED_AMOUNT` and `PROJ_YEAR` fields, by right-clicking on them in turn, and selecting **Remove Target** from the menu. Then remove the mapping for `AMOUNT` and `YEAR` also, this time by selecting **Remove Mapping** from the context menu on the field in the **Target(s)** list.

> One target field in a union cannot be linked to two or more source fields from the same source block, which is why we need to delete the mappings for the `YEAR` and `AMOUNT` fields, so we can re-map them to `PROJ_YEAR` and `PROJ_AMOUNT`, respectively.

Now, map the `PROJECTED_AMOUNT` field in the **Projection_2** block to the `AMOUNT` field in **Target(s)**, and the `PROJ_YEAR` field in **Projection_2** to the `YEAR` field in **Target(s)**. You can use either the **Map to Target** dialog, or drag-and-drop, as we saw earlier. You also need to re-map `YEAR` from **Projection_1** to `YEAR` in the **Target**, and `AMOUNT` from **Projection_1** to `AMOUNT` in the target.

Your final **Target(s)** field list should look like the following screenshot:

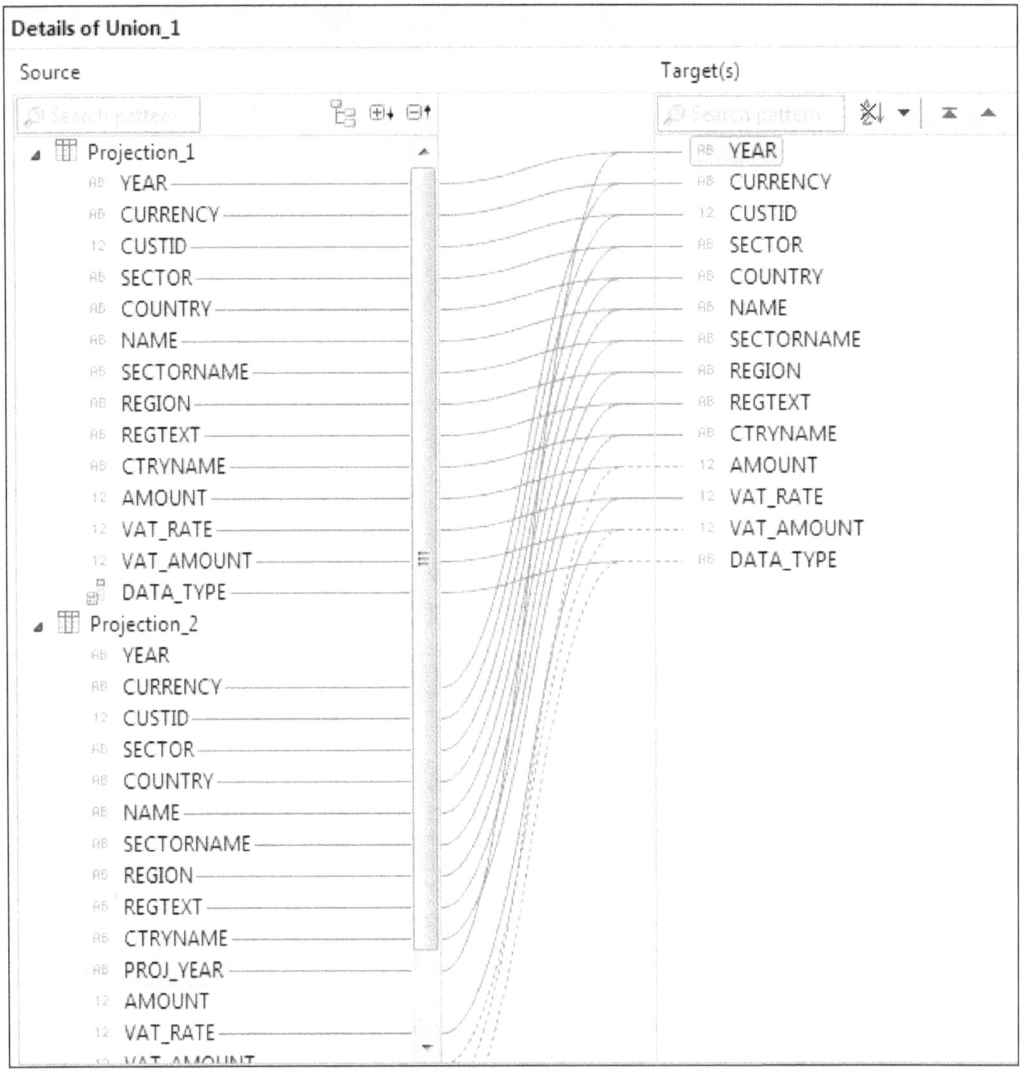

Note how we have mapped `YEAR` from `CUST_REV` to `PROJ_YEAR` from `PROJ_REV` in the union, in exactly the same way as we did in the join, and how the `AMOUNT` and `YEAR` fields provided by **Projection_2** are not mapped to any target fields. These two fields, not referenced in the view, will not be visible.

Output

Now that we have added our source views and tables to our view, used either aggregation or projection blocks to select the source columns with the data which interests us, and combined the different sources together in either a join or a union, we can determine the final output to present to our user.

Defining an output block is done in exactly the same way as we have defined the other blocks in our view. We select the source, draw a line from its output node to the input node of the output block, and then select our fields.

In our case, the source is our union block (or maybe the join block, if you left it in the view and didn't create the union). Please join the output node of the union block to the input node of the output block, to obtain the following (final!) version of our view:

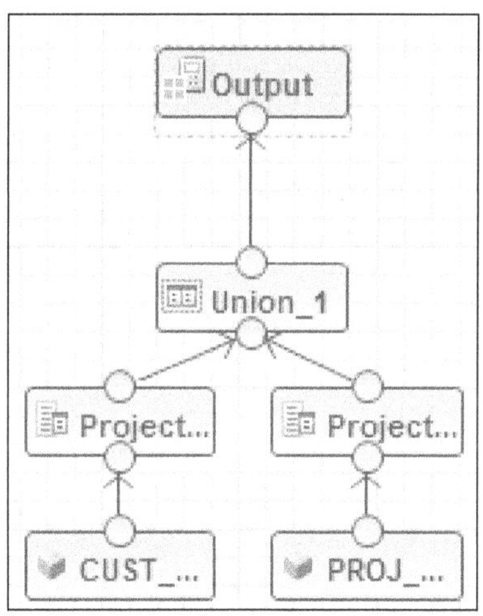

Now that the junction has been made, we can define the final output fields of our view. Click on the output node to see the list of available fields, then right-click on a field and select either **Add as Attribute**, or **Add as Measure**, to select it for output of our view.

Please add the `AMOUNT` and `VAT_AMOUNT` fields as measures to the output of the view and then add all the other fields as attributes.

Your output panel for the view should now look like the following screenshot:

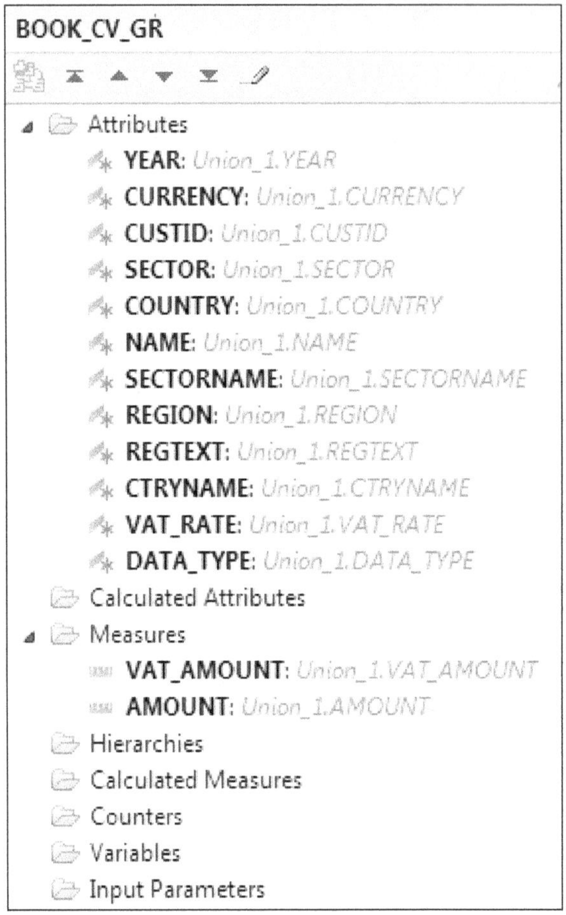

> You will notice that all the fields defined as attributes in the view are automatically considered to be key attributes, indicated by the little green star icon next to their name. Readers familiar with SAP's BW system will recognize this as being analogous to a BW cube, where all non-numeric data is a key.

At this point our calculation view is almost done. We have just one more action we need to perform, and that is to activate our view. Activation is done, as always, with the round green **Activate** button at the top-right corner of the view definition screen. We can activate the view now.

Results

Let's take a look at the results of our view. To do so, request a data preview, either by right-clicking on the view in the **Content** node of the **Navigator** panel and selecting **Data Preview** from the context menu, or by using the dedicated **Data Preview** button, which is immediately to the right of the activate button in the view definition screen.

The first thing you will notice when asking for a data preview is that the system requests a value for the `PERCENTAGE` input parameter. This is as expected—this input parameter is necessary when the initial instantiation of the underlying `PROJ_REV` view takes place. In the following screenshots, the data shown represents a `PERCENTAGE` value of 10 percent.

If we add the `YEAR` and `DATA_TYPE` fields to the **Labels axis** in the data preview, and the `AMOUNT` field to the **Values axis**, we will obtain the following result:

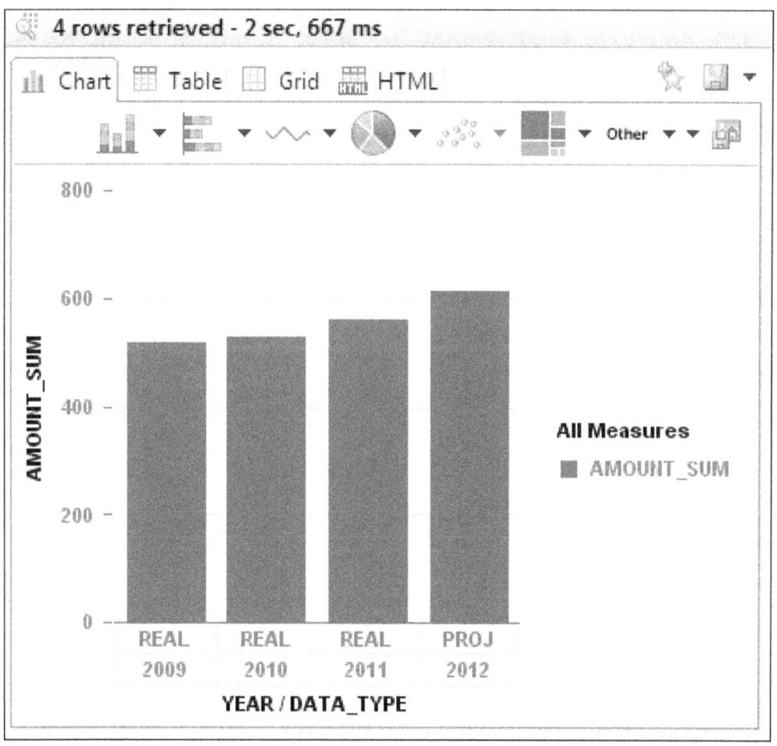

As we can see we have three columns for `REAL` data in years `2009`, `2010`, and `2011`. This data is being provided by the `CUST_REV` view. The data for year `2012` is `PROJ` (projected) data, and is being provided by the `PROJ_REV` view. If we check the figures, data for `2011` amounts to `560`, and for `2012` amounts to `615`, which is 10 percent higher.

> Actually the sum of 560 and 10 percent equals 616, the difference is due to rounding errors, since the numbers involved in the calculations are all whole numbers (Integers).

Feel free to play with the data preview, in order to ensure that all the data shown by the view is coherent. Calculation views will form the basis of the objects you use to present data to your users, so it's important to ensure that your projections, joins and other development blocks are working as you expect them to.

Summary

In this chapter, we took a look at what a graphical calculation view is, how it works, and how to build one. We started by importing our two analytic views, `CUST_REV` and `PROJ_REV`, and, using projection blocks, selected those fields with which we wanted to work, and created a new field to indicate the type of data we were using. We then joined the data in the two fields together, using first a Join block, then a Union block, in order to present a single list of fields. Finally, we took the output of the union, and added our fields to the Output block of the view. Using the Studio's **Data Preview** function, we confirmed that the calculation view we had just built was working as we expected.

In the next chapter, we'll be learning that SAP HANA provides two ways to create calculation views - first the graphical way, as we have just seen, and secondly by using an inbuilt language, SQLScript. In order to better understand how SQLScript works and how to use it in a calculation view, we'll be building another calculation view, using SQLScript. This new view will do exactly the same job as the one we've just built.

Quick reference

Here is a quick overview of the main topics covered in this chapter.

Object	Usage	Creation
Graphical calculation view	Allows you to work with data from different sources at once, combining and, filtering data as you require	**Quick Launch** | **Calculation View**, Provide **Name** and **Description**, select type as **Graphical**. Add source(s), map fields to output node, **Activate**.
Aggregation block	Sums data from raw tables, filters view on requested fields	In view definition, add block type of aggregation. Map source fields.
Projection block	Same as aggregation, but no summing of data lines from input (no difference when source is a view)	In view definition, add block type of projection. Map source fields as required.
Join block	Joins data from several sources in a view	In view definition, add block type of join. Link to source blocks. Create junctions between fields as required.
Union block	Like a join, combines data from different sources. Data should have the same format for optimum performance.	In view definition, add block type of union. Link to source blocks. Add fields to output from one source, then map to remaining sources as required.
Output block	Defines which fields will finally be visible to the user, and their type, attribute or measure. All attributes are key fields.	Output block is always present in a view. Link it to source block—output block can have only one source, use a join or union if necessary. Select input fields to use in output, and their type.

6

You Talking to Me? – Scripted Calculation Views

Writing actual code is not something we've had to do yet with SAP HANA; we've been using the graphical modeling tools provided in the Studio. This is one of the strong points of the system. Writing SQL code in itself is relatively easy. It doesn't take much training to be able to write a simple `SELECT` statement. After a couple of tries, we can add a `JOIN` or two, `GROUP BY`, `ORDER BY`, and we think that we've mastered everything SQL has to offer.

The truth of the matter is, of course, very different. Writing complex SQL is DIFFICULT. Writing a large SQL instruction to do *half* of what the graphical calculation view we built in the previous chapter can do, without bringing the machine to its knees, is not something that many developers can do, especially those who are not specialized database developers.

Graphical developments and wizards are great things; however, there are some things you just cannot do with them. Complicated developments with specialized business rules sometimes cannot simply be modeled by joining blocks to each other. If this is the case in a project you're working on, you'll have to write the SQL instructions to do the work yourself.

As touched upon briefly in the previous chapter, SAP provides a mechanism that allows you to create calculation views using SQL statements and an internal development language, **SQLScript**. In this chapter, we'll be building a calculation view with the same characteristics as the one we made in the previous chapter, only this time we'll be using SQLScript to create it, not the graphical editor.

Creating a scripted calculation view

The creation of a scripted calculation view is done in exactly the same way as a graphical calculation view:

1. Open the Modeler perspective of the Studio (see the previous chapter for detailed instructions on how to do this).
2. Open the **Quick Launch** panel.
3. Select **Calculation View** | **Create**. You will be presented with the **New Calculation View** dialog we saw for the first time in the previous chapter.
4. Enter a **Name** and **Description** values (we'll use `BOOK_CV_SC`, for Book, Calculation View, Script for both **Name** and **Description**).
5. Select our `book` package.
6. Set the **View Type** option to **SQL Script**, as we can see in the following screenshot:

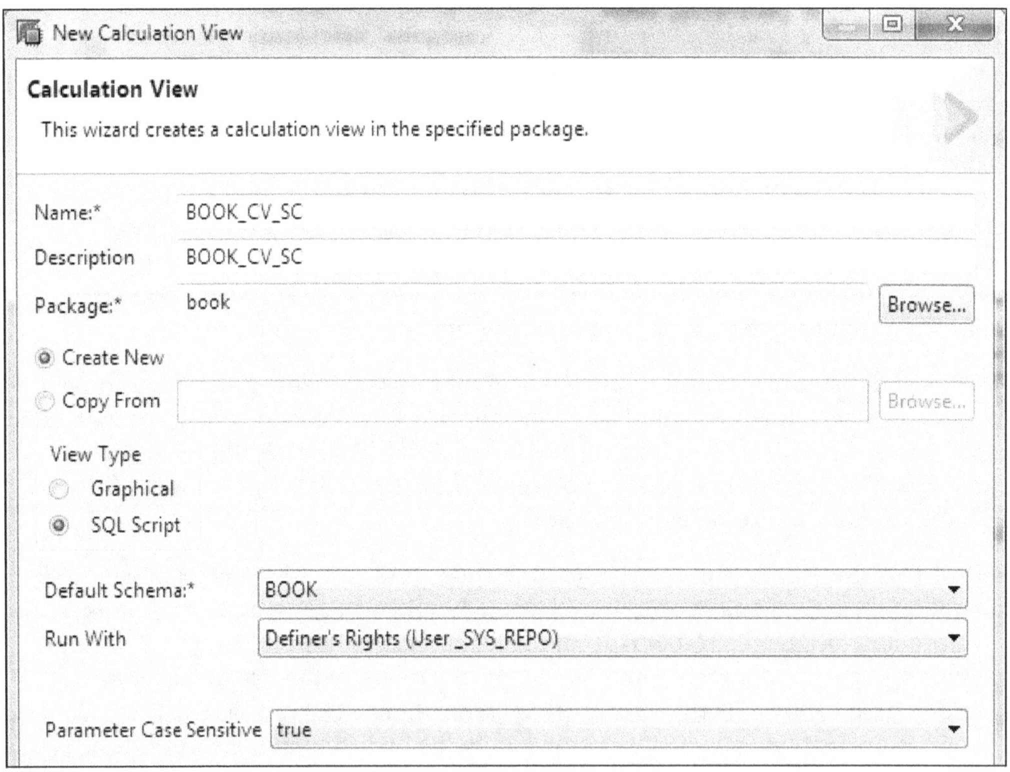

Setting the **View Type** option to **SQL Script** changes the options available at the bottom of the dialog. We now have the following options available to us:

- **Default Schema**: This option lets us define the database schema holding the tables that contain the data with which we want to work. In our case, this database schema is `BOOK`.
- **Run With**: Like for a graphical calculation view, this option defines whose authorization will be used to do the data selection in the database. A graphical calculation view can use only the authorization of the defining user, which, if you recall, is actually the system user `_SYS_REPO`. A scripted calculation view can use the authorization of the **invoker**, the user calling the view. This might be useful in some cases where data is user-sensitive. Authorizations in SAP HANA will be explained in full in *Chapter 7, Hey! That's My Data! - Authorizations in SAP HANA*.
- **Parameter Case Sensitive**: When set to **true**, parameter (user input parameters) names are case sensitive and therefore should be written in capital letters. If not, their case does not matter.

7. Click on the **Finish** button to create the view, and see the scripted view creation screen, shown here:

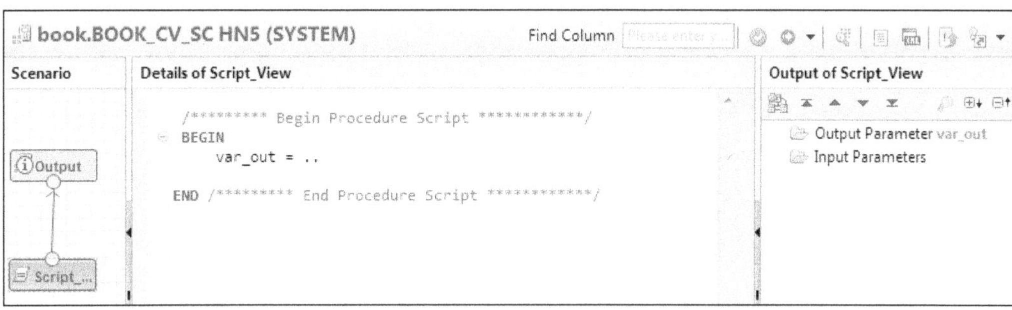

As we can see in the screenshot, a scripted calculation view starts life just like a graphical calculation view. We are given an output block (which in the scripted calculation view exists as a variable called `var_out`) and nothing else. All the work is left for us to do. Let's build our view in the same way we built our graphical calculation view in the previous chapter. The section headings toward the end of this chapter are exactly the same as those in the previous chapter, so that you can more easily compare the two ways of doing things.

Understanding CE functions

SQLScript provides a number of functions that enable optimized, parallel access to database objects. We can write native SQL to perform most tasks in the database, like this:

```
SELECT CUSTID, YEAR, SUM(AMOUNT)
  from BOOK.REVENUE
 where MANDT = 100
GROUP BY CUSTID, YEAR
```

It is, however, recommended to use the equivalent **CE** function to perform the task where possible. CE stands for **Calculation Engine**.

> CE functions are preferred to standard SQL firstly because they are a lot easier to work with, secondly because their use can be parallelized by the SAP HANA server, and finally because they don't require that the server use the SQL processor, which is time-saving. You can mix-and-match the use of CE functions and SQL inside your scripts; however, if there's a CE function that will do the job you need, it's a better idea to use it than to write the SQL yourself.

The CE function equivalent of the previous SQL statement would be something like the following screenshot. We'll be taking a look at the individual functions used in a minute.

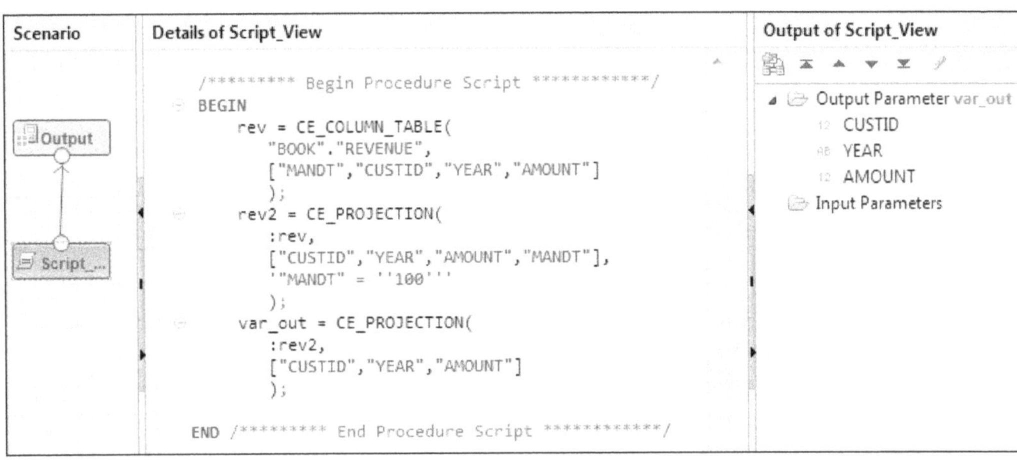

In this example, we use two CE functions, `CE_COLUMN_TABLE` and `CE_PROJECTION`. `CE_COLUMN_TABLE`, as its name suggests, is a function that selects data from a table and returns the requested columns in a **scalar** variable (here called `rev`).

> Note the syntax of the functions:
>
> - `output = function1(parameter1, parameter2, …);`
> - `output2 = function2(:output, parameter3, …);`
>
> `function1` returns its results, which we put in a variable called `output`. We can then use this variable in the call to `function2`, prefixing it with a colon.

The `CE_PROJECTION` function performs the same action as the projection block we saw in the previous chapter. It allows us to select the fields with which we want to work, and additionally, allows us to filter on them. The first `CE_PROJECTION` function filters the results of the `CE_COLUMN_TABLE` function, keeping only lines where the `MANDT` field has a value of `100`. The second `CE_PROJECTION` function presents to the user only the `CUSTID`, `YEAR`, and `AMOUNT` fields.

> For a full list of CE functions available in SAP HANA, and how you can use them in your developments, the SAP HANA SQLScript development guide is available for download from the `sap.com` website at `http://help.sap.com/hana/hana_dev_sqlscript_en.pdf`.

Now that we have had a first look at SQLScript and CE functions, let's create our scripted calculation view, and see in more detail the precise syntax of SQLScript.

Adding analytic views

Adding an analytic view to a scripted calculation view is, depending on your point of view, either easier or harder than adding one to a graphic calculation view. Rather than searching for the analytic view in the **Navigator** panel and dragging it to the view definition screen, in a scripted calculation view we just make a reference to the analytic view in our code.

The CE function allowing us to read the contents of an analytic view is `CE_OLAP_VIEW`. This function takes two parameters: the view name and the list of fields we wish to use. If we want to obtain the same results as in our graphical view from *Chapter 5, Let's Get Graphical - Graphical Calculation Views*, we need to select all the fields, except `EUROPE_REVENUE` and `row.count`. As you will have noticed in the previous screenshot, this means that we have to enumerate all the fields we wish to use.

The `CE_OLAP_VIEW` function call therefore looks like this:

```
cust_rev = CE_OLAP_VIEW(
   "_SYS_BIC"."book/CUST_REV",
   [
     "YEAR","CUSTID","CURRENCY","SECTOR",
     "COUNTRY","NAME","SECTORNAME","REGION",
     "REGTEXT","CTRYNAME",SUM("AMOUNT"),
     "VAT_RATE",SUM("VAT_AMOUNT")
   ]
   );
```

There are several things to note in this code snippet:

- The view name has been prefixed with a schema name. This is necessary since, as hinted-on earlier, SAP HANA transforms all your development objects into real SQL statements and views when you activate them. Your analytic view `CUST_REV` has been transformed into a real SQL view, in the `_SYS_BIC` database schema. All your development objects can be found in the `_SYS_BIC` schema. You can open it up in the **Navigator** panel to check for yourself if you like.
- The list of fields you select from the database is surrounded by square brackets. This is because SAP HANA expects one parameter, not a list of them. By surrounding your field list with square brackets, you turn the list of fields into a **set**.
- The order of fields you select from the view is unimportant. You can put them in any order you like (here, the fields have been listed in the same order they appear in the screenshots from the previous chapter).
- Any numeric fields (Measures) need to have an aggregation function associated with them. This can be seen in the case of the `AMOUNT` and `VAT_AMOUNT` fields, which have been summed. There are currently four aggregation functions available:
    - `count()` – returns the number of values
    - `sum()` – returns the sum of all values
    - `min()` – returns the smallest value in the list
    - `max()` – returns the largest value in the list
- The results of the `CE_OLAP_VIEW` function have been placed into a scalar variable, `cust_rev`. This variable can be used in further developments.

With the CUST_REV view being read by our calculation view, we can add the PROJ_REV view, in the same way, with the following code:

```
proj_rev = CE_OLAP_VIEW(
   "_SYS_BIC"."book/PROJ_REV",
   [
     "PROJ_YEAR","CUSTID","CURRENCY","SECTOR",
     "COUNTRY","NAME","SECTORNAME","REGION",
     "REGTEXT","CTRYNAME",SUM("PROJECTED_AMOUNT"),
     "VAT_RATE",SUM("VAT_AMOUNT")
   ]
   );
```

Your scripted calculation view should now look like the following screenshot. We cannot test it yet as no output has been defined, and in order to define output, more development work is required:

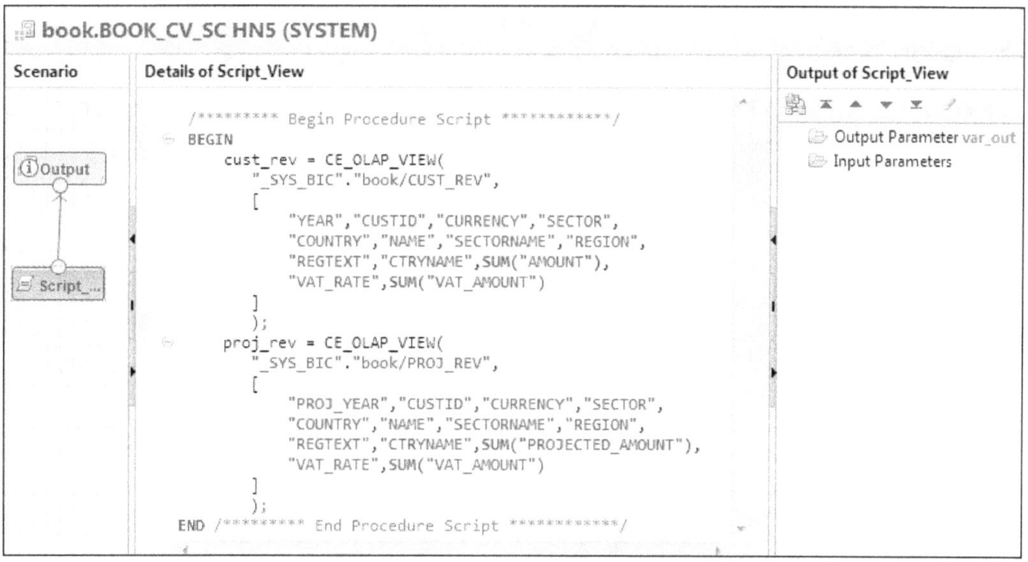

The projection block

Now that we have the contents of the analytic views in our calculation view, we need to add the DATA_TYPE field, as we did in the graphical view. To do this, we used a projection block, and we will be doing the same using SQLScript. The CE function we need to create a projection is called CE_PROJECTION, as we saw in an earlier screenshot.

The CE_PROJECTION function takes three parameters:

- The **source** of the data for the projection. This will usually be the result of another CE function, such as CE_COLUMN_TABLE or CE_OLAP_VIEW, for example. CE_PROJECTION cannot actually read data from the database as such, it only works with data which has already been read.
- The **data fields** to use in the projection. These fields must exist in the source, or be created dynamically in the projection. We'll be looking in a second at how to create fields dynamically.
- An optional **filter** to apply to the input fields.

In the previous section, we used the CE_OLAP_VIEW function to read the data from our CUST_REV and PROJ_REV views. The result of these data reads was put into two variables, cust_rev and proj_rev, respectively. We can now use these variables as input for the CE_PROJECTION function.

This is analogous to joining the input view block to a projection block in a graphical calculation view.

Let's use our cust_rev and proj_rev variables in our projections now. This will allow us to define the DATA_TYPE field, which should contain, as you recall, the word REAL for our CUST_REV view, and PROJ for PROJ_REV.

The SQLScript code we need to create the two projections is given as follows. This code is the equivalent of the definition of the two projection blocks in the graphical view we created in the last chapter.

```
projection_cust_rev = CE_PROJECTION(
    :cust_rev,
    [
      "YEAR","CUSTID","CURRENCY","SECTOR",
      "COUNTRY","NAME","SECTORNAME","REGION",
      "REGTEXT","CTRYNAME","AMOUNT",
      "VAT_RATE","VAT_AMOUNT",
      CE_CALC('''REAL''', VARCHAR(4)) AS "DATA_TYPE"
    ]
  );
projection_proj_rev = CE_PROJECTION(
   :proj_rev,
   [
     "YEAR","CUSTID","CURRENCY","SECTOR",
     "COUNTRY","NAME","SECTORNAME","REGION",
```

```
        "REGTEXT","CTRYNAME","AMOUNT",
        "VAT_RATE","VAT_AMOUNT",
        CE_CALC('''PROJ''', VARCHAR(4)) AS "DATA_TYPE"
    ]
);
```

As we can see in the code snippet, the `CE_PROJECTION` function lets us select fields from the underlying view (in our case we chose to work with all the fields we read in from the analytic view). It also allows us to create a calculated column, just like we did in the graphical view.

The creation of our calculated column `DATA_TYPE` is done using yet another CE function, this time `CE_CALC`.

The `CE_CALC` function takes two parameters:

- The **calculation expression**: This is exactly the same expression we enter in the calculated column dialog in the graphical calculation view creation wizard. In our example, we use the expressions `'REAL'` and `'PROJ'`. The expression itself needs to be enclosed by single quotes.

> Any single quote in the expression (such as the ones around the word `REAL`) need to be *escaped*. This means that we need to tell the SQLScript editor that it has not reached the end of the expression yet when it sees the single quote. To escape a single quote in the editor, we use another single quote. Hence the three single quotes in a row.

- The **data type** of the created column: Any valid SQL data type can be created. In our examples, the created columns are of type `VARCHAR`, and of length `4`.

The final action we have performed in our projection is to rename two fields. In the `PROJ_REV` analytic view, the data we are interested in is in the `PROJ_YEAR` and `PROJECTED_AMOUNT` fields, and not the basic `YEAR` and `AMOUNT` fields. When we read the underlying view with the `CE_OLAP_VIEW` function, we decided not to read the `YEAR` and `AMOUNT` fields, since we do not need them in our development. In the `CE_PROJECTION` function we have just seen, we have renamed the `PROJ_YEAR` field to `YEAR`, using the `AS` keyword. Similarly, `PROJECTED_AMOUNT` has been renamed to `AMOUNT`.

At this point, we have created two more variables in our view, `projection_cust_rev` and `projection_proj_rev`. These two projections have allowed us to create our calculated `DATA_TYPE` column, and to rename some columns from the underlying view.

The aggregation block

Once again, in this chapter we won't be using aggregation blocks in our view. However, if you need to create one in your developments, it is possible to do so in a scripted calculation view, just like it was using the graphical editor.

The CE function to create an aggregation block in a scripted view is called `CE_AGGREGATION`. This function takes the following three parameters:

- The **data source**: This needs to be the output of another CE function, such as `CE_OLAP_VIEW` or `CE_PROJECTION`. `CE_AGGREGATION` cannot read database data directly.
- The **aggregation columns**: This is a list, surrounded by square brackets, of the aggregations to perform. The four aggregation functions allowed are `COUNT()`, `SUM()`, `MIN()`, and `MAX()`. As you can guess, each of these functions takes a measure name as parameter.
- The optional **group by** column(s): These define the grouping of the aggregation. For example, perform `count()` of different `YEAR` values; the input parameter will be parsed, and each value of the `YEAR` column will be counted. The output will contain one line per unique value in the `YEAR` column, along with a column containing the number of times each value was present in the input.

As you can imagine, and in the same way as we saw in the previous chapter, `CE_AGGREGATION` defines an implicit projection on the data; any column from the input that is not present in the list of aggregation columns nor in the group-by list, will not be present in the output of the function.

The join block

In the previous chapter, we examined briefly how to use a join block in our graphical calculation view. We can create joins in a scripted calculation view also, and they can be of the following three types:

- **Inner Join**: The standard join type, where entries in the join field list from the left-hand table must exist in the right-hand table to be included in the output. This join type is created with the CE function `CE_JOIN`.

- **Left Outer Join**: Entries in the left-hand table will be included in the output whether they exist in the right-hand table or not. The CE function to create this join type is `CE_LEFT_OUTER_JOIN`.
- **Right Outer Join**: Similar to the left outer join, but with the right-hand table taking precedence. Entries in the right-hand table will always be included in the output, whether they have correspondence in the left-hand table or not. To create a join of this type, use the `CE_RIGHT_OUTER_JOIN` function.

> For readers familiar with SQL, you might like to note that SQLScript does not currently support the notion of `FULL_OUTER_JOIN` in CE functions.

Each of these functions uses the same syntax, and they all take four parameters:

- **Left-hand table**: The variable containing the data from the table considered to be on the left. Like `CE_PROJECTION` and `CE_AGGREGATION`, the CE join functions cannot read data from the database directly, so data needs to be contained in variables already.
- **Right-hand table**: The variable containing the data from the table considered to be on the right.
- **Join attributes**: A list of one or more fields on which to perform the join between the tables. The field or fields need to exist in both tables. If you need to create a join using tables with field names that are different (maybe `CUSTID` and `CUSTOMER_ID`, which mean the same thing but the names are just different), then you will need to use a `CE_PROJECTION` beforehand in order to rename one of the fields.
- **Projection list**: The CE join functions allow you to provide a list of field names that should be in the result of the function. This, in effect, allows you to create a projection on the result of the join. This parameter is optional. If you do not provide it, only the fields on which you create the join (the join attributes) will be present in the result. If you wish to use other fields from the input tables, you need to specify their names here. If you provide this parameter, you must include at least all of the join attributes, or the activation of your view will fail.

The union block

In our graphical calculation view, we used a union block to join our two projections, and we'll be doing exactly the same thing in our scripted view. In order to create a union between two tables, SAP HANA provides yet another CE function, `CE_UNION_ALL`, which will allow us to create a union between our two projections.

The `CE_UNION_ALL` function takes only two parameters; the two variables containing the data on which to perform a union. These two tables must have the same field names in them, or the activation of the view will fail.

The result of the `CE_UNION_ALL` function is yet another variable, which we can use elsewhere in our view.

Here is the `CE_UNION_ALL` statement used in our scripted calculation view:

```
union_result = CE_UNION_ALL(
  :projection_cust_rev,
  :projection_proj_rev
);
```

As you can see, the `CE_UNION_ALL` function is simple to use. This function is the direct equivalent of the union block we used in our graphical view earlier. At this stage, our view is almost finished. We just need to define the output of our view for it to be usable. It should look like the following screenshot at the moment:

Defining the view's output

In our graphical calculation view from the previous chapter, we were provided with an **output** block. We joined this output block to the output of the union block, and then added the fields from the union to the result field list of our view.

In a scripted calculation view, we do something similar. You will notice in the previous screenshot that we have an output block in the scripted calculation view, in the same way we had one in the graphical calculation view. This block works in exactly the same way; it is here that we define the output fields of the view.

The output block is linked to the script block in our view. What's more, the link between the two cannot be changed.

This means that the script block (which is the SQLScript code we've been writing) needs to give the data to the output block in some way.

It does this using the `var_out` variable you are given when you create the view. All we need to do is to assign a value to this variable, and then define the field names and types that we are assigning to the variable, and we will be able to pass data to our output block, and hence to our user.

Let's define our output variable first, then we can assign values to it. To define the output of the script, right-click on the right-hand pane of the display, the **Output of <Script_View>** panel, on the **Output Parameter** node, then select **Create** from the menu, to see the **Define Output Parameter** dialog, which is pictured as follows:

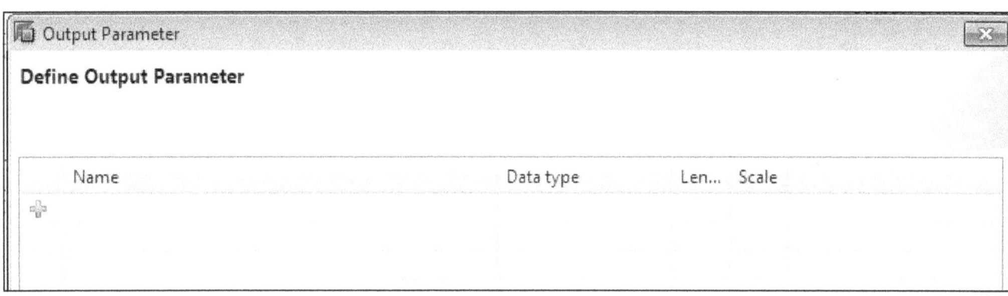

This dialog lets us specify the output fields of our script, their names, data type, and length. This will then let SAP HANA check that the values we assign in the script match the data we said we were going to assign. It makes syntax-checking for the SQLScript easier.

In the **Output Parameter** dialog, we need to list all the fields that are present in our `union_result` variable. This is somewhat fastidious as you need to list each field and its data type. To find the data type for the field you will need to go right back to the definition of the original tables that hold the base data.

To add a field to the output parameter, click on the green plus sign icon in the first column of the dialog to request a new line, then type the field name, its type and length. Here is the result of our **Output Parameter** dialog when completely filled-in for our view:

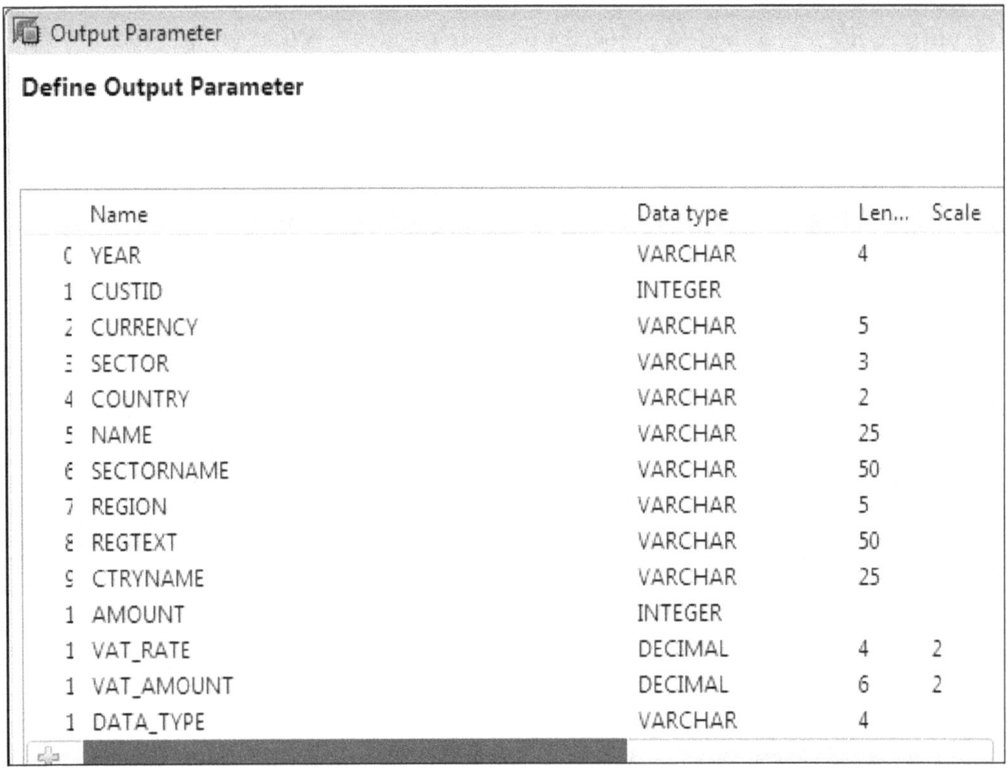

Once this has been done, click on **OK** to save the output parameter definition.

Now all that remains for us to do is to assign values to the `var_out` variable in order to be able to use them in our output block. This is done easily; we already have a variable containing the data we need - the `union_result` variable. It is enough that we rename the `union_result` variable to `var_out`, and we're done with the SQLScript.

The code for our `CE_UNION_ALL` function call therefore becomes:

```
var_out = CE_UNION_ALL(
  :projection_cust_rev,
  :projection_proj_rev
);
```

And our script is finished! We've read in the data from our analytic views, created projections on them, joined them together in a union, and indicated to SAP HANA what the output of the script will be in terms of field names, types, and lengths.

The complete code for the scripted calculation view is now as follows:

```
/********* Begin Procedure Script ************/
BEGIN
  cust_rev = CE_OLAP_VIEW("_SYS_BIC"."book/CUST_REV",
    ["YEAR","CUSTID","CURRENCY","SECTOR","COUNTRY","NAME",
    "SECTORNAME","REGION","REGTEXT","CTRYNAME",SUM("AMOUNT"),
    "VAT_RATE",SUM("VAT_AMOUNT")]);
  proj_rev = CE_OLAP_VIEW("_SYS_BIC"."book/PROJ_REV",
    ["PROJ_YEAR","CUSTID","CURRENCY","SECTOR","COUNTRY","NAME",
    "SECTORNAME","REGION","REGTEXT","CTRYNAME",
    SUM("PROJECTED_AMOUNT"),"VAT_RATE",SUM("VAT_AMOUNT")]);
  projection_cust_rev = CE_PROJECTION(:cust_rev,
    ["YEAR","CUSTID","CURRENCY","SECTOR","COUNTRY","NAME",
    "SECTORNAME","REGION","REGTEXT","CTRYNAME","AMOUNT",
    "VAT_RATE","VAT_AMOUNT",CE_CALC('''REAL''', VARCHAR(4)) AS
    "DATA_TYPE"]);
  projection_proj_rev = CE_PROJECTION(:proj_rev,
    ["PROJ_YEAR" AS "YEAR","CUSTID","CURRENCY","SECTOR",
    "COUNTRY","NAME","SECTORNAME","REGION","REGTEXT",
    "CTRYNAME","PROJECTED_AMOUNT" AS "AMOUNT","VAT_RATE",
    "VAT_AMOUNT",CE_CALC('''PROJ''', VARCHAR(4)) AS
    "DATA_TYPE"]);
  var_out = CE_UNION_ALL(:projection_cust_rev,
    :projection_proj_rev);
END /********* End Procedure Script ************/
```

If you now click on the output block in the graphical depiction of the view on the left-hand side of the view definition screen, you will see that the list of fields we defined as output for the script is available, and we can add them as output for our view. Please add, by right-clicking on the field and then selecting the appropriate entry from the menu, `AMOUNT` and `VAT_AMOUNT` as **measures** and all other fields as **attributes**. This will then give the following output definition for the view:

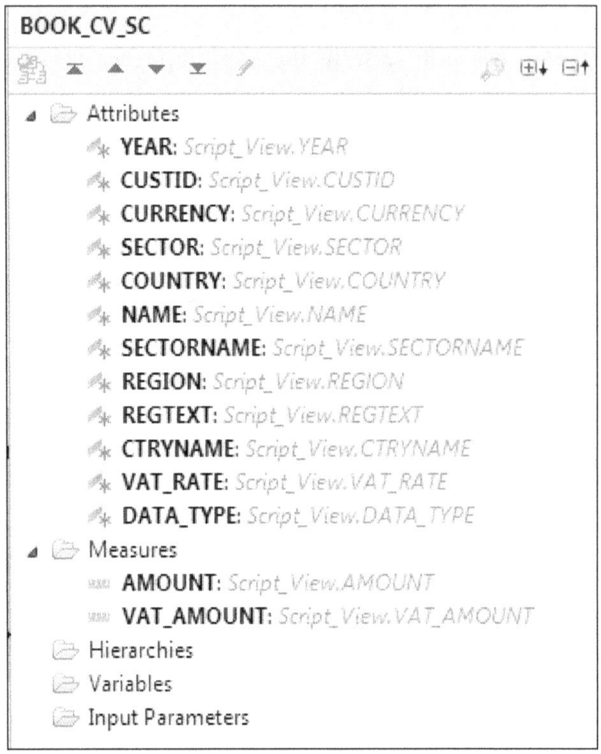

There's just one more thing we need in order to finish our scripted calculation view; as always we need to activate the view. The view is then finished, and we can test it to make sure it performs as we expect.

Results

If we now open a data preview for our scripted view, we can see the contents of the view, and compare these results with those given by the graphical calculation view we created in the previous chapter.

In the following screenshot, we have a data preview of the graphical calculation view on the left, side-by-side with a data preview of our scripted calculation view on the right.

As you can see from the screenshot, the data present in both of our views is identical; we now possess the knowledge enabling us to create calculation views, either using the graphical designer provided in the Studio, or using SQLScript:

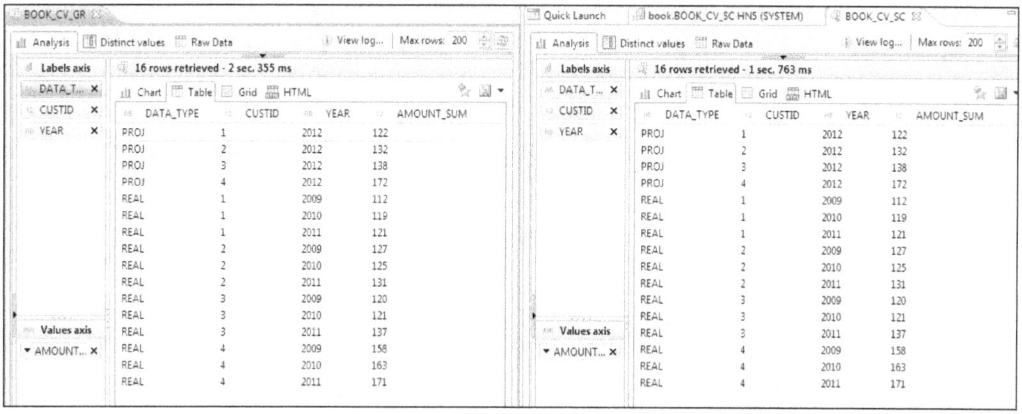

Summary

In this chapter, we have taken a look at the possibilities provided to us when we create **scripted calculation views** in SAP HANA. We have seen that scripted calculation views can achieve exactly the same results as graphical calculation views. Scripted calculation views are created by **writing code**, instead of by manipulating objects on the screen. We have been introduced to the **CE functions** provided by SAP HANA, and have used some of these, notably the `CE_OLAP_VIEW`, `CE_PROJECTION`, `CE_CALC`, and `CE_UNION_ALL` functions to **read data** from an analytic view, create a **projection** on the data read, **calculate columns** on the fly, and then **join data** from two views together. We have seen that the results of CE functions are assigned to **variables**, which we can then use in other functions, prefixing the variable name with a **colon**. Finally, we did a comparison of the output of our scripted view and its graphical counterpart, and saw that the view contents of both were identical.

In the next chapter, we'll be looking at an important part of any data modeling or reporting project, the concept of **authorizations**. It is very rare that we wish for all users to have access to all the data in the system, and so we need to restrict who can see what. SAP HANA provides very fine-grained authorizations we can implement to achieve this, as we will see in the next chapter.

Quick reference

Here is a quick overview of the main topics covered in this chapter.

Object	Usage	Creation
Scripted calculation view	Like a graphical calculation view, this allows development of complex data models, combining data from several sources, and presenting the data in one coherent place.	**Quick Launch** | **Calculation view** | **Create**. Give **Name** and **Description** values, select **SQLScript**. Write the appropriate script, define the output parameter, and activate.
CE functions	These allow us to interact with the database, and the data we have read from it, without writing SQL.	• `CE_OLAP_VIEW`: This reads an analytic view • `CE_COLUMN_TABLE`: This reads a database table (column table only) • `CE_PROJECTION`: This creates a projection on data read into a scalar variable • `CE_CALC`: This creates a calculated column in a projection • `CE_JOIN`, `CE_LEFT_OUTER_JOIN`, and `CE_RIGHT_OUTER_JOIN`: This joins two scalar variables together • `CE_UNION_ALL`: This creates a union of two scalar variables (which have the same field list)

7

Hey! That's My Data! – Authorizations in SAP HANA

At this stage in the book, you have learned how to create a database schema, import data, or create tables using SQL, then use that data in attribute, analytic, and calculation views. At no point have we examined the fact that some of your users might not be allowed to have access to all the data in the system, or might have specific rights, maybe to create data but not to see the data that is currently in the system. We'll see concrete example of access restrictions on both objects and their content in this chapter.

SAP HANA provides several different layers of security from which you can benefit, and in this chapter we'll be looking at each of them. We'll examine how we can create each type of object, how they interact with each other, and how we can use them.

The authorization concept in SAP HANA is comprised of different notions:

- Roles
- SQL privileges
- Analytic privileges
- System privileges
- Package privileges
- Users

We will take a look at each of these concepts in turn.

Roles

In SAP HANA, as in most of SAP's software, authorizations are grouped into roles.

A role is a collection of authorization objects, with their associated privileges. It allows us, as developers, to define self-contained units of authorization. In the same way that at the start of this book we created an attribute view allowing us to have a coherent view of our customer data which we could reuse at will in more advanced developments, authorization roles allow us to create coherent developments of authorization data which we can then assign to users at will, making sure that users who are supposed to have the same rights always have the same rights. If we had to assign individual authorization objects to users, we could be fairly sure that sooner or later, we would forget someone in a department, and they would not be able to access the data they needed to do their everyday work. Worse, we might not give quite the same authorizations to one person, and have to spend valuable time correcting our error when they couldn't see the data they needed (or worse, more dangerous and less obvious to us as developers, if the user could see more data than was intended).

> It is always a much better idea to group authorizations into a role and then assign the role to users, than assign authorizations directly to users.
>
> Assigning a role to a user means that when the user changes jobs and needs a new set of privileges; we can just remove the first role, and assign a second one.
>
> Since, we're just starting out using authorizations in SAP HANA, let's get into this good habit right from the start. It really will make our lives easier later on.

Creating a role

Role creation is done, like all other SAP HANA development, in the Studio. If your Studio is currently closed, please open it, and then select the **Modeler** perspective.

> In order to create roles, privileges, and users, you will yourself need privileges. Your SAP HANA user will need the `ROLE ADMIN`, `USER ADMIN`, and `CREATE STRUCTURED PRIVILEGE` system privileges in order to do the development work in this chapter.

You will see in the **Navigator** panel we have a `Security` folder, as we can see here:

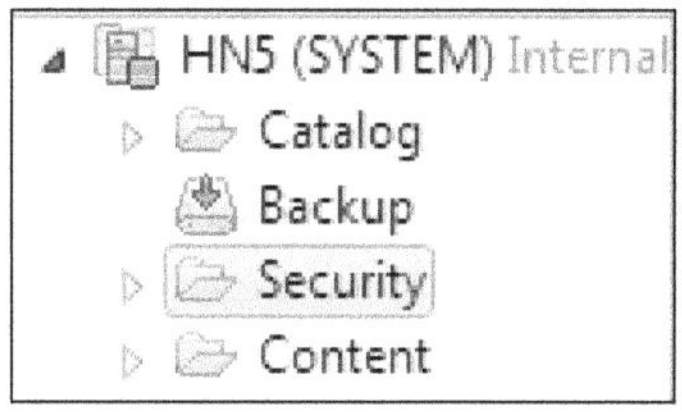

Please find the `Security` folder and then expand this folder. You will see a subfolder called `Roles`. Right-click on the `Roles` folder and select **New Role** to start creating a role.

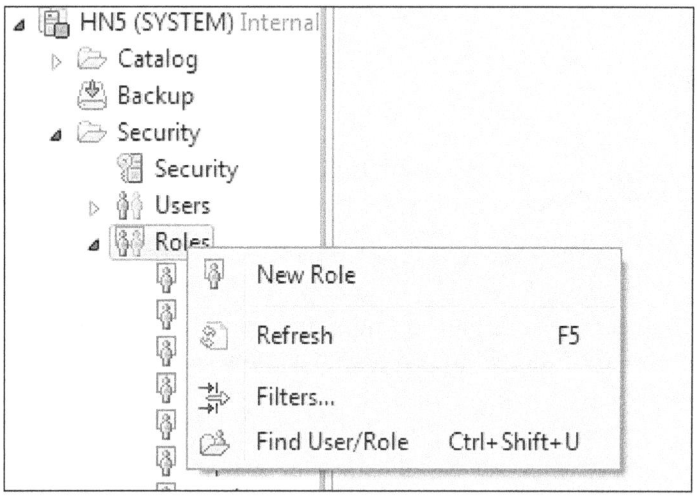

On the screen which will open, you will see a number of tabs representing the different authorization objects we can create, as we can see here:

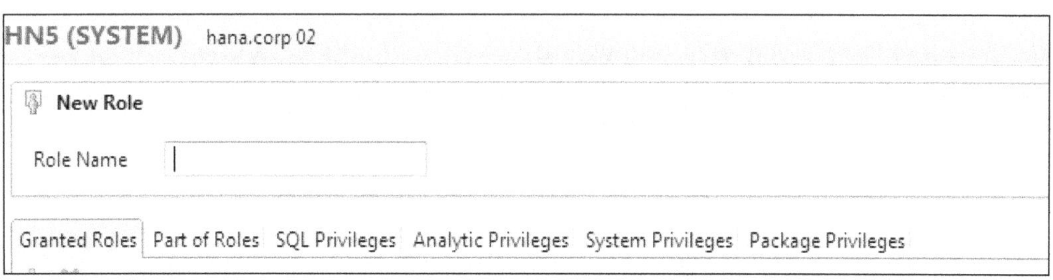

We'll be looking at each of these in turn, in the following sections, so for the moment just give your role **Name** (BOOKUSER might be appropriate, if not very original).

Granted roles

Like many other object types in SAP HANA, once you have created a role, you can then use it inside another role. This onion-like arrangement makes authorizations a lot easier to manage.

If we had, for example, a company with two teams:

- Sales
- Purchasing

And two countries, say:

- France
- Germany

We could create a role giving access to sales analytic views, one giving purchasing analytic views, one giving access to data for France, and one giving access to data for Germany. We could then create new roles, say Sales-France, which don't actually contain any authorization objects themselves, but contain only the Sales and the France roles.

The role definition is much simpler to understand and to maintain than if we had directly created the Sales-France role and a Sales-Germany role with all the underlying objects.

> Once again, as with other development objects, creating small self-contained roles and reusing them when possible will make your (maintenance) life easier.

In the **Granted Roles** tab we can see the list of subroles this main role contains. Note that this list is only a pointer, you cannot modify the actual authorizations and the other roles given here, you would need to open the individual role and make changes there.

Part of roles

The **Part of Roles** tab in the role definition screen is exactly the opposite of the **Granted Roles** tab.

This tab lists all other roles of which this role is a subrole. It is very useful to track authorizations, especially when you find yourself in a situation where a user seems to have too many authorizations and can see data they shouldn't be able to see.

You cannot manipulate this list as such, it exists for information only. If you want to make changes, you need to modify the main role of which this role is a subrole.

SQL privileges

An SQL privilege is the lowest level at which we can define restrictions for using database objects.

SQL privileges apply to the simplest objects in the database such as schemas, tables and so on. No attribute, analytical, or calculation view can be seen by SQL privileges.

> This is not strictly true, though you can consider it so. What we have seen as an analytical view, for example, the graphical definition, the drag and drop, the checkboxes, has been transformed into a real database object in the `_SYS_BIC` schema upon activation. We could therefore define SQL privileges on this database object if we wanted, but this is not recommended and indeed limits the control we can have over the view. We'll see a little later that SAP HANA has much finer-grained authorizations for views than this.

An important thing to note about SQL privileges is that they apply to the object on which they are defined. They restrict access to a given object itself, but do not at any point have any impact on the object's contents. For example, we can decide that one of our users can have access to the `CUSTOMER` table, but we couldn't restrict their access to only `CUSTOMER` values from the `COUNTRY` USA.

SQL privileges can control access to any object under the **Catalog** node in the **Navigator** panel.

Let's add some authorizations to our `BOOK` schema and its contents. At the top of the **SQL Privileges** tab is a green plus sign button. Now click on this button to get the **Select Catalog Object** dialog, shown here:

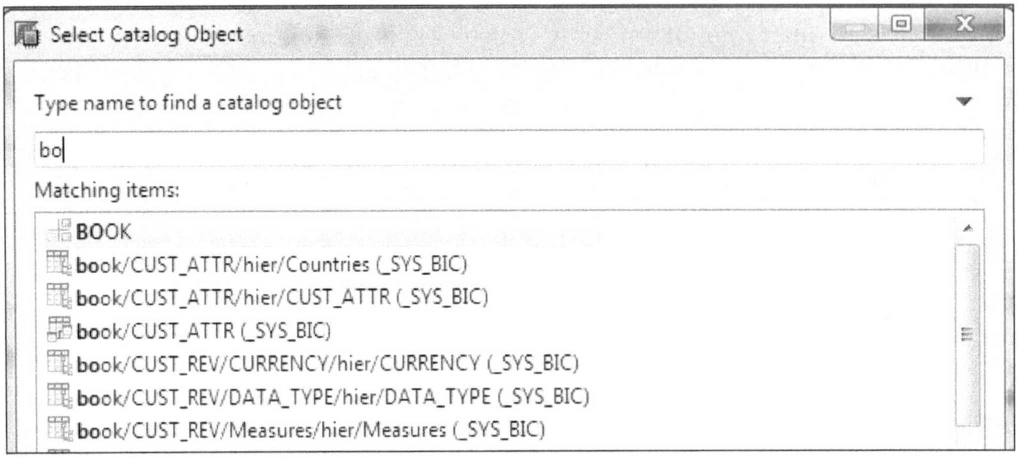

As you can see in the screenshot, we have entered the two letters `bo` into the filter box at the top of the dialog. As soon as you enter at least two letters into this box, the Studio will attempt to find and then list all database objects whose name contains the two letters you typed. If you continue to type, the search will be refined further.

The first item in the list shown is the `BOOK` schema we created right back at the start of the book in the *Chapter 2, SAP HANA Studio - Installation and First Look*. Please select the `BOOK` item, and then click on **OK** to add it to our new role:

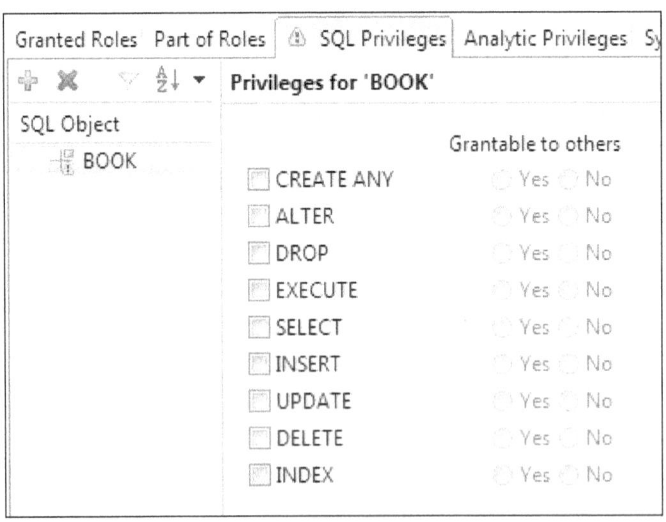

The first thing to notice is the warning icon on the **SQL Privileges** tab itself:

This means that your role definition is incomplete, and the role cannot be activated and used as yet.

On the right of the screen, a list of checkbox options has appeared. These are the individual authorizations appropriate to the SQL object you have selected. In order to grant rights to a user via a role, you need to decide which of these options to include in the role.

The individual authorization names are self-explicit. For example, the **CREATE ANY** authorization allows creation of new objects inside a schema.

> The **INSERT** or **SELECT** authorization might at first seem unusual for a schema, as it's not an object which can support such instructions. However, the usage is actually quite elegant. If a user has **INSERT** rights on the schema `BOOK`, then they have **INSERT** rights on all objects inside the schema `BOOK`.
>
> Granting rights on the schema itself avoids having to specify the names of all objects inside the schema. It also future-proofs your authorization concept, since new objects created in the schema will automatically inherit from the existing authorizations you have defined.

On the far right of the screen, alongside each authorization is a radio button which gives an additional privilege, the possibility for a given user to, in turn, give the rights to a second user.

This is an option which should not be given to all users, and so should not be present in all roles you create; the right to attribute privileges to users should be limited to your administrators. If you give just any user the right to pass on their authorizations further, you will soon find that you are no longer able to determine who can do what in your database.

For the moment we are creating a simple role to show the working of the authorization concept in SAP HANA, so we will check all the checkboxes, and leave the radio buttons at **No**:

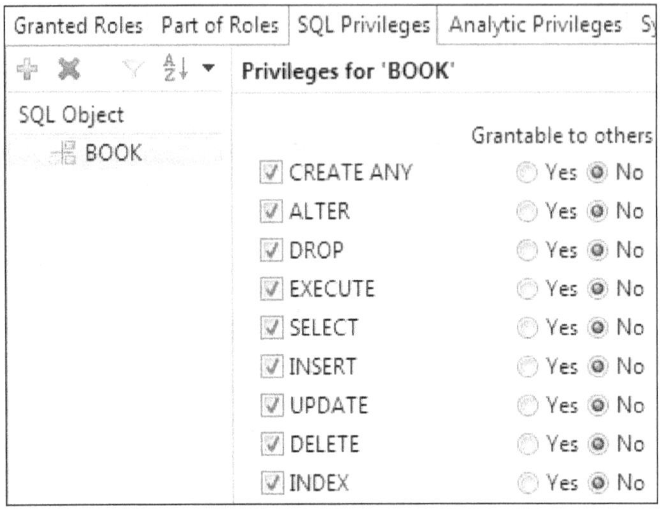

There are some SQL privileges which are necessary for any user to be able to do work in SAP HANA. These are listed below. They give access to the system objects describing the development models we create in SAP HANA, and if a user does not have these privileges, nothing will work at all, the user will not be authorized to do anything.

The SQL privileges you will need to add to the role in order to give access to basic SAP HANA system objects are:

- The **SELECT** privilege on the `_SYS_BI` schema
- The **SELECT** privilege on the `_SYS_REPO` schema
- The **EXECUTE** privilege on the `REPOSITORY_REST` procedure

Please add these SQL privileges to your role now, in order to obtain the following result:

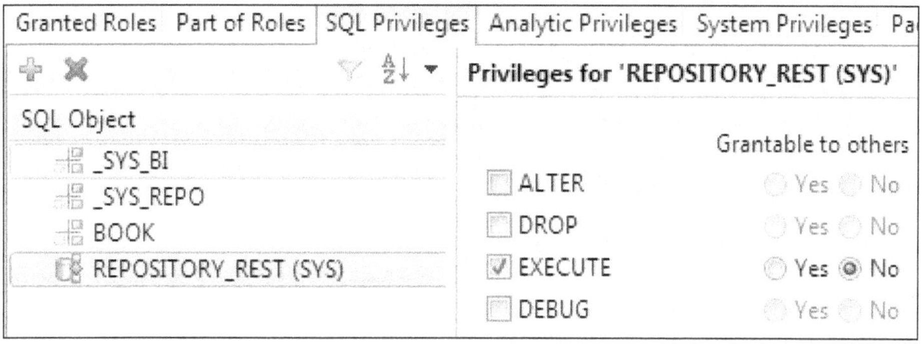

As you can see with the configuration we have just done, SQL privileges allow a user to access a given object and allow specific actions on the object. They do not however allow us to specify particular authorizations to the contents of the object.

In order to use such fine-grained rights, we need to create an analytic privilege, and then add it to our role, so let's do that now.

Analytic privileges

An analytic privilege is an artifact unique to SAP HANA, it is not part of the standard SQL authorization concept.

Analytic privileges allow us to restrict access to certain values of a given attribute, analytic, or calculation view. This means that we can create one view, which by default shows all available data, and then restrict what is actually visible to different users. We could restrict visible data by company code, by country, or by region. For example, our users in Europe would be allowed to see and work with data from our customers in Europe, but not those in the USA.

An analytic privilege is created through the **Quick Launch** panel of **Modeler**, so please open that view now (or switch to the **Quick Launch** tab if it's already open).

> You don't need to close the **role definition** tab that's already open, we can leave it for now, create our analytic privilege, and then come back to the role definition later.

From the **Quick Launch** panel, select **Analytic Privilege**, and then **Create**.

As usual with SAP HANA, we are asked to give **Name**, **Description**, and select a **package** for our object. We'll call it `AP_EU` (for analytic privilege, Europe), use the name as the description, and put it into our `book` package alongside our other developments. As is common in SAP HANA, we have the option of creating an analytic privilege from scratch (**Create New**) or copying an existing privilege (**Copy From**). We don't currently have any other analytic privileges in our development, so leave **Create New** selected, then click on **Next** to go to the second screen of the wizard, shown here:

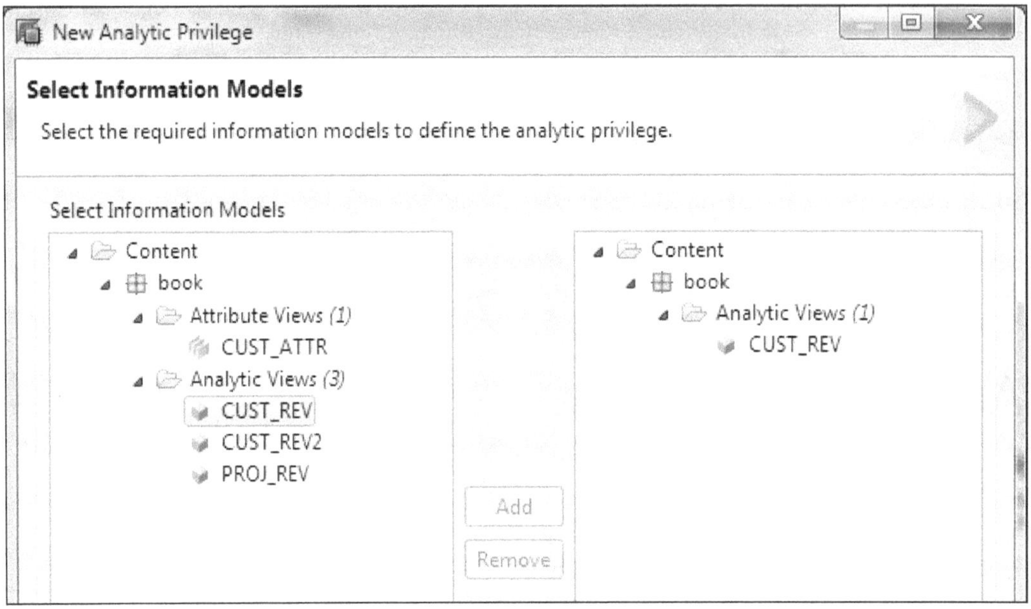

On this page of the dialog, we are prompted to add development models to the analytic privilege. This will then allow us to restrict access to given values of these models. In the previous screenshot, we have added the **CUST_REV** analytic view to the analytic privilege. This will allow us to restrict access to any value we specify of any of the fields visible in the view.

To add a view to the analytic privilege, just find it in the left panel, click on its name and then click on the **Add** button. Once you have added the views you require for your authorizations, click on the **Finish** button at the bottom of the window to go to the next step.

You will be presented with the analytic privilege development panel, reproduced here:

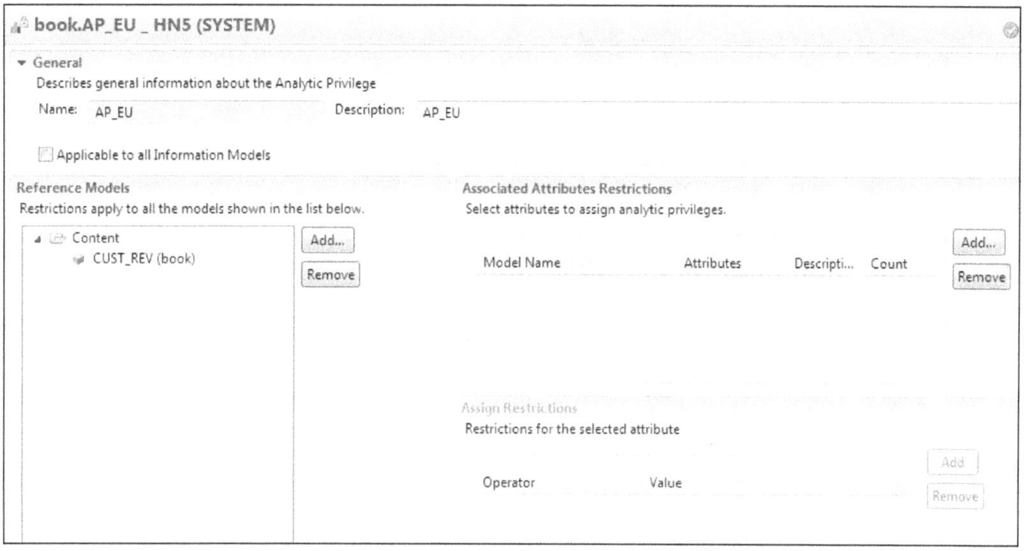

This page allows us to define our analytic privilege completely. On the left we have the list of database views we have included in the analytic privilege. We can add more, or remove one, using the **Add** and **Remove** buttons. To the right, we can see the **Associated Attributes Restrictions** and **Assign Restrictions** boxes. These are where we define the restrictions to individual values, or sets of values. In the top box, **Associated Attributes Restrictions**, we define on which attributes we want to restrict access (country code or region, maybe). In the bottom box, **Assign Restrictions**, we define the individual values on which to restrict (for example, for company code, we could restrict to value 0001, or US22; for region, we could limit access to EU or USA).

Let's add a restriction to the `REGION` field of our **CUST_REV** view now. Click on the **Add** button next to the **Associated Attributes Restrictions** box, to see the **Select Object** dialog:

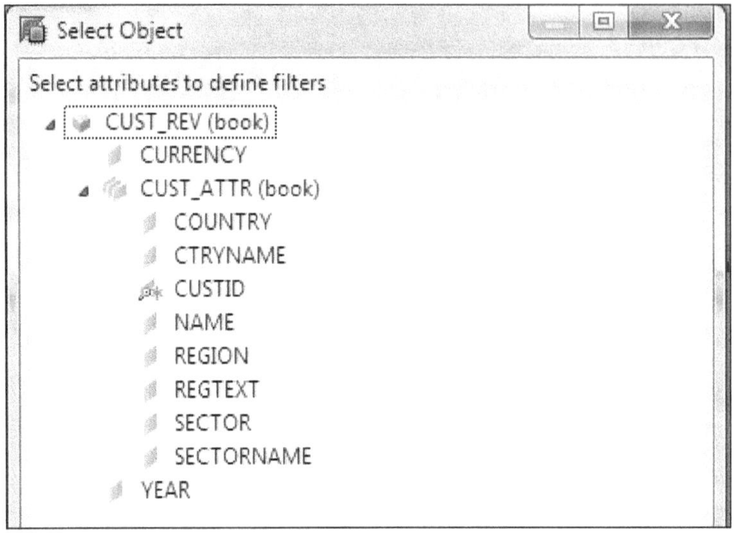

As can be expected, this dialog lists all the attributes in our analytic view. We just need to select the appropriate attribute and then click on **OK** to add it to the analytic privilege.

> Measures in the view are not listed in the dialog. We cannot restrict access to a view according to numeric values. We cannot therefore, make restrictions to customers with a revenue over 1 million Euros, for example.

Please add the `REGION` field to the analytic privilege now.

Once the appropriate fields have been added, we can define the restrictions to be applied to them. Click on the `REGION` field in the **Associated Attributes Restrictions** box, then on the **Add** button next to the **Assign Restrictions** box, to define the restrictions we want to apply.

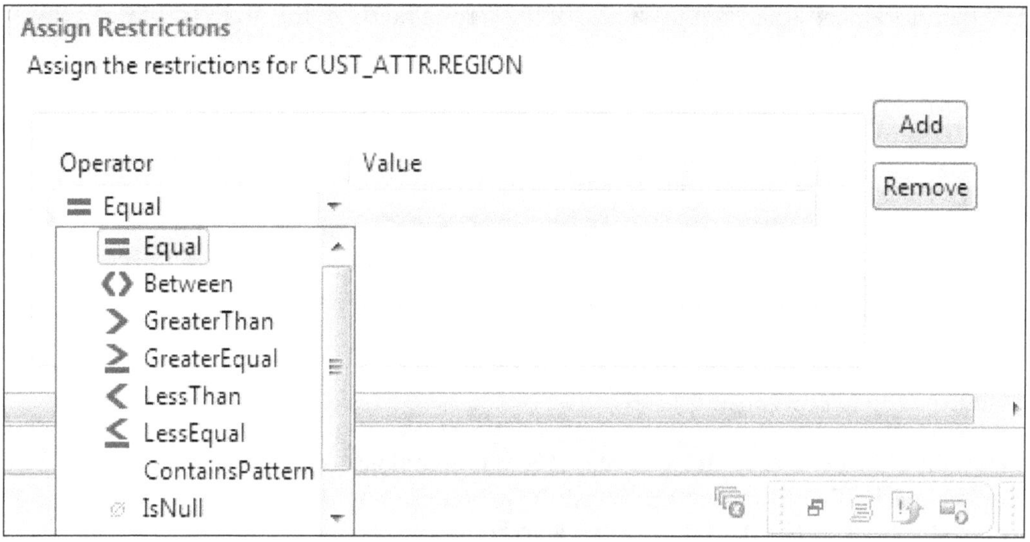

As we can see, restrictions can be defined according to the usual list of comparison operators. These are the same operators we used earlier to define a restricted column in our analytic views.

In our example, we'll be restricting access to those lines with a `REGION` column equal to `EU`, so we'll select **Equal**.

In the **Value** column, we can either type the appropriate value directly, or use the value help button, and the familiar **Value Help Dialog** which will appear, to select the value from those available in the view. Please add the `EU` value, either by typing it or by having SAP HANA find it for us, now.

There is one more field which needs to be added to our analytic privilege, and the reason behind might seem at first a little strange.

> This point is valid for SAP HANA SP5, up to and including (at least) release 50 of the software. If this point turns out to be a bug, then it might not be necessary in later versions of the software.

The field on which we want to restrict user actions (`REGION`) is not actually part of the analytic view itself. `REGION`, if you recall, is a field which is present in **CUST_REV**, thanks to the included attribute view **CUST_ATTR**. In its current state, the analytic privilege will not work, because no fields from the analytic view are actually present in the analytic privilege.

We therefore need to add at least one of the native fields of the analytic view to the analytic privilege. We don't need to do any restriction on the field; however it needs to be in the privilege for everything to work as expected.

> This is hinted at in SAP Note 1809199, SAP HANA DB: debugging user authorization errors.
>
> > *Only if a view is included in one of the cube restrictions and at least one of its attribute is employed by one of the dimension restrictions, access to the view is granted by this analytical privilege.*
>
> Not an explicit description of the workings of the authorization concept, but close.

Our analytic view **CUST_REV** contains two native fields, `CURRENCY` and `YEAR`. You can add either of these to the analytic privilege. You do not need to assign any restrictions to the field; it just needs to be in the privilege.

Here is the state of the analytic privilege when development work on it is finished:

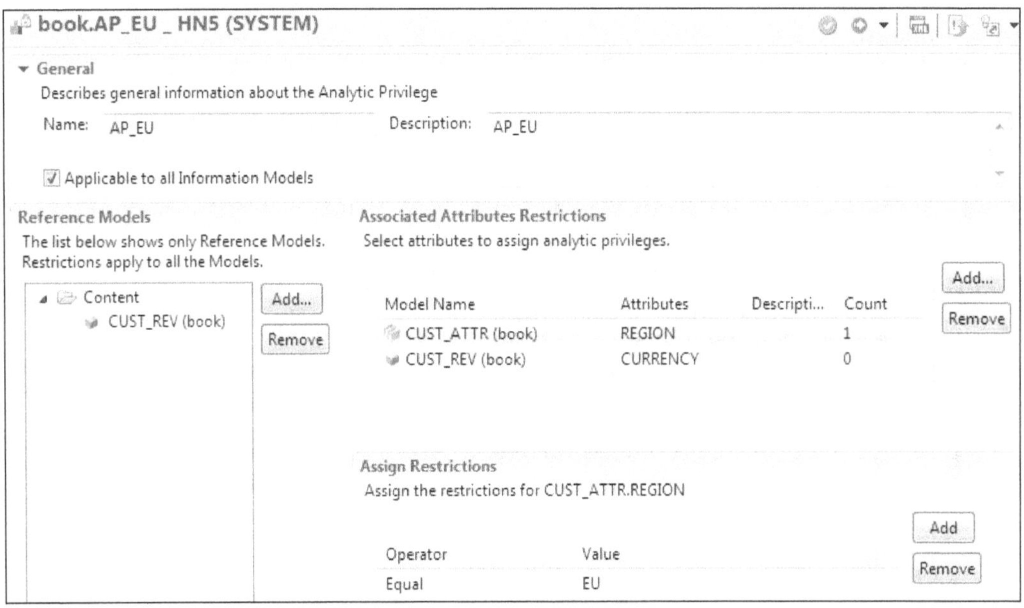

The **Count** column lists the number of restrictions in effect for the associated field. For the `CURRENCY` field, no restrictions are defined.

We just need (as always) to activate our analytic privilege in order to be able to use it. The activation button is the same one as we have used up until now to activate the modeling views, the round green button with the right-facing white arrow at the top-right of the panel, which you can see on the preceding screenshot.

Please activate the analytic privilege now.

Once that has been done, we can add it to our role. Return to the **Role** tab (if you left it open) or reopen the role now.

> If you closed the role definition tab earlier, you can get back to our role by opening the `Security` node in the **Navigator** panel, then opening `Roles`, and double-clicking on the `BOOKUSER` role.

In the **Analytic Privileges** tab of the role definition screen, click on the green plus sign at the top, to add an analytic privilege to our role. The analytic privilege we have just created is called `AP_EU`, so type `ap_eu` into the search box at the top of the dialog window which will open. As soon as you have typed at least two characters, SAP HANA will start searching for matching analytic privileges, and your `AP_EU` privilege will be listed, as we can see here:

Click on **OK** to add the privilege to the role. We will see in a minute the effect our analytic privilege has on the rights of a particular user, but for the moment we can take a look at the second-to-last tab in the role definition screen, **System Privileges**.

System privileges

As its name suggests, system privileges gives to a particular user the right to perform specific actions on the SAP HANA system itself, not just on a given table or view.

These are particular rights which should not be given to just any user, but should be reserved to those users who need to perform a particular task. We'll not be adding any of these privileges to our role, however we'll take a look at the available options and what they are used for.

Click on the green plus-sign button at the top of the **System Privileges** tab to see a list of the available privileges. By default the dialog will do a search on all available values; there are only fifteen or so, but you can as usual filter them down if you require using the filter box at the top of the dialog:

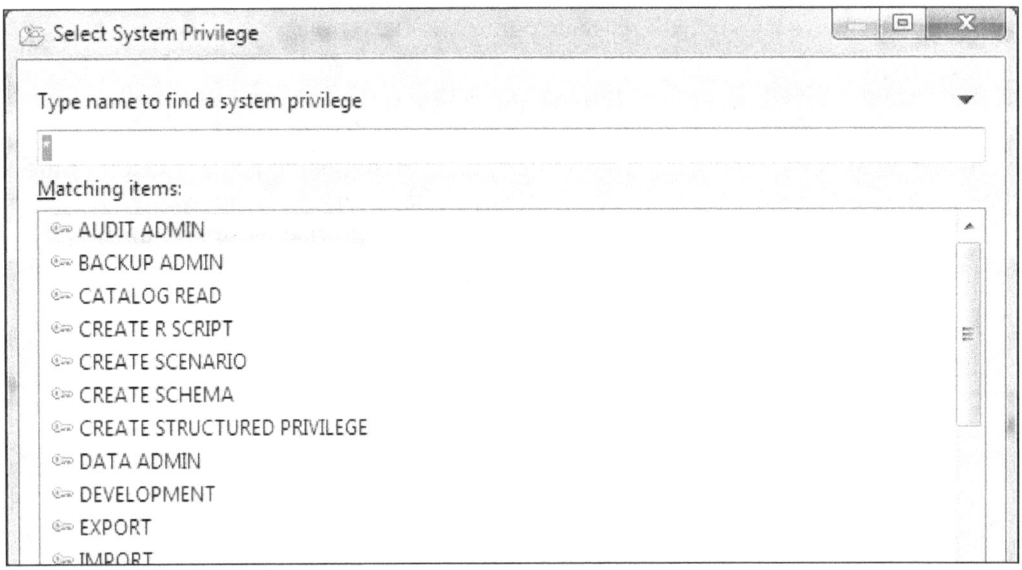

For a full list of the system privileges available and their uses, please refer to the SAP HANA SQL Reference, available on the `help.sap.com` website at `http://help.sap.com/hana/html/sql_grant.html`.

Package privileges

The last tab in the role definition screen concerns **Package Privileges**. These allow a given user to access those objects in a package.

In our example, the package is called `book`, so if we add the `book` package to our role in the **Package Privileges** tab, we will see the following result:

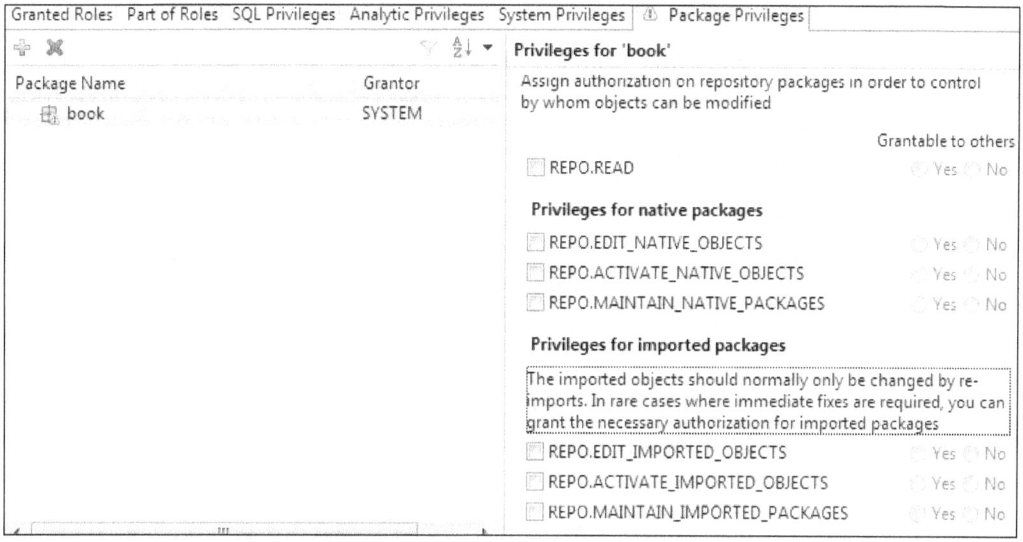

Assigning package privileges is similar to assigning SQL privileges we saw earlier. We first add the required object (here our `book` package), then we need to indicate exactly which rights we give to the role. As we can see in the preceding screenshot, we have a series of checkboxes on the right-hand side of the window. At least one of these checkboxes must be checked in order to save the role.

The individual rights have names which are fairly self-explanatory. **REPO.READ** gives access to read the package, whereas **REPO.EDIT_NATIVE_OBJECTS** allows modification of objects, for example.

The role we are creating is destined for an end user who will need to see the data in a role, but should not need to modify the data models in any way (and in fact we really don't want them to modify our data models, do we?). We'll just add the **REPO.READ** privilege, on our `book` package, to our role. Again we can decide whether the end user can in turn assign this privilege to others. And again, we don't need this feature in our role.

At this point, our role is finished. We have given access to the SQL objects in the `BOOK` schema, created an analytic privilege which limits access to the Europe region in our **CUST_REV** model, and given read-only access to our book package. After activation (always) we'll be able to assign our role to a test user, and then see the effect our authorizations have on what the user can do and see. Please activate the role now.

Users

Users are probably the most important part of the authorization concept. They are where all our problems begin, and their attempts to do and see things they shouldn't are the main reason we have to spend valuable time defining authorizations in the first place.

In technical terms, a user is just another database object. They are created, modified, and deleted in the same way a modeling view is. They have properties (their name and password, for example), and it is by modifying these properties that we influence the actions that the person who connects using the user can perform.

Up until now we have been using the `SYSTEM` user (or the user that your database administrator assigned to you). This user is defined by SAP, and has basically the authorizations to do anything with the database.

> Use of this user is discouraged by SAP, and the author really would like to insist that you don't use it for your developments. Accidents happen, and one of the great things about authorizations is that they help to prevent accidents. If you try to delete an important object with the SYSTEM user, you will delete it, and getting it back might involve a database restore. If however you use a development user with less authorization, then you wouldn't have been allowed to do the deletion, saving a lot of tears.
>
> Of course, the question then arises, why have you been using the SYSTEM user for the last couple of hundred pages of development. The answer is simple: if the author had started the book with the authorizations chapter, not many readers would have gotten past page 10.

Let's create a new user now, and assign the role we have just created.

From the **Navigator** panel, open the `Security` node, right-click on **User**, and select **New User** from the menu to obtain the user creation screen as shown in the following screenshot:

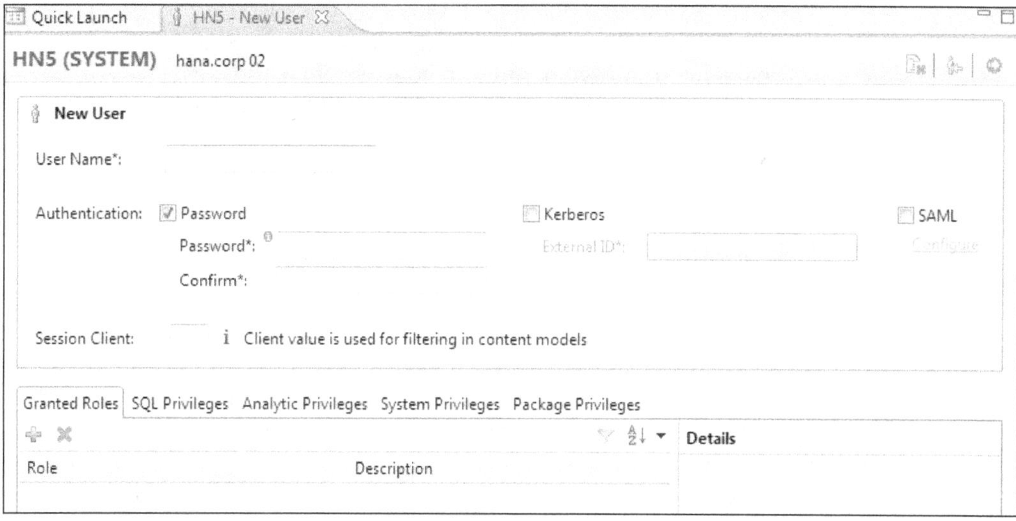

Defining a user requires remarkably little information:

- **User Name**: The login that the user will use. Your company might have a naming convention for users. Users might even already have a standard login they use to connect to other systems in your enterprise. In our example, we'll create a user with the (once again rather unimaginative) name of `BOOKU`.
- **Authentication**: How will SAP HANA know that the user connecting with the name of `ANNE` really is Anne? There are three (currently) ways of authenticating a user with SAP HANA.
    - **Password**: This is the most common authentication system, SAP HANA will ask Anne for her password when she connects to the system. Since Anne is the only person who knows her password, we can be sure that Anne really is `ANNE`, and let her connect and do anything the user `ANNE` is allowed to do. Passwords in SAP HANA have to respect a certain format. By default this format is one capital, one lowercase, one number, and at least eight characters.

> You can see and change the password policy in the system configuration. Double-click on the system name in the **Navigator** panel, click on the **Configuration** tab, type the word `pass` into the filter box at the top of the tab, and scroll down to **indexserver.ini** and then **password policy**. The password format in force on your system is listed as **password_layout**. By default this is `A1a`, meaning capitals, numbers, and lowercase letters are allowed. The value can also contain the # character, meaning that special characters must also be contained in the password. The only special characters allowed by SAP HANA are currently the underscore, dollar sign, and the hash character. Other password policy defaults are also listed on this screen, such as **maximum_password_lifetime** (the time after which SAP HANA will force you to change your password).

    - **Kerberos** and **SAML**: These authentication systems need to be set up by your network administrator and allow single sign-on in your enterprise. This means that SAP HANA will be able to see the Windows username that is connecting to the system. The database will assume that the authentication part (deciding whether Anne really is `ANNE`) has already been done by Windows, and let the user connect.

- **Session Client**: As we saw when we created attribute and analytic views back at the start of the book, SAP HANA understands the notion of client, referring to a partition system of the SAP ERP database. In the SAP ERP, different users can work in different Clients. In our development, we filtered on Client 100. A much better way of handling filtering is to define the default client for a user when we define their account. The **Session Client** field can be filled with the ERP Client in which the user works. In this way we do not need to filter on the analytic models, we can leave their client value at **Dynamic** in the view, and the actual value to use will be taken from the user record. Once again this means maintenance of our developments is a lot simpler.

> If you like, you can take a few minutes at the end of this chapter to create a user with a session client value of 100, then go back and reset our attribute and analytic views' default client value to Dynamic, reactivate everything, and then do a data preview with your test user. The result should be identical to that obtained when the view was filtered on client 100. However, if you then create a second user with a session client of 200, this second user will see different data.

We'll create a user with a password login, so type a password for your user now. Remember to adhere to the password policy in force on your system. Also note that the user will be required to change their password on first login.

At the bottom of the user definition screen, as we can see from the preceding screenshot, we have a series of tabs corresponding to the different authorizations we can assign to our user. These are the same tabs we saw earlier when defining a role.

As explained at the beginning of this chapter, it is considered best practice to assign authorizations to a role and then the role to a user, rather than assign authorizations directly to a user; this makes maintenance easier. For this reason we will not be looking at the different tabs for assigning authorizations to our user, other than the first one, **Granted Roles**.

The **Granted Roles** tab lists, and allows adding and removing roles from the list assigned to the user. By default when we create a user, they have no roles assigned, and hence have no authorizations at all in the system. They will be able to log in to SAP HANA but will be able to do no development work, and will see no data from the system.

Please click on the green plus sign button in the **Granted Roles** tab of the user definition screen, to add a role to the user account. You will be provided with the **Select Role** dialog, shown in part here:

This dialog has the familiar search box at the top, so typing the first few letters of a role name will bring up a list of matching roles. Here our role was called `BOOKUSER`, so please do a search for it, then select it in the list and click on **OK** to add it to the user account.

Once that is done, we can test our user to verify that we can perform the necessary actions with the role and user we have just created. We just need, as with all objects in SAP HANA, to activate the user object first. As usual, this is done with the round green button with the right-facing white arrow at the top-right of the screen. Please do this now.

Testing our user and role

The only real way to check if the authorizations we have defined are appropriate to the business requirements is to create a user and then try out the role to see what the user can and cannot see and do in the system.

The first thing to do is to add our new user to the Studio so we can connect to SAP HANA using this new user.

To do this, in the **Navigator** panel, right click on the SAP HANA system name, and select **Add Additional User** from the menu which appears.

This will give you the **Add additional user** dialog, shown in the following screenshot:

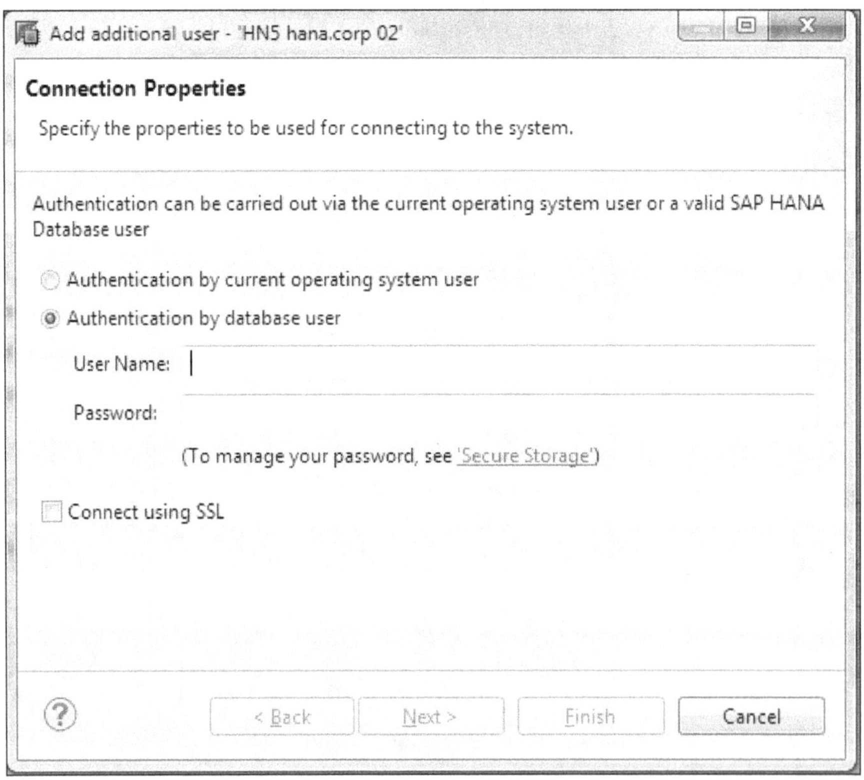

Enter the name of the user you just created (BOOKU) and the password you assigned to the user. You will be required to change the password immediately:

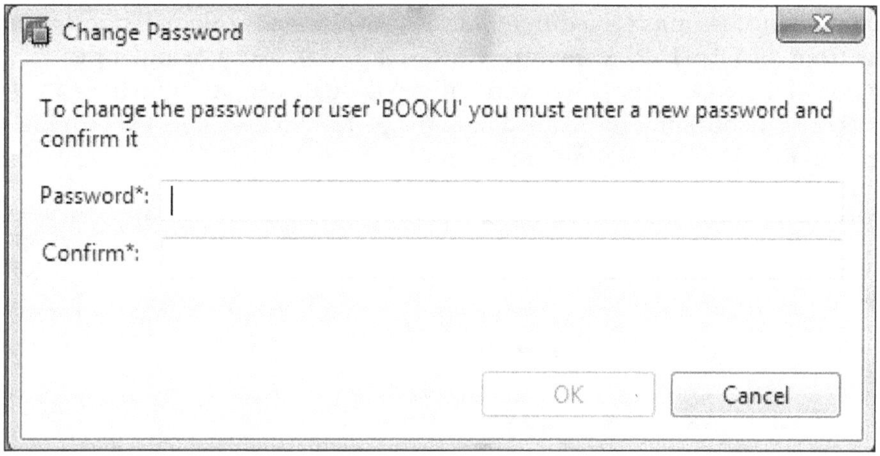

Click on **Finish** to add the user to the Studio.

You will see immediately in the **Navigator** panel that we can now work with either our SYSTEM user, or our BOOKU user:

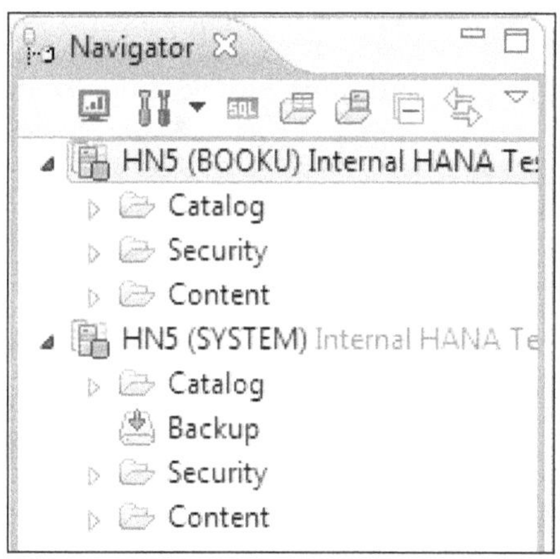

We can also see straight away that BOOKU is missing the privileges to perform or manage data backups; the **Backup** node is missing from the list for the BOOKU user.

Let's try to do something with our BOOKU user and see how the system reacts. The way the Studio lets you handle multiple users is very elegant, since the tree structure of database objects is duplicated, one per user, you can see immediately how the different authorization profiles affect the different users. Additionally, if you request a data preview from the **CUST_REV** analytic view in the book package under the BOOKU user's node in the **Navigator** panel, you will see the data according to the BOOKU user's authorizations. Requesting the same data preview from the SYSTEM user's node will see the data according to SYSTEM's authorizations.

Let's do a data preview on the **CUST_REV** view with the SYSTEM user, for reference:

12 rows retrieved - 234 ms — Add filter

test	SECTOR	NAME	SECTORNAME	REGTEXT	CTRYNAME	REGION	COU
2	ENT	Jacques	Enterprise Customer	Europe	France	EU	FR
4	SMB	Jones	Small and Medium ...	North America	United States of A...	NAR	US
1	SMB	Smith	Small and Medium ...	Europe	Great Britain	EU	GB
3	IND	Martin	Individual Owner	Europe	Great Britain	EU	GB
4	SMB	Jones	Small and Medium ...	North America	United States of A...	NAR	US
4	SMB	Jones	Small and Medium ...	North America	United States of A...	NAR	US
3	IND	Martin	Individual Owner	Europe	Great Britain	EU	GB
3	IND	Martin	Individual Owner	Europe	Great Britain	EU	GB
1	SMB	Smith	Small and Medium ...	Europe	Great Britain	EU	GB
2	ENT	Jacques	Enterprise Customer	Europe	France	EU	FR
1	SMB	Smith	Small and Medium ...	Europe	Great Britain	EU	GB
2	ENT	Jacques	Enterprise Customer	Europe	France	EU	FR

As we can see, there are 12 rows of data retrieved, and we have data from the EU and NAR regions.

If we ask for the same data preview using our BOOKU user, we can see much less data:

9 rows retrieved - 78 ms — Add filter

test	SECTOR	NAME	SECTORNAME	REGTEXT	CTRYNAME	REGION	CO
2	ENT	Jacques	Enterprise Customer	Europe	France	EU	FR
3	IND	Martin	Individual Owner	Europe	Great Britain	EU	GB
1	SMB	Smith	Small and Medium ...	Europe	Great Britain	EU	GB
2	ENT	Jacques	Enterprise Customer	Europe	France	EU	FR
1	SMB	Smith	Small and Medium ...	Europe	Great Britain	EU	GB
3	IND	Martin	Individual Owner	Europe	Great Britain	EU	GB
3	IND	Martin	Individual Owner	Europe	Great Britain	EU	GB
1	SMB	Smith	Small and Medium ...	Europe	Great Britain	EU	GB
2	ENT	Jacques	Enterprise Customer	Europe	France	EU	FR

`BOOKU` can only see nine of the 12 data rows in our view, as no data from the `NAR` region is visible to the `BOOKU` user. This is exactly the result we aimed to achieve using our analytic privilege, in our role, assigned to our user.

Summary

In this chapter, we have taken a look at the different aspects of the authorization concept in SAP HANA. We examined the different authorization levels available in the system, from SQL privileges, analytic privileges, system privileges, and package privileges. We saw how to add these different authorization concepts to a role, a reusable group of authorizations.

We went on to create a new user in our SAP HANA system, examining the different types of authentications available, and the assignment of roles to users.

Finally, we logged into the Studio with our new user account, and found out the first-hand effect our authorizations had on what the user could see and do.

In the next chapter, we will be working with hierarchical data, seeing what hierarchies can bring to our reporting applications, and how to make the best use of them.

Quick reference

Here is a quick overview of the main concepts we've seen concerning authorizations in SAP HANA:

Object	Usage	Creation
Role	Group authorization objects together	In the **Navigator** panel select `Security` folder and expand it, then select the `Roles` folder and **New Role**. Give a name, add other authorization objects, and Deploy.
SQL privileges	Grant access to base SQL objects in the database (tables and schemas for example)	In **role definition** go to the **SQL Privileges** tab click on **Add** select object by name, select desired SQL rights (**SELECT**, **INSERT**, and so on). Remember to give **SELECT** to `_SYS_BI` and `_SYS_REPO`, and execute to `REPOSITORY_REST`.

Object	Usage	Creation
Analytic privilege	Grant access to specific values returned by analytic models (attribute, analytic or calculation views)	In the **Quick Launch** panel under the **Analytic Privileges** tab and **Create**. Give name, description, select concerned models, select desired attribute name(s), appropriate value(s) for restriction, and activate. Remember to make sure at least one native field from the analytic view (not an included attribute view) is in the analytic privilege, and to assign to a user or to a role
System privileges	Give access to specific features of the SAP HANA system (backup, import & export, and so on)	In **role definition** go to the **System Privileges** tab, click on **Add**, select privilege from list and click on **OK**.
Package privileges	Give access to packages	In **role definition** go to the **Package Privileges** tab, click on Add, select **package**, check checkbox for rights to give, and click on **OK**.
User	Allows a person to connect to the SAP HANA Database system	In the Navigator panel go to `Security` folder, select **Users** and right-click then **Add User**. Give name, choose authentication method, and enter default password as appropriate. Assign roles and activate

8
On Another Level – Hierarchies in SAP HANA

Our SAP HANA application is at this point fairly rich. We have data in tables which we have used in attribute, analytic, and calculation views. We have authorizations defining who can see the data present in them. We're almost ready to deliver our application to our users so that they can work with the data themselves and do their own analysis.

One useful visualization option on data that users love is the notion of hierarchies. Hierarchies allow us to group objects together, and more importantly, give us subtotals along similar grouping lines. A hierarchy uses the parent-child analogy, where the child node is a logical subgroup of the parent node.

Probably the most common hierarchy that we use in our everyday life is the time hierarchy, even if we usually don't think of it in that way. If we were to look at time as a hierarchy, we could visualize it like this:

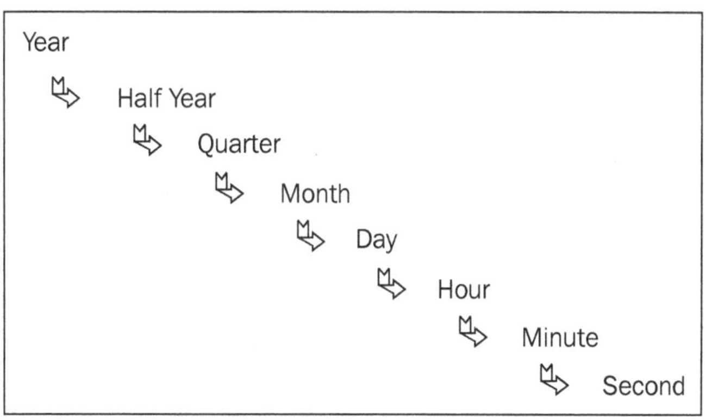

The advantage using hierarchies is the automatic aggregation of values they provide. Using the time hierarchy as shown in the preceding figure, any values for the day value of 01 January 2013 would automatically be aggregate into the total for the month of January, for the first quarter of 2013 (Q1-2013), for the half year of 1-2013, and for the year of 2013. No particular calculation is necessary on our part as developers to benefit from these automatic aggregations, and even more useful, each subtotal is dynamically calculated; it will depend on the particular data the user can see or on the data filtered at the time. It is a very useful function.

> These dynamic calculations can lead to some performance problems if you have hierarchies with hundreds of levels, to be applied to data sets with millions of lines, so usage of hierarchies should be done intelligently, according to the real needs of end users.

Hierarchy types in SAP HANA

SAP HANA can use two different types of hierarchy:

- Parent-child hierarchy
- Level hierarchy

Let's take a couple of minutes to look at these hierarchy types.

Parent-child hierarchies

A parent-child hierarchy is a simple, two-level hierarchy where the child element has an attribute containing the parent element. This hierarchy type is somewhat limited (to two levels, for example), though it does have some use in specific circumstances.

You might consider that an invoice having several lines is a parent-child hierarchy, where the invoice ID is the parent and the line item is the child, for example.

Level hierarchies

A level hierarchy, as its name suggests, does not limit the hierarchy to only two levels, making it much more flexible in terms of how many levels of data you can represent with one. You can define freely the hierarchy levels, as long as each child node has the parent node as an attribute. This allows us to create several different levels, where one node's child can be another node's parent, and so on.

To understand the notion of a parent being a child, take the following example.

If a supermarket has a list of products, such as this:

Food	Type
Cola	Soft Drink
Lemonade	Soft Drink
Chocolate	Snack Food
Crisps	Snack Food
Beer	Alcoholic Drink
Apples	Fruit

We could represent this as a simple hierarchy of food types with their associated contents:

- Soft Drink
  - Cola
  - Lemonade
- Alcoholic Drink
  - Beer
- Fruit
  - Apples
- Snack food
  - Chocolate
  - Crisps

However, the different food types are probably arranged in our supermarket into groups (usually in different aisles):

Food Type	Food Group
Soft Drink	Drinks
Alcohol	Drinks
Snack Food	Food
Fruit	Food

This in itself is a hierarchy of sorts:

- Drinks
  - Alcoholic Drink
  - Soft Drink
- Food
  - Fruit
  - Snack food

The Soft Drink category, which was the parent of Cola and Lemonade, is now itself a child, of Drinks. If we represent the full hierarchy, we can see the complete structure of our supermarket in the following figure:

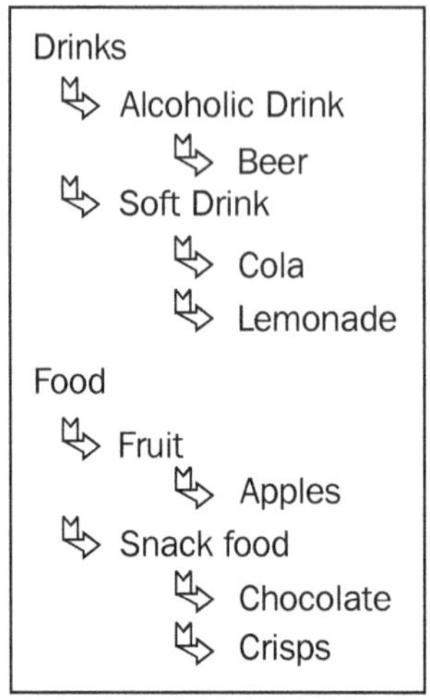

In our example, Snack Food, Fruit, Food, Soft Drink, Alcoholic Drink, and Drinks are not products, they are just grouping operators. They do not actually exist. However, they allow us to group our products and provide logical subtotal levels for our reports. This is the real power of hierarchies.

Let's look at the sales value for our products for one given day in the supermarket:

Product	Sales Value
Beer	$124
Cola	$73
Lemonade	$26
Apples	$54
Chocolate	$129
Crisps	$61

In themselves, the figures are interesting, and will allow our supermarket manager to do some analyses on his sales. However, if we represent these sales figures according to our supermarket hierarchy, we can have a much more visual, and useful view on the data:

Total				$467
↳	Drinks			$223
	↳	Alcoholic Drink		$124
		↳	Beer	$124
	↳	Soft Drink		$99
		↳	Cola	$73
		↳	Lemonade	$26
↳	Food			$224
	↳	Fruit		$54
		↳	Apples	$54
	↳	Snack food		$190
		↳	Chocolate	$129
		↳	Crisps	$61

The data is aggregated according to the hierarchy, and the system provides subtotals on the parent nodes. These in turn are aggregated into their own parent's total, and the overall total for the hierarchy is shown as well. Presenting data in this format is usually the most useful way for end users, and being able to do this naturally without any development on our part as developers is a real selling point for SAP HANA. Of course, as hinted earlier, these calculations have to be done by the backend server in SAP HANA, so don't overuse hierarchies or performance will suffer.

Creating a hierarchy in SAP HANA

SAP HANA provides us with the possibility to create hierarchies on top of several different objects. For example, if we create a hierarchy on an attribute view, we will automatically have access to the hierarchy in any analytic or calculation view we build.

> It is important to note here that it is not currently possible to use the Studio to see the results of hierarchy development. Hierarchies can only be visualized outside the Studio, in reporting software. Additionally, only reporting software which uses the MDX language to "talk" to SAP HANA can see and therefore use hierarchies. This means that reporting applications built upon SAP's BusinessObjects suite cannot currently (as of SPS5, revision 45 of SAP HANA) use hierarchies you build. If however you deploy your reporting application in Microsoft Excel or some other tool which uses MDX, you will be able to use your hierarchy. We will be looking in detail at the possibilities offered by different reporting tools in *Chapter 9, Deploying Your Reporting Application to Reporting Software*.

Please open your attribute view **CUST_ATTR** now, so that we can build a hierarchy on it.

> In case you've forgotten, an attribute view can be found on the **Navigator** panel, under your HANA system name, Content, your **Package** name (ours is called `book`), **Attribute views**, then double-click on the view name.

If you click on the **Semantics** block in the view designer, you'll see the current state of the view, as we left it a couple of chapters ago. It should look just as shown in the following screenshot:

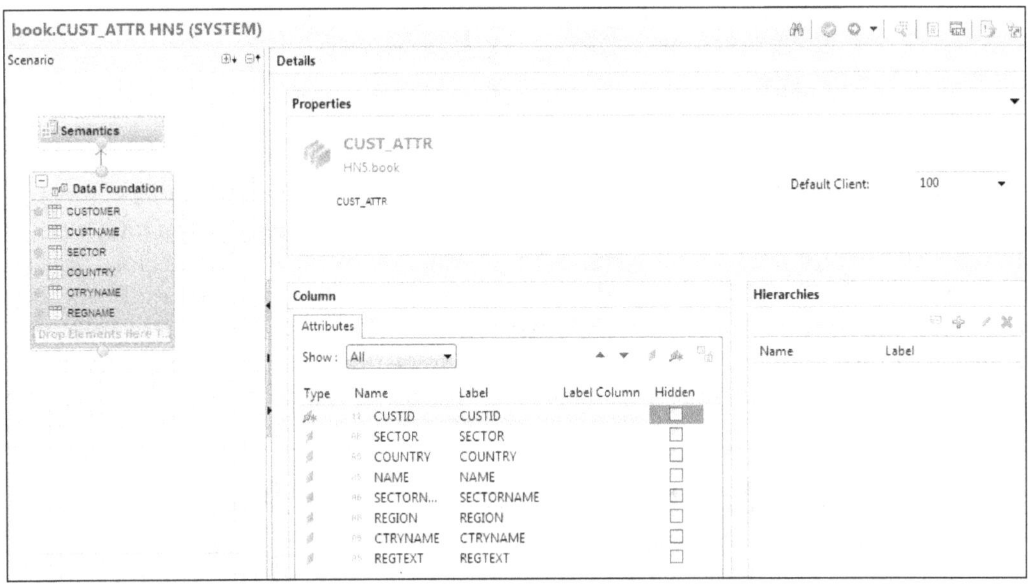

We can see the tables which make up the view (in the **Data Foundation** block on the left), as well as the final fields of these tables that the view uses (in the **Column** panel). The right hand panel is called **Hierarchies**, and it's here that we will be building our hierarchy.

The hierarchy we will be building uses three of the fields in our view:

- `REGION`: This represents basically a geographical region. In our data sample, we have data from the NAR (North America) and EU (Europe) regions.
- `COUNTRY`: As the name suggests, the country of our customer. Each country value is assigned to a region.

- `CUSTID`: The customer ID of our customer. Each customer from a country has a unique customer ID.

In the hierarchy panel of the view definition screen, click on the green plus-sign button to see the **Create New Hierarchy** dialog, shown here:

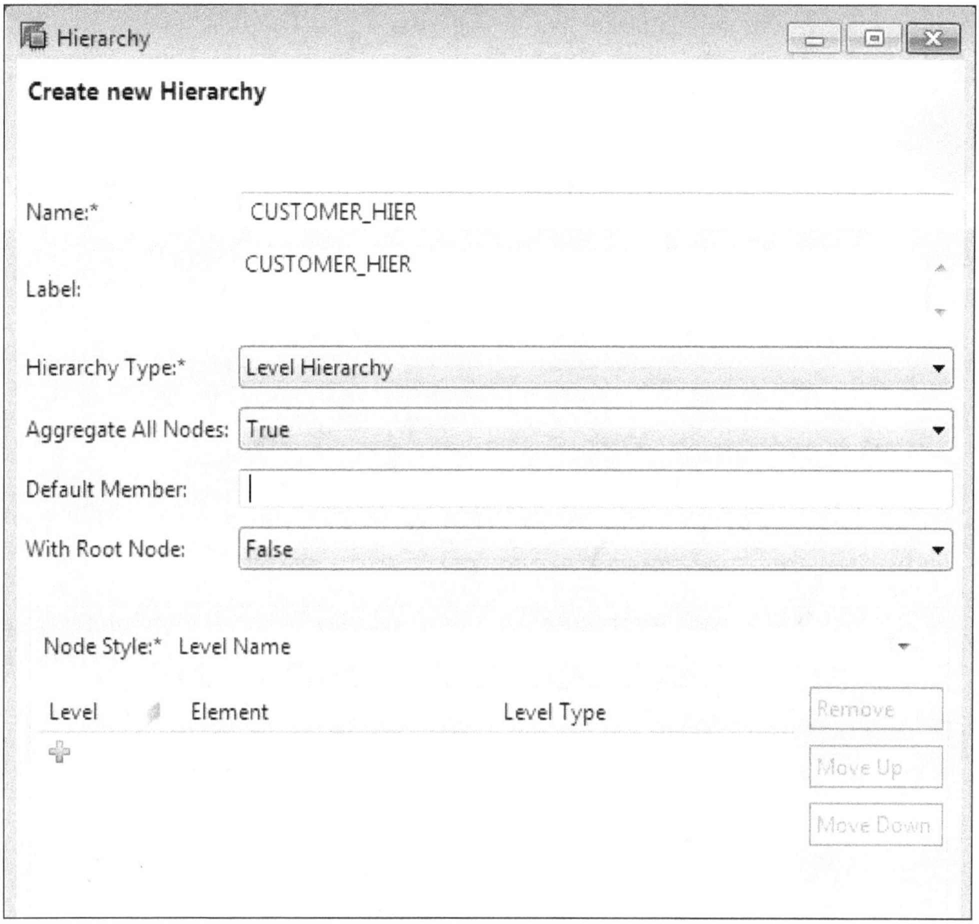

The information we need to provide when creating a hierarchy is:

- **Name**: As usual, a name meaningful to you. Names can be a combination of upper and lowercase letters, numbers, and the underscore character.
- **Label**: The description will automatically be filled in with the hierarchy name. You can enter any text you like here.

- **Hierarchy Type**: As we saw earlier, in SAP HANA, hierarchies can be either level hierarchies or parent-child hierarchies.
- **Aggregate All Nodes (True** or **False)**: This value indicates to SAP HANA whether intermediate nodes are allowed to contain values, and whether these values should be included in the total for the hierarchy or not.
    - In our supermarket example earlier in this chapter, we saw that Chocolate (sales value $129) belonged to the Snack Food category, which in turn belonged to the Food category.
    - By default, if there was only Chocolate in Snack Food, and only Snack Food in Food, then the values would aggregate simply (as we saw earlier)
    - Imagine however what would happen if Snack Food could itself hold a value. If **Aggregate All Values** was set to **True**, the aggregation would be done correctly:

Total					$181
↳	Food				$181
	↳	Snack food		($52)	$52
			↳ Chocolate ($129)		$129

    - If however, **Aggregate All Nodes** was set to **False**, then intermediate nodes would not be rolled-up into totals, only the lowest level node on the hierarchy would have its values counted, as shown in the following figure:

Total					$129
↳	Food				$129
	↳	Snack food		($52)	$129
			↳ Chocolate ($129)		$129

> As you can see, when we look at the sales volume for our supermarket along the hierarchy we have defined, we have now lost $52.
>
> Whether you set **Aggregate All Nodes** to **True** or **False** depends on your hierarchy, data, and requirements, however it is usually better to leave the value set to true, to ensure that your totals will always be correct, unless you are really certain that this is not what you want.

- **Default Member**: It tells SAP HANA (and more importantly MDX) which is the default member of the hierarchy. By default if left blank, this means "all members".
- **With Root Node**: It indicates to SAP HANA whether you wish for a root node to be created (useful if you don't have one). A root node allows you to have an overall total for your hierarchy.
- **Node Style**: The **Node Style** option indicates how each value in the hierarchy should be represented. This is purely cosmetic and depends on the preferences of your users. For our chocolate-in-a-supermarket example, the different values would give:
    - **Level Name**: [Snack Food].[Chocolate]
    - **Name Only**: Chocolate
    - **Name Path**: [Food].[Snack Food].[Chocolate]
- **Level**: Here you define the levels in your hierarchy. Levels defined on lower lines are automatically children of higher lines in the dialog. Click on the green plus-sign button to create a line, then select in the **Element** column, the appropriate field for the level you are creating. The list of available fields appears when you click on the column, as shown in the following screenshot:

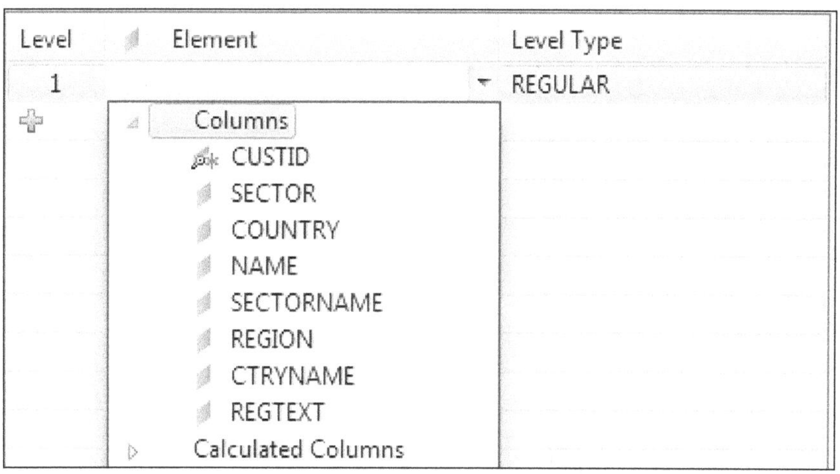

For the example we will be building, give your hierarchy a name and a description (`CUSTOMER_HIER` might be appropriate). Select **Level Hierarchy** value, and set **Aggregate All Nodes** to **True**. Keep **Default Member** blank, set **With Root Node** to **True**, set **Node Style** to **Level Name**, and the levels of `REGION`, `COUNTRY`, `CUSTID`, in that order. Your hierarchy definition dialog should look as shown ,when you have finished:

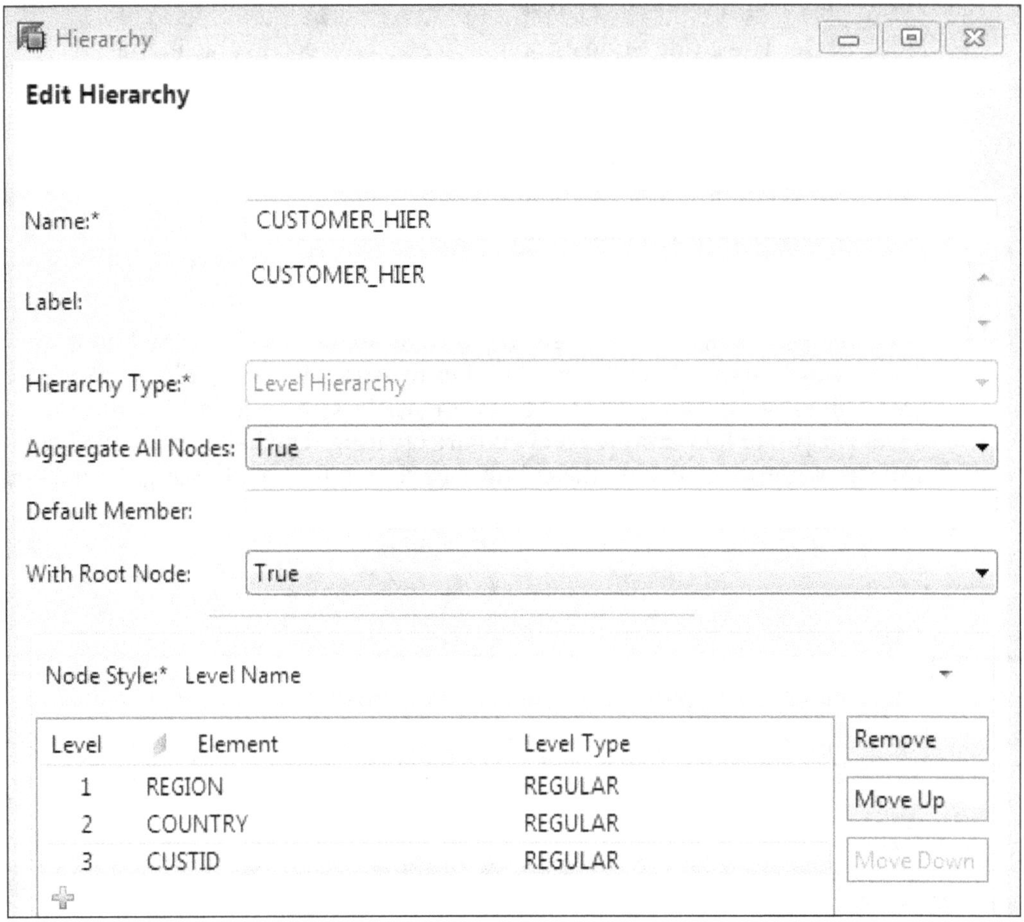

When you are ready, click on **OK** to save the hierarchy, then save and activate your attribute view.

Viewing data according to a hierarchy

As you recall, our **CUST_ATTR** attribute view is used inside our `CUST_REV` analytic view, it is the attribute view that provides all the information describing the revenue information.

> We can of course create a hierarchy at the calculation view (though not analytic view) level. This is done in the same way as for an attribute view, and will give the same results. Creating the hierarchy on the underlying attribute view however, makes it available wherever the attribute view is used, once again adhering to our philosophy of building blocks, trying to do the work only once and reusing it whenever possible.

If we now open our `CUST_REV` view in Excel using an Excel **PivotTable**, we can use our data, and the hierarchy will allow us to have automatic subtotals and grouping of data.

> As explained earlier, we cannot see the results of our hierarchy from the Studio, and as yet, we don't know how to access our views from an MDX tool, such as Excel. For that reason, no explanations on how to obtain the following results in Excel are provided here, but rest assured, we'll be learning how to reproduce the following section in the next chapter.

The PivotTable in Excel offers us, in the list of fields available for reporting, the customer hierarchy alongside the other fields in the view:

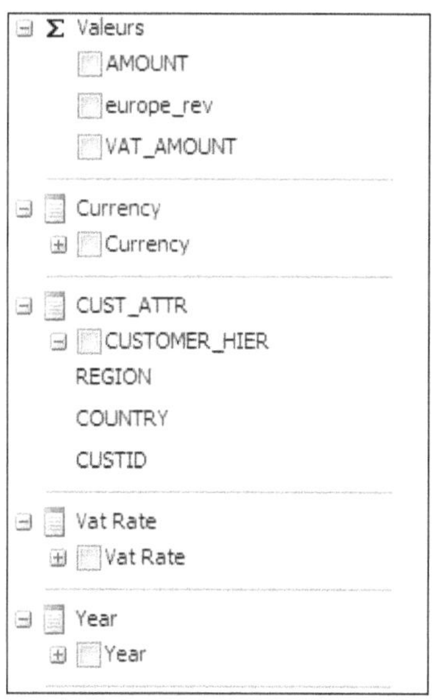

If we choose to view our data with `CUSTOMER_HIER` in the lines, and the `AMOUNT` field as a value, we obtain the following result:

Lines	AMOUNT
EU	**1113**
FR	**383**
2	383
GB	**730**
1	352
3	378
NAR	**492**
US	**492**
4	492
Total	**1605**

While this is exactly the correct result, it is not very presentable to our users, since we do not have access to the customer's `Name`, but their ID. The same is true for `Country` and `Region`. You will notice in the list of fields available for reporting, the different description fields are not available.

We can overcome this limitation by indicating, inside the Studio, which field is the description for which ID.

This is done in the definition of our **CUST_ATTR** view, in the **Semantics** block. If you open this block now, you will see that a column named **Label Column** is available in the **Column** table, as we can see here:

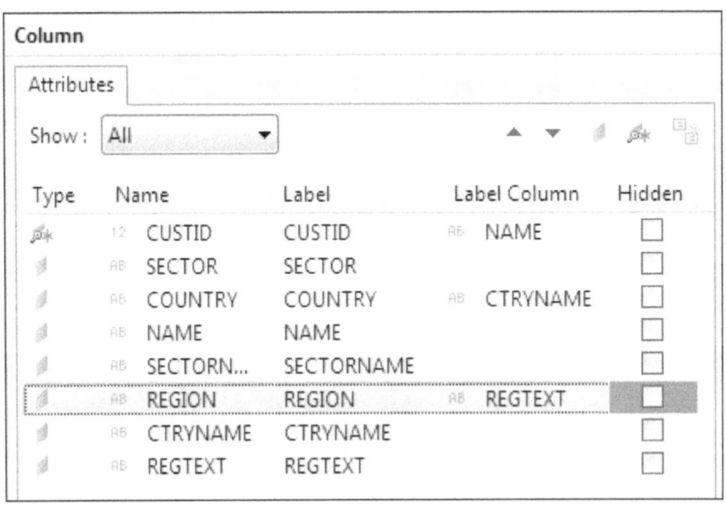

All we need to do is indicate in this column the appropriate **Label** for the corresponding ID field, to have this information made visible in Excel, and hence, make our hierarchy view a lot more useful.

To indicate the appropriate label for a given ID field, just click on the corresponding line in the table in the **Label Column** column, and select the field containing the description from the list of fields displayed.

The correct assignments for our view have been made in the previous screenshot. Once you have made these changes to your view, reactivate it, and we can see the results in Excel.

We don't need to do any further work in Excel to see the correct descriptions instead of the IDs, just refresh the PivotTable using the **Refresh** button in the ribbon:

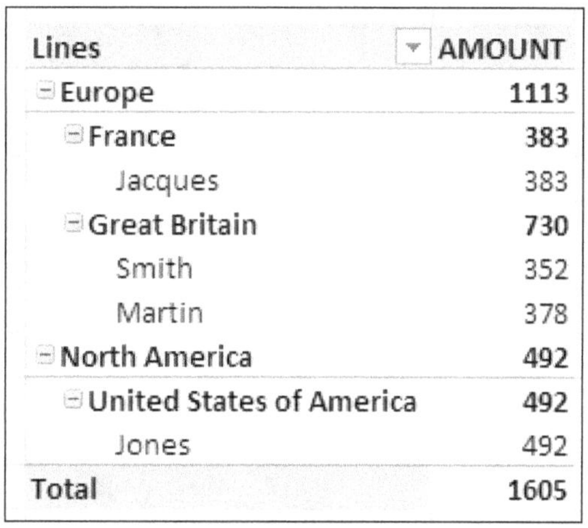

Lines	AMOUNT
Europe	1113
France	383
Jacques	383
Great Britain	730
Smith	352
Martin	378
North America	492
United States of America	492
Jones	492
Total	1605

Summary

In this chapter, we have taken a look at hierarchies, both the concepts, and how they can be used inside SAP HANA. We saw that hierarchies allow us to group data, to obtain subtotals automatically, and to perform aggregation of data.

We noted that hierarchies can only be used in reporting software, not inside the Studio, and that only reporting software using the MDX language can use them.

Finally, we examined the notion of label column, which creates a link between the ID column of an object in a view, and its description column, and how this link can be used to make our data more descriptive for our users.

In the next chapter, we'll be learning how to deploy our different views to reporting software, such as Microsoft Excel, of which we have just had a glimpse. We'll be taking a look at different reporting suites, and how the choice of software can provide different functionality to our users, even when we use the very same views for reporting.

Quick reference

Here is a quick overview of the main topics covered in this chapter.

Object	Usage	Creation
Hierarchy	Allows aggregation of data on levels defined according to enterprise structure.	In the attribute view: navigate to **Semantics** | **Hierarchies** | click on plus-sign. In graphical calculation view: in the **Output** dialog right-click on **Hierarchies** and **Create**. Enter **Name** and **Description**, choose type, and define levels.

9

Deploying Your Reporting Application to Reporting Software

So far in this book you have made the developments yourself as you've been going along, now you will have a reporting application which can be considered as finished. We've taken the data from our tables, and via different modeling views, have processed it for use. Authorizations are ready to handle different levels of data visualization, and we have hierarchies ready to display the data in a useful way.

It's now time for us to give our development to our users; our work as developers is done.

In this chapter we'll be taking a look at what we need to do to allow users access to our SAP HANA system, as well as some reporting tools we can use to visualize our data.

Getting software to talk to SAP HANA

In order to allow software to talk to SAP HANA and extract data from the system, a database driver is needed. A driver permits two things:

- Connection to the database using a given protocol
- Querying the database using a specific language

A connection protocol is the tool used to allow two pieces of software to talk to each other. It is basically a common language that SAP HANA and the reporting software use. SAP HANA includes some native drivers developed by SAP, and can also understand some more generic languages.

> Where possible, it is usually best to use a native driver provided by SAP to connect to your HANA system. Think of the communication protocols as languages humans speak. A German and a Hungarian might be able to communicate by both speaking English, but two Germans speaking their native language communicate much better and more efficiently. With SAP HANA it's the same; communication using a generic protocol will work, but won't be as optimized as a native protocol can be.

We've actually been using client software to work with our SAP HANA instance for a while already, the SAP HANA Studio is client software (and we, as developers, are the clients in this particular case). As you recall, the Studio is written in Java, and it communicates with the server using the Java Database Connectivity (JDBC).

The database protocols understood by SAP HANA are (currently):

- **ODBC**: Open Database Connectivity is a Microsoft developed protocol very popular in the Unix world. This is the most generic database connection protocol, understood by just about all databases and nearly all reporting software tools. The ODBC protocol uses a database-specific driver to convert ODBC instructions into a format the database understands. As such, it allows just about everything to talk to SAP HANA. However, this double-translation and being so generic means that the protocol knows nothing about SAP HANA at all, and is likely to be the least performant way of communicating with HANA.
- **JDBC**: Java Database Connectivity. This is also a generic database connection protocol, developed to allow any Java program to connect to and extract data from databases. Originally developed by Sun Microsystems, this protocol is now developed by the Java community effort.
- **ODBO**: OLE DB for OLAP (Object Linking and Embedding, Database for Online Analytical Processing). This protocol, developed and promoted by Microsoft, is designed to allow multidimensional reporting, such as accessing a cube rather than a table. In SAP HANA, this means accessing analytic and calculation views, rather than the base tables.

- **QaaWS**: Query as a WebService, a tool, and protocol developed by SAP for use with their BusinessObjects suite. Using a client-side tool to develop queries and then publish them as web services means that these queries can be consumed by any tool capable of using web services. This protocol is heavily used by SAP BusinessObjects dashboards (formerly known as Xcelsius) and Crystal reports.
- **BIWS**: Business Intelligence Web Services, a refinement of QaaWS, allowing either retrieval of the full query result, or only a subset (useful for drill down)
- **BICS**: Business Intelligence Consumer Services. A proprietary protocol developed by SAP to use with their BW and Business Objects software. BICS is designed to improve on and optimize communications, compared to the ODBO protocol.

Once the connection has been made to the database, the different query languages understood by SAP HANA are:

- **SQL**: Structured Query Language is the basic query language used by about every relational database. Originally developed in the 1970s by IBM. Used to manipulate and query tables.
- **MDX**: MultiDimensional eXpressions a Microsoft developed language, introduced in 1997 alongside the ODBO specification. Software which 'uses MDX' usually connects to the database using ODBO, and vice versa. Used to query multidimensional data models, such as analytic and calculation views via SAP HANA's OLAP processor.
- **BICS**: As we saw earlier, BICS is a connection protocol developed by SAP, and whose specification has not been made available for use by third parties. BICS is also the language used to extract data from the SAP BW or SAP HANA system using the native OLAP processing engines. The OLAP engine gives access to the multidimensional data models, and is solicited by BICS in the same way as by MDX.

Over the next couple of sections we'll take a look at some different ways of accessing SAP HANA data using various reporting tools, and see what each has to offer.

> This chapter is not a fully blown training for the different tools presented; it aims to give an overview of some tools which can be used to access SAP HANA, and the advantages and disadvantages of each.
>
> Furthermore, the list of tools is not exhaustive. There are many more reporting suites on the market, at different price levels and with different sets of functionality. Feel free to use any given tool to access your data in SAP HANA; any tool capable of using one of the database protocols and languages listed above should be able to work with SAP HANA, even if the tool has not been certified for use with the system.

SAP Lumira

One of the easiest reporting tools used to connect to SAP HANA and analyze data is SAP's Lumira tool. It allows ad hoc analysis of data, without any particular formatting. If you require rapid data analysis along different axes but don't require production of formatted reports (for distribution or presentation, for example) then Lumira is the ideal tool for the job.

> Lumira is a tool which used to be called Visual Intelligence. On the `sap.com` website, and in the software, the term Visual Intelligence still appears at times. Don't be surprised if you see the product being referred to as Visual Intelligence and not Lumira.

Downloading and installing

A trial version of Lumira, valid for 30 days, can be downloaded from the `sap.com` website at `https://www.sap.com/campaign/ne/free_trial/visual_intelligence/index.epx`.

As you can see in the following screenshot, two different versions of the software are available; **32-bit** and **64-bit**. The version you need to download depends on the version of Windows you are running:

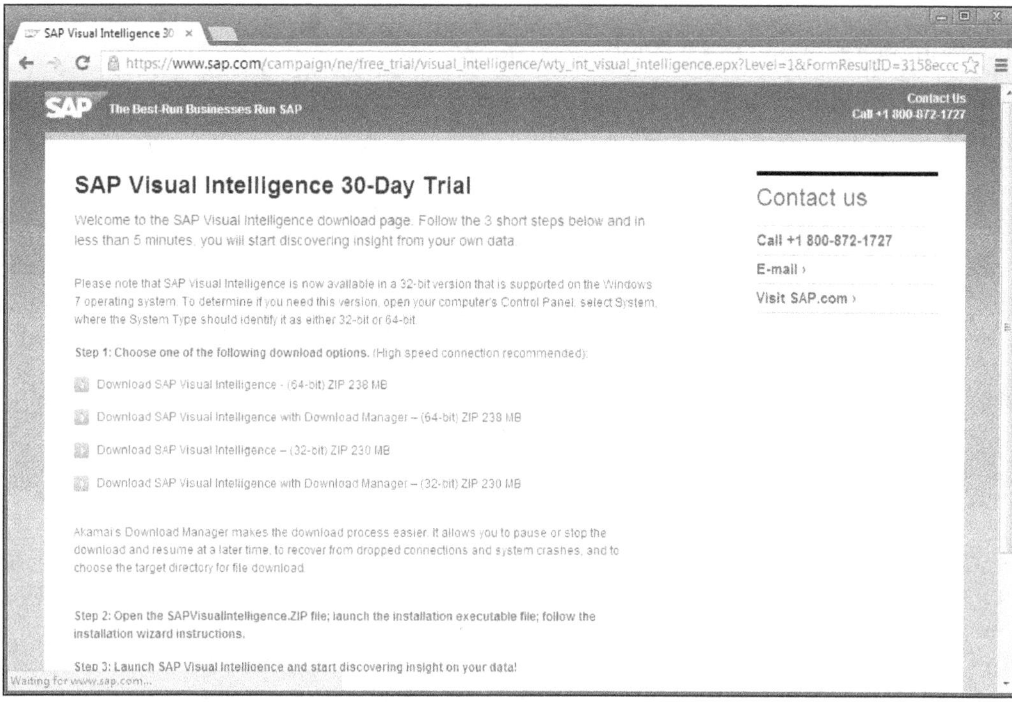

Install the product by following the instructions in the installer. The only information you will need to provide is the installation path.

> The installer will refuse to run if your Windows version does not correspond to the version of Lumira you have downloaded.

Upon running the software for the first time, you will see the evaluation code dialog, shown in the following screenshot:

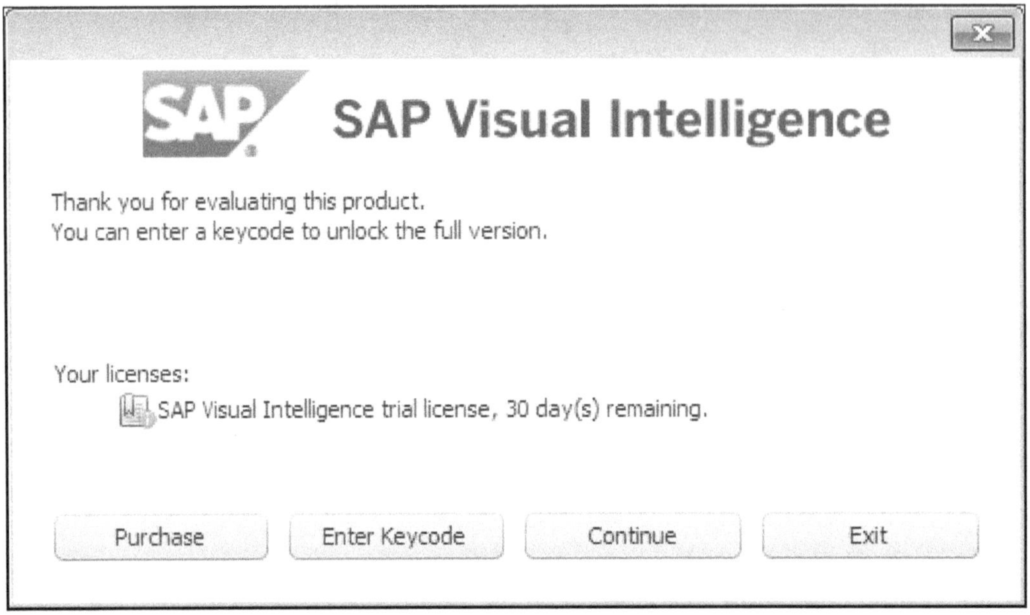

To try out Lumira, just click on the **Continue** button, and benefit from a 30-day trial of the software.

Connecting to SAP HANA

At the main Lumira screen, click on the **New Document** button at the top-left corner of the window to create a connection to a data source, using the **New Document** dialog you can see here:

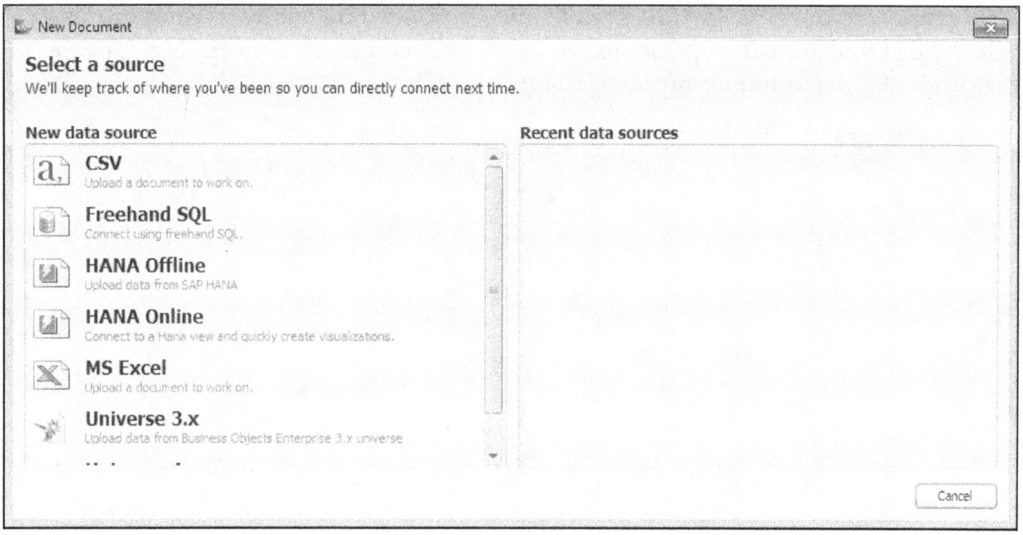

This dialog allows connection to various data sources, not just SAP HANA. The principal data sources are, of course, SAP products, notably HANA, and BusinessObjects. You can also use **Excel** files, **CSV** (text) files, or use the **Freehand SQL** option to connect to an SQL database such as Microsoft's SQL server.

Connection to SAP HANA can be done in two ways:

- **HANA Online**: Connect to your SAP HANA server using a live connection, and "slice and dice" your data as you wish. Your network connection must always be available, and the data is retrieved from the server as you request it. This is the simplest option, and the one you will probably use most while in the office.
- **HANA Offline**: Connect to your SAP HANA server only once when the connection is created, and download all the data in the relative view to the PC running Lumira. This allows for the network connection to be severed as no further communication with the server is necessary to do data analysis. This is a useful option for meetings with no network access, or for demonstrations. Note that however the data volume could be potentially huge, so care must be taken when using this option.

Let's connect to our SAP HANA system and do some data analysis using Lumira. Select the **HANA Online** option, to see the **New Document from HANA Online** dialog shown in the following screenshot:

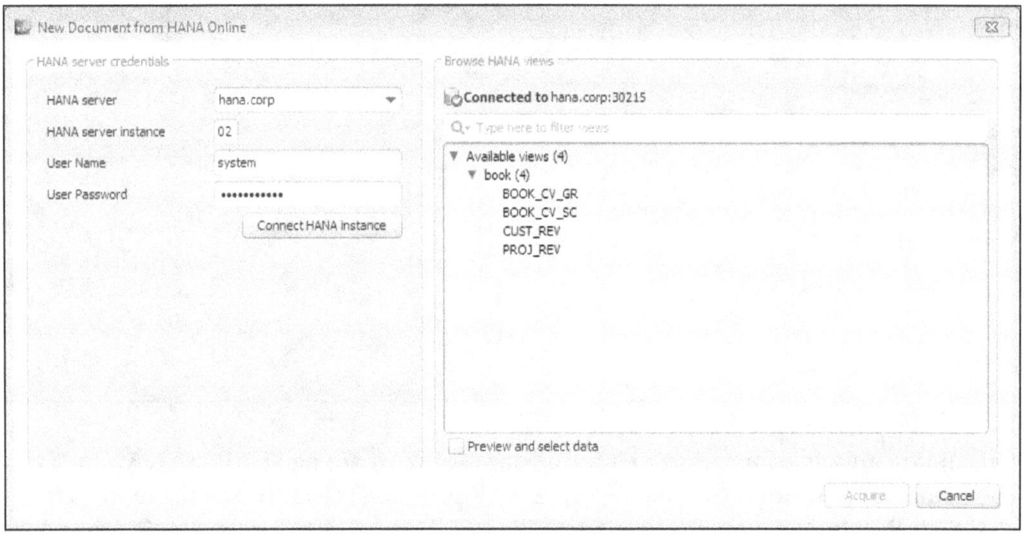

On the left is a pane requesting the server credentials. These are the same as those you gave when configuring the Studio right back at the start of the book. When you have entered the server address, instance number, and your **User Name** and **User Password**, click on **Connect HANA instance** to see the list of available views in the right-hand pane.

As you can see in the screenshot, we have access to our two analytic views and two calculation views. Our attribute view we created is not listed as it does not contain data as such (there are no measures in an attribute view).

Analyzing data with Lumira

Select `BOOK_CV_GR` (our graphical calculation view) and then click on **Acquire** to start data analysis on the view.

As you might recall, we have in our calculation view a user input variable called `PERCENTAGE` which asks our user for an estimated revenue increase in percent. The first thing that Lumira asks from us is that we fill this variable, by presenting us with the **Hana Variables** dialog, shown here:

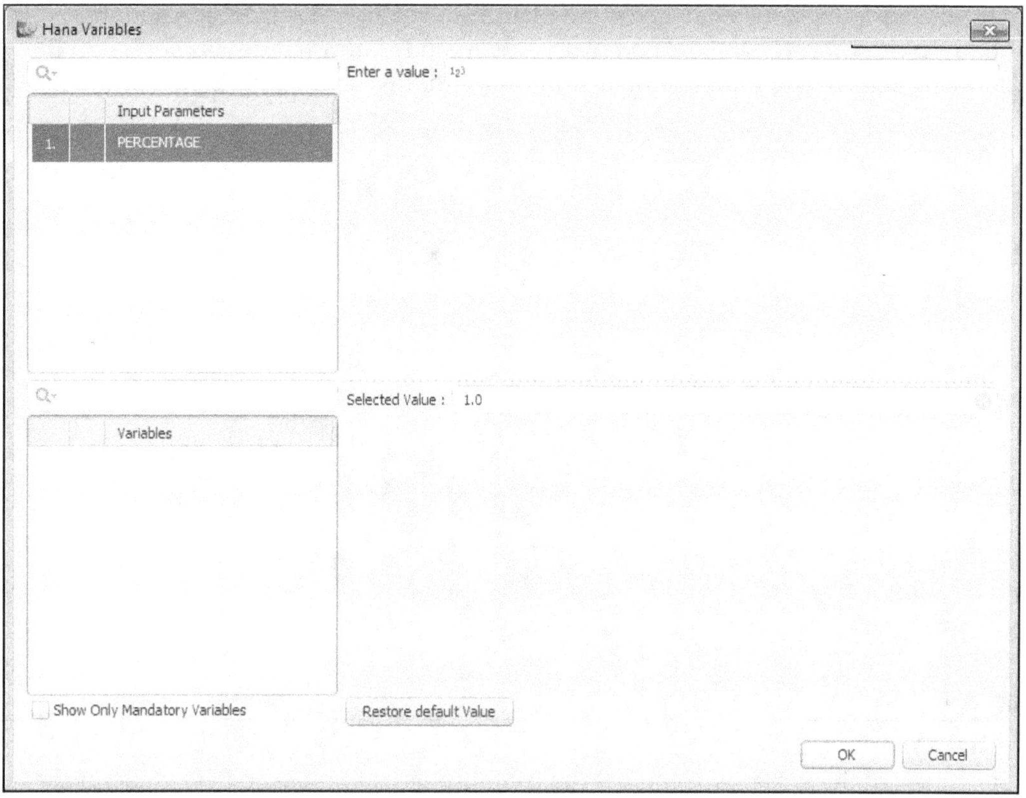

This dialog lists the variables in the view we request, and prompts us for a value for each of them. As you can see in the screenshot, we need to enter a value for our `PERCENTAGE` variable, and the system proposes the default value we defined, 1 percent.

Once the variable values have been filled and we've clicked on **OK** to validate them, we can proceed with our analysis. The main Lumira window is shown in the following screenshot, and it is via this interface that we can manipulate our data:

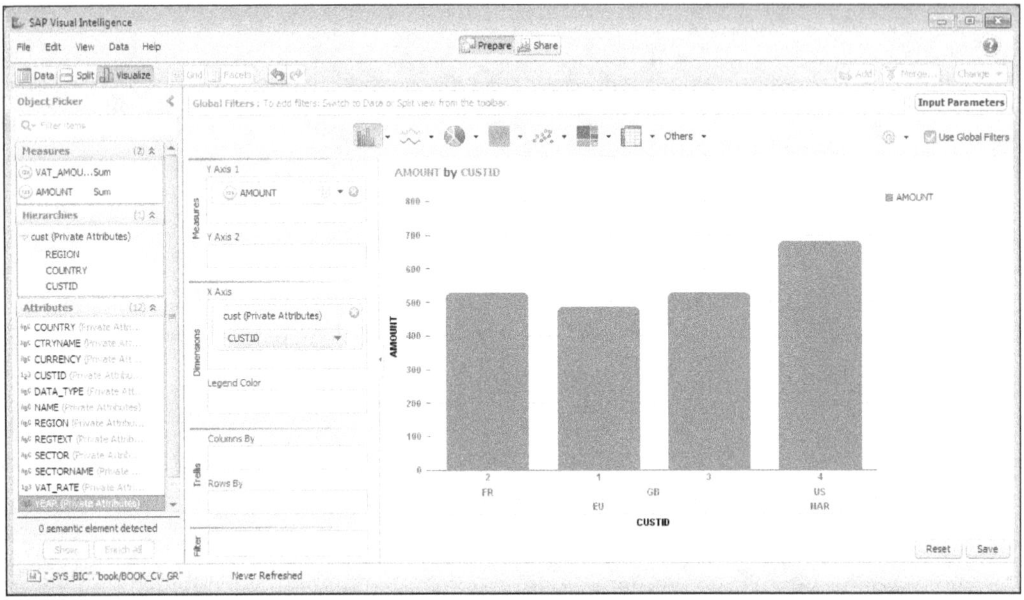

On the left of the screen, we can see the list of fields in the selected view and at the top, the list of **Measures** available, followed by any visible **Hierarchies** (here we can see our **cust** hierarchy created in the previous chapter), followed by the remaining fields in the view.

The remainder of the window is given over to the analysis currently being done. The main part of the window on the right is the graphical representation of the data, and on the left of this (the second column in the screenshot), we can see the fields being used.

Visualizing data is done simply; just drag at least one measure to either the X or Y axis of the graph as you prefer to see the value this measure represents. Then by dragging attributes or hierarchies to the other axis, you will see this value decomposed.

In our screenshot, you can see that the AMOUNT measure is being viewed on the Y axis. On the X axis, the **cust** hierarchy is used to see the decomposition of this value, down to the CUSTID level, which is the lowest, most fine-grained level of the hierarchy.

Visualization options and formatting concerns

Along the top of the screen in the previous screenshot we can see a series of pictogram buttons representing different types of graphs. These can be used to change the display of the data we have requested, and operate in real-time; clicking on a different representation type will change the output immediately. This makes Lumira a very flexible product, ideal in the hands of key users who need to make quick, dynamic analyses of data.

One thing that Lumira cannot do however is produce a formatted report on your data. The tool is just not designed for that requirement. If you need formatted reports, then you will need a different tool (and probably lose the dynamic data analysis features in the process). Some other tools which might fit the bill are SAP's crystal reports (you can get a free trial at `http://www54.sap.com/solutions/sme/software/free-trials.html`) or MicroStrategy (their reporting software can be downloaded for free at `http://www.microstrategy.com/freereportingsoftware/`). Both of these tools can connect to SAP HANA and both are very powerful reporting tools.

Microsoft Excel®

One of the most common pieces of reporting software in use today is Microsoft Excel. This is true in just about every company, whether they have a BI suite or not. Ask any financial controller which tool they prefer to use and their answer will nearly always be Excel, just because it allows not only to visualize data, but to do rapid simulations on that data as well, all in a familiar interface.

Excel can be used to connect to SAP HANA, as we saw in the previous chapter. Using Excel to interact with data in your SAP HANA system means that whenever you open your Excel file, you can update the data and it will always be fresh.

Connecting to Excel requires that the SAP HANA driver for Excel be installed on the PC. This will need to be done on every PC which will connect to SAP HANA, and so in general will be done by your IT department.

Installing the SAP HANA client for Excel

The client software for Excel can be found in the SAP Service Marketplace Download Center (SWDC) by following this path:

Go to `http://service.sap.com/swdc` and navigate to **Support Packages and Patches** | **A - Z Index** | **H** | **SAP HANA Platform Edition** | **SAP HANA Platform Edit. 1.0** | **Support Package Stack Download** | **Next Step** | Open **SAP HANA Client for Microsoft Excel 1.00** | Tick the appropriate version | **Next Step** | **Add to Download Basket**.

You can then download the Excel client using the SAP Download Manager application, and can extract the installation media using the SAPCAR tool, available on the SWDC site (visit `http://service.sap.com/swdc` and navigate to **Support Packages and Patches** | **A - Z Index** | **S** | **SAPCAR** | **SAPCAR 7.2** | **Windows server on IA32 32bit** | Click on the `SAPCAR.exe` file whose name will appear at the bottom of the window). Once the SAPCAR file and the client SAR file have been downloaded, copy them both to a suitable directory (your desktop maybe), and then from a command-line window type the following command to extract the archive:

```
Sapcar.exe -xvf IMDB_CLIENT.SAR
```

Replace `SAPCAR.exe` with the name of the SAPCAR file you downloaded, and `IMDB_CLIENT.SAR` with the full filename of the client software archive.

You will need to download the appropriate client software for your version of Excel. Check the Excel version installed on your machine before downloading and installing, as it's the version of Excel which is important, no matter the version of Windows you use. If you have a 64-bit edition of Windows, you may still have a 32-bit edition of Excel.

Check your Excel version using the menu entry **File** and go to **Help**. The Excel edition is listed on the right of the screen, as shown here:

In this screenshot we can see that we have a 32-bit edition of Excel, so we need to download the 32-bit client software.

Once the client software has been downloaded, you can install it by running the installer and following the onscreen instructions. The installer will ask only that you specify the destination folder for the software on your PC.

Connecting to SAP HANA using Excel

After installing the client software, you can connect to your SAP HANA instance using Excel.

Open up Excel, and create a new file. Now go to the **Data** tab, and then select **From Other Sources, From Data Connection Wizard**, as shown here:

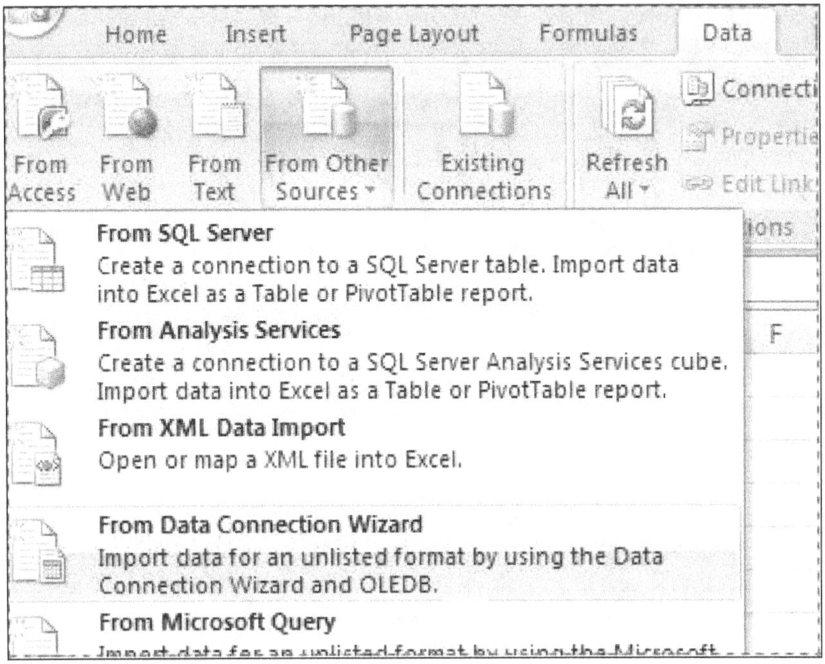

The **Data Connection Wizard** dialog box, shown in the following screenshot, will open:

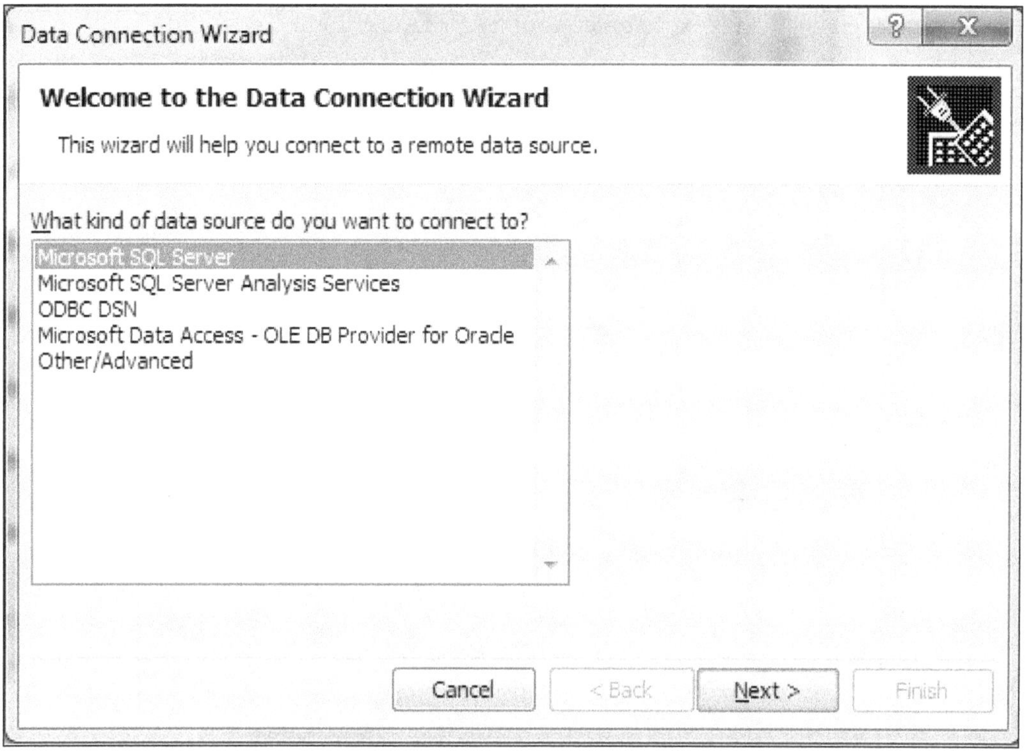

Select the last entry in the list, **Other/Advanced** to see the full list of data source types; the connection to SAP HANA will be listed as **SAP HANA MDX Provider**. Select this option, and then click on **Next** to enter your SAP HANA login credentials:

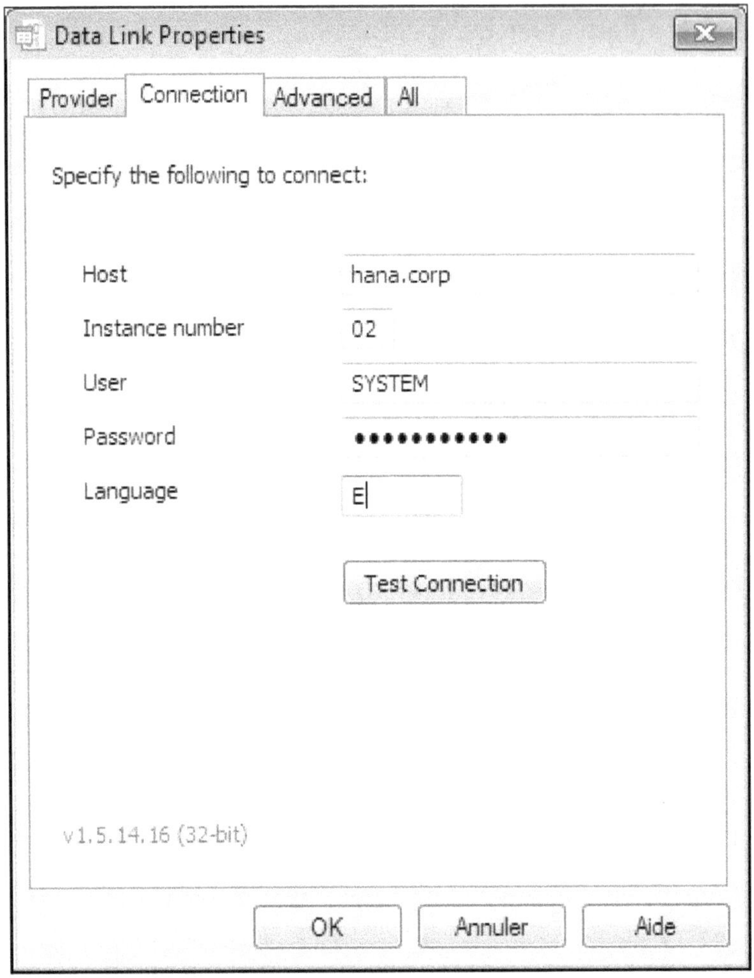

Use the **Test Connection** button to check your login info if you wish; this is not required but helps detect at least that you can connect to the SAP HANA server and your login information is correct. It can be useful if you have data retrieval problems later.

If the connection test worked, or if you decide not to do a connection test, you can click on **OK** to see a list of available views in your SAP HANA instance:

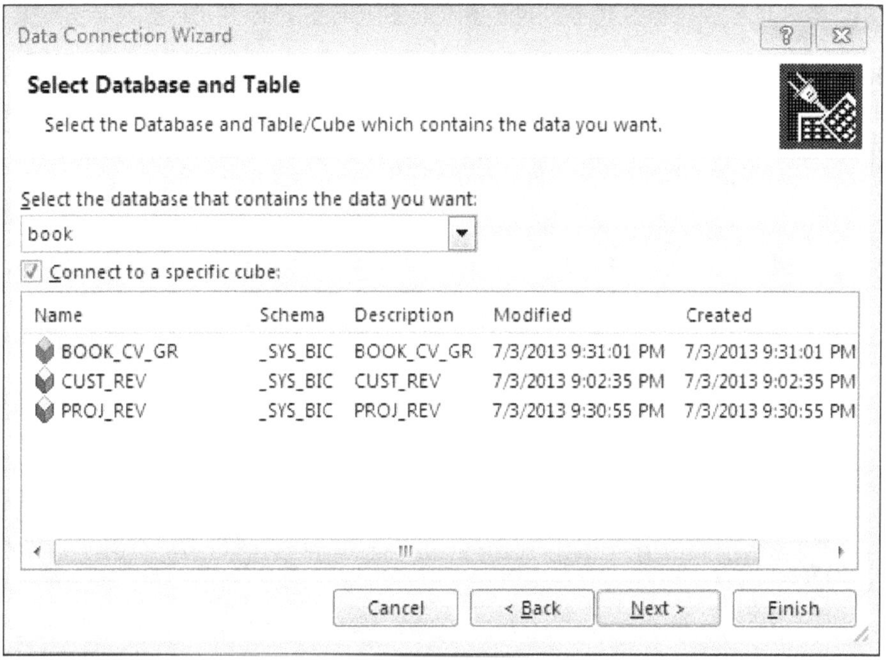

The list of views (termed CUBES here by Excel) is the same as that provided by Lumira earlier; only analytic and calculation views are listed, not attribute views.

Select the BOOK_CV_GR view in order to do data analysis on the information it contains.

> You will be asked whether you wish to save the login password in the Excel file you use to connect to SAP HANA. This is a potential security risk if other people can use your PC, so don't check this checkbox unless you are sure.

Click on **Finish** to add the connection to SAP HANA to your Excel file, and Excel will ask where you want to add the PivotTable in the file. All data from SAP HANA is presented as a PivotTable, and you'll need to specify the top-left corner of the table. You can usually leave this option at its default, and just click on **OK** to start working with your SAP HANA data in Excel.

> If you chose not to save the password to the connection in the Excel file, you will be asked once again to log in to your SAP HANA instance; this is normal.

You will be presented with your Excel sheet containing a PivotTable with your data from SAP HANA. In our case, this will be the data from the graphical calculation view we created back in *Chapter 5, Let's Get Graphical – Graphical Calculation Views*. Your Excel file should look as shown in the following screenshot:

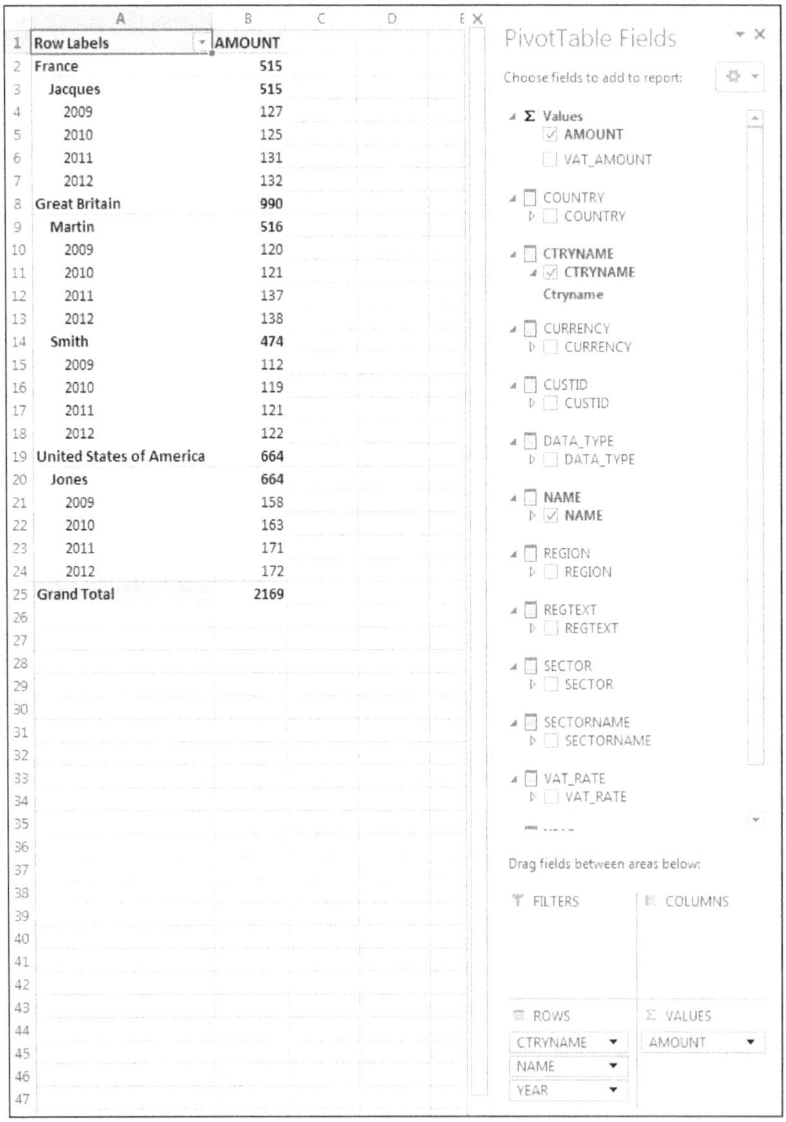

In order to add fields to your PivotTable report, either check the checkbox next to their name, or drag them to the **Lines**, **Columns**, **Filter**, or **Values** box. The PivotTable here is showing the `AMOUNT` measure, according to the `Ctryname`, `Name`, and `Year` fields. The different options available allow you to select data according to your needs from the view, filtering it and arranging the fields as you require. Once you have the required data in your Excel file, you can use Excel's formatting options to present it however you like (maybe using lookup functions such as `VLOOKUP()` in Excel to rearrange the layout).

Using Excel as a data presentation tool is a relatively powerful and cost-efficient way of giving your users free reign on their data presentation needs; once the initial development of the modeling views has been done in the Studio, your users can access the data, arrange it, and present it as they need.

Furthermore, since Excel is a nearly ubiquitous tool, the chances are that it is already installed (so no further licenses are required) and your users are already familiar with it (so no particular training is needed). Since users work with Excel all the time, they are much more likely to be autonomous using it as a reporting tool (needing much less time from IT support).

Tableau software

One interesting data analysis tool, similar to SAP's Visual Intelligence product, is Tableau. Tableau is a data visualization and dashboard generation tool; like Visual Intelligence, you can use it to analyse data rapidly. You can however use your data analyses in dashboards, making Tableau an interesting choice, especially for fast prototyping needs.

Tableau is a commercial product, costing upwards of one thousand dollars. A free 14-day trial version of the software can be downloaded from the Tableau software website at `http://www.tableausoftware.com/products/trial`.

After downloading the software, install it using the installer (just follow the prompts and select a destination folder for installation, no other information is necessary).

When the program has installed, run it and on the first screen select the **Connect to data** option at the top-left of the window to select a data source:

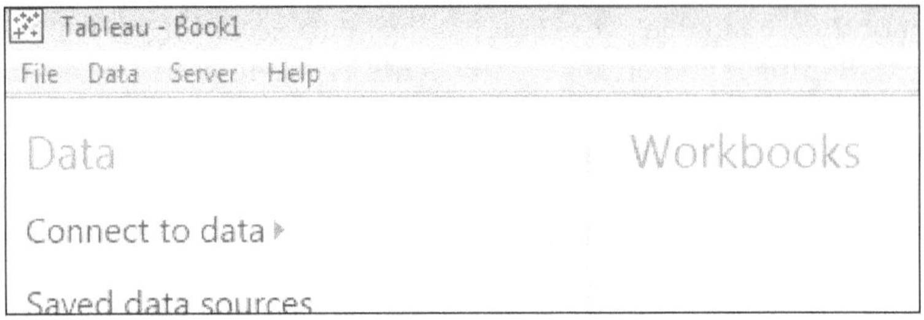

You will be presented with a list of data source types. You can use two of these to connect to your SAP HANA server, either the SAP HANA option, or the last option in the list, **Other Databases (ODBC)**.

Installing the SAP HANA client driver

In order to use either of the connection options available in Tableau, a SAP HANA driver needs to be installed, in much the same way as a driver was necessary for connection via Excel.

In this case, however, the driver needed is the SAP HANA Client 1.0, which you can download from the Sap Service Marketplace at `http://service.sap.com/swdc` and navigate to **Support Packages and Patches** | **A - Z Index** | **H** | **SAP HANA Platform Edition** | **SAP HANA Platform Edit. 1.0** | **Support Package Stack Download** | **Next Step** | Open **SAP HANA Client 1.0** | Tick **Windows Server on IA32 32bit** | **Next Step** | **Add to Download Basket**.

Even if you have a 64-bit version of Windows, Tableau requires the 32-bit version of the driver to be installed, since Tableau is a 32-bit program.

You will need to extract the client driver archive file using the `sapcar` tool, as explained earlier in the section concerning Microsoft Excel.

Once you have downloaded and extracted the client software, you can install it by running the `hdbsetup` tool in the extraction folder. This installer requires only that you specify a destination directory for the program, as you can see here:

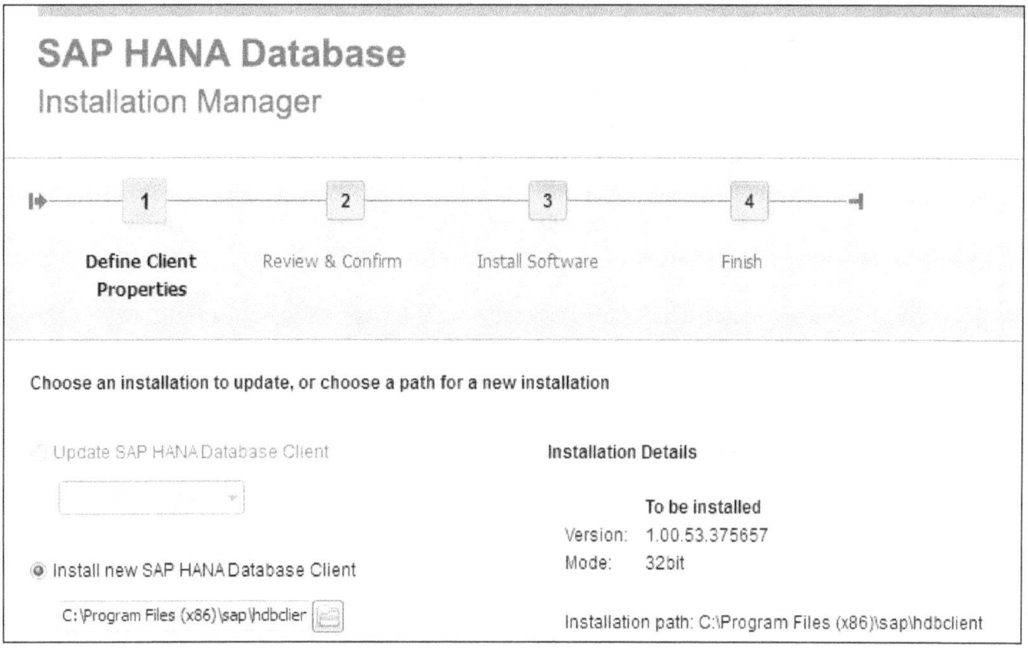

Just follow the prompts to install the driver. It only takes a couple of minutes.

After installation, you will not see any new programs on your PC; no start menu group will have been created, and no new icons will be sitting on your desktop, but the driver is installed, and ready for use.

Creating an ODBC DSN in Windows

Now that the SAP HANA client is installed, we will use it to configure a connection in Windows. This is called DSN: a data source same. This DSN will let us use our connection in any tool capable of using the ODBC protocol.

Windows offers a control panel applet to use to configure ODBC connections; you can find it by going to **Control Panel** | **Administrative Tools** | **ODBC Data Source Administrator**.

> As we explained earlier, Tableau is a 32-bit program, and as such, if you have a 64-bit edition of Windows, you will need to use the 32-bit ODBC configuration tool to create your DSN. Unfortunately, the 32-bit ODBC configuration does not have a handy icon to call it up, so you'll need to run it from the Windows directory if this is your case.
>
> The 32-bit ODBC configuration is called `odbcad32`, and can be found in the `c:\Windows\SysWOW64` directory. You can see the file to run in the following screenshot:
>
> 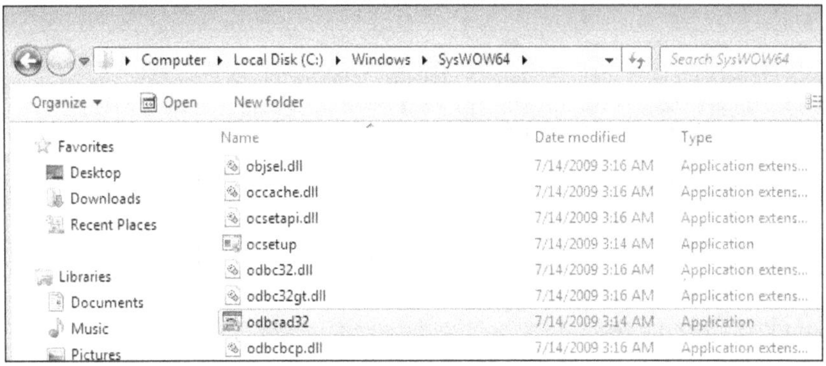
>

Using the ODBC configuration tool is relatively simple. On the main screen, switch to the **System DSN** tab, and click on the **Add** button, to see the list of drivers installed on your machine. The SAP HANA driver is called `HDBODBC32`, as you can see here:

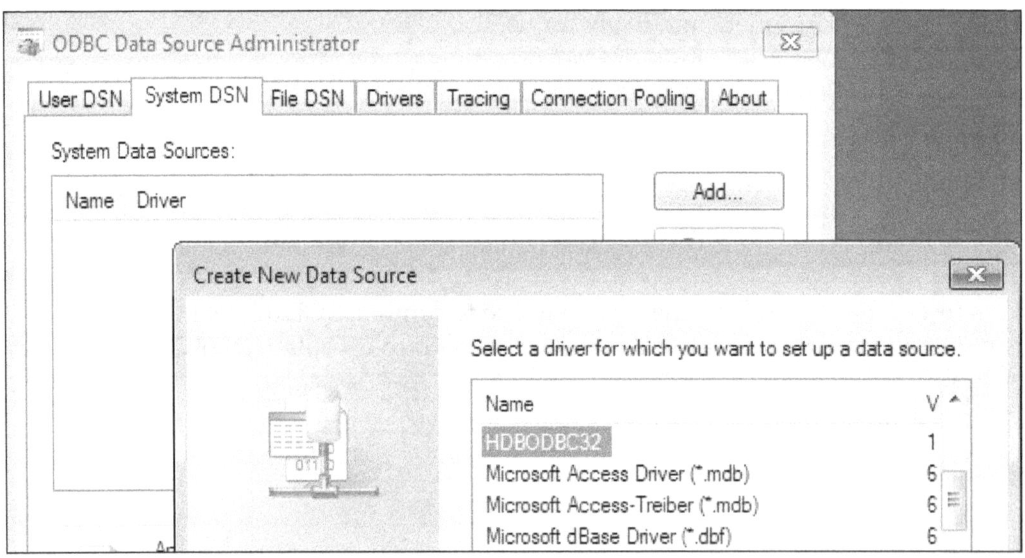

Click on **Finish** to select the driver and enter the connection information in the pop-up window which will appear. This is the same connection information we've been using throughout the book, and it consists of the server address, port, and your login information. You can see the connection information dialogs here:

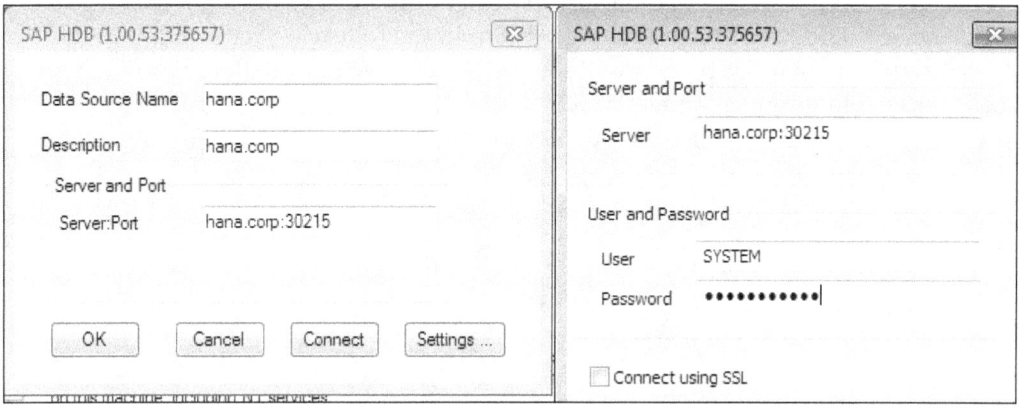

You are first asked for **Data Source Name**. This information is very important, as it's what you will use in your different tools connecting to SAP HANA. In our example, we've used the SAP HANA server name, `hana.corp`.

The format you will need to use to enter the address information is **Server:Port**, where server is the server address, and port is the SAP HANA instance number, surrounded by 3 and 15. In the preceding screenshot, our SAP HANA instance number is `02`, giving a port value of `30215`.

Use the **Connect** button to pass from the first dialog (server name and address) to the second (login information).

When your connection information is entered correctly, click on **OK** to close the dialogs. At this point you can close the ODBC configuration tool, and return to Tableau.

Connecting to SAP HANA using Tableau

Now that we have an ODBC connection ready for use, we can use it to analyze our data in SAP HANA using Tableau.

From the Tableau **Connect to data** screen, select **Other Databases (ODBC)** to see the **Generic ODBC connection** dialog, shown in the following screenshot. In the dropdown list next to **DSN**, you will see the DSN we've just created. Select it, and click **Connect** to use it to connect to SAP HANA. You will need to specify (once more) your username and password, as you can see in the screenshot:

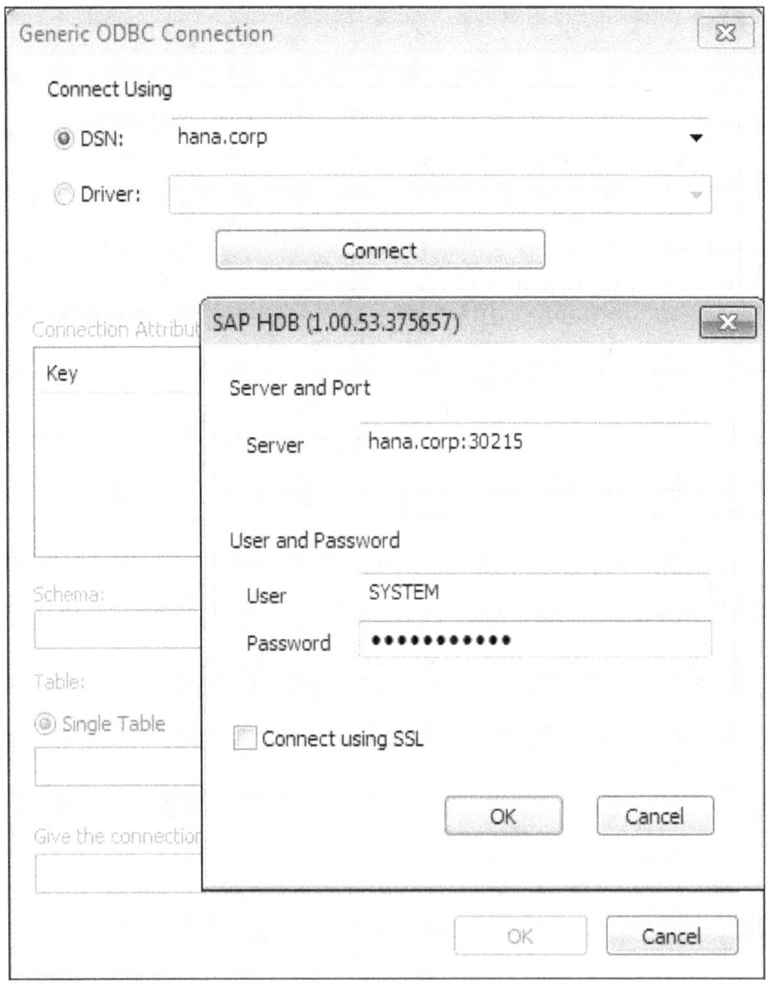

Click on **OK** to make the connection to SAP HANA.

The next information we need to provide is the database schema, in the **Schema** list. You might be tempted to select the `BOOK` schema, as this is where our tables are located, however in order to use our different views, we need to select the `_SYS_BIC` schema instead.

If therefore you select the `_SYS_BIC` schema, and then request the list of available tables in the **Single Table** list (in Tableau, our views are considered to be tables, unlike in Excel where they are cubes), you will see all of our developments, as you can see here:

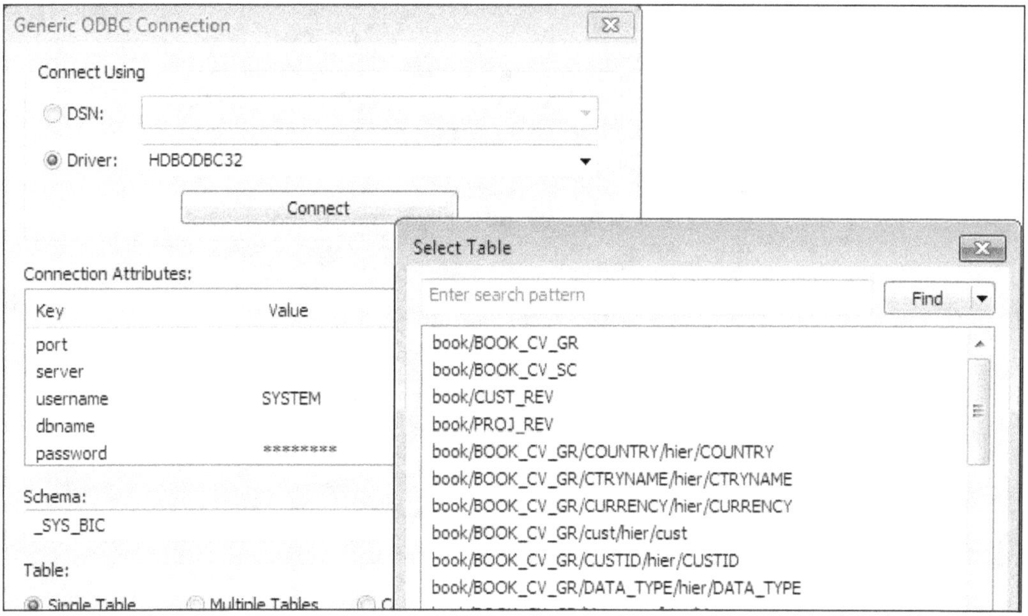

Let's use our graphical calculation view `BOOK_CV_GR` as a data source. Select it from the list, and click on **OK** to use it in Tableau. Dismiss the **Create an extract** popup (which is just a best practice notification for Tableau), and then select **Connect Live** to connect to SAP HANA.

You will receive the main Tableau report designer screen, and the different fields available for use will be those in your SAP HANA view. As with other tools we have seen before (including the Studio), just drag the different fields to the part of the report you wish to use. In the following screenshot, we have done a simple analysis of `AMOUNT` by `CTRYNAME`, customer `NAME`, and `YEAR`, in much the same way we did using Excel.

> It is important to note that we were not prompted for a value for our `PERCENTAGE` variable. Tableau does not understand SAP HANA variables at this point, so the default value (1 percent) was used automatically.

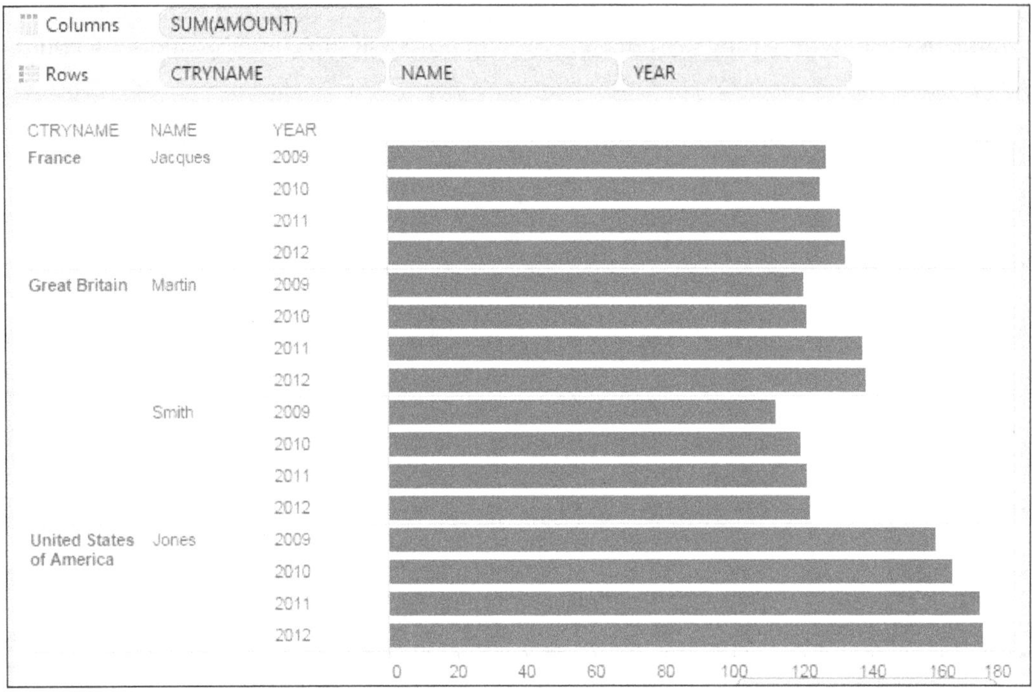

At this point, we have created a simple data visualization chart using Tableau, in much the same way we did using Excel or Lumira. Tableau however, allows us to use this visualization in a dashboard, which is a formatted display of the data.

Navigate to **Dashboard** | **New Dashboard** from the menu to create a new dashboard in Tableau. Your visualization will be listed at the top-left of the screen as `Sheet1`. Drag this to the right-hand part of the screen to use it in your dashboard, as you can see in the following screenshot:

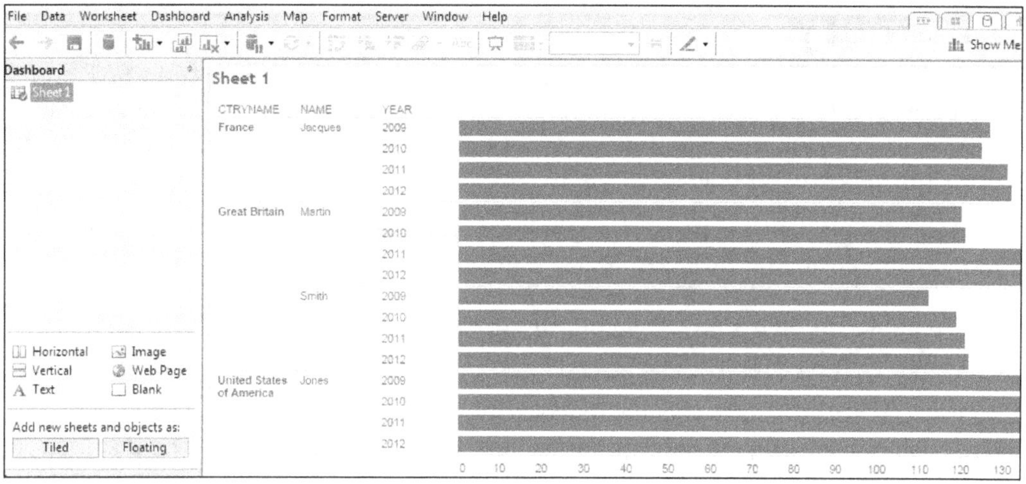

At first view, it looks exactly the same as the previous screenshot. However note that the definition options (**Columns**, **Rows**, and **Filter**) are not present; we are in a final view screen here with the display we will be using to communicate our figures.

If you click on the **Show Me** tab at the top of the screen, you can access different visualization types (raw grid, the bar chart we can see in the screenshot, or a pie chart, for example). These allow us to display the data differently according to our needs. The basic fields displayed (`AMOUNT`, `CTRYNAME`, `NAME`, and `YEAR`) are still the same however.

As we have seen, Tableau takes the simple data analysis options we saw in SAP's Visual Intelligence tool a little further, allowing us to create reports simply using drag and drop for the different fields to be used, and then incorporate the visualization in dashboards.

Summary

In this chapter, we have taken a look at several reporting tools (both from SAP and from other vendors) we can use to connect to SAP HANA and extract and analyze our data. We've seen that SAP has a tool, Lumira, allowing for rapid analysis of data using drag and drop of fields making it simple to do slice and dice analysis.

In a similar vein, Tableau allows us to create reports using drag and drop of fields, and then allows us to incorporate these reports in graphical dashboards.

We also looked at data analysis using Microsoft Excel, probably the most ubiquitous tool in use today, and one that most users are familiar with.

Lumira does not need any specific driver to be installed to connect to SAP HANA, as it's built into the tool. Excel and Tableau, however, need a driver to be installed.

We also saw some limitations of reporting tools; Lumira can see and use our input parameters and hierarchies, whereas Tableau and Excel cannot see the input parameters. Excel can use our hierarchies, whereas Tableau cannot.

These are of course only some of the different reporting tools available for use; there are many more, from many more vendors, such as MicroStrategy. All these tools have strengths and weaknesses and you will need to choose for yourself the best tool for the job.

In the next chapter, we'll be taking a look at how we can insert data into our SAP HANA instance; at the start of the book, we imported some tables using the Studio, but if we need to import data on a more industrial scale, we'll need a dedicated tool for the job. SAP provides such a tool in Business Objects Data Services (BODS).

Quick tool comparison

Rather than a quick reference, in this chapter we present a comparison of the tools examined:

Tool	Usage	Hierarchies Supported?	Driver Needed?	User Training required	Save reports for later use
Lumira	Quick data analysis, drag and drop analysis primarily for data discovery, not reusable reports.	Yes	No	-	No
Excel	Data analysis using pivot tables, creating formatted reports using Excel formatting options.	Yes	Yes (driver for Excel)	---	Yes (in Excel)
Tableau	Create reports and dashboard for data analysis. Simple lists can be added to formatted dashboards for distribution.	No	Yes (HANA Client)	++	Yes

10
Data Provisioning Using Data Services

Until now, we have been looking at how to use data we have in our SAP HANA system. We have seen that tables and their contents can be used in myriad ways to sort, filter and otherwise process data for analysis by users with reporting software.

At the start of the book, we imported some sample data. It was provided in a self-contained archive file of some tables and their data. We've been using this as the basis for our examples since. This data has been useful; there are only a handful of tables, and 10 to 15 lines of information in all. Understanding the tables, the links between them, and checking that our modeling objects work correctly is relatively easy with such a small dataset.

In the real world, of course, especially with SAP HANA, datasets are much larger. Tens or even hundreds of millions of lines of data are not uncommon; they are even the main reasoning behind the SAP HANA product.

The question we need to ask, when we have such huge amounts of data, before we start analyzing it, is how we can get it in to SAP HANA. Importing an archive is not really feasible, and indeed with more than a couple of megabytes of data, any attempt to import via the Studio would fail.

What's more, in general, a dataset is a living thing. New data will arrive; some old data lines might change, or be deleted. Depending on our needs, we might want to be able to load in only the changes to our data, rather than reload in everything. In other words, we might need to load data in delta mode rather than full-load mode.

We need to find a tool capable of importing large amounts of data into SAP HANA in a reasonably automated way, and luckily, such tools exist on the market. Tools designed to **Extract** data from one system, maybe perform **Transformations** on that data, and then **Load** it into another system, are called **ETL** tools. SAP has an ETL tool, called **SAP Business Objects Data Services** (or **BODS** for short), which we can use to load data in a simple way into our SAP HANA instance. BODS is the SAP-preferred tool for data loading into SAP HANA. There are, of course, many other ways of importing data, using other ETL tools (IBM has a product called **DataStage**, Microsoft has **Integration Services**, for example), or by writing your own solution that connects to your SAP HANA instance, maybe. In this chapter we'll be looking exclusively at SAP's Business Objects Data Services.

In this chapter we'll take a look at loading bulk data into SAP HANA using BODS. We'll create a data load job in BODS, loading data from a flat file of just over 5 million lines and using the structure of the file to create a table in SAP HANA on the fly.

> This chapter is not intended to be a full introduction to BODS, which is a very rich tool, capable of performing a great deal of transformations, filters, and other actions on data as it is transferred from one system to another. A full BODS introduction is outside the scope of this book. However, you will see how the main data flow objects in BODS are created, and how they relate to one another in order to create an ETL job, and you will be able to adapt this technique to create your own ETL jobs.

It is assumed that you have a BODS server installed in order to use the information in this chapter. If your SAP HANA license is for either the SAP HANA Enterprise or SAP HANA Enterprise Extended edition, you have a license for BODS, and can download and install it from the SAP Service Marketplace (`http://service.sap.com/swdc`). Go to **Installations and Upgrades** | **A - Z Index** | **D** | **SAP Data Services** | **SAP Data Services 4.1** | **Installation**.

About the sample data

The data we will be using in this chapter is a large dataset, downloaded from a U.S. Government "public data" website at `http://www.transtats.bts.gov/DL_SelectFields.asp?Table_ID=236&DB_Short_Name=On-Time`.

The data concerns commercial flights inside the USA, starting in 1998 and going right through to the present day.

This is the same data we glimpsed back in *Chapter 1, So, What Is This SAP HANA Thing Anyways?*, which demonstrated the relative speed of SAP HANA compared to other database systems.

We'll only be looking at the data for 1988, which represents over 5 million lines. This data for 1988, initially 12 files (one per month) has been compiled into one single CSV file of just over 1.2 GB of raw data.

> As explained in *Chapter 1, So, What Is This SAP HANA Thing Anyways?*, the sheer size of the data (57 MB compressed for 1988 alone) means it is not possible to distribute the dataset with the book. However, you can download it yourself from the given URL; it's publicly-available data. Alternatively, readers who wish to acquire the whole dataset can feel free to contact the author, who can make a download link available.

Understanding the BODS main screen

When we run the Data Services Designer tool for the first time, we will be presented with the main screen, as shown in the following screenshot:

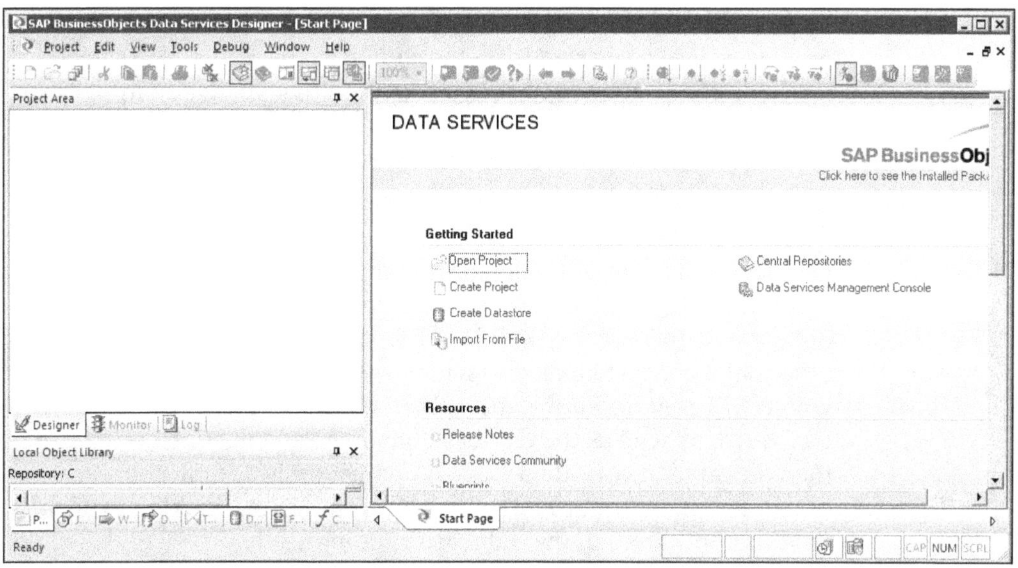

The screen layout is as follows:

- At the top of the screen, the menu and button bar with buttons representing the main options are available according to the selected object in the tool.
- On the left of the screen is the **Project** panel. This panel lists the contents of the current project (think of it as the equivalent of the **Navigator** panel in the SAP HANA Studio).
- Underneath the **Project** panel we can see **Local Object Library**, which has at the bottom a series of tabs, listing the different object types available. These are as follows:
    - **Projects**: This lists the projects that exist in the BODS Repository, and allows you to create new projects.
    - **Jobs**: This lists jobs on the server. A BODS job defines which actions (data flows and/or work flows) need to be performed, and in which order.
    - **Work Flows and Data Flows**: A data flow describes one particular ETL (Extract, Transform, Load) action. This will list the source of data, the transformations needed on the data, and the destination. Since data flows are independent objects, they can be reused in different jobs, or different work flows. A work flow is a group of one or more data flows, performing a logically-grouped action. Creating work flows as independent objects makes them reusable in different jobs.
    - **Transforms**: This tab lists the different actions that can be performed on data as it is transiting from the source to the target. At a simple level, we can perform case-transformation (converting to upper case, for example) on text data. Transforms can be much more complex, however, including selecting the destination according to the input data (lines concerning the year 2000 should go to table T2000, from year 2001 to T2001, maybe), and other transformation types.
    - **Datastores**: This lists the database connections that have been configured in Data Services. In order to be able to use a particular database connection (to SAP HANA, MySQL, SQL Server, or some other database instance), you will need to create a datastore object, which will contain information about the server, port, username and password, as well as the database type. These datastore objects are then reusable in your data flows. A datastore is a connection to a database. The datastore object handles listing, and making available, the different tables in the database, automatically.

- **Formats**: This shows the different file formats Data Services knows about. Here you can define the structure of any flat files (CSV files, XML files, or Excel workbooks, for example) that you might want to use as either source or target in a data flow. This will allow Data Services to understand the file format automatically when the file is opened. Once more, you define the files once in the **Formats** tab, and can then re-use the definition in any of your data flows.
- **Functions**: **Functions** allow you to perform specific actions on data as it is being transferred. More precise than transforms, functions allow you to write code to clean up or verify data. You might like to make sure that phone numbers are all formatted correctly (`(xxx) yyy-zzzz` in the USA, `aa.bb.cc.dd.ee` in France, for example). This can be done using **Functions**.

* On the right-hand side of the screen, taking up most of the space, is the object manipulation panel. This is where you interact with, create and modify data flows, projects, workflows, and so on.

Creating a Data Services project

In the next couple of sections we'll take a look at the steps necessary to load a CSV file into SAP HANA using Data Services. This presumes that neither the format of the CSV file, nor the SAP HANA instance, are known to Data Services, so we'll create all the individual objects necessary to perform our data flow.

Creating a project

As we saw earlier, a project in BODS is used to hold all the individual actions we need to perform.

In order to create a project, switch to the **Projects** tab, and right-click on some empty space inside that tab. Then select **New** from the context menu that will appear. You will see BODS' **New Project** dialog, which just asks for a name for your project. In this example, we'll call the project `flight`. Click on **OK** to dismiss the **New Project** dialog, and your new project will appear in the list of available projects:

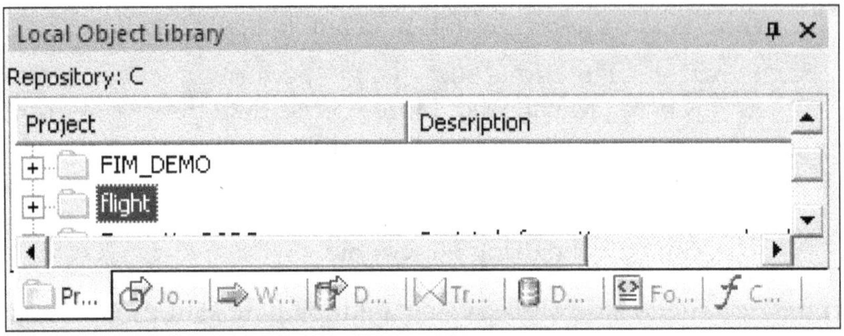

Your project is now ready for use, so we can proceed to create a job, which will handle execution of our data transfer, once it's finished.

Creating a BODS job

A **job** in BODS is used to launch a data transfer. It is this object that can be run, or scheduled, and will call up any contained data flows or work flows.

Job creation is done simply from within the project we have just created. Right-click on the project name (`flight`), and select **New Batch Job** from the menu that will appear, as you can see here:

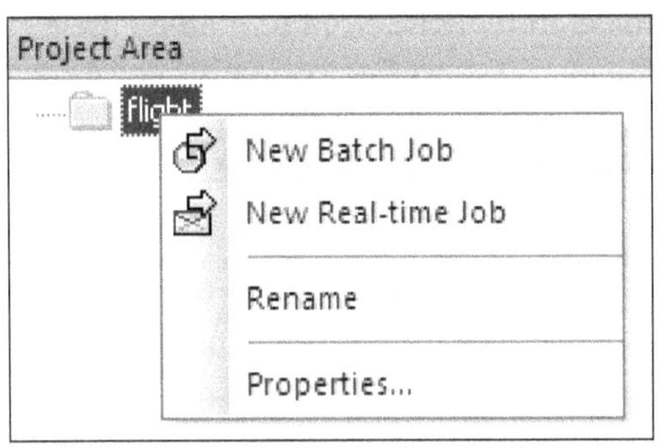

You will be prompted for a name for your new job. In BODS, job names are unique, so you cannot use a name that exists already. In our example, the job is called `flight_1988`, so type the job name, and just press *Enter* to create your job, which is initially empty.

We are now in a position to create the objects that will comprise the job, starting with the connection to our SAP HANA instance.

Creating an ODBC connection to SAP HANA from within BODS

In order to connect our BODS system to our SAP HANA instance, we must first create an **Open DataBase Connectivity** (**ODBC**, a database connection protocol) connection. As you recall from *Chapter 9, Deploying Your Reporting Application to Reporting Software*, in order to enable ODBC connections to SAP HANA, the SAP HANA Client software must be installed on the machine. In the case of BODS, this means that we need to install the SAP HANA Client on the BODS server itself (not the client).

> Refer back to the previous chapter for instructions on downloading and installing the SAP HANA Client. Remember that it will need to be installed on the server that runs the BODS Job Server. The Job Server is a 64-bit program, so you'll need to install the 64-bit version of the SAP HANA Client. You might need to ask your system administrator to perform the installation, in which case, you can show him/her the appropriate section of the book (the section concerning using Tableau Software with SAP HANA).

Once you have installed, or have ensured that the SAP HANA Client software is installed on your BODS Server machine, you can create an ODBC connection to your SAP HANA instance from within the software.

Switch to the **Datastores** tab and right-click on some empty space within the **Datastores** tab. You will be presented with the **Datastores** context menu, shown in the following screenshot:

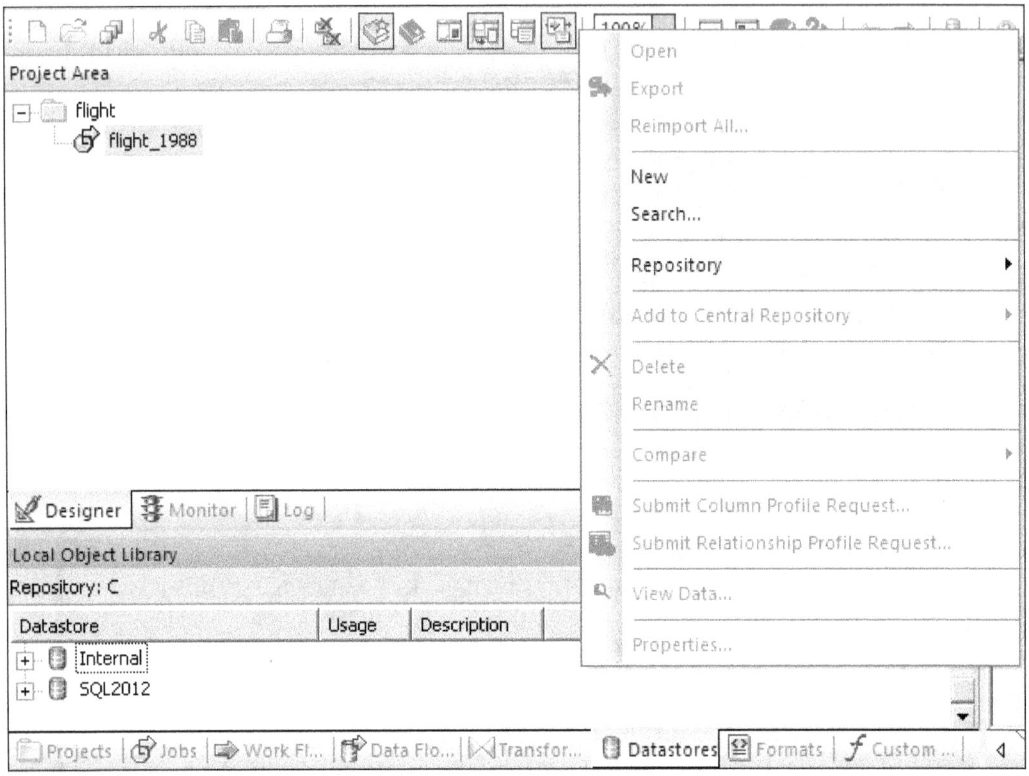

From this menu, select **New** to see the **Create New Datastore** dialog:

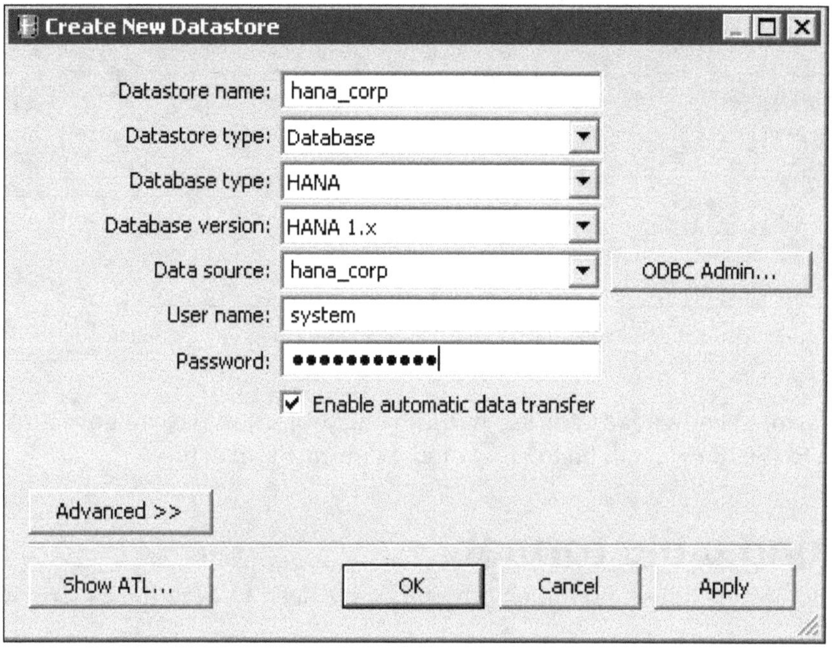

[The dialog will initially only contain the first three fields. The others appear automatically when you select **Database type** of **HANA**.]

You will need to enter the name you wish to give to your datastore, as well as a type (**HANA**) and the ODBC DSN name. If you don't currently have an ODBC connection configured to your SAP HANA instance, use the **ODBC Admin...** button to open the ODBC configuration panel to create one. Full instructions for DSN creation are given in the previous chapter. In this example, we are using the **hana_corp** DSN, and have specified our SAP HANA username of `SYSTEM`, with that user's password.

Click on **OK** to request BODS to verify that the information you have entered is correct (it will attempt to connect to your SAP HANA instance to make sure), and save the entry. Your new datastore will appear in the list in the **Datastores** tab:

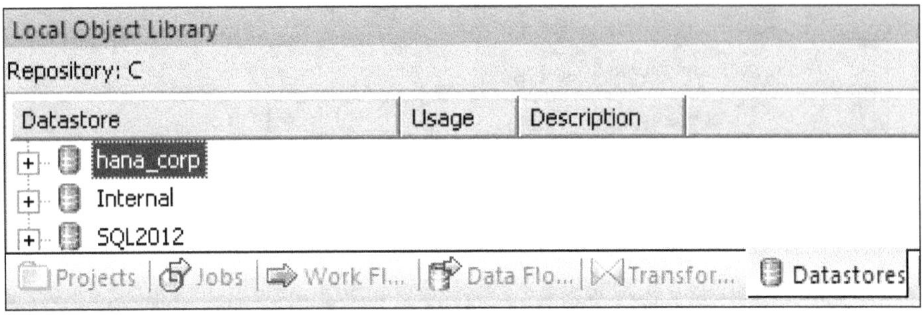

Your datastore is now ready for use within your project, so we can now turn our attention to the file we will be loading, and examine its structure.

Defining a file format

In order to be able to use a flat file with BODS, we need to describe its structure.

The file we will be loading into our SAP HANA instance is a data file containing some public data concerning commercial flights in the USA, in 1988. This file contains just over five million lines, and here are the first two:

```
1988;4;10;25;2;1988-10-25;UA;19977;UA;0;248;10713;1071301;30713;
BOI;Boise, ID;ID;16;Idaho;83;11292;1129201;30325;DEN;Denver, CO;CO;08;
Colorado;82;1240;1249;9;9;0;0;1200-1259;0;0;0;0;1422;1420;-2;0;0;-1;
1400-1459;0;0;0;102;91;0;1;642;3
1988;4;10;26;3;1988-10-26;UA;19977;UA;0;248;10713;1071301;30713;BOI;
Boise, ID;ID;16;Idaho;83;11292;1129201;30325;DEN;Denver, CO;CO;08;
Colorado;82;1240;1238;-2;0;0;-1;1200-1259;0;0;0;0;1422;1405;-17;0;0;
-2;1400-1459;0;0;0;102;87;0;1;642;3
```

The file is a CSV file; we can see that the field separators are semicolons, and the lines end at a paragraph (or newline) marker.

The structure of each line is described in the following screenshot:

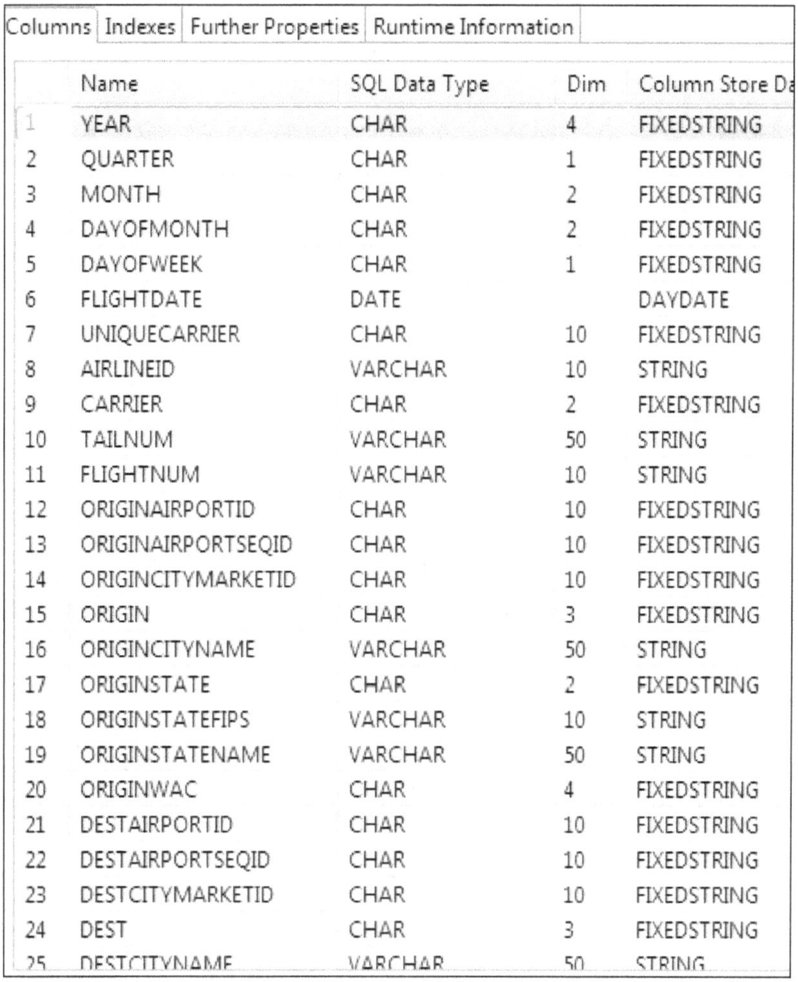

Columns | Indexes | Further Properties | Runtime Information

	Name	SQL Data Type	Dim	Column Store Da
1	YEAR	CHAR	4	FIXEDSTRING
2	QUARTER	CHAR	1	FIXEDSTRING
3	MONTH	CHAR	2	FIXEDSTRING
4	DAYOFMONTH	CHAR	2	FIXEDSTRING
5	DAYOFWEEK	CHAR	1	FIXEDSTRING
6	FLIGHTDATE	DATE		DAYDATE
7	UNIQUECARRIER	CHAR	10	FIXEDSTRING
8	AIRLINEID	VARCHAR	10	STRING
9	CARRIER	CHAR	2	FIXEDSTRING
10	TAILNUM	VARCHAR	50	STRING
11	FLIGHTNUM	VARCHAR	10	STRING
12	ORIGINAIRPORTID	CHAR	10	FIXEDSTRING
13	ORIGINAIRPORTSEQID	CHAR	10	FIXEDSTRING
14	ORIGINCITYMARKETID	CHAR	10	FIXEDSTRING
15	ORIGIN	CHAR	3	FIXEDSTRING
16	ORIGINCITYNAME	VARCHAR	50	STRING
17	ORIGINSTATE	CHAR	2	FIXEDSTRING
18	ORIGINSTATEFIPS	VARCHAR	10	STRING
19	ORIGINSTATENAME	VARCHAR	50	STRING
20	ORIGINWAC	CHAR	4	FIXEDSTRING
21	DESTAIRPORTID	CHAR	10	FIXEDSTRING
22	DESTAIRPORTSEQID	CHAR	10	FIXEDSTRING
23	DESTCITYMARKETID	CHAR	10	FIXEDSTRING
24	DEST	CHAR	3	FIXEDSTRING
25	DESTCITYNAME	VARCHAR	50	STRING

We can see when we compare the file data and the structure data that the first field does correspond to the year, and the fifteenth field (`ORIGIN`) does at least seem in the file data to be an airport ID (`BOI`).

In order to define this structure in BODS, we need to create a **Format** object. Switch to the **Formats** tab of the main BODS screen, right-click on the **Flat Files** line, and then select **New** from the context menu to see BODS' **File Format Editor** dialog:

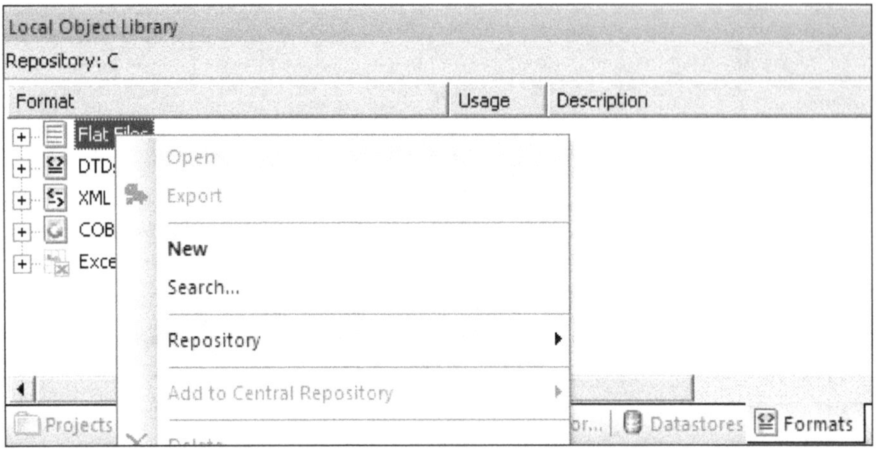

The **File Format Editor** dialog is shown in the following screenshot. When it initially appears, the dialog is nearly empty. We will first give our **Format** object a name (`flight_data`). Entering the name of the directory containing the data file, and the file name in the **Root Directory** and **File Name(s)** fields on the left of the screen will cause BODS to ask you if you wish to have it attempt to analyze your file:

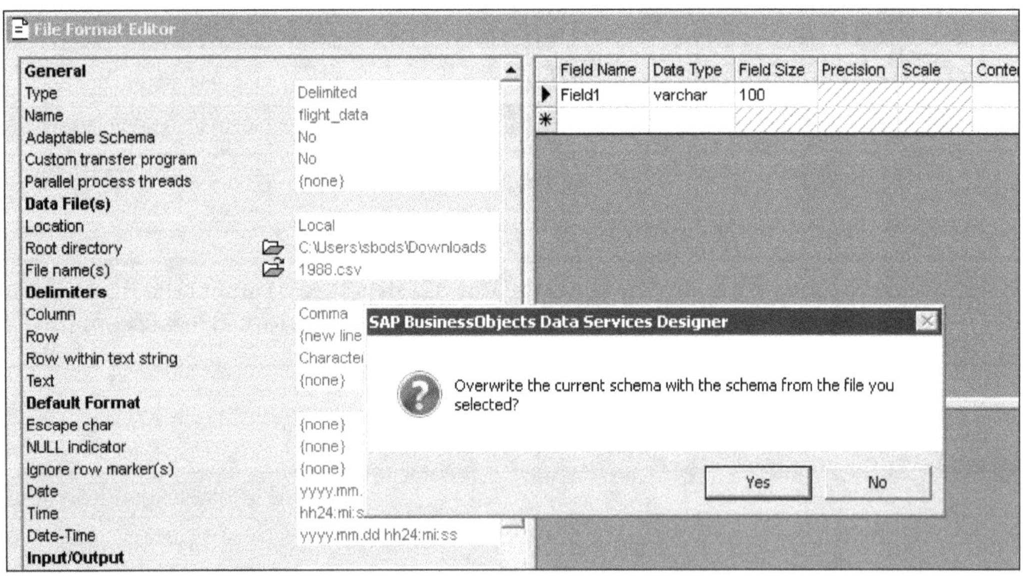

Initially, BODS will not manage to correctly interpret the file for you, as you can see here:

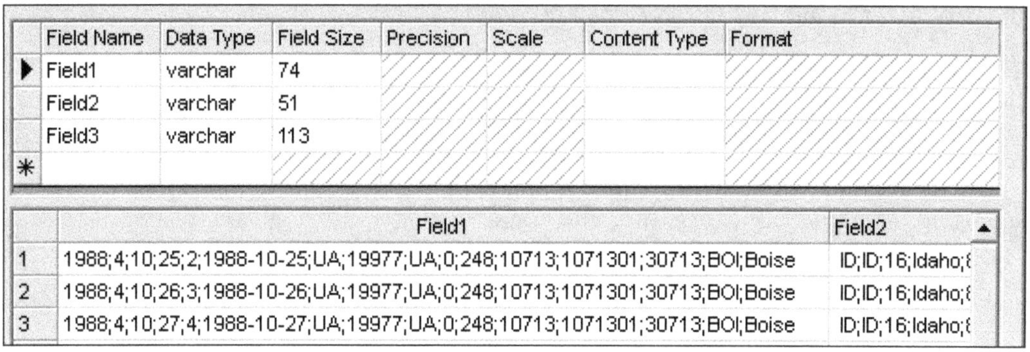

This is due to the field separator. Its default value is **Comma**, which does not correspond to our file. Change the value to **Semicolon**, by clicking on the **Comma** value next to **Column**, in the **Delimiters** section on the left-hand side of the dialog, and BODS will correctly interpret the file for you:

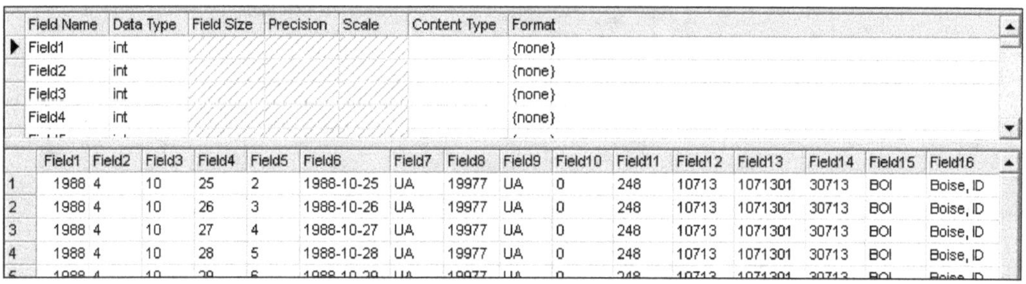

At this point, the **Format** object is usable; we can use it as-is. However, you might like to rename the different fields, which BODS has automatically named **Field1**, **Field2**, and so on.

> The field names in BODS will become the field names in SAP HANA when we transfer the data in a minute, so using explicit field names is always recommended.

Either change the field names to something more meaningful, or leave them as-is, as you prefer, for this example. Once you are done, click on the **Save & Close** button to save your **Format** object.

Creating a data flow

At this point, we have created the basic objects we will need to load our data from the CSV file into our SAP HANA instance using BODS.

The object that will handle the data load is a data flow. This defines the source of the data (our CSV file), any transformations needed on the data (we don't have any), and the target of the transformation (a new table in SAP HANA).

To create a data flow, switch to the **Data Flows** tab of the BODS main screen. You will see two types of data flow:

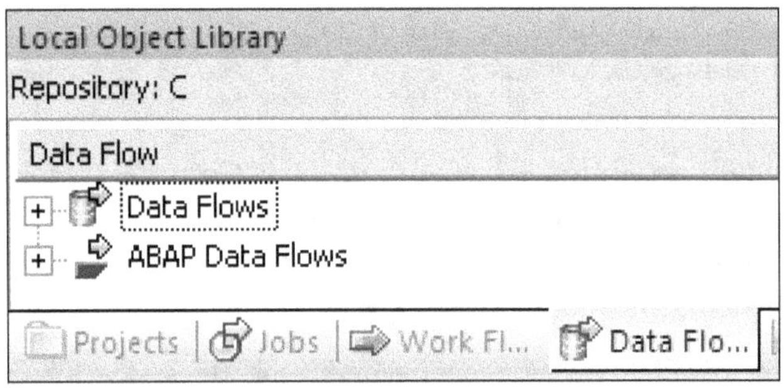

> **ABAP Data Flows** are used when transferring data into an SAP ERP or SAP BW instance; we are not concerned with them here.

Right-click on the **Data Flows** line in the list, and select **New** from the menu, to create a new data flow. You will be presented with a default name for your data flow (something like **New_DataFlowxx**), which you should change to something meaningful. In our example, the data flow is called `Flight_data`. Press *Enter* to accept your data flow name, and the data flow will be created.

Double-click on it to see the data flow designer, which is represented by a new tab opening on the right-hand side of the screen, and this tab being initially empty.

Adding a source object

Our data flow, conceptually, is very simple. Take the data from our CSV file (represented in BODS by our **Format** object), and transfer it to a new table in SAP HANA (the instance is defined in our `hana_corp` datastore object).

Creating this data flow is as simple as it sounds (fortunately!). Leave the **Data Flow** tab open on the right-hand side of the screen, and on the left-hand side, switch to the **Formats** tab, and find your **Format** object in the list (ours is called `flight_1988`). Click on it, and drag it to the data flow designer panel on the right.

As you can see in the following screenshot, BODS will ask whether you want this **Format** object to be the source or the target of a data transfer:

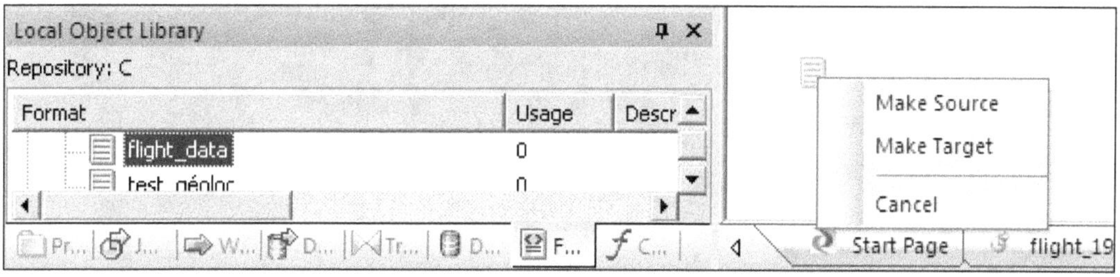

In our case, the file is the source of the data, so select **Make Source** from the menu.

Adding a target object

The target of our data flow is a table in SAP HANA. We know the instance information; it's in our `hana_corp` datastore. However, we don't yet know the table's name and schema; we'll have to define this as the flow runs.

What's more, the target does not actually exist as yet; it will be created by BODS as the job runs.

Usually, BODS requires, as for the **Format** object, that we define beforehand the exact structure and identity of our objects, but in this case, we cannot since it does not exist yet.

To fulfill this requirement, BODS introduces the notion of a **Template Table**. This table will take the structure of the input data (the structure of our CSV file). We only need to give our table a name and a schema, and BODS handles the rest for us.

To add a template table as a target for our data transfer, switch to the **Datastores** tab on the left-hand side of the BODS main screen, and find your `hana_corp` datastore. Click on the plus sign next to the `hana_corp` name to expand the object, and you will see **Template Tables** listed. Drag the **Template Tables** line to the main data flow designer panel:

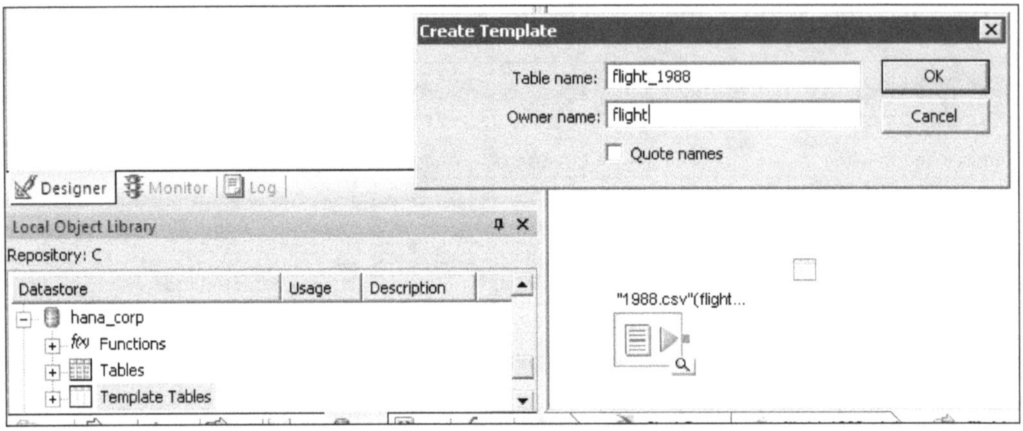

As you can see in the screenshot, you will be asked, in a pop up window, the name for your destination table and its schema inside SAP HANA. In our example, the table is called `flight_1988` and the schema is called `flight`.

> At this point, you should note that if the schema itself does not exist in your SAP HANA instance, the data transfer will fail when we run it later.
>
> To create the `flight` schema in your SAP HANA instance in the Studio, in the **Navigator** panel, right-click on your instance name, select **SQL Editor** from the list, and enter the following SQL code:
>
> ```
> CREATE SCHEMA FLIGHT;
> ```
>
> Now run the SQL command, and if you refresh the **Catalog** node of **Navigator**, you will see your `FLIGHT` schema appear.

At this point your data flow should look something like this:

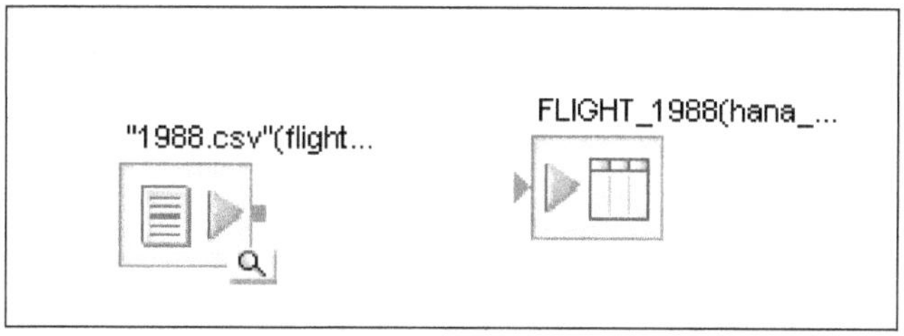

As you can imagine, we need to link the source object (the block with the arrow on the right pointing out of the block) and the target (the block with the arrow on the left pointing into the block). We can do this simply by clicking on the square just outside the source block, and drawing a line to the arrow connected to the target block, to make a link:

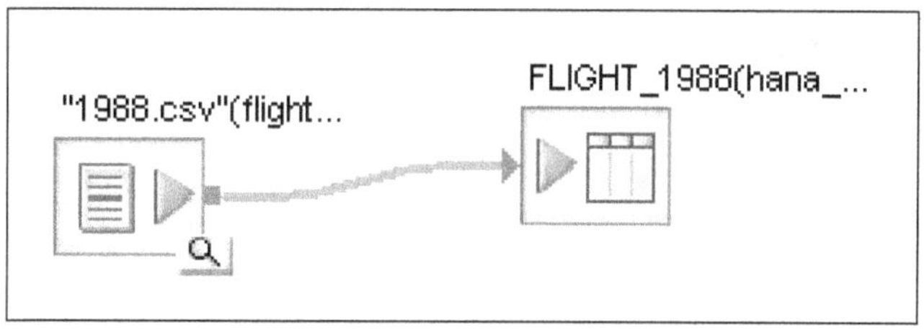

And our data flow is finished! We have a flow that will read data from our CSV file and send it to SAP HANA, creating the destination table on the fly.

All we need now is to run it, and for this, we will need to add it to our job.

Adding a data flow to a job

As you can imagine, given the simplicity of creation of the different objects we have just made, adding a data flow to a job is simple.

Switch to the **Jobs** tab, and double-click on your job, to make sure that its definition is open in the designer panel on the right-hand side of the screen.

Now switch to the **Data Flows** tab, and find the data flow you have just created. It is called `flight_data` in our example.

Just drag the name of the data flow to the job definition panel on the right-hand side of the screen to add it to the job:

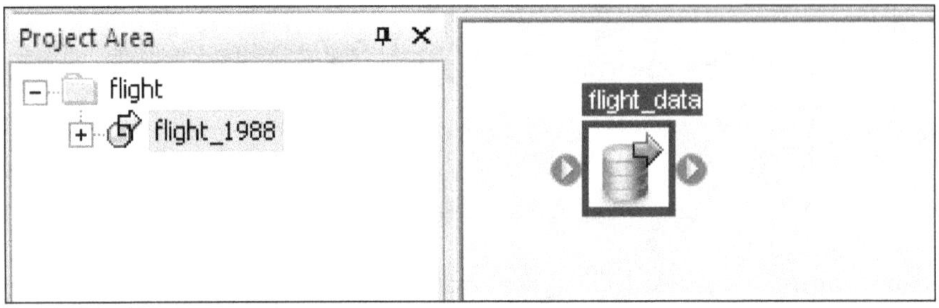

Using the `flight_data` data flow in our `flight_1988` job means that all the objects we have created are now collected together in our project, as they are all referenced.

Running a BODS job

If you now right-click on the job name, you can run it, by selecting **Execute** from the menu:

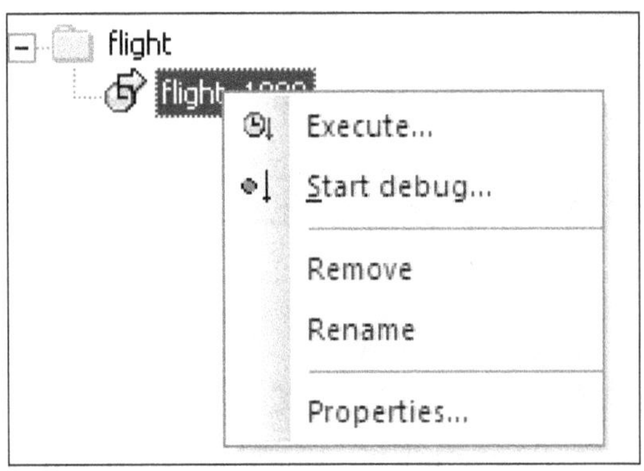

You will be asked to save all objects that need saving, which in our case means all the objects we have just created since we haven't saved any of them yet:

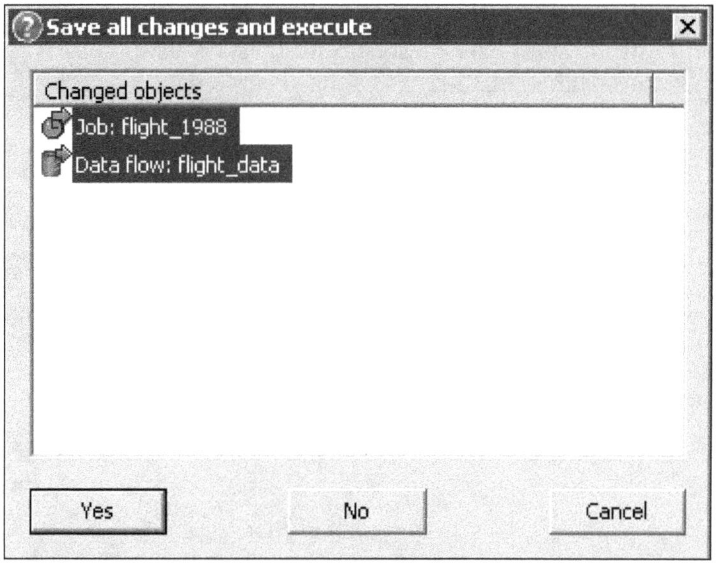

The system will propose several options concerning the execution of the job; you can leave these at their default values, and click on **OK** to run the job.

A detailed job log will appear, and update itself as the job runs:

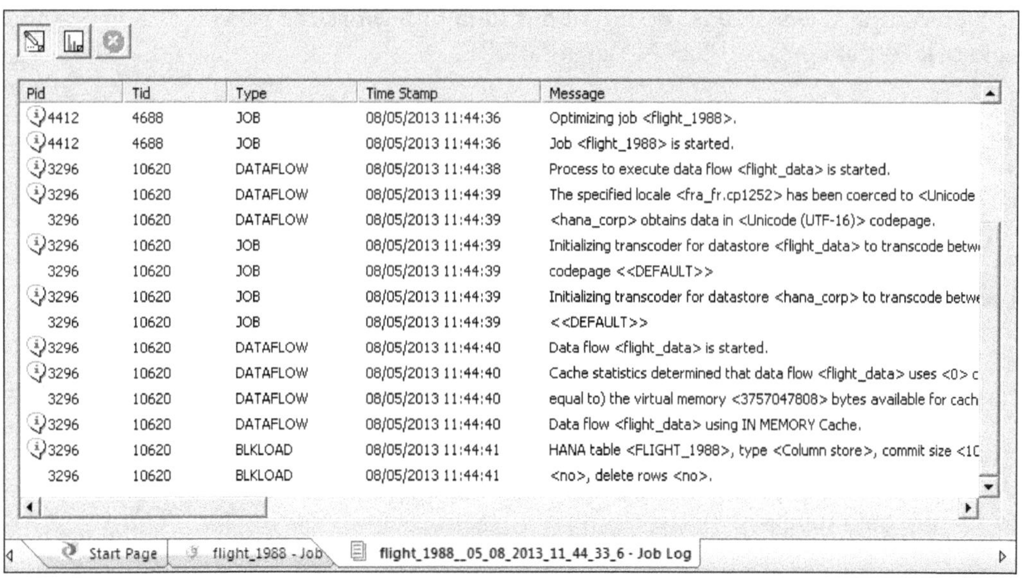

Once the job has completed, you will be able to see the results in your SAP HANA instance. If you return to your SAP HANA Studio and refresh your **Navigator** panel, you will see that a new table, `FLIGHT_1988`, has been created:

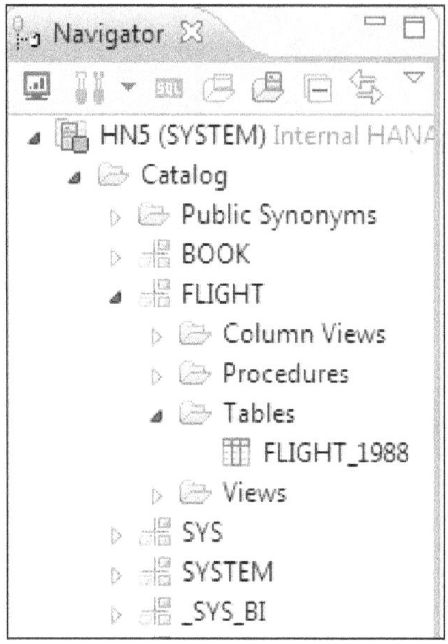

The preceding screenshot is proof that our data flow works as expected! You are now able to load data into SAP HANA using BODS.

Summary

In this chapter, we have taken a look at Business Objects Data Services (BODS). We have seen that it is an ETL (Extract, Transform, Load) tool, developed by SAP.

We have seen that a data transfer needs a **source**, an optional **transformation**, and a **target**. Sources and targets can be flat files (**formats**), or database tables (**datastores**), and **transformations** can do simple things such as text case changes, or more complex transformations, maybe complex enough to require coding via the use of **functions**.

A **data flow** can be included in a **work flow** if it needs to be reusable, and either **data flows** or **work flows** can be included in a **job**, which can then be executed to run the data transfer.

We have now examined both data modeling in SAP HANA in the first few chapters, creating attribute, analytic and calculation views, and have seed accessory functions such as authorizations and (in this chapter) how we can load data into our SAP HANA instance. In *Chapter 11, Application Development Using the XS Engine*, we will be doing some real coding, developing a web application using SAP HANA's inbuilt application server, the **XS Engine**.

Quick reference

In this section we present a quick reference to the objects covered in this chapter.

Object	Usage	Creation
Format	This describes a flat file for use with BODS	The **Formats** tab, right-click, and click on **New**. Define the file format, location, field types, and names. Formats can be either source or target in data flows.
Datastore	This defines a link to a database	The **Datastore** tab, right-click, and click on **New**. Choose datastore type, database type, and enter connection information. Use a datastore as either source or target in data flow. Use existing tables as a source, use template tables or existing tables as targets. Template tables will be created, then take the structure of input data.
Transformation	This describes a modification to make to data as it is transferred	In a data flow, add a transformation of appropriate type according to business needs between source and target. Several transformations can be linked in series in a data flow.
Function	This allows complex transformations to be defined in code	The **Functions** tab, right-click, and click on **New** Write function code (take inspiration from existing functions!)

Object	Usage	Creation
Data flow	This describes one data transfer, from a source to a target, optionally passing via a transformation	The **Data Flow** tab, right-click, and click on **New**. Add source, transformation, function, and target. Link all together. Add to a work flow or a job.
Work flow	This defines a list of one or more data flows to be run in series	The **Work Flow** tab, right-click, and click on **New**. Add one or more data flows, and link them together. Add a work flow to a job.
Job	This is the object that can be executed, or scheduled, to do the data transfer	Create a project, right-click on project name, and select **New Batch Job**. Add one or more data flows and/or work flows, and link them together
Project	This allows grouping of objects together in a group for development	The **Projects** tab, right-click, and click on **New**. Create a job in the project.

11

Application Development Using the XS Engine

Over the course of the last couple of hundred pages, we've taken a look at the SAP HANA system. Right back at the start of the book, we saw that SAP HANA is basically just a database (albeit one with bells, whistles, and go-faster stripes). We've seen that we can make tables, attribute, analytic, and calculation views using various artifacts to provide calculation and other functionality. We can do reporting on our tables using several reporting tools, and import and export data using certified ETL software such as SAP's Data Services.

One aspect we haven't looked at yet is doing actual development work; that is, writing a program, not necessarily just some SQL construction. What if we want, say, a web application to interact with our data, maybe with a form to let a user enter data themselves?

The good news is that we can do this with SAP HANA in several different ways.

Since the start of the book, whenever we have connected to SAP HANA to do development work, create tables, views, import and export data, we've been using the SAP HANA Studio. This software is a Java application, based on the Eclipse IDE, onto which SAP has added some functionality specific to SAP HANA.

This functionality connects to the database using the credentials we entered, and executes SQL statements. These turn our graphically-designed objects into SQL objects. In order to let the Eclipse software talk to SAP HANA, SAP provides a connector library, the SAP HANA JDBC connector. **JDBC** means **Java Database Connector**. Since JDBC is a standardized API, if we were to write software in Java, we could make it work with SAP HANA just by using the SAP HANA JDBC library in our software. We could then make our software work with MySQL just by replacing the SAP HANA JDBC library with a MySQL JDBC library, if we wanted.

Using libraries such as these is called **database abstraction**. Rather than making an application that talks directly to SAP HANA or MySQL, or SQL Server, we make an application that understands JDBC. Then, by plugging in the correct JDBC library, our application can talk to any given database—the database itself has been abstracted away.

As we saw in *Chapter 9, Deploying Your Reporting Application to Reporting Software*, other database protocols can be used with SAP HANA, such as ODBC.

We won't be looking at the ODBC connector in itself, but it is useful to know that it exists. ODBC is often used to write web-based applications that need database persistence. For example, Facebook is a web-based application, written in PHP, which is a scripting language designed for the web. The PHP program needs to store data between user connections, and it does this using a large collection of MySQL servers. (Maybe we could suggest SAP HANA to the guys at Facebook?) If the connector that Facebook uses to talk to MySQL is the PHP-MySQL-ODBC connector, they could swap it for the SAP HANA-ODBC connector with little effort to use SAP HANA instead of MySQL.

What we'll be seeing in this chapter however, is that SAP HANA doesn't need an external web server or language to write applications. One is provided in the default installation of the server; this server is called the XS Engine (for SAP HANA eXtended Application Services). We'll be looking at several aspects of this server and what we can do with it:

- Creating a simple Hello World application with XS Engine
- Creating an XS Engine application that connects to the SAP HANA database and pulls some data
- Using the SAPUI5 user interface library with an XS Engine application

At the end of the chapter you will possess the basic building blocks you will need to build your own applications on the XS Engine, connect to your own SAP HANA database and present and work with your own data.

Checking the XS Engine

Let's start by checking whether the XS Engine is running on your SAP HANA instance.

Open up a browser and point it to the address `http://<server>:80<instance>`.

So, for example, if your server was at the address `hana.corp`, and your SAP HANA instance number was `02`, the address for your server would be:

```
http://hana.corp:8002
```

You should see the XS Engine default webpage, as shown in the following screenshot:

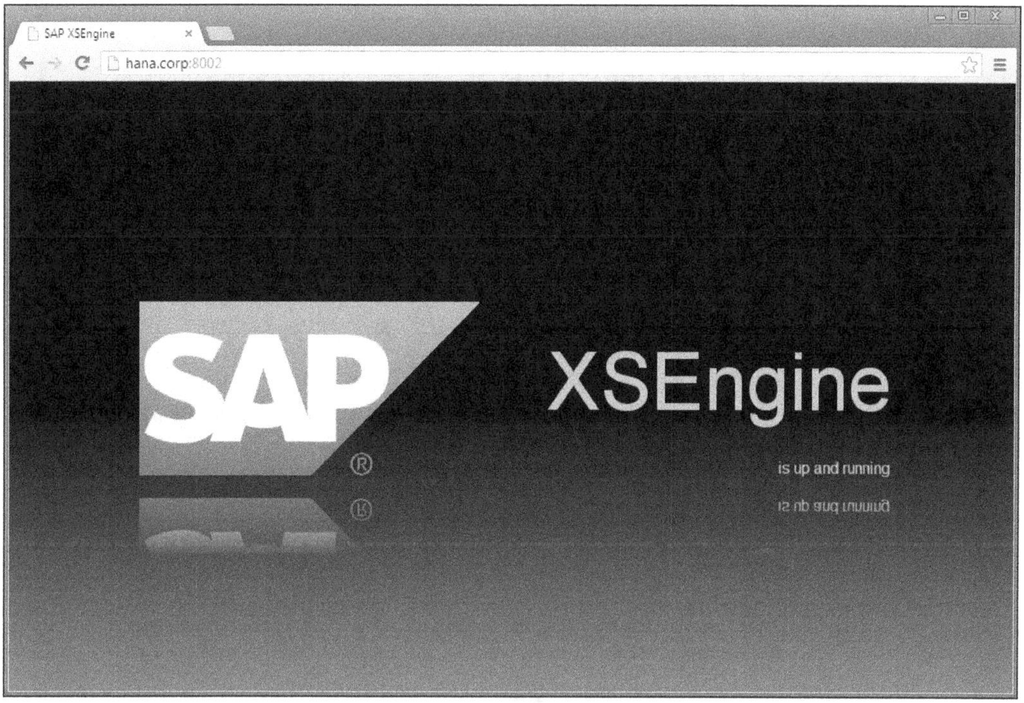

If you can see this screen, then all is well! You'll be able to follow the application development instructions in this chapter.

If you get an error or the XS Engine page doesn't load, you have a problem. Check whether your network is correctly configured, whether you have access to the correct website port (maybe port 8002 is blocked by your proxy, for example). Also, check whether your system administrator has deactivated the XS Engine, or has set it to run on a nonstandard port.

Understanding XS Engine applications

Applications written using the XS Engine are written in JavaScript. That is, server-side JavaScript, not the kind that makes annoying pop ups appear on webpages after ten seconds.

> Of course, since XS Engine applications are webpages in themselves, we could write an application in JavaScript on the server that creates JavaScript in the browser, and still open that annoying pop up, if we so desired. In fact, we will be doing something like this later—minus the annoying pop up.

As usual, SAP provides a development environment capable of connecting to the XS Engine, and we already have a copy installed—it's the SAP HANA Studio.

Developing applications with the XS Engine takes a little setting-up, but once that's done, writing the application code itself is relatively straightforward.

In the Studio, open the **SAP HANA Development** perspective, from the menu option **Window** | **Open Perspective** | **Other** | **SAP HANA Development**.

The **Navigator** panel will change to a more filled-out panel with three tabs, seen here:

- **Project Explorer** will display applications we develop, and the source files that comprise them.
- **SAP HANA Repositories** will show source code repositories we create on the server, as well as the contents of these repositories. The XS Engine includes a **version control system** (**VCS**) for all development objects, allowing projects to be stored on the server (not on the local PC), shared between members of a development team, locked for editing by one member (preventing anyone else from making changes to the object), and giving the possibility to recover previous changes to an object.
- **Navigator** is the familiar tree list of objects on the server, which will include our development objects.

> In the Studio revisions 45 to 48 (at least), the **Navigator** panel has a few bugs when there are development objects of the XS Engine stored in the system. It can see that there are objects on the server, but doesn't manage to correctly display them, and if they are selected, sometimes error messages appear in the Studio. For this reason, if you see strange objects with no name, or names that half resemble objects in your projects in the **Navigator** panel then it is probably easier to ignore the **Navigator** panel when doing XS Engine development, and ignore the XS Engine objects in the **Navigator** panel when doing database modeling.

Creating an application using XS Engine

Application creation using the XS Engine is done in four steps:

1. **Create a delivery unit**: Just like when we created our modeling objects right back at the start of the book, a delivery unit is used to transport objects from one instance of SAP HANA to another.
2. **Create a package**: The same notion that we saw earlier, a package groups objects together. In XS Engine development, a package can contain one or several projects, as well as any modeling objects (attribute, analytic, and calculation views) used by the project(s).
3. **Create a project**: Any given web application is made up of several source files. Main pages, utility function files, graphics, and third-party libraries all need to be kept together in a project.
4. **Create application descriptor files**: These files are needed by the XS Engine, and are used to describe the project, the authorizations it uses and needs, and so on.

Let's start with a simple XS Engine application—the same application you've probably created or seen created in about any given development language, our old favorite, the Hello World application.

Creating a delivery unit

A delivery unit, when used for transport of an XS Engine application, is exactly the same as the one we created earlier in order to be able to transport SAP HANA modeling objects.

From the **Modeler** perspective, in the **Quick Launch** panel, select **Setup** | **Delivery Units** | **Create** and then give your new delivery unit a name. In this example, we've created a delivery unit called `XSTEST`:

For the delivery unit, that's all that needs to be done. Click on **Close** to dismiss the dialog.

Creating a package

In order to create an XS Engine application (**XSapp**), it must be stored inside a package. This, once more, is just like any other SAP HANA modeling object. From the **Modeler** perspective, the **Quick Launch** panel, select **Package** | **Create** and give your package a name (once again, we've used `xstest` here, though in lowercase this time, as all package names are in lowercase). Select `XSTEST` as the delivery unit:

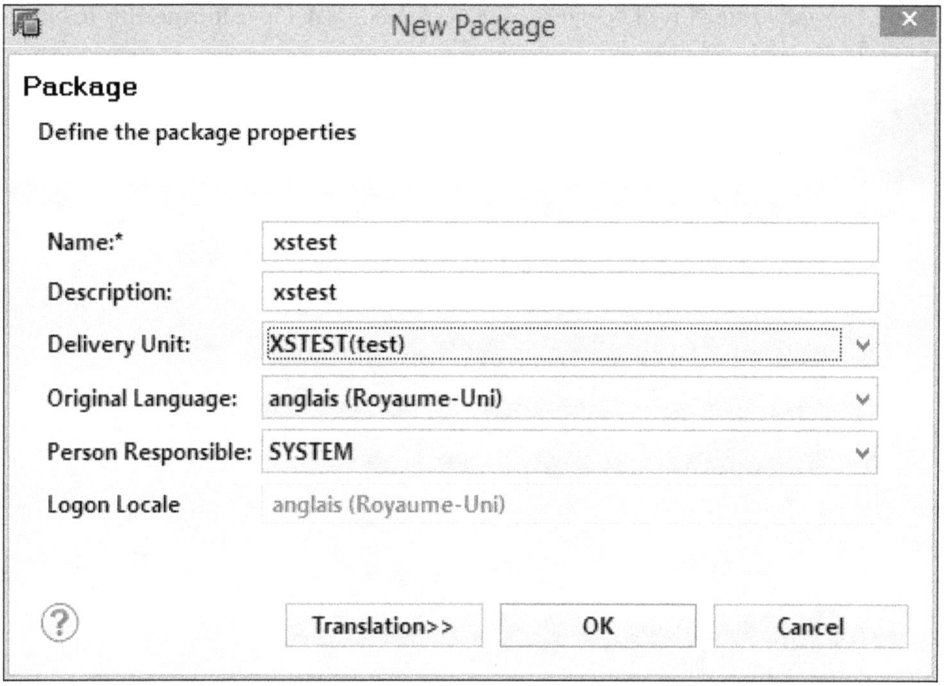

You can now click on **OK** – the package has been created. If you refresh the **Navigator** panel, you'll see it listed under the **Content** node. It is currently empty, but we'll be filling it up soon enough!

Creating a project

An XSapp needs a project to function. This can be created from the **SAP HANA Development** perspective (**Window** | **Open Perspective** | **Other** | **SAP HANA Development**).

Right-click inside the **Project Explorer** panel (by default on the left-hand side of the screen, where the **Navigator** panel is usually found) and select **New** | **Project** from the menu.

The **New Project** wizard will appear. Select **SAP HANA Development | XS Project**, as shown here:

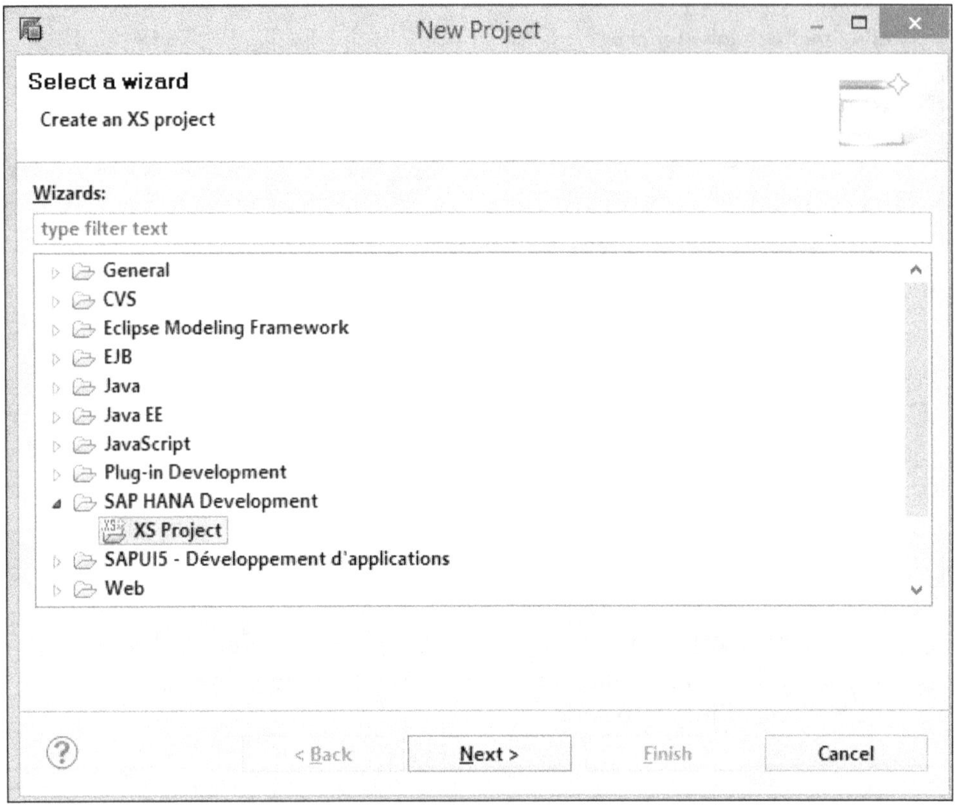

Click on **Next** to enter the project name (in this example, we'll call the application `xstest`), then click on **Finish** to have the Studio create the basic project skeleton for you. At this point your **Project Explorer** panel should look like this:

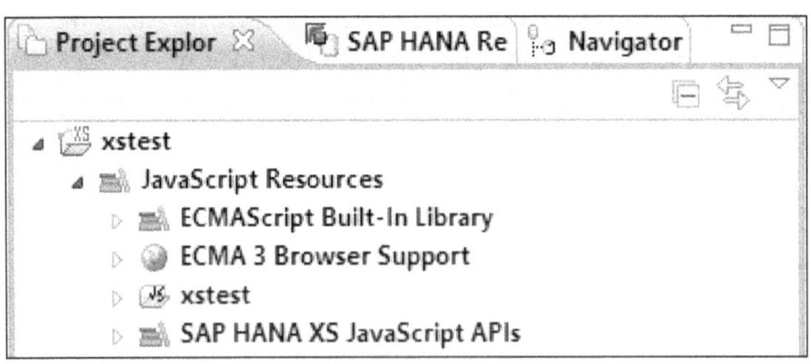

Sharing your project on the SAP HANA Server

We now need to insert the project into the XS Engine's version control system. All projects on the XS Engine are stored on the server, not on your PC. This allows projects to be shared between developers, development machines, and makes them always available.

> Developers familiar with ABAP development in the SAP ERP or SAP BW will find this familiar – the programs are always stored on the server.

To create the project on the server, right-click on its name and select **Team | Share project** from the menu.

> Depending on your SAP HANA server configuration, you might be presented with a list of repository types, as shown in the following screenshot:
>
> 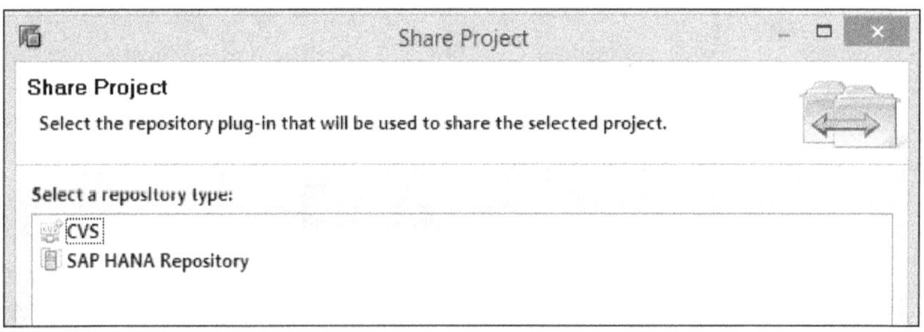
>
>
> If this is the case, select **SAP HANA Repository** from the list, and click on **Next** to continue.

You can now select a repository workspace for your project. You might need to ask your system administrator for the correct workspace to use. You might even need to create one, if you are the first (or only) developer on your SAP HANA system.

Creating a repository workspace

You will be presented with a list of existing repositories on your server, in the **Share Project** dialog, which we can see in the following screenshot:

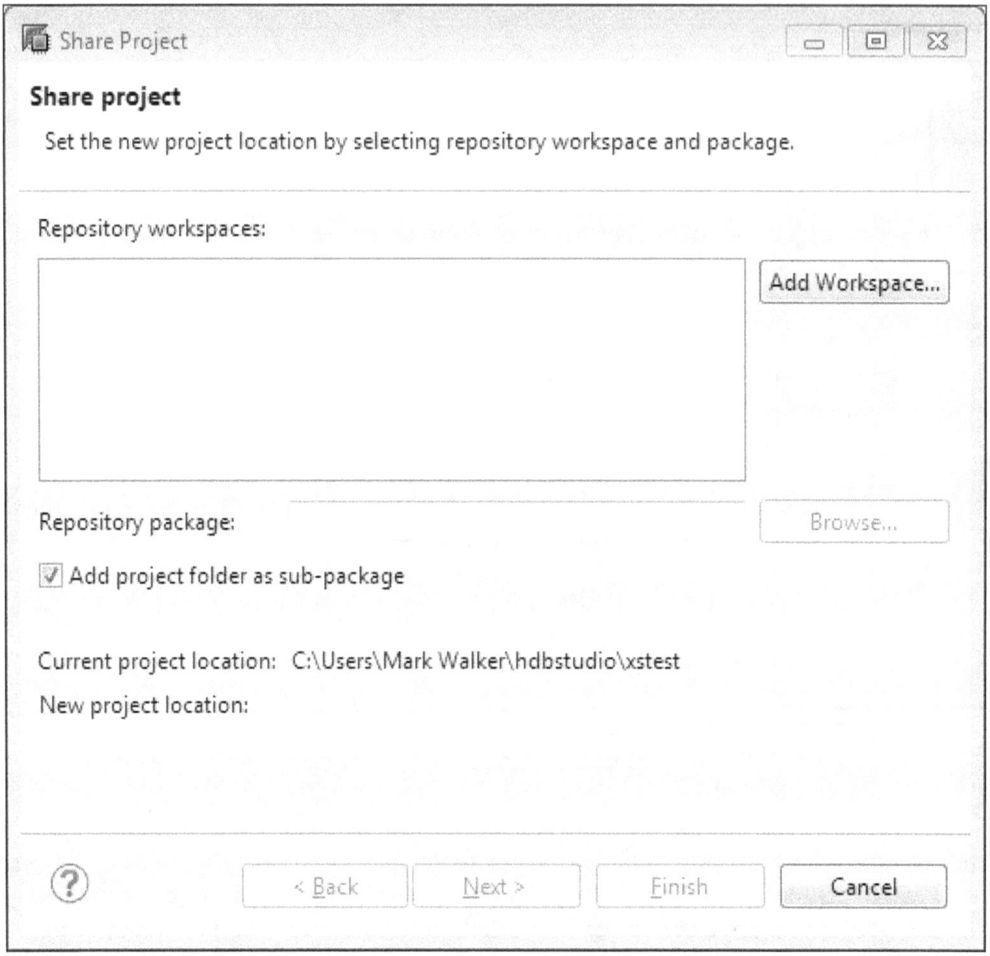

As this is your first development project in the Studio, and unless your system administrator has configured your installation for you, you will probably receive and error message at this point, complaining about the repository client version:

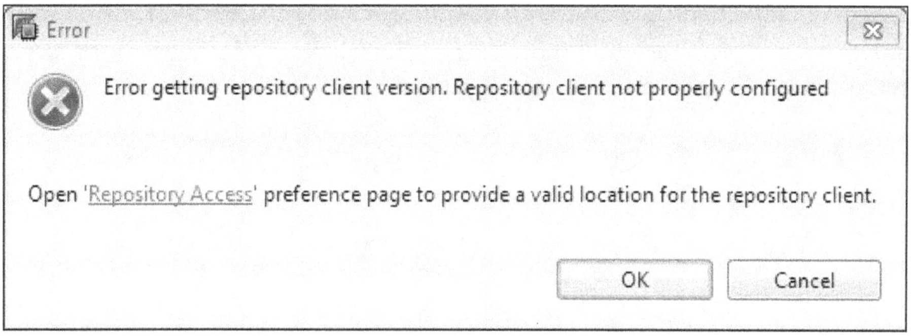

This error is due to a missing configuration option in the Studio.

The Studio needs a tool—`regi.exe` (on Windows) or `regi` (on Linux)—to connect to the SAP HANA server's VCS system. This tool is not included in the installation of the Studio, and hence is not configured for use.

In order to install this tool, you need to install the SAP HANA Client software. This was discussed back in *Chapter 9*, in the section concerning Tableau Software (which also needs this client software). You might like to skip back to that section for download and installation instructions for the client.

Note a couple of points:

- `regi.exe` is only included in the 64-bit installation of the client software, so even if you installed the client for use with Tableau, there is a fair chance that you will need to download and install the 64-bit version of the client software anyway.
- `regi.exe` can only be used with 64-bit versions of the Studio, so if you are using a 32-bit Studio version on Windows, either by choice or because your Windows version is 32-bit, then you are out of luck. You will need to upgrade to a 64-bit version of the Studio to use the functions in this chapter. (Linux users are not concerned by this problem, as the `regi` software for Linux is 64-bit, and only a 64-bit version of the Studio is made available by SAP).

Once you have installed the 64-bit version of the SAP HANA Client software, you can configure the repository tool with the Studio. Click on the **Repository Access** link in the error message to see the configuration page for the tool:

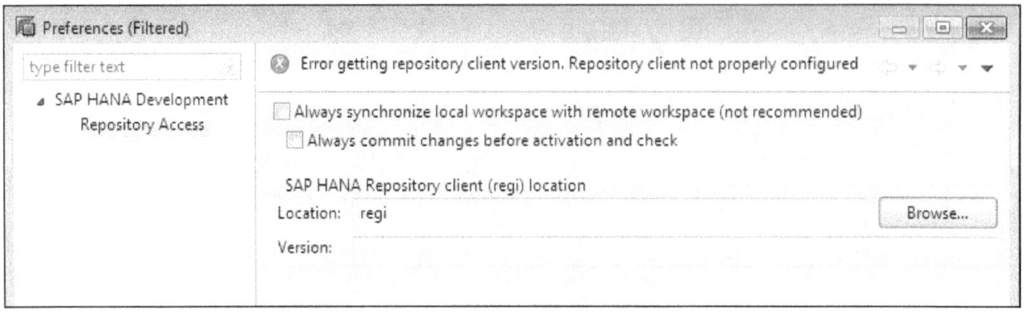

Click on the **Browse** button to find and select the `regi.exe` file. The file is located in the main installation folder you selected for the client software. By default this is `c:\Program Files\SAP\hdbclient`, as you can see in the following screenshot:

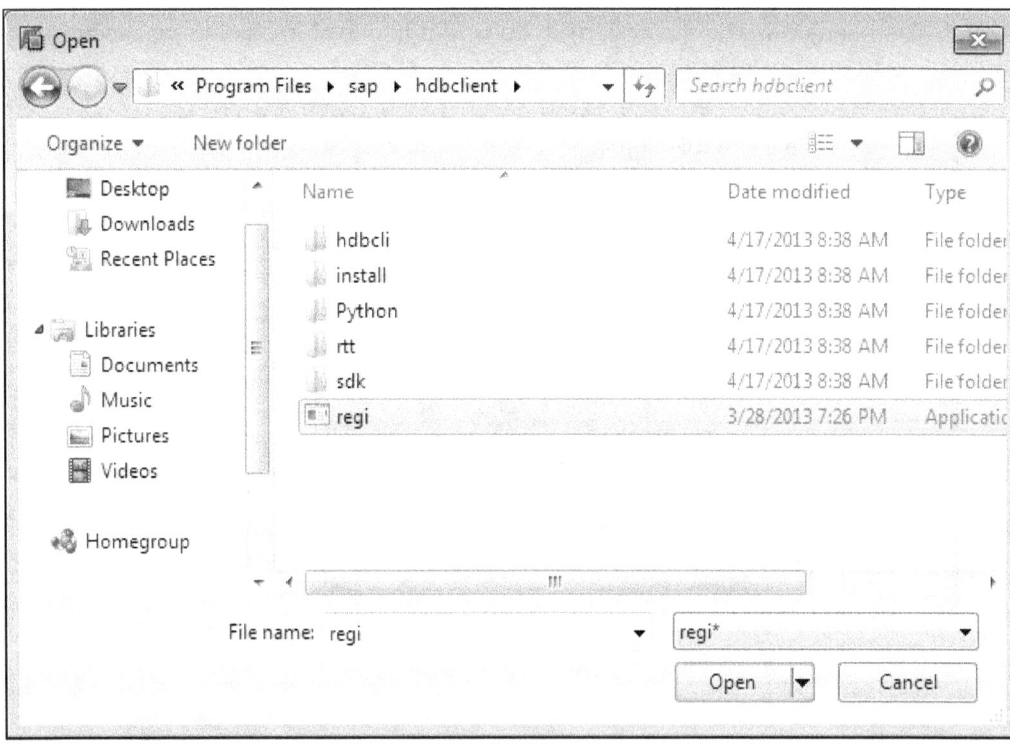

Select the `regi` file, and click on **Open** to validate your choice. You can then click on the **OK** button to dismiss the **Configuration** dialog, and then on **OK** to dismiss the error message. Now click on **Cancel** in the **Repository Workspaces** dialog, and try once more to right-click on your project name (`xstest`) in the **Navigator** panel, and select **Team** | **Share project**. The **Share project** dialog will appear once more, this time without the error message, and you can continue configuring your project.

As you can see in the screenshot, there are currently no repositories in this SAP HANA system, so we'll need to create one. Click on **Add Workspace** to do this.

You will see the **Create New Repository Workspace** dialog, which will ask for the SAP HANA user to use (you can see in the screenshot that both our `SYSTEM` user and our `BOOKU` user, which we used to test our authorizations, are listed). You will also need to give the workspace a name (here, `xstest`) and a directory on your PC to hold the files you are working on currently:

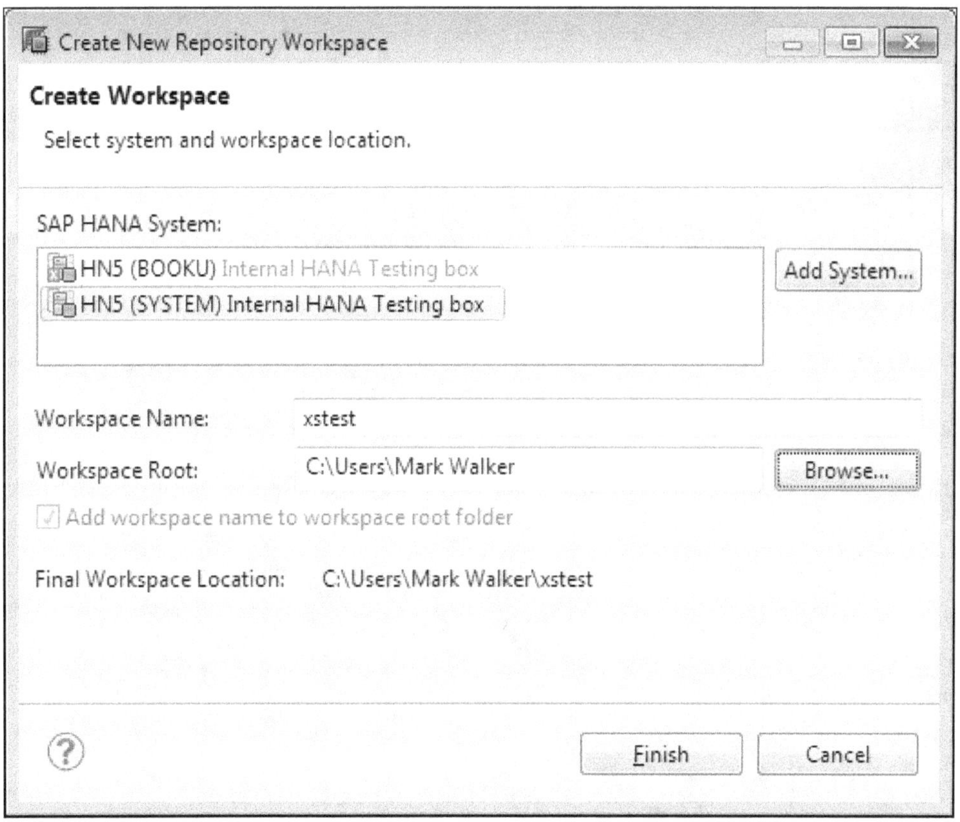

Once you have entered the identification information for your workspace, click on **Finish** to see it listed in the list of available workspaces, as you can see here:

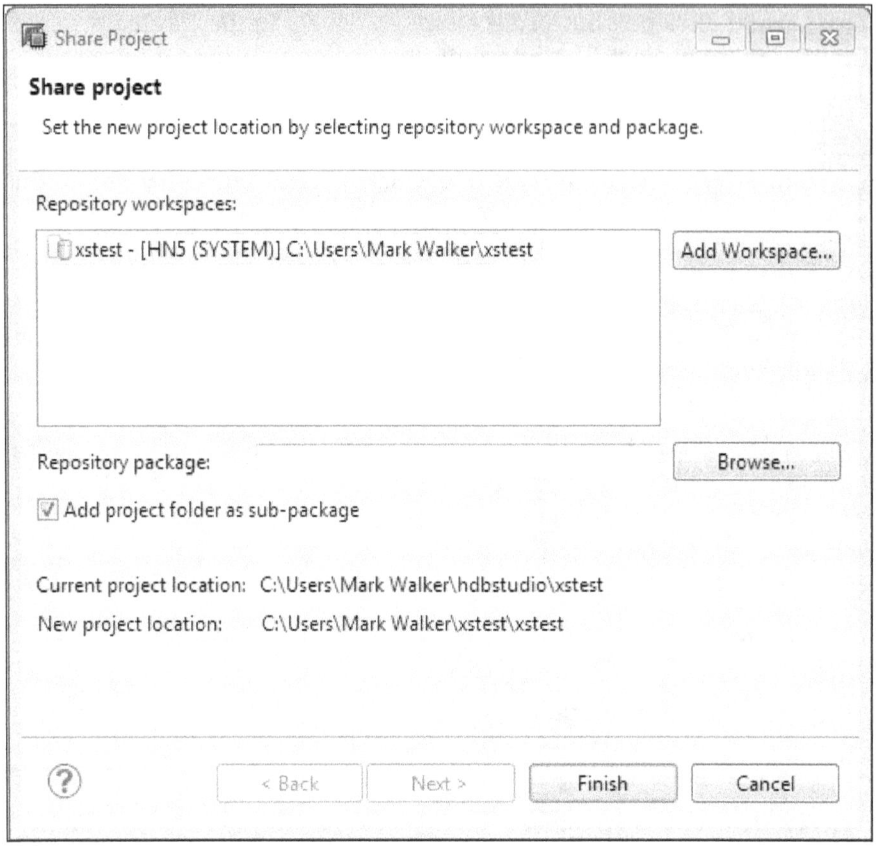

At this point we can add our `xstest` package to our workspace, using the **Browse** button, as shown in the following screenshot:

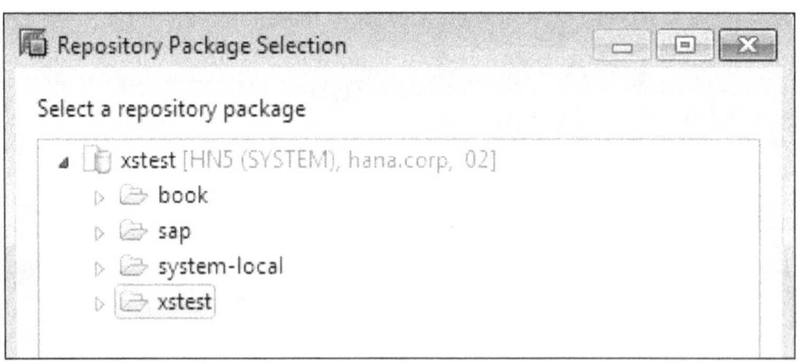

Once you have selected the package for your project and chosen the workspace in which you wish to work with the project files, you can click on **Finish** to dismiss the dialog, and share your project.

A project shared on the server is indicated in the **Project Explorer** panel with the package name alongside the server name. In the following screenshot, we can see that our `xstest` project has been shared on the server in our `xstest` package, and the `dummy` project has not been shared yet:

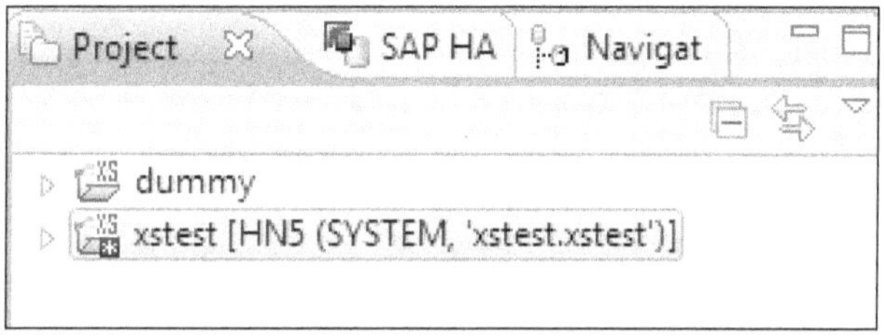

Checking the status of your project files

When a project exists on the SAP HANA server, files in the project can be in one of several different states:

- **New on the PC, inexistent on the server, or changed on the PC**: Files or projects in this state will be shown with a black square icon with a white star. You can see this is the case of the whole `xstest` project in the previous screenshot. To commit items in this state to the server, right-click on them and select **Team** | **Commit** from the menu. Do this for your `xstest` project now, so that the version on the server will be synchronized with that on the PC.
- **Committed to the server, but inactive**: Like all items in SAP HANA, an XS Engine object must be activated before it can be used. Activation for programs will check that the syntax of the program is correct; for projects it will try to ensure that all required files referenced are present and will indicate to the XS Engine that the project can be run. Objects needing activation will have a gray diamond icon. If you make any changes you will need to remember to activate your object before it will be usable. Please take a minute or two to activate your `xstest` project now.
- **Active**: Like our modeling objects in previous chapters, active objects are those that will be used when called upon, either in the Studio or in other developments. They are the only objects that will return values to users.

Understanding application descriptor files

Before we can use our project we need to do some work with it. First, we have to create some special files on the server, which will indicate what type of project we have created, so that the XSEngine can process it correctly. Then we'll write some actual content.

XS Engine applications have three possible application descriptor files:

- **The application descriptor file**: This tells the XS Engine that in the package being referenced (our package here is called `xstest`), there is an XS Engine application (as opposed to a SAP HANA modeling development).
- **The application access file**: This tells the XS Engine who can see and do what in your application. This file defines, among other things, URL rewriting rules for your application and indeed whether the application itself is exposed by the web server; that is, whether it is an application that can be called from a web browser.
- **The application privileges file**: This defines the authorizations for your development. Privileges defined in this file are converted into SAP HANA authorizations when you activate the file.

Creating the application descriptor file

An application descriptor file is a file called `.xsapp`. It has no name, just the extension, and no content. It serves to tell the XS Engine that the package containing the `.xsapp` file contains an XS Engine application. To this extent, no content is necessary; the existence of the file is enough.

To create the file, right-click on your project name in the **Project Explorer** panel (ours is called `xstest`), and select **New | File** from the menu, as shown in the following screenshot:

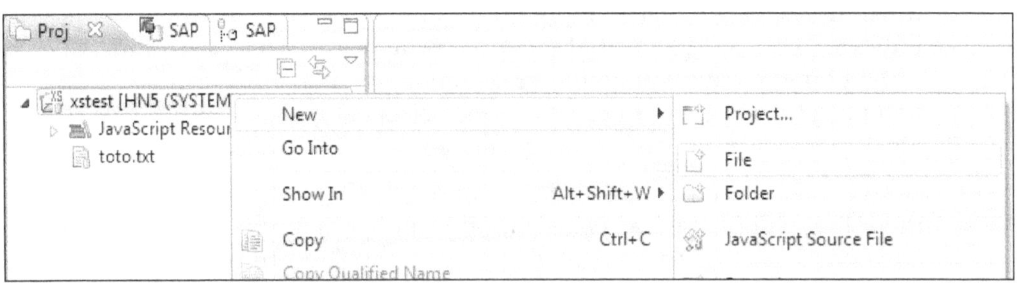

In the **New File** dialog, leave the parent folder at its default value of the project, and enter a filename of `.xsapp` (just the extension). Click on **Finish** to create the file.

As explained earlier, we'll leave the file empty, and just commit it to the server, then activate it. Right-click on the filename in the **Project Explorer** panel, and select **Team | Commit** from the menu to add it to the project on the server. You can now right-click on it once more, and select **Team | Activate** to activate the file.

> Remember that a file must be activated before it is usable by the server. If you have made changes to a file and it is not listed in the **Project Explorer** panel as uncommitted, yet you don't see your changes reflected in the development when you test, then it is more than likely you didn't activate the file.
>
> It is usually a good idea to activate the whole project when you have committed changes to existing files, or have added new files to the project. This makes sure that the project is coherent.

We now have a package containing an XS Engine application, and have created the first application descriptor file, the `.xsapp` file, telling the XS Engine that there is an application in the given package. Next, we need to create the application access descriptor file.

Creating the application access descriptor

This file, like the application descriptor file, is necessary for the XS Engine to present our application to users via the web interface. Whereas the `.xsapp` file tells the XS Engine that a package contains an application, the application access descriptor, `.xsaccess`, tells the XS Engine how the application should be called up. It indicates whether the application is visible, whether users need to log in, and other basic configuration options for the application.

Like the `.xsapp` file, the `.xsaccess` file has no name, just the extension. Unlike the `.xsapp` file, however, the `.xsaccess` file does have some contents. The file consists of statements defining the application. These are basically name-value pairs, with the name being the configuration option, and the value, the particular configuration value.

The `.xsaccess` file needs to be a valid **JSON** (**JavaScript Object Notation**) file, meaning that the format needs to respect JSON syntax. Since all JSON sentences are surrounded by curly braces {}, the `.xsaccess` file needs to contain at least one pair of braces.

Configuration options in the .xsaccess file

The `.xsaccess` file can contain one or more configuration options for your application. If a particular configuration parameter is not present in the file, its default value will be used. The available configuration options, their default values, and meanings are listed as follows:

- **exposed** (default: **false**): This indicates to the XSEngine that the given application should be visible (**true**) or invisible (**false**). If your application configuration does not contain an `exposed` line, or the line is set to `"exposed" : false`, users will receive an HTTP error of 404 (file not found) if they try to access your application. The `exposed` configuration line should appear like this in your `.xsaccess` file:

```
{
  "exposed":true
}
```

- **authentication** (default: **Basic**): This tells the XS Engine that you require users log in to your application in order to use it.

  Available authentication options are as follows:

  - **null** (`"authentication" : null`): This will disable login checks for your application.
  - **Basic** (`"authentication" : Basic`): This will cause the browser to display a login prompt and will require the user to enter a valid database username and password to be able to use your application.
  - **SAP Logon Ticket** (`"authentication" : LogonTicket`): This option tells the XS Engine to accept valid SAP Single sign-on (SSO) tickets, usually sent via browser cookies to the web server.
  - **Form-based login** (`"authentication" : Form`): This redirects your user to a form to fill in in order to log in. This option requires a special setup in the XS Engine configuration.

  If you wish, you can list different authentication options as an array, allowing login using any of the available methods. You could therefore choose to accept an SSO login if one is presented, or require that the user log in using their username and password, as follows:

```
{
  "authentication":
    [
      {
```

```
            "method":"LogonTicket"
          },
          {
            "method":"Basic"
          }
        ]
    }
```

- **authorization** (no default value): This lists the authorization values you require that your users possess in order to use your application. These values need to be listed in the application privileges file. If you create a package called `xstest` as we have done, and inside this package you create another package called `admin`, you can require special privileges for the `admin` package, allowing you to split your users into two groups of **user** and **admin** easily. Authorization can be implemented with something like the following code snippet:

```
{
  "authorization":
      [
          "xstest::Reader",
          "xstest::Admin"
      ]
}
```

- **rewrite_rules** (no default value): Readers familiar with website development will most likely have come across this notion before. Rewrite rules allow you to give URLs to your users that are easier to read, and usually shorter. For example, instead of an URL of `http://hana.corp:8002/xstest/xstest/index.xsjs?client=tom&country=FR&action=list`, you could use something like `http://hana.corp:8002/xstest/xstest/list/FR/tom`.

  To achieve this, you would use the following configuration snippet:

```
{
  "rewrite_rules" :
  [
    {
      "source": "/list/(\\d+)/(\\d+)/",
      "target": "/index.xsjs?client=$2&country=$1&action=list"
    }
  ]
}
```

- **mime_mapping** (no default value): This allows you to define the mapping between a file's extension, and the mime type with which this file will be sent to the server. For example, you could force the XS Engine to transfer all PNG images with the `.png` extension as the mime type `image/png` with the configuration:

  ```
  {
    "mime_mapping" :
      [
        {
          "extension":"png", "mimetype":"image/png"
        }
      ]
  }
  ```

- **force_ssl** (default: **false**): This tells the XS Engine whether to accept connections using standard HTTP (`"force_ssl" : false`), or only secure connections using HTTPS (`"force_ssl" : true`) should be accepted for your application. `force_ssl` is written as follows in the configuration file:

  ```
  {
    "force_ssl":true
  }
  ```

- **enable_etags** (default: **true**): If enabled, this option will generate entity tags (**etags**) for all static content sent by the server (such as text files or images). This can help browser caches, since it is easier for the browser to tell if content has changed, and avoid asking for the same, unchanged content twice. Use `enable_etags` as follows:

  ```
  {
    "enable_etags":true
  }
  ```

- **prevent_xsrf** (default: **false**): This will enable checking by the XS Engine against cross-site request-forgery (**xsrf**) attacks on your application. This requires that you first initialize the background security token, then use it in all communication with the XS Engine. If you activate this configuration option but do not send the security token to the server on all communication, the XS Engine will refuse the communication with an error. You can activate this option with the following configuration snippet:

  ```
  {
    "prevent_xsrf":true
  }
  ```

We have looked at all available configuration options for our `.xsaccess` file, so let's create one for our project now. This is done in the same way as for our `.xsapp` file, just right-click on the project name in the **Project Explorer** panel, select **New** | **File** from the menu, enter a filename of `.xsaccess`, then commit and activate it on the server.

In our configuration file, we want to expose our application (since if we don't, we won't be able to call it up), and tell the XS Engine that we don't require that the users log in to use our application. To do this, we will use the `exposed` and `authentication` keywords, as follows:

```
{
     "exposed" : true,
     "authentication" : null
}
```

Please type this content into the `.xsaccess` file that has opened as an editor window when you created the file, as shown in the following screenshot:

Once you have made these changes, commit and reactivate the file once more (right-click, and navigate to **Team** | **Commit**, right-click, and navigate to **Team** | **Activate**).

At this point, we have a skeleton application that is usable by the XS Engine. Everything is in place to be able to create our web application, the only thing missing is the application itself!

Hello, World!

Let's start our development by creating the standard first application used in every language under the sun; the Hello, World application. This will allow us to ensure that our development environment is functioning correctly, that our application descriptor files (`.xsapp` and `.xsaccess`) are correct and that the XS Engine is working correctly.

To do this, we'll create a new file in our application, called `hello.xsjs`. This file will be our application's main file, the one we'll call from our browser.

An XS Engine program is written in JavaScript, and the program generates HTML for the browser. Our program will be very simple—it will just tell the browser that we're sending some HTML, and then output the `Hello, World` text.

Our program code is therefore as follows:

```
$.response.contentType = "text/html";
$.response.setBody( "Hello, World !");
```

Type this code into the `hello.xsjs` file, then commit and activate it on the server.

The `$` annotation at the start of each line tells the XS Engine we are accessing the XS Engine JavaScript API. It basically means "the web application". Following that, we have a period, and then the word `response`.

> The full documentation concerning the XS Engine JavaScript syntax and APIs can be found on the **help.sap.com** site at `http://help.sap.com/hana/jsapi/index.html`.

This syntax (`$.response`) means the response object (`response`) of (`.`) the web application (`$`). It is a standard way of accessing different properties and methods of an object. Give the object's name, a period, and then the property or method name.

As we can see in the previous code, this logic can be extended further, where in the first line, we access the `contentType` property of the `response` object of the web application. Reading the lines backwards is usually the easiest way of figuring out what is going on.

The first line of our code is as follows:

```
$.response.contentType = "text/html";
```

As we have just seen, we're manipulating the `contentType` property. This indicates to the browser what kind of information we're sending it. By giving a value to the `contentType` property, we can influence how the browser will interpret the response. In our example, we set the value to `text/html`, which is the **MimeType** for an HTML document.

We could have set the value to `text/plain` if we were sending a text document that the browser shouldn't try to interpret as HTML, for example.

> Just about every type of content imaginable on the Internet has an associated MimeType, from the PNG images (`image/png`) we saw in the previous section, to HTML files (`text/html`), Shockwave Flash files (`application/x-shockwave-flash`), and so on. Setting the correct MimeType helps the user's browser display your content correctly. For more information on the meaning and usage of MimeTypes, see the Wikipedia article on the subject at `https://en.wikipedia.org/wiki/Internet_media_type`.

The first line of our code sets the MimeType, but does not give any output to the user. The actual output of our application is handled by the second line:

```
$.response.setBody( "Hello, World !");
```

Here, we're accessing the `setBody` method of the `response` object. We can tell it's a method because of the brackets. The content of the brackets are the argument we pass to the method—in our case, the argument is the HTML page.

> A property does nothing, but stores a value for later use. A method performs an action, with or without parameters, and maybe using property values set previously.

So our program, in English, reads something like this:

Set the output type to `html`, and then send "Hello, World !" to the browser.

Let's see if it works!

Calling up our XS Engine application in a browser

As we saw at the beginning of this chapter, the XS Engine is running on our SAP HANA Server, and will respond to requests on the port `80<instance>` (in the example of the server running at the address `hana.corp` with an instance number of `02`, the address for the XS Engine is `http://hana.corp:8002`).

In order to call up our application, we need to tell the XS Engine where it is located. In our case, the file we want is called `hello.xsjs`, in the `xstest` project, in the `xstest` package.

The XS Engine expects for URLs to follow the following syntax:

```
<server>:<port>/<package>/<project>/<file>
```

In our case this gives an URL of:

```
http://hana.corp:8002/xstest/xstest/hello.xsjs
```

> You will need to change the address to that of your SAP HANA Server, and change the port, if your instance number is not 02.

If we type this address into our browser, we will see our XS Engine application in all its glory:

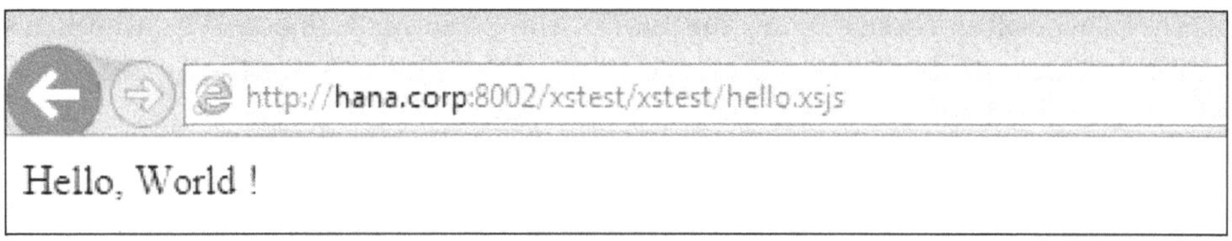

Congratulations! We have a functioning XS Engine application.

Let's move on to something a little more complex—accessing data in the SAP HANA database from an XS Engine application.

XS Engine database access

Accessing the database itself from within an XS Engine application is done simply, from JavaScript. In this section, we'll take a look at what needs to be done on the backend to get this to work.

The first thing that SAP HANA requires in order to give access to the database is that a user should be logged into the system. For that reason, the authentication-less application we've just built cannot be used as-is for database access.

You, therefore, have two options at this point:

- Use the application skeleton we've just built as a template for new applications, and copy it to initialize applications as you create them
- Modify the application we've just made, building upon it and adding more features as we go

The option you choose is really up to you. If you will be building a great deal of XS Engine applications, it can be interesting to have a basic template you use (especially if you need to create and use an HTML template, maybe with some images and company-specific CSS files).

If you're just playing with the XS Engine and seeing how it works, you might not need to create application templates at this point.

Copying an XS Engine application

In order to copy an application we've built, in the Studio, right-click on the application name in the **Project Explorer** panel and select **Copy** from the menu that appears.

Then, right-click somewhere in the empty space in the **Project Explorer** panel, and select **Paste**. This will bring up the **Copy Project** dialog, as shown in the following screenshot:

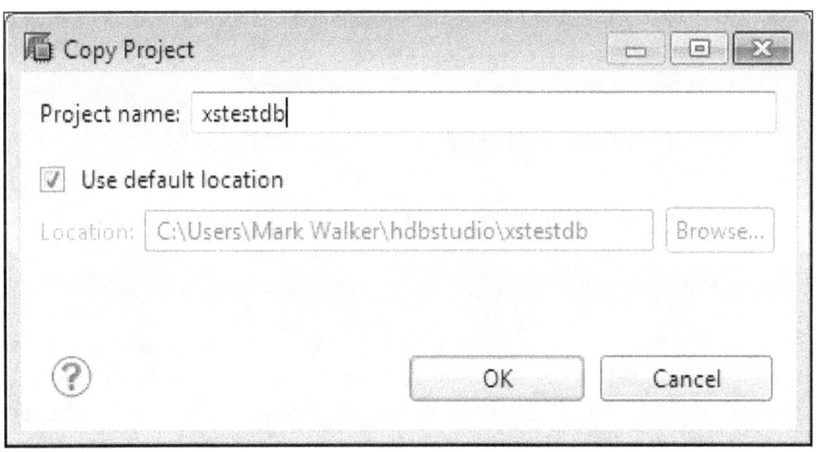

Give your project copy a name (by default it will be `Copy of <project>`, in this case we've called it `xstestdb`), and click on **OK**. You will see an error (at least in all Studio versions up to revision 52):

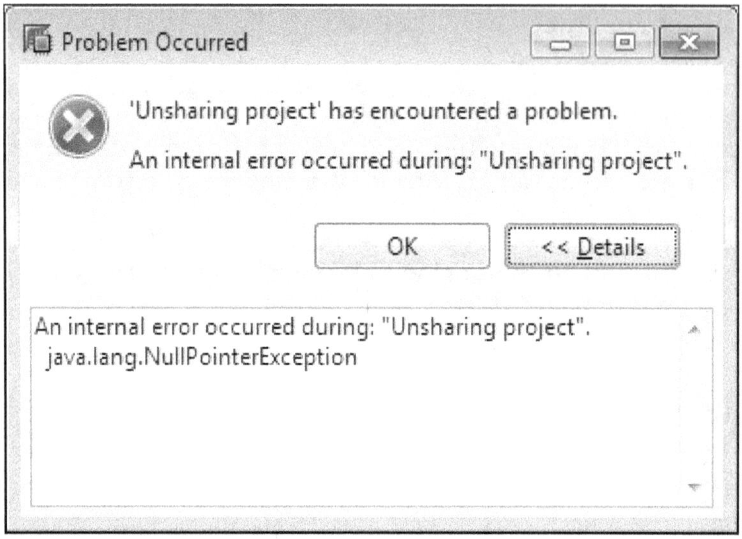

You can ignore this error, just click on **OK** to make it go away.

Your project will now be listed in the **Project Explorer** panel, with a red warning symbol:

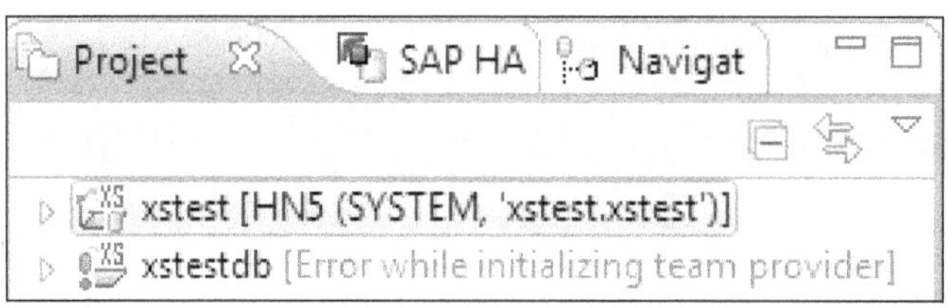

In order to make the project usable, we need to unshare it from the server (we haven't shared it yet, but the fact that we copied it leads the Studio to think the project is shared, leading to the undefined situation we can see in the **Project Explorer** panel). We can then share the project, commit it, and activate it.

Therefore, please perform the following actions on your new project (`xstestdb`):

- **Unshare the project**: Right-click on the project name and select **Team** | **Unshare project** from the menu.

- **Share the project**: Right-click on the project name and select **Team** | **Share Project**. Select your repository workspace and package in the dialog that will appear.

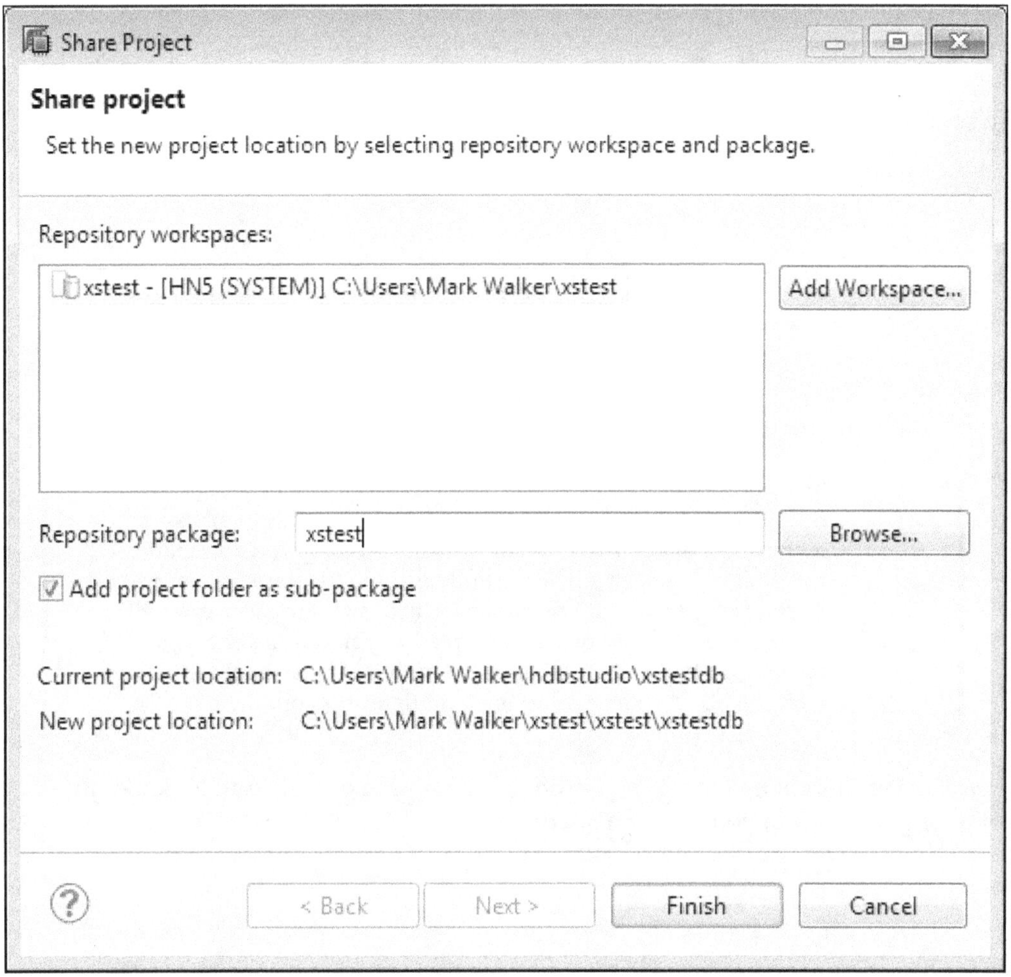

- **Commit the project**: Right-click on the project name, select **Team** | **Commit**.
- **Activate the project**: Right-click on the project name, select **Team** | **Activate**.

After executing this list of actions (in order…), your project is present on the SAP HANA Server, and is callable from a browser. We can now make the necessary changes to use the SAP HANA database from within our application.

Enforcing login in an XS Engine application

As explained earlier, we need to have our user logged in in order to enable database access. We can enforce login, by making a change to the `.xsaccess` file. Changing the line:

```
"authentication" : null
```

To something as follows:

```
"authentication":
  [
    {
      "method":"Basic"
    }
  ]
```

This will enforce login by the XS Engine, and will have the browser take care of creating a login dialog box, showing it to the user, and then handling the response.

> Be aware that Basic authentication is a barebones authentication method. As explained, everything is handled for you automatically, and so it isn't a very advanced authentication system. For example, it won't encrypt communications for you, so your password will be sent over the network unencrypted. If you require encrypted communications, you will have to handle that elsewhere—maybe with the XS Engine's `force_ssl` configuration option.

Please make this change to your `.xsaccess` file now. Your file will look like the following code when you have finished:

```
{
     "exposed" : true,
     "authentication":
     [
       {
         "method":"Basic"
       }
     ]
}
```

If you now commit and reactivate your file on the server and then call up your project file in the browser, you will be asked to log in. In the following screenshot, we're calling up the `hello.xsjs` file, which does not allow database access, but the project has been changed to enforce login, as we can see:

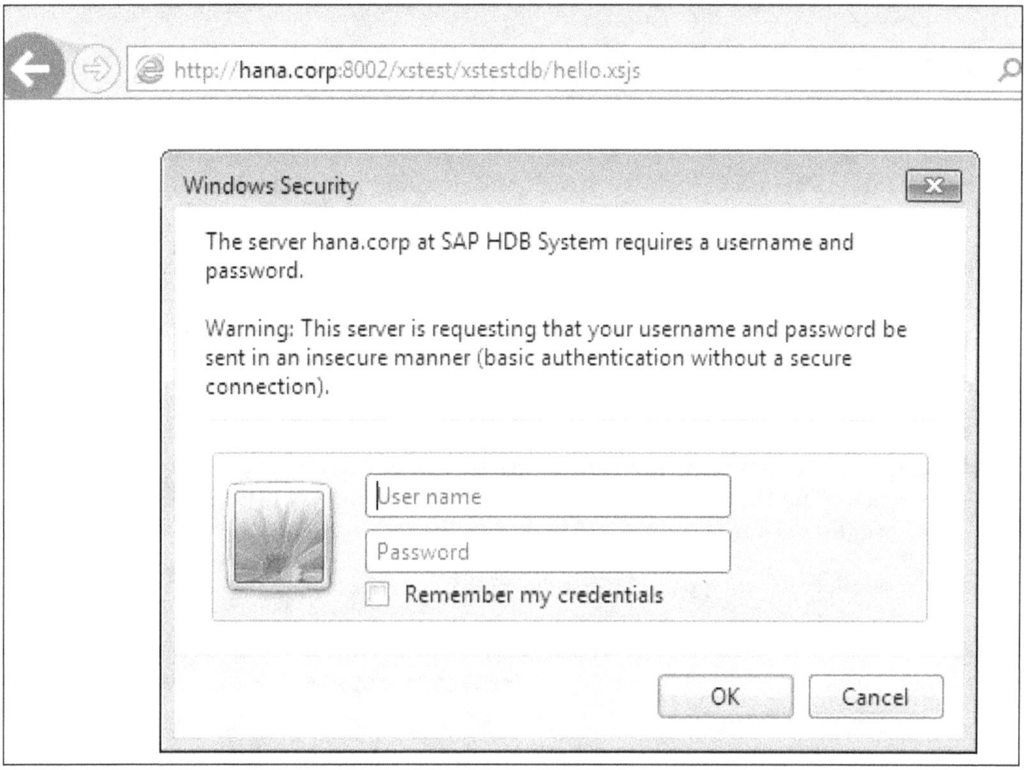

You can log in using your SAP HANA `SYSTEM` username and password (or even use the `BOOKU` user we created in *Chapter 7, Hey! That's My Data! - Authorizations in SAP HANA*, if you like!), and you will once again see the `Hello, World` text.

Accessing the database

With system login being enforced by the application server, we are in a position to request database access from the XS Engine. As you can imagine from an integrated system such as SAP HANA and its XS Engine, accessing the database from your programs is rather simple.

The XS Engine Javascript API provides several objects to handle database access:

- `$.db` handles database connectivity, and will create a connection object using `$.db.getConnection()`
- The connection object (the result of `getConnection()`) allows you to create prepared statements using `prepareStatement()`
- The prepared statement object (the result of `prepareStetement()`), which represents a query, allows you to send queries to the server and get the query results back using `executeQuery()`
- The query result object (the result of `executeQuery()`) allows you to check result sets, loop over available rows, and so on

The full list of the properties and methods of `$.db` can be found in the SAP HANA JavaScript reference (`http://help.sap.com/hana/jsapi/index.html`) but the most important are those we've just seen; they will allow you to get started using the database in your XS Engine programs.

The following is a sample XS Engine program that will access the SAP HANA database, query an attribute view, and then loop over the results, writing results to the webpage. The program code is printed in full here, we'll run it first, then examine how it works in detail:

```
$.response.contentType = "text/html";
var conn = $.db.getConnection();
var pstmt = conn.prepareStatement(
  "select * from \"_SYS_BIC\".\"book/CUST_ATTR\""
  );
var rs = pstmt.executeQuery();
var body="";

if (!rs.next())
{
   body="Failed to query attribute view " +
      "CUST_ATTR in book package";
} else {
   body = rs.getString(4) + "<br>";
   while (rs.next())
   {
      body = body + rs.getString(4) + "<br>";
   }
}
```

```
$.response.setBody(body);
rs.close();
pstmt.close();
conn.close();
```

If we create this file in our project (call it `custlist.xsjs`), save it, commit it, and activate it (or just commit the file and then reactivate the whole project, which will automatically activate the file for us), we will obtain the following results:

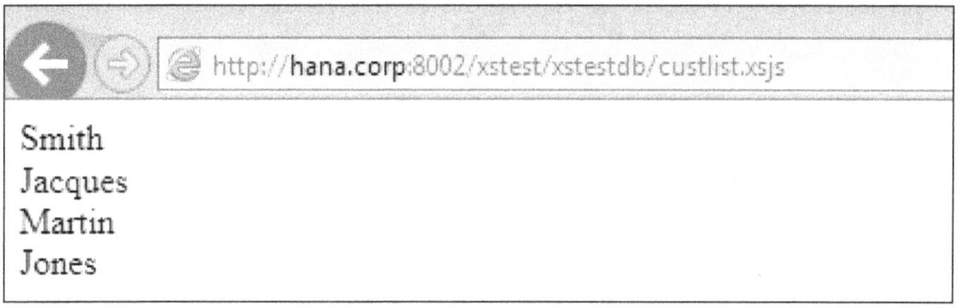

If you recall, this list is the list of customer names in our `CUST_ATTR` view, which we created right back in *Chapter 3, Your First SAP HANA Development - An Attribute View*!

So we can create XS Engine applications and can have them access the database—the sky is the limit! But how exactly did we achieve this result? Let's dissect the program to see the details.

As we saw in our first XS Engine JavaScript application, we indicate to the user's browser that we will be returning HTML code:

```
$.response.contentType = "text/html";
```

This second line of code creates a variable called `conn`. We assign to this variable the result of the `getConnection` method of the `db` object of the web application. This is the line that connects our XS Engine application to the underlying SAP HANA database. It will use the credentials of the currently-connected user. This information is determined at runtime by the browser with the aid of the `authentication: { "method":"Basic" }` line in the `.xsaccess` file:

```
var conn = $.db.getConnection();
```

Once a connection to the database has been opened by the previous line of the program, we can use it to prepare a query for use. We create a `pstmt` variable, to which we assign the result of the `prepareStatement` method of the `conn` variable. A **prepared statement** is an SQL query in which you can replace **placeholders** with variable values at runtime. Since the SQL query we are using does not contain any placeholders, we do not strictly need to use a prepared statement, but it is a good habit to use them generally, for security reasons:

```
var pstmt = conn.prepareStatement(
  "select * from \"_SYS_BIC\".\"book/CUST_ATTR\""
  );
```

> Prepared statements using placeholders are, from a security viewpoint, the preferred way of accessing the database, rather than generating your SQL code at runtime.
>
> If we wanted to enable our users to pass a customer ID as a parameter to our program, and then use that parameter to see the customer revenue, we could write the following code:
>
> ```
> var conn = $.db.getConnection();
> var pstmt = conn.prepareStatement( " SELECT
> * FROM REVENUE WHERE CUSTID='" + $.request.
> parameters.get("id"));
> var rs = pstmt.executeQuery();
> ```
>
> Here you can see that we create our query using some fixed code (`SELECT * FROM REVENUE WHERE CUSTID=`) and we concatenate with that `ID` given as a parameter. Call the program in our browser with the following URL:
>
> `http://hana.corp:8002/custrevenue.xsjs?id=3`
>
> We will obtain the revenue for the customer with ID of `3`.
>
> This is a very simple way of using user input in our programs, but it is one of the biggest security holes we could introduce into our program.

A malicious user could change the URL of our program in an attempt either to see unauthorized data (here trying to see data for all users by adding a condition to our `WHERE` clause, which will always evaluate to true):

```
http://hana.corp:8002/custrevenue.xsjs?id=3 'or
1=1'
```

Or worse, using the security hole to corrupt our database (here by adding some custom SQL):

```
http://hana.corp:8002/custrevenue.xsjs?id=3 ';
delete from revenue;'
```

This type of security hole is called an **SQL Injection flaw**, because any user can inject any SQL they wish into our application. Using placeholders in your SQL code is the easiest way to protect against this type of attack in your program, since user input is checked for correct typing and content, and your program will fail rather than execute unwanted code.

We could change our sample program to the following to use a placeholder:

```
var conn = $.db.getConnection();
var pstmt = conn.prepareStatement( " SELECT *
FROM REVENUE WHERE CUSTID=?' );
pstmt.setInt(1, $.request.parameters.get("id"));
var rs = pstmt.executeQuery();
```

As you can see, the user input (the `id` variable) is used in the `setInt` call, which will replace the first placeholder in the SQL statement (the first question mark) with the value of the user input. If the user's input is not an integer, this call will fail, but your application will be protected.

Once our prepared statement has been created, we can execute it on the database, and return the results of the SQL in a variable we call `rs`:

```
var rs = pstmt.executeQuery();
```

The following line creates a variable called `body`, and makes sure it is empty. This variable will be used to hold the HTML page we are creating before we send it to the browser at the end of our program:

```
var body="";
```

The following code snippet checks whether the SQL query was correctly executed. If the SQL failed, the `rs` variable (which is the result of the SQL query; in technical terms an object of type `ResultSet`, according to the SAP documentation) will not have a method called `next()`. You should always check whether the action you attempt to execute succeeded or not:

```
if (!rs.next())
{
  body="Failed to query attribute view " +
    "CUST_ATTR in book package";
```

At this point in the program, inside the `else` statement, we know that the SQL query was correctly executed. In the `rs` variable, therefore, we have the lines of data in the `CUST_ATTR` view. More specifically, `rs` will contain at any moment in time one line of the contents of `CUST_ATTR`. We need to loop through the results in order to use each line:

```
} else {
    body = rs.getString(4) + "<br>";
```

The `rs` variable, being of type `ResultSet`, has various methods available for reading the values of the fields in the result line. You can find a complete list of these methods in the SAP Help on the `ResultSet` object, at `http://help.sap.com/hana/jsapi/classxsruntime_1_1db_1_1ResultSet.html`. In our example, we use the `getString` method to recover the value of the fourth field in the view. This corresponds to the Customer Name field, as we can see here in the definition of the `CUST_ATTR` view:

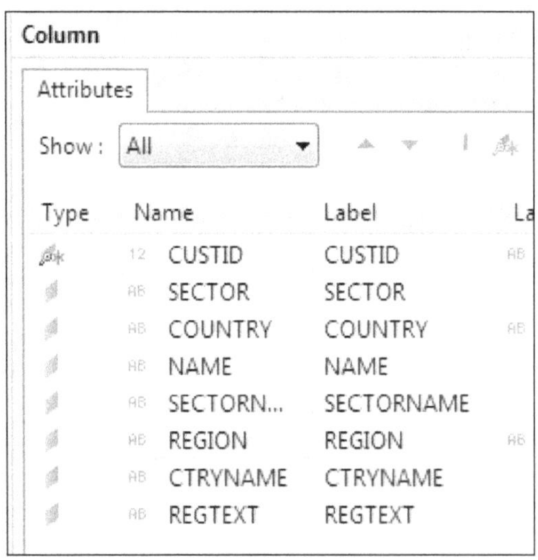

Column numbers in XS Engine JavaScript start at 1 (not 0 as in many computing languages), so column number 4 corresponds to the NAME column. We recover this value, and add it to the body variable (the output of our page), along with an HTML line break (<br>):

```
while (rs.next())
{
  body = body + rs.getString(4) + "<br>";
}
```

This loop (which will execute as long as the rs variable has a next() method, so for each row read from the database) recovers the names for all the other customers, and adds them all to the page output:

```
}

$.response.setBody(body);
```

We return the webpage to the browser using the setBody method of the response object, with our body variable:

```
rs.close();
pstmt.close();
conn.close();
```

Finally, we close (and free the memory) of the result of our query, then the query, and then the database connection itself. Be careful to release these objects in the reverse order you create them—you cannot close the connection to the database, and then free the prepared statement, because the prepared statement refers to the database connection internally. Closing these objects in the wrong order could lead to your program crashing.

In this section, you've seen how to do simple database access using the XS Engine, and how you can loop over the result of a query in order to present the results to the user in a simple list. Next we'll take a look at a real **user interface (UI)** development using a framework provided by SAP just for that purpose.

Developing user interfaces using SAPUI5

SAP has developed and made available a user interface framework for use with its products. Using this framework, which is called **SAPUI5**, you can create rich interfaces for your users, with a consistent look and feel.

Documentation for the SAPUI5 toolkit is available directly from your SAP HANA Server at the following address:

```
http://server:port/sap/ui5/1/sdk/index.html
```

In our case, the documentation is available at:

```
http://hana.corp:8002/sap/ui5/1/sdk/index.html
```

The documentation provides a complete list of available functionality, as well as detailed examples for each of the user interface controls available, how they can be created in your programs, and how their parameters change their function.

Here's a quick glimpse at one of the pages in the documentation detailing the **Value Holders** type of control:

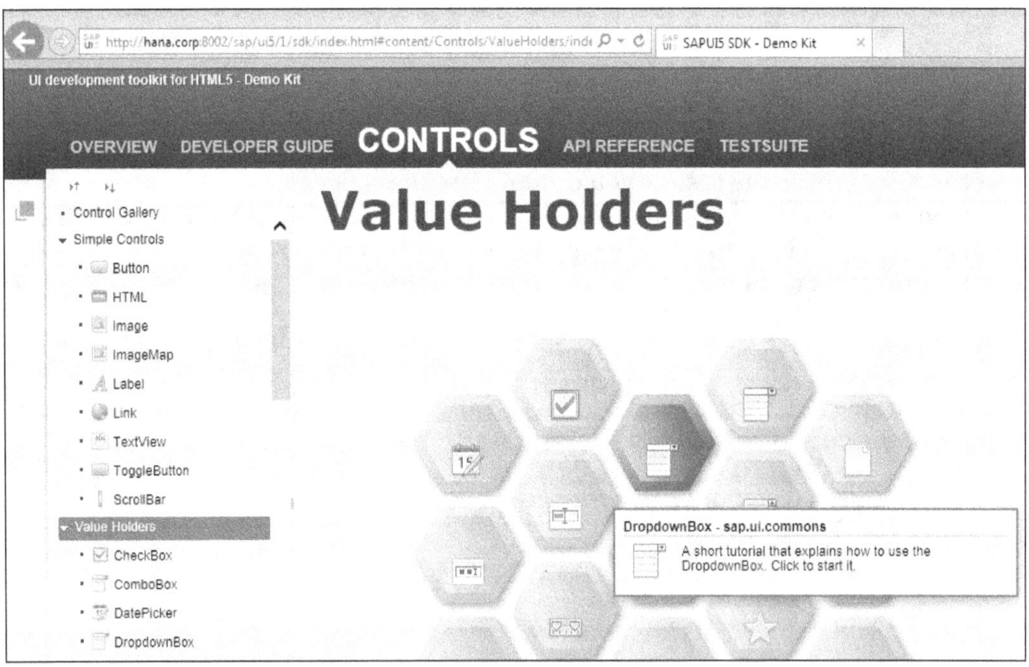

It is worth taking some time to get familiar with the different controls SAPUI5 makes available, it'll be time saved later when you create your own applications.

Here's an example of the user interface we'll be creating in this section:

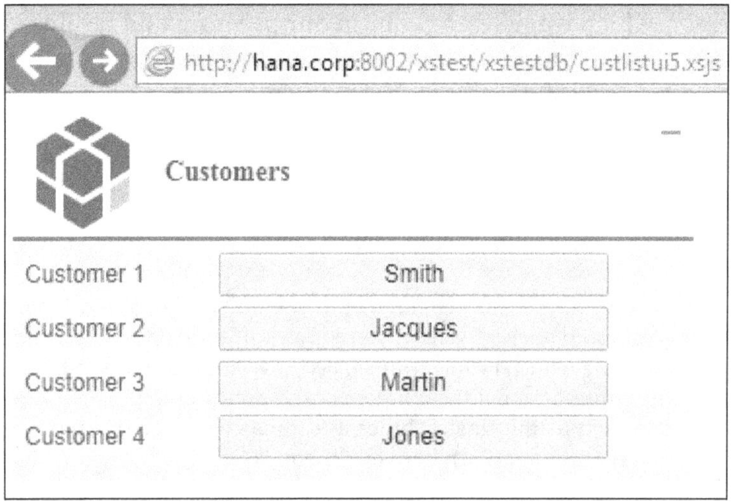

We have made a list of customers, with each customer name being a button; when the user clicks on it, some details about the customer will be shown, as we can see here:

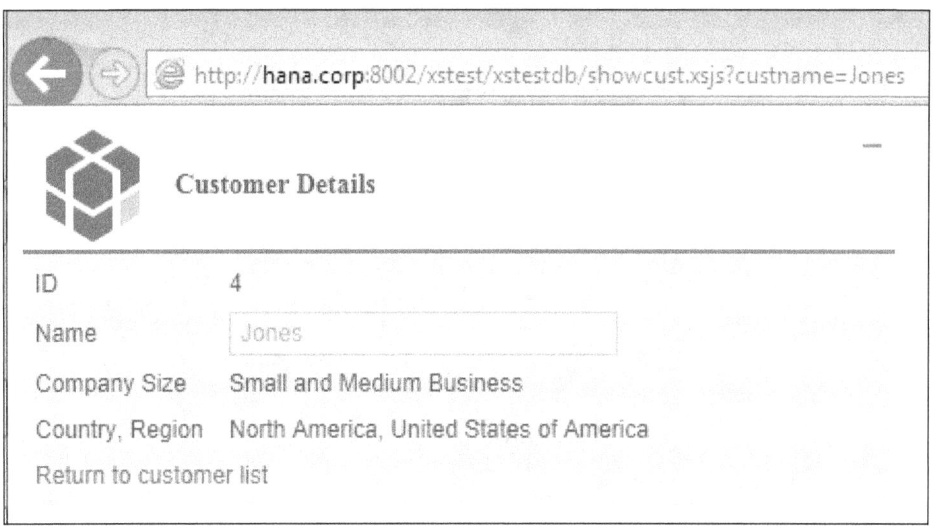

As you can see from the screenshots, we'll be building upon our existing customer list program, filling it out with a real user interface, and making it link to a new program that will show some information about the selected customer.

The most important thing to note about using SAPUI5 is that the framework is a JavaScript library, which we will reference in our program and be able to use in the web pages we create. This leads to an interesting situation where our server program (the `custlist.xsjs` program), written in JavaScript, is generating a web page that is JavaScript in itself. This can at times be somewhat hard to read, especially when we need to determine which closing bracket belongs to which opening bracket, or when we need to *escape* a bracket, since it is used by the browser on the frontend, and not by the server on the backend.

> When you are writing code, and especially when it is a language such as JavaScript, where there is a multitude of braces, brackets, and single and double quotes, if you want to be sure to have the right number of closing braces corresponding to the opening braces, type the closing brace as soon as you type the opening brace, and then fill in between them.

Adding an image resource to an XS Engine project

In the screenshots we have just seen, you can see an image representing a cube:

This image is available in the code supporting the book, and you will need to upload it to the SAP HANA Server as part of your project in order to be able to use it in your developments.

The easiest way of uploading a file to the server is by using drag-and-drop, from your computer to the **Project Explorer** panel of the Studio.

First let's create a subfolder in our project to hold the image files we will be using (there will be only one image in our example). Right-click on your project name, and select **New** | **Folder** to create a new subfolder:

You will be presented with the **New Folder** dialog, as shown in the preceding screenshot. Make sure your project is selected in the list (here, `xstestdb` is selected), type a name for your folder (`images`) and select **Finish** to create it on the server.

Once the folder has been created, you will need, like for any other object we create, to commit and activate it before you can use it. As usual, right-click on the folder name and select **Team** | **Commit**, then **Team** | **Activate** to do this.

Once the folder has been created, we can upload our image. Make sure that you can see, on your computer screen, the **Project Explorer** panel of the Studio, as well as a **Windows Explorer** view of the folder containing your image to upload, as we can see in the following screenshot:

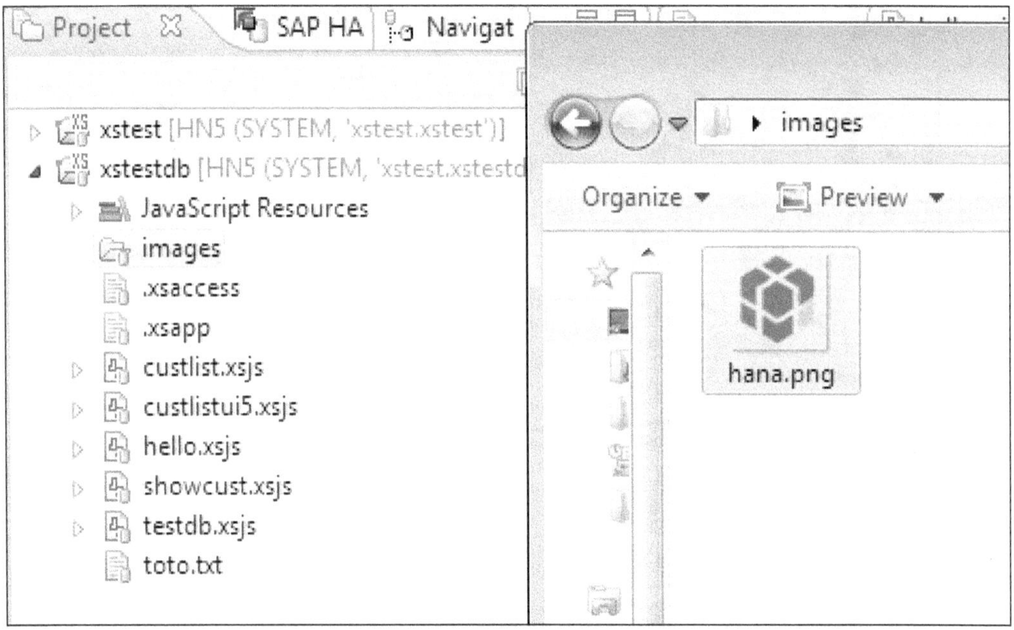

You can now click on your image, drag it to the `images` folder in the **Project Explorer** panel of the Studio, and drop it. The Studio will ask what you want to do with the dropped object, with a **File Operation** dialog:

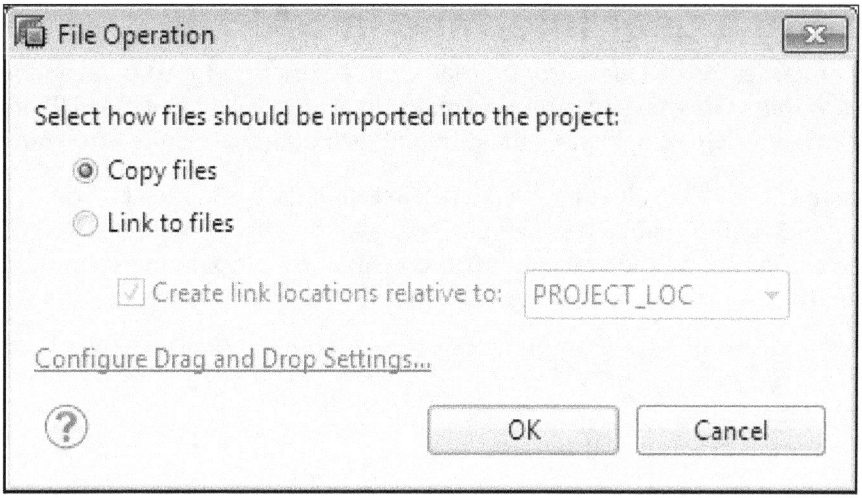

Leave **Copy files** selected, and click on **OK** to upload your image. As usual, commit it and activate it so we can use it later.

> You can upload other file types to your project in the same way (maybe you have a PDF file you want your users to be able to access). You can even select a whole directory (maybe your corporate identity images that you will need to use in your project) and upload the directory and all its contents at once.

Your image has now been uploaded into the `images` directory of your project. If you call the URL with a browser, you will see the image displayed correctly:

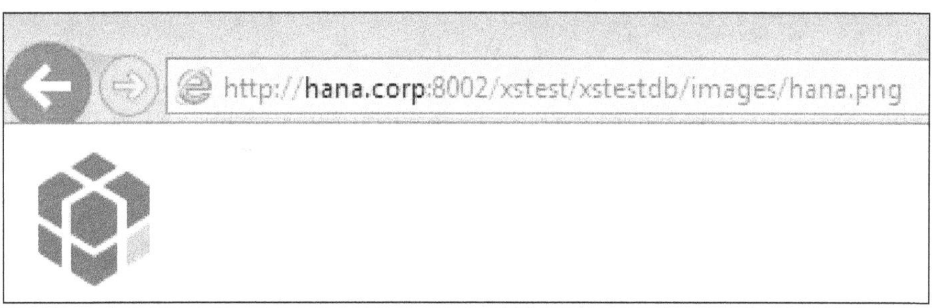

Creating a user interface in SAPUI5

As we saw earlier, SAPUI5 is a user interface framework developed in JavaScript. This means that your web pages need to make JavaScript calls to the SAPUI5 library in order to have it create and show the different user interface elements to your users.

In our example, we'll be creating a `Panel` item (which is basically a box on the screen), which will contain a number of `Rows`, each of which will have two `Columns`, with a `Label` control in the first column and a `Button` control in the second. As a reminder, the desired output for our customer list page is shown here once again:

Prototyping the interface in static JavaScript

If we are to use the SAPUI5 library in a web page, the web page itself will need to be written in JavaScript, since this is the base language for the library. Any XS Engine application it itself written in JavaScript, meaning we have a JavaScript program that creates a JavaScript program. Since writing JavaScript, which in turn writes JavaScript, is relatively difficult, at least in the beginning, you might want to start with a static page calling the SAPUI5 framework. This will allow you to have an overview of the result you wish to obtain before integrating it with the database access, and before generating it dynamically.

Doing your development this way will also allow you to ensure that the different options do what you think they should do (and what the documentation claims they do), without taking the risk of breaking your code. It helps you understand the library and get everything clear in your head.

Here is a static HTML page with an example of panel creation and usage, giving output similar to the result we wish to obtain:

```
<html>
<head>
  <script
      src="/sap/ui5/1/resources/sap-ui-core.js"
    id="sap-ui-bootstrap"
    data-sap-ui-libs="sap.ui.commons"
    data-sap-ui-theme="sap_goldreflection" >
  </script>
</head>
<body>
  <div id="uiArea">
  </div>

  <script>
    var oPanel = new sap.ui.commons.Panel(
      {
        width: "350px"
        }
      );
      oPanel.setTitle(
        new sap.ui.commons.Title(
          {
            text: "Customers",
            icon: "images/hana.png"
          }
        )
      );
      var oMatrix = new
        sap.ui.commons.layout.MatrixLayout(
        {
```

```
                layoutFixed: true,
                width: '300px',
                columns: 2
            }
        );
        oMatrix.setWidths('100px', '200px');
        var customer=1;
        var oLabel = new sap.ui.commons.Label(
            {
                text: 'CustID '+String(customer)
            }
        );
        var oButton = new sap.ui.commons.Button(
            {
                text: 'Button',
                width: '200px',
                press: function()
                    {
                        alert('Pressed');
                    }
            }
        );
        oLabel.setLabelFor(oButton);
        oMatrix.createRow(oLabel, oButton);
        oPanel.addContent(oMatrix);
        oPanel.placeAt("uiArea");
      </script>
    </body>
</html>
```

Running this web page on the server will obtain the following result. The screenshot shows what happens when the button is pressed:

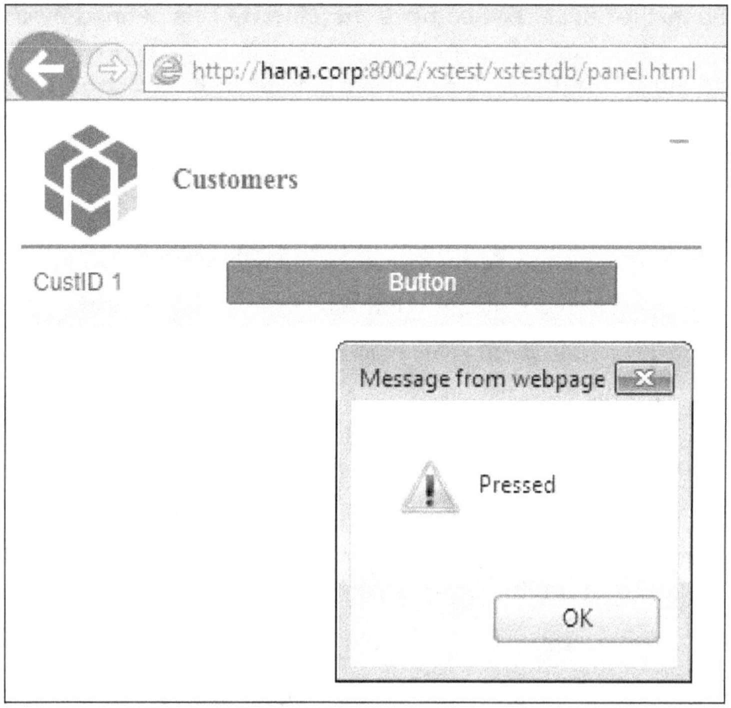

The interesting points in the aforementioned program are listed. The numbers refer to the line numbers in the code:

- 3 to 7: These lines cover including and initializing the SAPUI5 library in the HTML web page. This call will be similar in all programs you write. The path to the library is fixed by SAP. There are three different screen themes (`data-sap-ui-theme`) available: `sap_goldreflection`, `sap_platinum`, and `sap_mvi`. They all have the same functionality, only the design on the screen changes.
- 11: A SAPUI5 application on the frontend is represented by an HTML `div` element. This `div` element is initially empty. The SAPUI5 framework will create the contents for the `div` element at runtime.
- 14 to 57: This is the main client-side JavaScript program. It generates the `panel`, `button`, and many other controls at runtime, using the SAPUI5 library.
- 24: The `panel` item has a `header` block (we can see it in the different screenshots) with some text and an optional icon. Here we indicate that the icon to display is the one we uploaded to our project earlier (`hana.png`).

- 40: The text for the `label` component (**CustID 1**) is defined here. Note we use the counter variable `customer`, transform its value to a string, and use that. It will be useful for us when we have several lines in a moment.
- 47: When the user clicks on the `button` item, we can have SAPUI5 call a function. This can either be a JavaScript function defined in our program with a function name (making it reusable), or, as here, by using what's called an **anonymous function**. This function can only be called by clicking on this button. It doesn't exist elsewhere in the program.
- 53: Note the syntax to indicate that the label is a label for the `button` item.
- 55: We add the matrix (the row/column layout) to the `panel` item.
- 56: Then add the `panel` item to the page, which will make it (and all its content) visible for the user. It is here that we indicate that SAPUI5 should place our panel and its contents inside the `uiArea div`.

Take a moment to familiarize yourself with the syntax and usage of the different objects in the program. We'll be using them in the next section, creating them dynamically in our program to output a variable number of lines for our customer list.

Transforming the static JavaScript into dynamically generated code

Once your user interface prototype is satisfactory in static code, you can transform it into a dynamically-generated version, which you can then combine with database access routines. In this way you will create your end result of a web page whose user interface is dynamically generated in the browser using JavaScript, based upon a web page that is generated on the fly on the server, and whose content depends on user actions and database tables. (It sounds complicated, but it's not that hard to get grips with really!).

Creating dynamic output is relatively easy; we saw it earlier with our database access. Put the content in a variable, and at the end of the page, give the variable's contents into the `$.response.setBody()` method.

We'll not detail the transformation of the whole of the static JavaScript code into dynamically created JavaScript as it is a little repetitive, however, here is the start and the end of the program so you can get the idea of how it's done. The complete program is included in the source code accompanying the book, and is called `dynamicpanel.xsjs`.

```
var header=
"<html>"+
"  <head>"+
"    <script src=\"/sap/ui5/1/resources/sap-ui-core.js\""+
"      id=\"sap-ui-bootstrap\""+
"      data-sap-ui-libs=\"sap.ui.commons\""+
"      data-sap-ui-theme=\"sap_goldreflection\" >"+
"    </script>"+
"  </head>"+
"  <body>"+
"      <div id=\"uiArea\">"+
"      </div>";

var body="      <script>"+
"        var oPanel = new sap.ui.commons.Panel("+
"          {"+
"            width: \"350px\""+
"          }"+
"        );";

…
body=body+"          oPanel.placeAt(\"uiArea\");";
var footer="        </script>"+
"  </body>"+
"</html>";
$.response.contentType = "text/html";
$.response.setBody(header + body + footer);
```

The important thing to note in this program is that the JavaScript generates JavaScript code for the browser to interpret. Since both the server and the browser will be using single and double quotes, any which are destined for the browser must be *escaped*. Escaping means indicating to the server that it should ignore a character. In the fourth line of the program snippet shown, the double quotes that are needed on the browser side, for example, are escaped using the **backslash** character, so that the server will ignore them:

```
"    <script src=\"/sap/ui5/1/resources/sap-ui-core.js\""+
```

The whole of the program generates three variables: `header`, `body`, and `footer`. These three variables contain:

- `header`: The top of the HTML page, including the call to initialize the SAPUI5 library

- `footer`: The bottom of the page, notably the closing elements of the `<body>` and `<html>` tags
- `body`: The main HTML page

At the end of the program, we output these variables to the main web page as usual, by giving them to the `$.response.setBody` method.

At the end of this stage, we have a server-side program generating a browser-side JavaScript page, which will generate our user interface at runtime.

We are now in a position to combine this with our database accessing code, to finalize our program.

Integrating the user interface and the database access routines

Integration of the user interface program with the database access is done simply. In the initial database access program we output the customer name directly to the screen:

```
body = body + rs.getString(4) + "<br>";
```

We just need to replace this with the JavaScript code, which will create a line in our panel to generate our interface depending on the table contents:

```
body = body + "var customer=1;";
body = body + "var oLabel = new sap.ui.commons.Label({text: 'Customer
'+String(customer)});\n";
body = body + "var oButton = new sap.ui.commons.Button({text: '" +
rs.getString(4) + "', width: '200px', press: function() {document.
location.href='showcust.xsjs?custname=" + rs.getString(4) + "'}});";
body = body + "oLabel.setLabelFor(oButton);";
body = body + "oMatrix.createRow(oLabel, oButton);";

body = body + "oPanel.addContent(oMatrix);";
```

Admittedly, this new code is much more long-winded, but it does a lot more!

We've basically just copied our panel creation code into our new program and integrated the result from the database read. You can see that we still use the `rs.getString(4)` call to retrieve the customer name, just as we did before. This time it is included in some fancy user interface code, but the actual work done is the same.

We've also used our simple counter variable, called `customer`, in the code. This variable only exists on the browser-side. It will allow us to print out the line number of the table.

Finally, we have changed the anonymous function called when the user presses the button. Instead of just creating a pop-up alert, we will use the button press to redirect the user to a new page (which we haven't created yet). The URL for this new page contains a variable, `custname`, which will contain the name of the customer whose button was pressed. It will allow us to display some information about the customer.

> Note here how we have removed the spacing from the program. You can write your code however you like, indenting the code or not. The spacing and indents (and any blank lines) are for your benefit, not for the server's. You will find that indenting your code, and including blank lines from time to time, you make your code much more readable. This might not seem so important right now, but when you come back to your program in six months, you'll appreciate having taken the time to improve the readability of your code, especially if like here it's a program that creates another program, with numerous brackets, braces, escaped characters, and so on.

The final customer-list program is printed here. It includes the database read operation from the start of the chapter and the SAPUI5 user interface we've just built. Comments have also been added to explain just what we're doing and why:

```
$.response.contentType = "text/html";
var conn = $.db.getConnection();
var pstmt = conn.prepareStatement( "select * from \"_SYS_BIC\".\"book/
CUST_ATTR\"" );
var rs = pstmt.executeQuery();
var body;
body = "";
var head="<html><head>" +
      "<script src=\"/sap/ui5/1/resources/sap-ui-core.js\" id=\"sap-
ui-bootstrap\" data-sap-ui-libs=\"sap.ui.commons\" data-sap-ui-
theme=\"sap_goldreflection\" ></script>"+
      "</head>"+
      "<body>"+
      "<div id=\"uiArea\"></div>";
var footer = "</body></html>";

if (!rs.next())
```

```
{
  $.response.setBody("Oops");
} else {
  //Create a panel instance
  body = "<script>var oPanel = new sap.ui.commons.Panel({width:
\"350px\"});";

  //Set the title of the panel
  body = body + " oPanel.setTitle(new sap.ui.commons.Title({text:
\"Customers\", icon: \"images/hana.png\"}));";

  //Create a matrix layout with 2 columns
  body = body + "var oMatrix = new sap.ui.commons.layout.
MatrixLayout({layoutFixed: true, width: '300px', columns: 2});";
  body = body + "oMatrix.setWidths('100px', '200px');";

  //Begin of main loop on database results
  body = body + "var customer=1;";

  //Create a simple form within the layout
  body = body + "var oLabel = new sap.ui.commons.Label({text:
'Customer '+String(customer)});\n";
  body = body + "var oButton = new sap.ui.commons.Button({text: '" +
rs.getString(4) + "', width: '200px', press: function() {document.
location.href='showcust.xsjs?custname=" + rs.getString(4) + "'}});";
  body = body + "oLabel.setLabelFor(oButton);";
  body = body + "oMatrix.createRow(oLabel, oButton);";

  //Add the form to the panels content area
  body = body + "oPanel.addContent(oMatrix);";
  body = body + "customer=customer + 1;";

  while (rs.next())
  {
    //Create a simple form within the layout
    body = body + "var oLabel = new sap.ui.commons.Label({text:
'Customer '+String(customer)});\n";
    body = body + "var oButton = new sap.ui.commons.Button({text: '"
+ rs.getString(4) + "', width: '200px', press: function() {document.
location.href='showcust.xsjs?custname=" + rs.getString(4) + "'}});";
    body = body + "oLabel.setLabelFor(oButton);";
    body = body + "oMatrix.createRow(oLabel, oButton);";
```

```
        //Add the form to the panels content area
            body = body + "oPanel.addContent(oMatrix);";
            body = body + "customer=customer + 1;";
         }

         //Attach the panel to the page
         body = body + "oPanel.placeAt(\"uiArea\");</script>";
      }

   $.response.setBody(head + body + footer);
   rs.close();
   pstmt.close();
   conn.close();
```

This program is included in the source code accompanying the book. It's called `custlistui5.xsjs`.

We've now built half of our final program. With just one more source file, we'll have built a full customer record display program.

Passing information from one source file to another

A real program needs to pass information from one stage to another; it needs to accept information from the user and act upon it.

As you have seen in the first page of our website, when the user clicks on a button corresponding to a customer, a call is made to a new page, passing the customer name as a parameter to the page:

```
      body = body + "var oButton = new sap.ui.commons.Button({text: '"
   + rs.getString(4) + "', width: '200px', press: function() {document.
   location.href='showcust.xsjs?custname=" + rs.getString(4) + "'}});";
```

In this section we'll create the receiving page, showing how we can access data passed as a parameter, how we can use it safely and avoid the dangers of user-supplied data.

The first thing to do is create the new source file. It is called `showcust.xsjs`. Remember to commit and activate it.

We'll not list the whole of the source code for the `showcust.xsjs` page here, only the parts of it that introduce new concepts. The complete source code for the file is included in the accompanying code for the book.

Since the page's URL will contain a parameter, the customer name, in the `custname` parameter, we will start by recovering this value for use in our program. The XS Engine API provides a method for reading page parameters with the `get` method of the `parameters` object of the `request` object. The `request` object represents the HTTP request, or (put more simply) information about the URL used to call our application. We'll use this `get` method to read the value passed in the URL and save it to a variable called, rather unimaginatively, `custname`:

```
var custname = $.request.parameters.get("custname");
```

As we saw earlier in the chapter, we need to be very careful with user input. Trusting parameters passed to a web page is a very dangerous practice.

To combat this, we'll use a placeholder in the SQL query, and have the XS Engine check that the `custname` variable is really a string and not some other data type. This check will also ensure that the URL does not contain any malicious code.

In order to create a placeholder in the SQL code, we need to write our query, and put a question mark where we will place the variable:

```
var pstmt = conn.prepareStatement( "select * from \"_SYS_BIC\".\"book/
CUST_ATTR\" where name=?" );
```

As before, we are selecting data from our `CUST_ATTR` attribute view, only this time specifying which customer name we are interested in. As such (in our example) the query will return only one row.

To use the placeholder, we need to replace it with the contents of our `custname` variable. To do this securely, the XS Engine provides, once again, a method to achieve this. The `preparedStatement` object (in our program the `pstmt` variable contains an object of type `preparedStatement`) has a number of methods allowing placeholder replacement according to required data type. The `custname` variable should hold a `String` value (representing the customer name), so we'll use the `setString` method, with our `custname` variable, and ask it to replace the first placeholder in the SQL statement:

```
pstmt.setString(1, String(custname));
```

Once the placeholder has been replaced, we can execute the query and use the results in our program in the same way as we did for the `custlistui5.xsjs` file.

The rest of the `showcust.xsjs` file is concerned with the user interface creation, and is not listed here. Take a moment to read through the code in order to confirm to yourself that you understand how we have used the server-side JavaScript once more to create client-side code, creating and using different SAPUI5 objects.

When we run the `showcust.xsjs` file passing a customer name in the URL, we will obtain details concerning our customer:

If, however, the user tries to request information about a customer unknown to the database, an error will be listed:

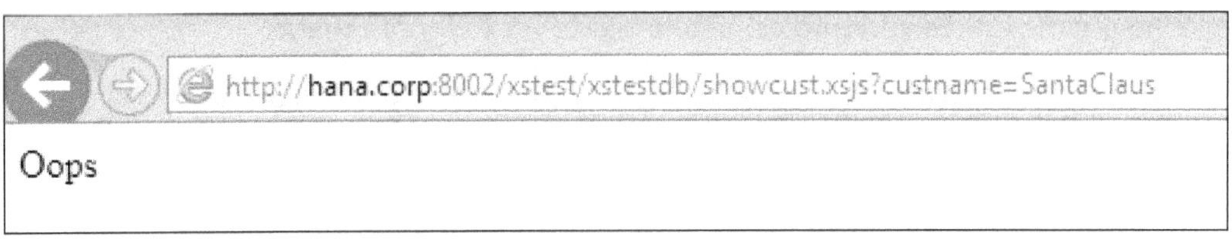

You can, of course, use the SAPUI5 library to personalize the error page, maybe telling the user what they have done wrong.

At this stage, our example XS Engine application is finished. We have created a two-page application using the SAPUI5 framework, accessing the database, presenting the information to the user in a simple but efficient manner.

Summary

In this chapter, we have taken a long journey together examining the XS Engine and the possibilities it offers.

We have seen that the XS Engine is an application server allowing us to write server-side JavaScript programs.

We created a delivery unit, a package, and a project for our developments. The package and project names become the path part of the final web URL.

An XS Engine project requires application descriptor files in order to function; an `.xsapp` file telling the server that the package contains an application, and the `.xsaccess` file describing notions such as **authentication** and whether the application is callable by users or not.

The XS Engine provides a rich API allowing us to create and access our web applications. The starting point of this API is the `$` object. Subobjects of the `$` object give us access to the output web page (`$.response`), to the request URL (`$.request`), and to the SAP HANA database (`$.db`), among other things.

We have seen that we can create a server-side program that can create either a simple HTML page, or a complex web page using client-side JavaScript. In the case we create client-side JavaScript, our code becomes more complex and we need to escape braces and quotes, to tell the server to ignore them.

The XS Engine provides a rich user interface framework in the SAPUI5 library. We took a look at a static web page using the library, creating a panel layout with two columns containing a label and a button.

We then saw how we can transform this static, client-side JavaScript into a server-side program generating the client-side JavaScript. Once this was done, we integrated our JavaScript-generating JavaScript with some database access routines to create a list of customers that the user can interact with.

We saw that when we pass information from one web page to another we must be careful not to trust information coming from outside the application. Using the notion of **placeholders** and **placeholder replacement** in our SQL queries, we protect ourselves and our application from possibly malicious data.

We now possess the basic building blocks necessary to use SAP HANA's XS Engine to do real development work, making web-based applications able to leverage the power of the SAP HANA system to provide functionality for our users.

Quick reference

In this section we present a quick reference to the objects covered in this chapter.

Object	Usage	Creation
XS Engine	Server-side JavaScript-based web application server for SAP HANA.	Installed by default. Runs at http://<server>:80<instance number>.
Project	Groups together all files necessary for an XS Engine application.	Got to the Studio and then to the SAP HANA development perspective. In the Project Explorer panel, right-click in the design area and click on **New** | **Project**. Give a name, save, share on server, commit, and activate.
.xsapp	Application descriptor file. Tells XS Engine that a package contains an application.	Right-click on project name, **New** | **File**; create a .xsapp file, and save, commit, and activate.
.xsaccess	Configuration of the application.	Right-click on project name, then click on **New** | **File**, .xsaccess. Enter configuration parameters (exposed, authentication, rewrite_rules, and so on), save, commit, and activate.

$.db	Gives access to the SAP HANA database from an XS Engine application.	var conn = $.db.getConnection();
		var ps = conn.prepareStatement("select * from table");
		var rs = ps.executeQuery();

placeholder	Replaces parts of a predefined SQL query with variables at runtime, checking their type and validity.	var sql = "select * from revenue where custid=?";
		var custid = 3;
		ps = conn.prepareStatement(sql);
		ps.setInt(1,custid);

SAPUI5	User interface framework developed by SAP.	Documentation and example programs for all objects is available at http://server:80<instance>/sap/ui5/1/sdk/index.html.

So Long and Thanks – Where To Go from Here

What we've covered

Well, I think we're about done.

Our journey over the last three hundred pages (or thereabouts) has taken us through most of the development options in SAP HANA.

This book was split up into four main parts:

- Chapters 1 and 2: Introduction and installation
- Chapters 3, 4, 5, and 6: Database development in SAP HANA
- Chapters 7, 8, 9, and 10: Ancillary functions useful to most developments
- Chapter 11: The XS Engine for website development

Let's take a quick moment to see what we learned together.

In *Chapter 1, So, What Is This SAP HANA Thing Anyways?*, we looked at the **architecture** of SAP HANA. We saw that it is a **massively parallel, in-memory** database which uses **column-based storage** and **data compression**. We noted that SAP only sells SAP HANA as an **appliance**, meaning a software/hardware bundle, helping to guarantee performance levels since the software is running on certified hardware combinations.

We did a couple of tests on a large dataset (140 million lines), comparing performance of SAP HANA and MySQL using simple SQL statements. Rather unsurprisingly, we saw that SAP HANA could satisfy our example queries up to 160 times faster than the venerable MySQL database.

In *Chapter 2, SAP HANA Studio – Installation and First Look*, we started looking at SAP HANA from the inside.

We saw that accessing SAP HANA is relatively easy, either by purchasing a **license**, creating a virtual machine at a **cloud** hosting service, or by asking SAP for a **free trial** of the system.

Next we started a tour of the SAP HANA **Studio**, the modeling software used to work with the SAP HANA server. We saw the different **perspectives** (groups of windows) and **panels** available, and how to use them.

Finally, we **imported** some sample data, had a look at its structure, and checked that everything was correctly present in our system, using the **Data Preview** feature.

Our development journey proper started in *Chapter 3, Your First SAP HANA Development – An Attribute View*. We created a **Delivery Unit** and a **Package** to contain our future developments, then went on to create an **attribute view**, permitting the display of master data (non-numeric data).

Our attribute view started by exposing only some fields of a base table, then we improved it, adding a second table to show a customer's name alongside their ID.

Filtering on the **Client** field allowed us to automatically exclude certain rows from the view's output.

Junctions between tables, as well as joins, according to the user's connection language to display textual descriptions were explained also (**text join**).

Analytic views were what we discovered in *Chapter 4, Painting with Numbers – An Analytic View*. We saw that analytic views are views on base tables, allowing us to work with numeric data (**measures**) as well as nonnumeric data (**attributes**).

Measures allowed us to define the default **aggregation** of fields, such as SUM, MIN, or MAX, and after **adding an attribute view** to our analytic view, we were able to benefit from all the work we had already done, making the best use of these reusable objects.

We also learned about **restricted** and **calculated columns**, and how they could help us do low-level calculations automatically in the view, making the results available everywhere the view is used.

Lastly in *Chapter 4, Painting with Numbers – An Analytic View*, we created an **input parameter**, allowing user input in our view (a projected revenue increase). We used the input parameter in a calculated column, making the result of our view dynamic at runtime.

Chapters 5, Let's Get Graphical – Graphical Calculation Views, and *Chapter 6, You Talking to Me? – Scripted Calculation Views*, introduced the notion of **calculation views**, both **graphical** and **scripted** using **SQL Script**. We learned that calculation views allow us to extract data from two or more analytic views or tables at once, group the data together, and display one vision to the user. We used this notion to combine real data from one analytic view and projected data we created using our input parameter to another, together in one view with the aid of projections and a union.

In order to show that calculation views could be built either using the graphical designer available in the Studio, or in SQL Script, we built the same view using both methods.

Chapter 7, Hey! That's My Data! – Authorizations in SAP HANA, started the section on **helper functions** rather than pure database development, introducing the notion of **authorizations** in SAP HANA.

We saw that we could **restrict** access to database objects at the **SQL level** (tables and schemas), which defines who can work with an object but doesn't consider the object's contents, or at an **analytic level**, allowing limiting by field values. **System privileges** allowed access to certain system functions for our users.

We created a **role**, allowing us to ensure that attribution of privileges to users was done coherently across the system, and then created a **test user** having the role we'd just created. We were then able to connect to the SAP HANA system using our test user and do some tests, confirming that our restrictions worked as expected.

When we moved on to *Chapter 8, On Another Level – Hierarchies in SAP HANA*, we discovered **hierarchies** and how they could help **presentation** of data, especially for calculation of **subtotals** according to the data being displayed. We discovered that unfortunately, many reporting systems are unable to use the hierarchies we develop in SAP HANA, and we were only able to see the results of our development in **Microsoft Excel**.

Chapter 9, Deploying Your Reporting Application to Reporting Software, allowed us to look at SAP HANA from a user's viewpoint, discussing the relative merits of some of the more prominent **reporting software** compatible with SAP HANA. We examined SAP's Visual Intelligence tool, Microsoft Excel and Tableau, showing how each of these tools could be used to **display** the **contents** of the **data models** we'd developed together.

We saw that some tools (especially those developed by third-parties) require that we install SAP's SAP HANA **Client software** in order to be able to use them, while others (those made by SAP, unsurprisingly) don't require extra drivers to connect natively to SAP HANA.

For those pieces of software requiring the Client drivers, we had to make sure that the correct version (**32-bit** or **64-bit**) was installed, depending on our Windows version, and whether the tool itself was 32-bit or 64-bit.

In *Chapter 10, Data Provisioning with Data Services*, we took a while to look at exactly how we could load our SAP HANA database with our datasets sometimes totaling millions of lines. We created a **datastore** (connection to our SAP HANA instance, using an ODBC connection), a **format** (flat file definition), a **data flow**, a **job**, and a **project** to perform the data load of a CSV file of five million lines. We saw that a **template table** in **BODS** was able to create a table automatically in SAP HANA, before loading the table with data.

The fourth and final section of the book, website development, was covered in *Chapter 11, Application development with the XS Engine*. We spent a little time examining the **XS Engine**, then went on to write a simple two-liner, the Hello, World! application, seeing that the XS Engine is **JavaScript**-based on the server side.

We used application descriptor files, `.xsapp` and `.xsaccess` to enable our users to see and call up our application, and had a look at the different configuration options available to us as application developers.

We then added **database access** to our sample application, reading data from the attribute view we created back in *Chapter 3, Your First SAP HANA Development – An Attribute View*, and displaying it on the output webpage.

Finally, we took a look at the **SAPUI5** user interface framework, first creating a **static webpage** showcasing some of the functions of SAPUI5 then **integrating** the static webpage with our database accesses in order to create a pleasing user interface for our users displaying data from our SAP HANA database. A **second webpage** allowed us to **pass parameters** from one page to another securely, using **placeholder replacement** in our SQL query to protect our application against **malicious users**.

Now it's your turn

And there we are! We've taken a look at most of the features and functionalities of the SAP HANA system from a development perspective. You now possess the tools necessary to build your own database models, and integrate these in reporting software for your users to be able to analyze the data. You can create a simple XS Engine application, and you know where to look to see what other functions the XS Engine provides, especially if you want or need to use the SAPUI5 toolkit.

Where you go from here really depends on you. SAP HANA is a powerful system, allowing us to do data analysis work a lot faster than was ever possible in other systems. Switching a database from any given vendor to SAP HANA will see immediate gains, even if you don't change the data model. If, however, you spend some time building attribute and analytic views, calculation views on your data, you'll see even more speedups.

Whether you use SAP HANA as a database in its own right or just as the underlying data store for a SAP BW or ERP system, you now understand how development done at the database level can have positive impact in the application layer. Remember that the basic principle behind the SAP HANA system is to push as much calculation and workload as possible right down to the database layer, in order to limit the amount of data transiting across the network, and to avoid post-processing in your application (be it SAP's ABAP, an XS Engine application, or something else).

It is important to correctly define your data model, and to carefully design your SQL statements, just as with any other database. If your SQL requires that the entire database be read just to discover one figure or two, even the high speed of SAP HANA will not be enough to save your application!

Of course the question remains; what do we do with this extra speed? It's not just about getting information to your users faster, it's about what they can do with that data once they have it. Remember that all the work that we do as developers and consultants, only serves to enable our users to do their jobs faster, better and more efficiently.

Good luck making your users' jobs faster, better and more efficient with SAP HANA!

Mark Walker, June 2013

Index

Symbols

A

B

C

D

S

[PACKT] PUBLISHING enterprise
professional expertise distilled

Thank you for buying
Software Development on the SAP HANA Platform

About Packt Publishing

Packt, pronounced 'packed', published its first book "Mastering phpMyAdmin for Effective MySQL Management" in April 2004 and subsequently continued to specialize in publishing highly focused books on specific technologies and solutions.

Our books and publications share the experiences of your fellow IT professionals in adapting and customizing today's systems, applications, and frameworks. Our solution based books give you the knowledge and power to customize the software and technologies you're using to get the job done. Packt books are more specific and less general than the IT books you have seen in the past. Our unique business model allows us to bring you more focused information, giving you more of what you need to know, and less of what you don't.

Packt is a modern, yet unique publishing company, which focuses on producing quality, cutting-edge books for communities of developers, administrators, and newbies alike. For more information, please visit our website: `www.packtpub.com`.

About Packt Enterprise

In 2010, Packt launched two new brands, Packt Enterprise and Packt Open Source, in order to continue its focus on specialization. This book is part of the Packt Enterprise brand, home to books published on enterprise software - software created by major vendors, including (but not limited to) IBM, Microsoft and Oracle, often for use in other corporations. Its titles will offer information relevant to a range of users of this software, including administrators, developers, architects, and end users.

Writing for Packt

We welcome all inquiries from people who are interested in authoring. Book proposals should be sent to author@packtpub.com. If your book idea is still at an early stage and you would like to discuss it first before writing a formal book proposal, contact us; one of our commissioning editors will get in touch with you.

We're not just looking for published authors; if you have strong technical skills but no writing experience, our experienced editors can help you develop a writing career, or simply get some additional reward for your expertise.

www.ingramcontent.com/pod-product-compliance
Lightning Source LLC
LaVergne TN
LVHW080025210926
848481LV00011B/3104
* 9 7 8 1 8 4 9 6 8 9 4 0 3 *